DEGROWTH & STRATEGY

how to bring about social-ecological transformation

Published by Mayfly Books. Available in paperpack and free online at www.mayflybooks.org in 2022.

© Authors remain the holders of the copyright of their own texts. They may republish their own texts in different contexts, including modified versions of the texts under the condition that proper attribution is given to Degrowth & Strategy.

ISBN (Print)   978-1-906948-60-3
ISBN (PDF)   978-1-906948-61-0
ISBN (ebook) 978-1-906948-62-7

This work is licensed under the Creative Commons Attribution-Non commercial-No Derivatives 4.0 International (CC BY-NC-ND 4.0).
To view a copy of this license, visit
http://creativecommons.org/licenses/by-nc-nd/4.0

Cover art work by Dana Rausch who retains the image copyright.
Layout by Mihkali Pennanen.

DEGROWTH & STRATEGY

how to bring about social-ecological transformation

Edited by Nathan Barlow, Livia Regen, Noémie Cadiou,
Ekaterina Chertkovskaya, Max Hollweg,
Christina Plank, Merle Schulken and Verena Wolf

Praise for this book

"This book is what the degrowth movement needed the most: a well-reasoned and empirically grounded compendium of strategic thinking and praxis for systemic transformations. This is a true gift, not only to degrowthers, but to all those who understand the need for radical change. In an era of unprecedented challenges as the one we are living through, this book should become essential reading in every higher-education course across the social sciences and humanities."
Stefania Barca, University of Santiago de Compostela, author of *Forces of Reproduction – Notes for a Counterhegemonic Anthropocene*

"Emerging amidst the ruins of the destroyed (some call it developed) world, degrowth is a powerful call for transformation towards justice and sustainability. This book takes degrowth's ideological basis towards strategy and practice, relates it to other movements, and shows pathways that are crucial for the Global North to take if life on earth has to flourish again."
Ashish Kothari, co-author of *Pluriverse: A Post-Development Dictionary*

"The book is an exciting source of hope for degrowth futures. It is a thoroughly readable and ambitious book that sets out what degrowth wants to do and what it is actually achieving. It contains many inspiring examples of new ways of living together, illustrating how to share resources, create caring institutions, fair infrastructures, and new ways of relating to humans and more-than-humans."
Wendy Harcourt, International Institute of Social Studies of Erasmus University Rotterdam

"In contrast to previous works on the topic the focus is firmly placed on the challenge of how to achieve social-ecological transformation in the face of economic structures and powerful vested interests committed to a utopian vision of sustaining economic growth without end; a vision that pretends to be concerned for the poor while exploiting them and destroying Nature. An alternative multi-faceted vision is outlined in the most comprehensive exploration of the topic available, including addressing the role of money, mobility, energy, food, technology, housing, and most importantly how to change modernity's various growth–obsessed social–economic systems."
Clive Spash, Vienna University of Economics and Business, editor of *Handbook of Ecological Economics: Nature & Society*

"We live in times of great despair and danger, but also great promise. This book is the perfect gateway to strategy and action for our time, written by some of the very top thinkers in the degrowth movement. It will help you create possibilities to transform our world for the better."
Julia Steinberger, University of Lausanne

"This is a book everyone in the degrowth community has been waiting for. Moving beyond the diagnosis about the costs and limits of growth, this volume asks the question of what is to be done and puts forward an ambitious political program of how we go from here to there. The authors present a coherent vision of how different mobilisations at different scales can come together and steer societies to what now seems politically impossible – degrowth."
Giorgos Kallis, ICREA Professor, ICTA-UAB, author of *Limits* **and** *The Case for Degrowth*

"What is to be done about the Global North? Young economists of the degrowth generation share strategies on food, housing, energy, transport, technology, and money. Practical, stimulating, and provocative."
Ariel Salleh, author of *Eco-Sufficiency & Global Justice*

"How do we go from here to there? Read this book and you will find how societies can undertake a transformation towards degrowth."
Federico Demaria, University of Barcelona, co-author of
The Case for Degrowth

"Above all, *Degrowth & Strategy* is a work of revolutionary optimism. The range of visions offered in this text teaches us that we are better off finding a common ground in our strategies and tactics than dwelling on our differences, so that we may step into the future together. With this text, the degrowth movement shifts its central focus from the what and the why to the how. Be warned: this is for those to whom degrowth is an everyday commitment and not a mere thought exercise!"
Jamie Tyberg, co-founder and member of DegrowNYC

"*Degrowth & Strategy* is an important collection of essays on a subject of the greatest significance and urgency. Particularly impressive is the emphasis on public communication, workable political strategies and practical solutions."
Amitav Ghosh, author of *The Great Derangement: Climate Change and the Unthinkable*

"The most critical challenge is *implementing* degrowth – to ensure that production and consumption meet basic needs, neither more (waste) nor less (poverty). This collection confronts *strategy* head-on, with a singular unity of purpose and a rich variety of approaches. A must-read for all concerned about our uncertain future."
Anitra Nelson, University of Melbourne (Australia), co-author of *Exploring Degrowth*, **and co-editor of**
Food for Degrowth **and** *Housing for Degrowth*

"This book makes a timely and essential contribution to a number of intersecting debates regarding the *how* of social-ecological transformation. Expertly edited, the book's emphasis on philosoph*ies*, struggle*s* and strateg*ies* in more 'in principle' terms complements very effectively the consideration of concrete practices across a wide range of societal sites and sectors. A must-read for scholars and activists alike."
Ian Bruff, University of Manchester

"That we need to move to a degrowth economy is becoming ever more obvious. How we go about achieving it has hitherto been less clear, and less discussed in degrowth literature. This comprehensive and astute survey of transformative strategies, both those already in train and those that need to come into force, provides an essential guide."
Kate Soper, London Metropolitan University

"Nothing grows forever, and the same is true of economies. In this urgently needed book, an impressive group of academics and activists consider how we get to an economic system that operates within natural limits and with regard to social justice. Illustrated with inspiring case studies, the authors focus on the *how*, because the planet and our natural world are already showing us the *why*."
Martin Parker, Bristol University, author of *Shut Down the Business School*

"The structural, cultural and ideational barriers to degrowth have long been recognised by its advocates. Contributors to this collection respond to the challenges positively and creatively by thinking about strategy and how this concept can be harnessed by diverse social movements to initiate, inspire and institute bottom-up social-ecological change."
Ruth Kinna, Loughborough University

"We need to go beyond envisioning degrowth but identify pathways towards it. This is the first book that provides a comprehensive and in-depth engagement with strategies for degrowth, definitely leading us closer to a degrowth future. Required reading for anyone who aims to realise degrowth."
Jin Xue, Norwegian University of Life Sciences

"The Western growth model becomes increasingly untenable as a societal project, thereby urging communities, researchers, and decision-makers to find alternative pathways. To guide us through these turbulent times and towards a future beyond growth, the authors of *Degrowth & Strategy* provide a much-needed map – unprecedented in detail but also aware of the yet unknown."
Benedikt Schmid, University of Freiburg, author of *Making Transformative Geographies*

"How can we better organise to achieve social and ecological justice in a finite world? This is a big question with no easy answer. In an honest and thoughtful way, this book brings multiple voices expressing diverse pathways to pursue social-ecological transformation. What emerges from the presentation of different perspectives and strategies is not the suggestion of one right way to bring about change but a healthy, pluralistic, thought-provoking and respectful dialogue that can lead us in new and promising directions."
Ana Maria Peredo, Professor of Social and Inclusive Entrepreneurship, University of Ottawa & Professor of Political Ecology, University of Victoria

"In my classes, students keep circling back to the question – how do we move from the current world driven by the logic of capital, endless growth, needless production and consumption to a world that centres on justice, care, and living well in a way that amplifies life? This book provides what so many of us are craving for – thought-provoking engagement with the issue of strategies for materialising social-ecological transformation. The book offers theoretical frameworks, pathways, and practical examples of diverse strategies for social-ecological transformations at work. It is a must-read for academics, activists, practitioners, and ordinary people striving for an equitable and sustainable world. I am grateful to the editors and authors for creating this excellent resource for thinking and acting to facilitate a 'strategic assemblage for degrowth'."
Neera Singh, Geography & Planning, University of Toronto

Table of Contents

Forewords by Brototi Roy and Carola Rackete — 5 & 7

Introduction: Strategy for the multiplicity of degrowth by Merle Schulken, Nathan Barlow, Noémie Cadiou, Ekaterina Chertkovskaya, Max Hollweg, Christina Plank, Livia Regen and Verena Wolf — 9

Part I: Strategy in degrowth research and activism

The importance of strategy for thinking about transformation

Chapter 1 Radical emancipatory social-ecological transformations: degrowth and the role of strategy by Ulrich Brand — 37

Chapter 2 A strategic canvas for degrowth: in dialogue with Erik Olin Wright by Ekaterina Chertkovskaya — 56

Chapter 3 Taking stock: degrowth and strategy so far by Nathan Barlow — 72

Degrowth movement(s): strategising and plurality

Chapter 4 Strategising within diversity: the challenge of structuring by Viviana Asara — 93

Chapter 5 Degrowth actors and their strategies: towards a *Degrowth International* by Andro Rilović, Constanza Hepp, Joëlle Saey-Volckrick, Joe Herbert and Carol Bardi — 110

Chapter 6 Who shut shit down? What degrowth can learn from other social-ecological movements by Corinna Burkhart, Tonny Nowshin, Matthias Schmelzer and Nina Treu — 129

Strategising with our eyes wide open

Chapter 7 Social equity is the foundation of degrowth by Samantha Mailhot and Patricia E. Perkins — 145

Chapter 8 Evaluating strategies for emancipatory degrowth transformations by Panos Petridis — 160

Chapter 9 Rethinking state-civil society relations by Max Koch — 170

Chapter 10 Strategic entanglements by Susan Paulson — 182

Part II: Strategies in practice

Provisioning sectors

Chapter 11 Food — 200

Overview by Christina Plank

Case: The movement for food sovereignty by Julianna Fehlinger, Elisabeth Jost and Lisa Francesca Rail

Chapter 12 Urban housing — 219

Overview by Gabu Heindl

Case: Deutsche Wohnen & Co. Enteignen by Ian Clotworthy and Ania Spatzier

Chapter 13 Digital technologies — 246

Overview & Case: Low-Tech Magazine and Decidim by Nicolas Guenot and Andrea Vetter

Chapter 14 Energy — 268

Overview by Mario Díaz Muñoz

Case: The struggle against energy extractivism in Southern Chile by Gabriela Cabaña

Chapter 15 Mobility and transport — 289

Overview by John Szabo, Thomas SJ Smith and Leon Leuser

Case: The Autolib' car-sharing platform by Marion Drut

Economic and political reorganisation

Chapter 16 Care — 311

Overview by Corinna Dengler, Miriam Lang and Lisa M. Seebacher

Case: The Health Centre Cecosesola by Georg Rath

Chapter 17 Paid work   332

    Overview & Case: Just Transition in the aviation sector by Halliki Kreinin and Tahir Latif

Chapter 18 Money and finance   351

    Overview & Case: The Austrian Cooperative for the Common Good by Ernest Aigner, Christina Buczko, Louison Cahen-Fourot and Colleen Schneider

Chapter 19 Trade and decolonisation   375

    Overview by Gabriel Trettel Silva

    Case: Litigation as a tool for resistance and mobilisation in Nigeria by Godwin Uyi Ojo

About the Authors   393

About the Editors   403

Acknowledgements   405

Forewords

By Brototi Roy, co-president of *Research and Degrowth (R&D)* and co-founder of the Degrowth India Initiative

I first came across the term degrowth in 2014 while I was a master's student in economics in New Delhi, India. I was in my third semester and decided to take an elective course called "Key concepts in Ecological Economics." This course was the start of my engagement with the term, the movement and the academic scholarship on degrowth. With my friend and co-conspirator Arpita, I started the Degrowth India Initiative to have discussions and conversations on degrowth. Why, you ask? Because I was frustrated with the way a lot of people in Delhi had embraced the "imperial mode of living." And although I didn't know it at that time, the Degrowth India Initiative was a strategy to link the research carried out by the students in the university on sustainability and environmental justice with ideas about degrowth, with the hope of repoliticising the debate on social-ecological justice and equity in the Indian context.

Fast forward to October 2021, when I was in a public debate on degrowth in Antwerp, Belgium. One of the questions asked about the non-feasibility of degrowth was "What about the poor garment workers in Bangladesh? Will you ask them to degrow?" In the audience, there were quite a few of us who have been a part of various degrowth initiatives and actions over the years, and we shared our frustrations about this, and many other similar questions often being asked about degrowth and how it harms the poor in the Global South. Some go so far as to claim that people in the Global North should continue consuming fast fashion because of these garment workers, who are being done a favour and are kept in jobs because of this.

But has anyone asked the garment workers if this is what they really want, instead of just assuming and speaking on their behalf? Is this their idea of meaningful employment? What led them to work in these exploitative positions? And what would they consider a meaningful transformation of their lives and livelihoods? For me, a radical social-ecological transformation can only be achieved when it is anti-colonial and feminist. A degrowth strategy for me is to allow for the garment workers to speak their truths, collectively find solutions together, and never assume we know better.

This public event, despite being one of the most frustrating ones in terms of misrepresenting degrowth, did help in bringing a bunch of people together and has led to the creation of a degrowth group in Belgium. Would the group be able to engage with the colonial history of the country and strategise about what degrowth in the Belgian context means? I remain hopeful about it.

Both the Indian and the Belgian initiatives were born out of frustration with the current system and the need for social-ecological transformation, due to the exploitative patterns of capitalism, based on oppression and exploitation of marginalised communities and nature by some sections of the world and society. Both initiatives found degrowth ideas could help inform strategy while being critical and self-reflective.

From these two small anecdotes, I now turn to this edited volume. In the last couple of decades, degrowth has flourished as an academic sub-discipline and movement, with multiple books, articles, special issues, conferences, talks, and debates being organised around the topic. Yet not enough has been written on how one can go about creating long-lasting changes towards justice and equity.

This is precisely what the book does. It is a very important and impressive collection of strategies, which might or might not have stemmed from similar frustrations as mentioned above, experienced by the editors and authors, but which will definitely help, in the years to come, others who are trying to find solutions for social-ecological transformation in their own contexts.

By looking at the different strategies for a degrowth pathway and focusing on different aspects of the globalised world economy, this book provides concrete proposals for social-ecological transformations – albeit with a focus on the Global North. At the same time, the book also engages with critical ideas of feminist and decolonial degrowth in tangible ways – such as through the case of global trade or considerations around the organisation of care. The degrowth movement has been criticised for paying lip service to feminist and decolonial ideas; this book shows that once we move from the "why "question to the "how" question, one can't ignore the need for a holistic framework that is serious about its feminist and decolonial views.

All in all, the book is a step forward in thinking together with different degrowth initiatives and actors about how radical social-ecological transformation can be realised. By bringing degrowth in conversation with different other actors and movements fighting for social-ecological justice and equity, such as the climate justice movement, and providing concrete ways of engagement, I hope to see this book create ripples for change towards radical societal transformation towards justice and equity.

By Carola Rackete, Sea-Watch captain, and social and environmental justice activist

I am staring at my tomatoes. I didn't grow them, I rescued them from a trash bin where they were suffocating in plastic. I wonder what happened to them before I found them, how they were shipped from far away, who planted, harvested and processed them. I am sure they were dreaming of a better place. Me too.

I am dreaming of agriculture that regenerates the soil instead of depleting it. That sustains life for future generations and non-humans alike. That provides people with meaningful work and collective ownership of the land. A place where care for the community of life is valued more than its destruction. I am dreaming of a world where the tomatoes in my hands have come to me in a completely different way.

It's easy to imagine that better world once I start thinking about it. But how do we transition from one tomato to the other? How do we make that better tomato a reality? If degrowth is to have a part in our future we need to draw a map for how to move on from one place to the other. We need to define not only the destination at the end of that path, but also be able to share with other people how to find the trailhead and get started in a very practical way. This pathway of transformation must be as credible and real as the tomatoes in front of me.

This book is about these pathways of transformation – about mapping what is ahead, how to find the trailhead, what to bring on the journey, how to get from one trail marker to the next, and how to overcome expected obstacles. It is not only about ecological transformation – which is how I got connected to the degrowth movement – but about pathways towards better housing, care, mobility and energy, and global social justice. All these pathways intersect and lead us into the same direction of a future based on justice, decolonialism and care for one another, based on the choice of limiting economic and social practices that are set up to destroy everyone.

If we can envision not only where we want to get to, but also how we are going to get there, others might feel safe and confident enough to join us on that journey. At first, that path of transformation may only be taken by those who already share our vision of a just social-ecological future and who feel they have the skills, motivation and opportunity to make a start. But one of our most important challenges will be to practically demonstrate how walking that path of transformation will be beneficial for everyone in our societies beyond those already engaged.

Therefore, this book about degrowth transformation and strategy is important as a tool to prepare for getting underway towards the world of better tomatoes.

Introduction

Strategy for the multiplicity of degrowth

By Merle Schulken, Nathan Barlow, Noémie Cadiou, Ekaterina Chertkovskaya, Max Hollweg, Christina Plank, Livia Regen and Verena Wolf

We live in troubled times: climate emergency, rising inequality and the COVID-19 pandemic are just some of the grand challenges we are faced with. These are not unfortunate coincidences caused by humanity as a whole but the outcomes of a system oriented toward perpetual economic growth and capital accumulation. It is a system characterised by brutal injustices within and across societies – based on class, gender and racial divisions, and uneven relations between the Global North and the Global South. Addressing the current multifaceted ecological, social and economic crisis requires not just incremental but systemic change, which in this book we refer to as social-ecological transformation (see Chapter 1 for a definition).

Institutional responses to this crisis from those in power are not enough to meet the scale of the social-ecological transformation required. When it comes to climate change, for example, we are well into the third decade of high-profile UN Climate Change Conferences, where member states negotiate how to reduce global greenhouse gas emissions. Meanwhile, emissions are only rising. With states and corporations joining hands as the threat of climate change becomes increasingly real, false solutions are being proposed, including dangerous technologies and further financialisation to keep the economic engine running at full speed. These supposed solutions are wrapped into creative accounting to make them appear effective and are communicated using elusive terminologies, such as "net-zero" or "climate neutrality", which create a sense of change while continuing business as usual.

Parallel to this, many social movements have risen and keep rising to oppose the current state of things. From anti-austerity, Black Lives Matter, climate and environmental justice movements, to autonomous, feminist, indigenous and peasant movements, people across the world are boldly protesting against injustices, resisting entrenched structures of domination and building alternatives. This book emerged from discussions on degrowth, a burgeoning research area and an emerging social movement that critiques the pursuit of economic growth and capital accumulation and strives to reorganise societies to make them both ecologically sustainable and socially just. The degrowth vision of social-ecological transformation connects with a mosaic of progressive bottom-up movements across the world (Akbulut et al. 2019, Burkhart et al. 2020). Together, we see these movements as key agents of an urgently needed social-ecological transformation.

In order to be effective, social movements have to confront the agendas driven by corporate and state actors, who have the power to ignore, water down, co-opt and criminalise transformative efforts. Social movements often lack time and energy, capacities and resources, and it is easy to run out of steam and feel that efforts to bring change are futile. But there is no time for despair! What we need to do is to organise better within and across the movements we are a part of and to develop a more clear-eyed perspective on how to confront the powerful interests and structures standing in the way of systemic change. This is why the question of strategy is so important for anyone engaged in efforts for social-ecological transformation. This book aims to tackle the question of *how* systemic change can be fostered despite the constraints we face.

Degrowth & Strategy: how to bring about social-ecological transformation builds on existing research on degrowth and its vision for a society with ecological sustainability and social justice at the core. But it also takes this research further to dig more deeply into the question of strategy. The book offers a conceptual discussion of strategy and its relation to degrowth and social movements more generally and investigates strategies in practice, drawing on a variety of examples. In doing this, it brings together multiple voices from degrowth and related movements, to create a polyphony that reflects the multiplicity of degrowth. This discussion, we hope, will help the readers reflect on questions of strategy and empower them to apply this thinking in practice, contributing to more effective and concerted efforts for social-ecological transformation.

The remainder of this introduction will be structured as follows. We start by outlining a degrowth vision for social-ecological transformation. Second, we trace the existing discussion on strategy in the degrowth movement and explain why it is important to think about strategy. Third, we turn to conceptualising how we understand strategy in this book, which builds on and is closely aligned with our understanding of degrowth. Finally, we introduce the book and its structure, followed by a conclusion.

What is degrowth, and why does it need strategy?

We understand degrowth as a democratically deliberated absolute reduction of material and energy throughput, which ensures well-being for all within planetary boundaries. Contrary to perpetuating economies driven by growth and profit, degrowth offers an alternative vision for societies, centred on life-making, ecological sustainability and social justice. Since degrowth is based on the principles of autonomy, solidarity and direct democracy, bottom-up organising is seen as key to making an equitable and just transformation happen (Asara *et al.* 2013). Crucially, degrowth also acknowledges the historical inequities of colonialism and neo-colonialism, and therefore demands that the Global North reverse the social and ecological burdens it imposes on the Global South. Degrowth is a concept that comes from the European context, but it connects to a pluriverse of ideas from around the world that advocate for a good life beyond economic growth, capitalism, and development (Kothari *et al.* 2019), where living well also means not living at anyone else's expense (Brand *et al.* 2021).

The term degrowth was coined in 1972 as *décroissance* by André Gorz, a French philosopher whose thought has been an important source of inspiration for those working on degrowth (Kallis *et al.* 2015, Leonardi 2019). In the early 2000s, it was mobilised as an activist slogan in France, Italy (*decrescita*), Catalonia (*decreixement*) and Spain (*decrecimiento*), and décroissance as a social movement emerged in Lyon and spread across France (Demaria *et al.* 2013). In 2008, the first International Degrowth Conference for Ecological Sustainability and Social Equity took place in Paris, which is also when the term was translated into English. Since then, degrowth has gained further traction in academic and (some) activist circles. International degrowth conferences serve as key spaces for academic-activist discussion and have been hosted from multiple locations (Barcelona, Venice, Montreal, Leipzig, Budapest, Malmö, Mexico City, Vienna, Manchester, The Hague).

Within the academic realm, degrowth today is a burgeoning area of interdisciplinary research with the publication of hundreds of articles and a growing number of books on the topic in the last decade (Kallis *et al.* 2018, Weiss and Cattaneo 2017). Multiplicity is a key characteristic and arguably a strength of degrowth research, as it draws from different theoretical perspectives and currents of thought, and there is an acknowledgement that degrowth is not a unified scientific paradigm (Paulson 2017). This allows degrowth to be an inclusive conversation and a space for multiple voices that share the basic premise that the growth imperative must be overcome to ensure a good life for all (Barca *et al.* 2019). There are also some asymmetries and blind spots in the degrowth discussion. Critiques from, for example, decolonial, ecosocialist and feminist perspectives have pointed some of these out and have put forward paths for acting upon them (e.g. Andreucci and Engel-Di Mauro 2019, Dengler and Seebacher 2019, Gregoratti and Raphael 2019, Nirmal and Rocheleau 2019). In this volume, we embrace the multiplicity of degrowth, which, as the readers will notice, means that contributing authors will sometimes take different stances on degrowth's diverse manifestations.

Besides being a field of interdisciplinary research, degrowth has also been described as an emerging international social movement with close connections to other social-ecological movements (Chapter 4, Chapter 6; see also Akbulut *et al.* 2019, Demaria *et al.* 2013). Others prefer to describe degrowth as a community of activist scholars, or a network of networks. Whatever one's take on how to characterise the institutional set-up of degrowth, we can see that multiple international and regional groups have emerged and stabilised as relevant actors within degrowth activism, albeit mostly in Europe. International groups include, for example, *degrowth.info* (a web platform for information related to degrowth), the Support Group (a team supporting degrowth conferences) and Research & Degrowth (a group of degrowth researchers). Many regional groups, in turn, have organised themselves around research and activist communities, and some of these have also hosted international degrowth conferences or even formed a political party. However, groups and organisations coming together around degrowth ideas have not yet found concerted ways to collectively act together.

In this book, we argue that it is time to seriously address the question of strategy for degrowth, whilst respecting its multiplicity. This is not an easy path. It will involve a lot of negotiation and deliberation and is likely to come with different and contradictory views on how to bring about social-ecological transformation. Without seriously addressing the question of strategy for degrowth, the efforts of degrowthers and others fostering compatible visions around the world risk remaining marginal and fragmented, staying in the realm of ideas and fragile oases of alternatives. Or, when entering spaces beyond the movement, they risk being co-opted or engaged with in a one-sided way by actors opposed to systemic change. Concerted actions and coordination would help to amplify the efforts for social-ecological transformation and create more powerful ways to act collectively. Thus, we believe that only a rigorous discussion on strategy can help avoid this fragmentation or co-optation.

Degrowth and strategy so far

The lack of engagement with questions related to strategy by, for, and within the degrowth movement first became apparent during the 2018 Malmö Degrowth Conference. A more or less coherent degrowth vision of social-ecological transformation had, by then, emerged. This vision covers different spheres of life, exemplified by multiple existing small-scale initiatives and ideas for institutional and policy interventions that would help them flourish. However, the difficult question of *how* to foster degrowth – i.e., the question of strategy – was conspicuously missing from this debate. In October 2018, a new generation of academic activists in the degrowth movement vocalised this gap by publishing a piece entitled "Beyond visions and projects: the need for a debate on strategy in the degrowth movement" (Ambach *et al.* 2018) on the blog of *degrowth.info*. The authors argued that the degrowth community of academics and activists should critically reflect on degrowth researchers' then predominant and implicit approach to strategy, which the authors described as *strategic indeterminism*. To further this discussion, *degrowth.info* launched a ten-part series on degrowth and strategy (see Chapter 3). Finally, a group of young activists and academics – today known as Degrowth Vienna – decided to organise the first degrowth conference that had an explicit focus on strategies for social-ecological transformation. The objective of this conference was two-fold: first, to create a space that would allow for an exchange on, analysis of, and critical discussion about the role of strategy for the degrowth movement and research; second, to strategically advance degrowth as a concept within Austrian media, institutions, and organisations.

The *Degrowth Vienna 2020 Conference: Strategies for Social-Ecological Transformation* took place from 29 May to 1 June 2020. It explored obstacles, pathways, and limitations of ongoing and past transformations. The conference drew on the city of Vienna's intellectual history, from Red Vienna in the 1920s and the legacy of Karl Polanyi to the vibrant discussion of social-ecological transformation taking place in the city today. Conference contributions were grounded in the work of many academic and activist groups in and around Vienna and supported by an interdisciplinary body of knowledge. The conference opened up a virtual space for an exchange on functioning, abandoned and promising strategies for social-ecological transformation. These, the conference revealed, must include reflections on the degrowth movement's own internal organisation and strategic orientation, as well as alliance-building with other social-ecological movements, in addition to the continuous work of decolonising the degrowth vision and its praxis (Asara 2020).

By switching, relatively quickly, to an online format due to the COVID-19 pandemic, the Degrowth Vienna organising team widened the imagination of how the degrowth movement could gather as a community. Moreover, despite the challenges of the pandemic, the shift to an online conference allowed the discussion around strategy to be more inclusive than an in-person format would have allowed, with over 4,000 participants from both the Global North and the Global South joining the conversation.

The editorial team of this book was initiated by some of the organisers of the Degrowth Vienna 2020 conference and then joined by fellow degrowth researchers interested in the issue of strategy. Together, we concluded that the *degrowth.info* series and the Vienna conference were only the first steps for addressing strategy in relation to degrowth and that much more discussion was still needed. We drew on contributions to the blog series and the conference as a point of departure for selecting key issues that we thought could be deepened. The result was an 18-month process of coming to a shared understanding of the selected issues, contacting authors, reviewing drafts, asking for feedback, scrutinising our understanding of strategy, revising our timeline (several times), and learning from the diversity of perspectives and knowledge present in the degrowth movement and the social-ecological movements that degrowth is aligned with. In this sense, our book does not offer a comprehensive survey of the existing literature on degrowth and strategy, but rather puts forward our approach to selecting, framing and advancing key debates.

Conceptualising strategy for social-ecological transformation

In order to bring about social-ecological transformation in the face of powerful actors who employ various strategies of their own to oppose change, we believe that an honest and critical discussion about strategies must take place. In this section, we present the understanding of the term "strategy" that we have developed for and adopted throughout this book. That said, the conceptualisation proposed here should not be misinterpreted as an attempt to close the debate about what strategy is and what it should be about in the context of degrowth. Quite to the contrary, we hope that our contribution will be one helpful reference point that can sharpen future engagement with strategy. Before we introduce our conceptualisation, however, it is important to acknowledge that by engaging with strategy we are dealing with a contested concept.

Dealing with a contested concept

Applying the concept of strategy to degrowth thinking and activism is not a straightforward endeavour. In the history of Western thought, engagement with strategy started in the modern era in the context of efforts to apply rational methods of organisation to warfare (Freedman 2013). From the 1960s onwards, metaphors and concepts surrounding strategy travelled from military thought to the realms of business and management (*Ibid.*). Until today, strategy is primarily associated with the military or the corporate world, and hierarchical chains of command – contexts and characteristics that are alien to the degrowth vision.

The source we have just cited, Sir Lawrence Freedman, is also not your usual scholar to be quoted in a degrowth book. Freedman is most known for his writings about and political involvement in military matters. He has contributed to justifying powerful imperial forces that we – as degrowth scholars and activists – condemn and oppose. At the same time, he is the author of one of the most comprehensive books on strategy in English, which is hard to miss or ignore if one is trying to dig into the concept. In that book, he also proposes the most encompassing and elaborated definition of strategy we could find, which we engage with later in this section.

We are aware that a progressive movement like degrowth needs to be careful when dealing with the concept of strategy, and referencing sources engaging with it, so as not to reproduce what we advocate against. Examples of potential dangers of an unreflective application of strategy to degrowth thinking might include creating a vanguard group concerned exclusively with strategising that stands in hierarchical relation to the rest of the movement, thereby stifling attempts to build more horizontal forms of governance and potentially depriving the strategising process of feedback and creativity. Talking about change in terms of strategy might also invoke the notion that social-ecological transformation is only an antagonistic process and downplay the importance of deliberative practices or cultural change.

That said, within the debates on degrowth, the term strategy already appears now and again, especially more recently given the rising attention to the issue of strategy (e.g. Asara *et al.* 2015, Koch 2022, Nelson 2022). So far, however, the term is rarely clearly defined, is often used as a metaphor, and has not yet been subject to conceptual and critical scrutiny (see Chapter 3). Meanwhile, attempts to engage with strategy for a bottom-up transformation are by no means confined to the degrowth movement. Scholars and activists in a variety of contexts have been tackling or at least touching upon this uneasy terrain, trying to reclaim and rethink strategy for progressive social change (e.g., Maeckelbergh 2011, Maney *et al.* 2012, Mueller 2003, Parker 2021). The question of strategy has also been raised in relation to various allied social movements, ranging from agroecology, through the climate and environmental movements, to Occupy and the Zapatista (e.g.,

Smucker 2017, Staggenborg 2020, Stahler-Sholk 2017, Val *et al.* 2019).

Despite the challenging roots of the concept, strategy is thus *de facto* an ongoing concern for progressive movements, including degrowth. Grappling with the concept in a clearly defined manner, we argue, can foster already existing discussions and organising, with cautious engagement being better than shying away from the topic due to its challenges. In working with strategy, we want to offer a conceptualisation of it that avoids the problematic aspects we have highlighted and is also in tune with degrowth while preserving the important and at times challenging insights it brings.

Strategy – a thought construct and a flexible mental map

We understand strategy as a *thought construct* that details how one or several *actors* intend to bring about systemic change towards a desired end state. When applied in practice, a strategy serves as a *flexible mental map* that links an analysis of the status quo to a vision of a desirable end state by detailing different *ways* of achieving (intermediate) goals on the journey towards that envisioned future as well as certain *means* to potentially be employed along these *ways* (Freedman 2013). *Ways* refer to different pathways through which the transformation from the status quo to the desired end-state may come about. These pathways can be distinguished from one another, among other things, by the relations they envision between the strategising actor and other actors or between the actor and the structures they intend to change. *Means*, in turn, are concrete actions that actors may undertake when pursuing a strategy. Strategy may encompass antagonistic and consensual processes, where actors involved in strategising engage with adversaries or allies, anticipating their actions and responding to the opportunities or obstacles these create (Maney *et al.* 2012).

We are aware that, especially in progressive social movements and organisations, strategies are not always explicitly discussed. Instead, the ways and means pursued by an organisation in their everyday activities always at least partly emerge organically out of past experiences of their members and the narratives created by them (de Moor and Wahlström 2019). Research that looks at strategies-as-practice highlights the diverse and sometimes unconscious processes out of which strategies emerge in real-world organisations (Golsorkhi *et al.* 2010). For example, peasant-to-peasant processes can be seen as key to La Via Campesina's strategy for spreading peasant agroecology (Val *et al.* 2019). Furthermore, the very participation in building alternatives has a strategic element as "the creation of new political structures [i]s intended to replace existing political structures" (Maeckelbergh 2011, 7).

While we acknowledge such an understanding of strategies, in this book we argue for thinking about strategies analytically as well as deliberately and then applying this thinking in practice. Conceptualising strategies as *thought constructs* allows us to engage in analytical discussions about opportunities and challenges presented by a given context, to organise ourselves internally and with potential allies, and to evaluate different strategies for their ex-ante desirability and their ex-post efficacy.

By understanding strategy as a *flexible mental map*, in turn, we highlight that a strategy in practice is necessarily context-specific and dynamic. A strategy in practice, while still being a thought construct, is always defined in relation to the circumstances of the strategising actor. This includes their goals, their (limited) resources, how they are situated within broader social structures and processes, as well as what they anticipate other actors (allies and opponents) will do. Crucially, a strategy is thereby more than a mere plan. While a plan outlines a concrete list of steps an actor intends to take to reach a goal, a strategy comprises a set of considerations for how one might bring about change more generally, the details of which may later change. Indeed, the ways, the means and even intermediate goals foreseen in a strategy may need to be adapted as a strategy plays out and one must react to the actions of allies and opponents and to changing circumstances more broadly.

To add yet another layer of complexity to the discussion of strategy as a *flexible mental map*, strategies over time must also be able to reflect changes in the strategising actor's understanding of their surroundings. Indeed, how an actor analyses the status quo and the levers and mechanisms available to enact change is never complete and must thus be updated over time (Wright 2012). Strategies for degrowth at any one point in time can only ever reflect an informed guess about how transformation may come about. Working towards social-ecological transformation thus requires us to acknowledge uncertainty, complexity, and possible unintended consequences when strategising, and to create institutions for reflecting on and responding to these issues (Barca *et al.* 2019).

Thinking analytically and deliberately about strategy

Thinking analytically and deliberately about strategy, we argue, can enhance organising and action towards social-ecological transformation. To foster such thinking, it is necessary to differentiate distinct *ways* from *means* and *means* from *ends*.

Separating different *ways* from the *means* employed along those ways allows different strategies to be sorted and grouped, and their distinctions to be discussed analytically. The vocabulary of Erik Olin Wright is particularly helpful for thinking of different *ways* in which an actor may choose to work toward transformation. Wright (2009, 2019) discerns three "modes of transformation" within anti-capitalist movements – interstitial, ruptural and symbiotic. These are each accompanied by respective "strategic logics" (Wright 2019). The popularity that Wright's framework enjoys within and beyond degrowth for thinking about different ways of bringing about progressive change is one reason why we – at times also critically – engage with it in our book, hoping to create continuity with broader debates. Another reason for building on Wright's framework is that it highlights synergies between distinct modes of transformation and thus potentially facilitates collaboration between distinct political factions within degrowth and allied movements. We engage with

Wright's work at greater length later in the book, by setting out a strategic canvas that degrowthers and allies can engage with to identify and coordinate strategic priorities and tensions between different groups, and to think about how to avoid co-optation (see Chapter 2). We have also asked authors, especially in chapters dealing with strategies in practice (Chapters 11 to 19), to deliberately reflect on strategies employed in their fields and organisations by drawing on the analytical vocabulary of Wright or the way we have furthered (and diverged from) it in this book.

Separating *means* from *ends* in our definition of strategy creates space for debating about which means (and intermediate ends) should be considered conducive to social-ecological transformation, and which should not. This analytical process of separating means from ends is not a common approach within degrowth, but one which we think would be beneficial. Crucially, we do not wish to imply that the desirable end of reaching a socially just and ecologically sustainable society justifies using all possible means available to degrowth actors. As mentioned in the previous section, given the complexity of social change, it is impossible to foresee with certainty which means would lead to what ends. Calling for brutal means to achieve a peaceful end, for example, would ignore the great uncertainty attached to whether that end will come about because of these means. Instead, undesirable means may become ends in themselves (Parker 2021). Therefore, we maintain that it is vital that the strategising process itself as well as the ways and means discussed in degrowth strategies are guided by degrowth values like autonomy, care, conviviality, democracy, and equity even as their applicability in a specific context might be challenged.

Simply conflating means and ends when discussing and evaluating strategies is also problematic. Even for practices where means and ends seem to be in concert – sometimes referred to as prefigurative strategies – this is never completely the case. For example, a local bicycle repair cooperative engaged in prefigurative organising might still be using bicycle parts from factories that suppress organised labour or that use metals gained in exploitative extraction processes (see also Parker 2021). An open discussion about means and ends is thus needed to argue why a particular practice might nevertheless be considered part of a degrowth strategy.

Another reason for making a conceptual distinction between means and ends is that conflating them limits our thinking about how social-ecological transformation can be achieved. To drive the kind of change prefigured by running a bicycle repair coop at a systemic level, a broader set of strategic actions would be needed – such as cooperation with other initiatives for alternative transport, pushing for favourable regulation and redistribution, blocking unsustainable forms of transport, and supporting international workers' movements (Maney *et al.* 2012, Parker 2021, drawing on Boggs 1977). Analytically separating means and ends may also help in thinking about framing and communication, which are important elements of strategy in social movements (Smucker 2017, Staggenborg 2020). As Smucker (2017, 168–171) points out, when framed only in moral terms that reflect the ends, rather than, for example, showing how a particular action has a believable chance of making a difference, communication may fail to mobilise those sympathetic to the cause but struggling to see how it can be achieved. In other words, many strategic actions are primarily means to a greater end and may not always already embody the structures and processes characterising the end. They may nevertheless be important for driving social-ecological transformation and are thus not to be omitted from our thinking about strategies.

Strategy through organisation

Social-ecological transformation must be informed by a multiplicity of different knowledges and practices and involve many people – most of them not self-proclaimed proponents of degrowth and potentially not even self-proclaimed progressives (see Chapter 10). Strategies for social-ecological transformation are bottom-up and focused on building counter-power to dominant actors who focus on reproducing business as usual (see also Mueller 2003). Rather than trying to wield power for a single vision of a coordinated transformation, they primarily deal with dismantling existing power relations and organising alternatives.

By including multiple *actors* in the definition of strategy adopted in this book, we foreground the organisational capacities required for the strategising process (Staggenborg 2020). In other words, the creation and execution of strategies depend on the existence of collective actors (e.g. activist groups, social movements, economic organisations) that engage in organising. Thus, a key element of strategy is "building organisation in order to achieve major structural changes in the political, economic and social orders" (Breines 1989, 7). In tune with degrowth principles, organisation "needs to be able to take forms other than hierarchical and fixed" (Maeckelbergh 2011, 6), whilst acknowledging the necessity of action on a global scale (Parker 2021). This involves both "developing new social practices and autonomous structures of authority", like the Zapatista (Stahler-Sholk 2017, 24), and applying movement pressure to reshape the existing institutions that constrain the spectrum of what is possible, whether international organisations or the state (see Chapter 9). The question of how to organise can thus be seen as both the foundation for and a deliberate part of a successful strategy (Maney *et al.* 2012, Parker 2021).

We admit that there is a risk of creating hierarchies and closures when strategising, slipping into the problematic aspects of strategy that we started this section with. For example, this can happen through the emergence of "elite" groups or individual actors within a movement, specialised in strategising, and their separation from the rest of the movement. Such alienation could be mitigated by continued attention being paid to degrowth values like autonomy, care, conviviality and direct democracy in the strategising process, reflecting and acting upon any closures as they arise (Barca *et al.* 2019). Moreover, the necessity of embedding the strategising process in specific contexts and practices involves drawing on the experiences of members and allies already engaged in various fields of practice (Smith *et al.* 2021). An open and analytical exchange about strategies can thereby potentially help build coherence within different strands of the movement and beyond by forming narratives and enabling storytelling (de Moor and Wahlström 2019). However, the usefulness of clearly defining and discussing strategies in fostering movement participation and coordination rather than leading to alienation always hinges on how these dialogues are conducted. For degrowth, with strategic action becoming more important, good organisation and coordination are thus key to mitigating risks of developing distant leadership and misguided solutions.

Beyond its focus on bringing about "external transformation", a significant part of the book focuses on "internal movement building" (Maney *et al.* 2012) – in other words, the strategic coordination among degrowth actors, and with allied movements. The term "strategic assemblage" (see Chapter 3) points to three areas for deliberate coordination in relation to degrowth and strategy that are discussed in this book. First, while strategic plurality is essential for degrowth, plurality is not strategic in itself, but can become strategic through coordinated efforts of multiple actors involved in the degrowth movement and beyond. Explicitly denoting different strategic considerations will render the plurality of approaches that necessarily make up struggles for social-ecological transformation more effective, by highlighting synergies and acknowledging incompatibilities. Second, internal coordination within the degrowth movement, and an open discussion about it, may facilitate participation of more people in the movement, help build relations and create shared definitions, and avoid the reproduction of hierarchies (see Chapter 5). Finally, and crucially, actors who self-identify with degrowth only play a humble role in fostering social-ecological transformation and are meaningful only as part of larger joint efforts with allied movements. Thus, coordination of degrowth actors with a mosaic of connected movements is needed (see Chapter 6).

To sum up, thinking about strategy analytically and deliberately, we argue, can enhance bottom-up organising and action towards social-ecological transformation. Explicitly discussing and categorising strategies allows us to deliberate about their desirability, mutual compatibility, or incompatibility. Further, it enables us to analyse their efficacy and to coordinate and communicate our vision for how to achieve transformation with others – inside and outside of degrowth. To be aligned with the multiplicity of degrowth, strategies need to be dynamic and plural, based on degrowth values and sensitive to power relations. Strategies are to be fostered through organising and coordination, within the degrowth movement itself and as part of larger efforts of allied groups and social movements. The book can be seen as a collective quest for building strategies that are in tune with the multiplicity of degrowth, and it is now time to introduce its content.

Summary of the book

This book presents the first comprehensive attempt at grappling with the intersection of degrowth and strategy while confronting the underlying challenges of such an endeavour. It scrutinises strategy theoretically, identifies key strategic directions for degrowth, and explores strategies that are already being practised to realise a degrowth society. Its main argument is that to bring about social-ecological transformation, an intentional mix of strategies needs to be collectively deliberated and critically reflected on, making sure that it is (re-)aligned with degrowth values and contributes to the ensemble of broader efforts for social-ecological transformation.

In line with this argument, it was crucial to us that the making of the book itself was a collective process, assembling many voices. At the same time, we wanted the book to be carefully crafted to not be just an edited volume on the topic of strategy, but a coherent whole, where each contribution has its specific role and space. Thus, when contacting authors for writing different chapters, we asked them to address a specific sub-topic that we as the editorial team had identified as important to cover and that we thought they could contribute to. The different chapters of the book were written by academics, activists, and practitioners from the degrowth movement as well as allied groups and disciplines.

Part I of this volume explores the meaning of strategy for degrowth as both a research area and an emerging international social movement with its own agency. It presents the first collective effort of degrowth scholars to engage with the questions of strategy explicitly and in-depth. The chapters within this part of the book are in productive dialogue with each other, not shying away from disagreement while building upon a common foundation and charting various paths forward.

Part II provides an analysis of strategies in practice and offers insights from various actors involved in strategies for social-ecological transformation. First, it covers degrowth strategies in relation to provisioning systems, focusing on food, housing, technology, energy and mobility. Second, it addresses strategies for re-organising economic and political systems, covering care, work and labour, money and finance, and trade and decolonisation. This selection is not exhaustive but rather illustrative, illuminating strategies within concrete areas of practice.

To ensure coherence across the book, we followed three key steps. First, we shared the terminology on strategy used within the book, the key elements of which have been elaborated on earlier in this chapter. Second, we dedicated one chapter of the book (Chapter 2) to mapping out an analytical framework for engaging with strategy, which builds on the helpful vocabulary of Erik Olin Wright, but also diverges from it, in line with degrowth thinking. We then asked the authors of Part II to engage with the framework developed in the book, or the original terminology of Wright, in their chapters. Third, in asking the authors to engage with the book's vocabulary and framework, we strived for consistency across the book whilst allowing room for interpretation and flexibility by the authors. We hope that these steps have made it possible for multiple voices to come together into a polyphony, making the book a coherent whole.

Part I: Strategy in degrowth research and activism

Part I consists of three sections, each dealing with a specific aspect of degrowth and strategy. The first section highlights the importance of strategy for thinking about social-ecological transformation. Chapter 1 positions degrowth within the broader discourse on social-ecological transformation and argues why it is important for degrowth to discuss the issue of strategy. Chapter 2 outlines a framework for thinking about strategy in degrowth and other social movements through a critical dialogue with Erik Olin Wright. It is this framework, or the ideas of Wright directly, that we asked authors in Part II to engage with. Chapter 3 summarises how strategy has been discussed in the degrowth movement and suggests a new term to advance the discussion of strategy in degrowth – a strategic assemblage for degrowth.

The second section focuses on degrowth as a movement. Chapter 4 discusses the challenges of devising a common strategy within degrowth given its plurality, drawing on social movement studies. Chapter 5 provides an overview of the degrowth movement, its history, loose organisational structure and processes, reflecting on its agency and possible strategic ways forward. Chapter 6 situates degrowth *vis a vis* other social-ecological movements; it both explores how degrowth actors could position themselves and highlights what the degrowth movement can learn from other movements.

The final section in Part I highlights the diversity of how strategy is thought about in a degrowth context. Chapter 7 makes the case that, to overcome current asymmetric power relations underpinning capitalist growth, social equity needs to be a core element of strategising for social-ecological transformation. Chapter 8 suggests emancipatory potential as a useful guiding criterion for degrowth strategies. Chapter 9 sheds light on how the state can be understood and engaged with from a degrowth perspective and uses such a conceptualisation to rethink how state-society relations could be transformed. Chapter 10 concludes the section by reconciling, on the one hand, the insights on the diversity in degrowth, and, on the other, the voices arguing for strategic action within the degrowth movement.

Part II: Strategies in practice

Part II consists of two sections, where the first section focuses on strategies for transforming provisioning sectors and the second focuses on strategies for economic and political reorganisation.

Each chapter in Part II is divided into two sub-chapters, starting with an overview of degrowth strategies in an area of practice and followed by a concrete case in that field. The overview provides background information on the interdependencies of degrowth and the field studied as well as insights on strategies that have already been practised, discussed in the literature, or could be promising. Following the overview, each case delves into concrete examples and discusses their strategic challenges and potential in detail.

The two sub-chapters for each field have different authors: for most chapters, the overview is written by an author with an academic background, while the case sub-chapter is written by an activist or practitioner who constructively reflects on a degrowth strategy in their field – a campaign, an action, a project and so on – of which they have first-hand experience. In some chapters, academics and activists have collaborated, resulting in a single, integrated chapter that fulfils both purposes.

In Section I of Part II, Chapter 11 reviews literature on food and degrowth and argues that apart from building local food alternatives, the inclusion of other strategies and learning from, for example, the food sovereignty movement are necessary for social-ecological transformation. The case explores the strategies implemented by the Nyéléni food sovereignty movement at different administrative scales. Chapter 12 focuses on housing and zooms into a series of strategies at the national and regional levels. The Berlin-based campaign against private speculation in the housing market,

Deutsche Wohnen & CO Enteignen, is the case in focus. Chapter 13 challenges the role of digital technologies in our lives and questions our social imaginary toward technology. Highlighting potential strategies to challenge this relationship, it proposes low-tech digital tools and platforms like Decidim as a promising pathway for action. Chapter 14 on energy portrays various strategies that have been used to oppose big fossil fuel and renewable energy schemes, including the divestment movement and the use of legal instruments. The case looks into strategic alliances in resistance to mega-energy projects in Chile. Finally, Chapter 15 tackles questions of degrowth strategy in relation to mobility. It investigates different approaches to transforming the mobility sector, from technology-based scenarios to others that question mobility itself. A Paris-based case is analysed to assess the extent to which car-sharing may represent a satisfactory degrowth strategy.

Moving on to Section II, Chapter 16 introduces care as an essential underpinning for all social relations and provisioning, presenting strategies to strengthen care and avoid exploitative structures. The Integral Health Centre Cecosesola in Venezuela is an example of how care work can be organised differently based on rethinking its meaning and value in society. In Chapter 17, strategies for the reorganisation of paid work are discussed. The chapter delves specifically into the transformation of work in the aviation sector and explores the potential of alliances between unions and activists as well as local institutions for bringing about transformative change. Chapter 18 reviews various strategies for transforming the monetary and financial system. The example of the Cooperative for the Common Good in Austria points to the struggle of transforming the financial system from below. The section closes with Chapter 19 on trade and decolonisation, which illustrates that strategies in the Global North can only be considered against the background of colonial structures. The case presents the use of litigation to fight fossil corporate power in Nigeria.

Conclusion

Despite the urgent need for systemic change and the many strong voices that call for it, we see very little consequential action, while many demands are simply being watered down by governments and corporate actors. Even as their discussion is often rather sophisticated – with talks about climate emergency, circular economy, and various governance frameworks to address the multifaceted crisis – we cannot expect change at the scale required to come from those in power. Instead, the degrowth movement and allied groups need to think about how to organise strategically within and across their movements to shape the bottom-up social-ecological transformation that would bring an equitable, ecologically sustainable and thriving world for all.

The interrelations between theory and practice are at the core of the book, as no theory prepares us sufficiently for the creativity needed for building strategy, and strategy without theoretically informed considerations risks being reduced to short-term objectives without a vision. While Part I offers a nuanced and cogent view for building transformative strategies, Part II shows how strategies are embodied in ongoing practices that are already enacted by multiple actors striving for social-ecological transformation.

This book offers a solid ground for thinking about strategy in degrowth and related social movements and will inform action and research for social-ecological transformation. We expect that this volume – the outcome of a truly collective effort – will be of interest to academics, activists, practitioners and anyone else striving for an equitable and ecologically sustainable world, where everyone lives well, not at anyone else's expense and within planetary boundaries (Brand *et al.* 2021). This volume addresses strategy in a way that lives up to the multiplicity of degrowth on the one hand, and the need for well-coordinated and ambitious action for social-ecological transformation on the other. It points to many open questions in relation to strategy and challenges to address by the degrowth movement and its allies. We hope that this book will only be the beginning of a wider debate about how to collectively build strategies for systemic change. May many ideas and efforts that illuminate and strengthen the *how* of social-ecological transformation flourish!

References

Akbulut, Bengi, Federico Demaria, Julien-François Gerber, and Joan Martínez Alier. 2019. "Who Promotes Sustainability? Five Theses on the Relationships between the Degrowth and the Environmental Justice Movements." *Ecological Economics* 165 (November), 106418.

Ambach, Christoph, Nathan Barlow, Pietro Cigna, Joe Herbert, and Iris Frey. 2018. "Beyond Visions and Projects: The Need for a Debate on Strategy in the Degrowth Movement." *Degrowth.info* (blog), October 3, 2018. https://degrowth.info/blog/beyond-visions-and-projects-the-need-for-a-debate-on-strategy-in-the-degrowth-movement.

Andreucci, Diego, and Salvatore Engel-Di Mauro. 2019. "Capitalism, Socialism and the Challenge of Degrowth: Introduction to the Symposium." *Capitalism Nature Socialism* 30, no. 2: 176–188.

Asara, Viviana, Emanuele Profumi, and Giorgos Kallis. 2013. "Degrowth, Democracy and Autonomy." *Environmental Values* 22, no. 2: 217–239.

Asara, Viviana, Iago Otero, Federico Demaria, and Esteve Corbera. 2015. "Socially Sustainable Degrowth as a Social-Ecological Transformation: Repoliticizing Sustainability." *Sustainability Science* 10, no. 3: 375–384.

Asara, Viviana. 2020. "Degrowth Vienna 2020: Reflections upon the Conference and How to Move Forward – Part II." *Degrowth.info* (blog), https://degrowth.info/en/blog/degrowth-vienna-2020-reflections-upon-the-conference-and-how-to-move-forward-part-ii.

Barca, Stefania, Ekaterina Chertkovskaya, and Alexander Paulsson. 2019. "The End of Growth as We Know It: From Growth Realism to Nomadic Utopianism." In *Towards a Political Economy of Degrowth*, edited by Ekaterina Chertkovskaya, Alexander Paulsson and Stefania Barca, 1–17. London: Rowman & Littlefield.

Brand, Ulrich, Barbara Muraca, Éric Pineault, Marlyne Sahakian, Anke Schaffartzik, Andreas Novy, Christoph Streissler, Helmut Haberl, Viviana Asara, Kristina

Dietz, Miriam Lang, Ashish Kothari, Tone Smith, Clive Spash, Alina Brad, Melanie Pichler, Christina Plank, Giorgos Velegrakis, Thomas Jahn, Angela Carter, Qingzhi Huan, Giorgos Kallis, Joan Martínez Alier, Gabriel Riva, Vishwas Satgar, Emiliano Teran Mantovani, Michelle Williams, Markus Wissen and Christoph Görg. 2021. "From Planetary to Societal Boundaries: An Argument for Collectively Defined Self-Limitation." *Sustainability: Science, Practice and Policy*, 17, no. 1: 264–291.

Boggs, Carl. 1977. "Marxism, Prefigurative Communism, and the Problem of Workers' Control." *Radical America* 11, no. 6: 99–122. https://libcom.org/library/marxism-prefigurative-communism-problem-workers-control-carl-boggs.

Breines, Wini 1989. *Community and Organisation in the New Left 1962–1968: The Great Refusal.* New Brunswick, NJ: Rutgers University Press.

Burkhart, Corinna, Matthias Schmelzer, and Nina Treu. 2020. *Degrowth in Movement(s): Exploring Pathways for Transformation.* Winchester: Zero Books.

De Moor, Joost, and Mattias Wahlström. 2019. "Narrating Political Opportunities: Explaining Strategic Adaptation in the Climate Movement." *Theory and Society 48*, no. 3: 419–451.

Demaria, Federico, François Schneider, Filka Sekulova, and Joan Martinez–Alier. 2013. "What Is Degrowth? From an Activist Slogan to a Social Movement." *Environmental Values* 22, no. 2: 191–215.

Dengler, Corinna and Lisa M. Seebacher. 2019. "What about the Global South? Towards a Feminist Decolonial Degrowth Approach." *Ecological Economics* 157: 246–252.

Freedman, Lawrence. 2013. *Strategy: A History*. Oxford: Oxford University Press.

Gregoratti, Catia and Riya Raphael. 2019. "The Historical Roots of a Feminist 'Degrowth': Maria Mies's and Marylin Waring's Critiques of Growth." In *Towards a Political Economy of Degrowth*, edited by Ekaterina Chertkovskaya, Alexander Paulsson, and Stefania Barca. London: Rowman & Littlefield, 83–89.

Golsorkhi, Damon, Linda Rouleau, David Seidl, and Eero Vaara. 2010. "What is Strategy-as-Practice?" In *Cambridge Handbook of Strategy as Practice*, edited by Damon Golsorkhi, Linda Rouleau, David Seidl, and Eero Vaara, 1–29. Cambridge: Cambridge University Press.

Kallis, Giorgos, Federico Demaria, and Giacomo D'Alisa. 2015. "Introduction: Degrowth." In *Degrowth: A Vocabulary for a New Era*, edited by Giacomo D'Alisa, Federico Demaria, and Giorgos Kallis. London: Routledge, 1–17.

Kallis, Giorgos, Vasilis Kostakis, Steffen Lange, Barbara Muraca, Susan Paulson, and Matthias Schmelzer. 2018. "Research on Degrowth." *Annual Review of Environment and Resources* 43: 291–316.

Koch, Max. 2022. "State-Civil Society Relations in Gramsci, Poulantzas and Bourdieu: Strategic Implications for the Degrowth Movement." *Ecological Economics* 193: 107275.

Kothari, Ashish, Ariel Salleh, Arturo Escobar, Federico Demaria and Alberto Acosta. 2019. *Pluriverse: A Post-Development Dictionary.* Delhi: Authors Up Front.

Leonardi, Emanuele. 2019. "The Topicality of André Gorz's Political Economy: Rethinking 'Ecologie et liberté' (1977) to (Re)connect Marxism and Degrowth." In *Towards a Political Economy of Degrowth,* edited by Ekaterina Chertkovskaya, Alexander Paulsson, and Stefania Barca. London: Rowman & Littlefield, 55–58.

Maeckelbergh, Marianne. 2011. "Doing is Believing: Prefiguration as Strategic Practice in the Alterglobalization Movement." *Social Movement Studies* 10, no. 1: 1–20.

Maney, Gregory M., Rachel V. Kutz-Flamenbaum, Deana A. Rohlinger, and Jeff Goodwin. 2012. "An Introduction to Strategies for Social Change." In *Strategies for Social Change*, edited by Maney, Gregory M., Rachel V. Kutz-Flamenbaum, Deana A. Rohlinger, and Jeff Goodwin. Minneapolis: University of Minnesota Press.

Mueller, Tadzio. 2003. "Empowering Anarchy: Power, Hegemony, and Anarchist Strategy." *Anarchist Studies* 11, no. 2: 122–149.

Nelson, Anitra. 2022. *Beyond Money: A Post-Capitalist Strategy.* London: Pluto Press.

Nirmal, Padini and Dianne Rocheleau. 2019. "Decolonizing Degrowth in the Post-Development Convergence: Questions, Experiences and Proposals from Two Indigenous Territories." *Environment and Planning E: Nature and Space* 2, no. 3: 465–492.

Parker, Martin. 2021. "The Romance of Prefiguration and the Task of Organisation." *Journal of Marketing Management*, DOI: 10.1080/0267257X.2021.2006755.

Paulson, Susan. 2017. "Degrowth: Culture, Power and Change." *Journal of Political Ecology* 24: 425–666.

Smith, Thomas SJ, Mariusz Baranowski, and Benedikt Schmid. 2021. "Intentional Degrowth and Its Unintended Consequences: Uneven Journeys towards Post-Growth Transformations." *Ecological Economics* 190: 107215.

Smucker, Jonathan. 2017. *Hegemony How-to: A Roadmap for Radicals.* Edinburgh: AK Press.

Staggenborg, Suzanne. 2020. *Grassroots Environmentalism*. Cambridge: Cambridge University Press.

Val, Valentin, Peter M. Rosset, Carla Z. Lomelí, Omar F. Giraldo, and Dianne Rocheleau. 2019. "Agroecology and La Via Campesina I: The Symbolic and Material Construction of Agroecology through the Dispositive of 'Peasant-to-Peasant' Processes." *Agroecology and Sustainable Food Systems*, 43, no. 7–8, 872–894.

Weiss, Martin, and Claudio Cattaneo. 2017. "Degrowth – Taking Stock and Reviewing an Emerging Academic Paradigm." *Ecological Economics* 137: 220–230.

Wright, Erik Olin. 2009. *Envisioning Real Utopias*. London: Verso.

Wright, Erik Olin. 2012. "Taking the Social in Socialism Seriously." *Socio-Economic Review* 10: 386–402.

Wright, Erik Olin. 2019. *How to Be an Anti-Capitalist in the 21st Century*. London: Verso.

PART I

Strategy in degrowth research and activism

The importance of strategy for thinking about transformation

Chapter 1:

Radical emancipatory social-ecological transformations: degrowth and the role of strategy[1]

By Ulrich Brand

The contributions to this book show that the term degrowth is used in manifold ways: For a movement or an ensemble of movements, for a field of research and a community of scholars, for concrete initiatives and experiences, and – in the broadest sense – for a vision or utopia for another society. A society – or societies – which enable(s) freedom, justice and a "good living for all" without destroying the bio-physical conditions of social life on earth. That means an organisation of social life with very different institutions, logics, imaginaries as well as societal and power relations, including society-nature relations. The transformations required to create such organisations of social life are subject to historical and current experiences, uncertain futures, social and technological innovations, very different and plural forms of knowledge. To enable a good living for all is thereby at least partly related to planned and effective actions. This is where the question of *strategy* comes in, i.e., the question of *how* (see Introduction). Thereby, transformative actions, and questions of how to strategise towards them, are oriented, not only by shared experiences, but also by new normative horizons and visions of an alternative future. Degrowth has, so far, been strong in proposing these new horizons and visions. It is also increasingly offering convincing approaches to strategic thinking and action. While it is mainly formulated against the background of experiences in the Global North, globally, degrowth is thereby part of a plurality of approaches, of a pluriverse (Kothari *et al.* 2019) which has the goal

---

1   I would like to thank the whole editorial team of the book for their fantastic work to make this important publication possible. I am particularly indebted to the two editors who commented several times on draft versions of this chapter, which led to important improvements and more clarity. Of course, I take full responsibility for the content.

of fostering radical emancipatory *social-ecological transformations*.[2]

In this chapter, I embed the emerging debate about degrowth and strategy within broader discussions about social-ecological transformations. This then allows me to provide some pointers to issues that I perceive to be important for degrowth's strategic orientation process. I start off by briefly introducing some major aspects of the debate around social-ecological transformations. I thereby suggest some conceptual and also political-strategic distinctions between different types of transformations. Then, I put the degrowth perspective into conversation with this debate and outline some ideas about the role of strategy. After some brief considerations on "the question of the state", which has gained importance in degrowth debates, I conclude with reflections and open questions.

On social-ecological transformation(s): What kind?

In the last ten years, within debates around the multiple crises we are facing – and particularly those focusing on their social-ecological dimensions – there have been important contributions that used the terms societal, social-ecological, sustainability or Great transformation.

Within this debate, it is broadly acknowledged that the context of struggles towards transformation has changed dramatically, compared to earlier periods when discussions about sustainability were just emerging. First, the complexity of problems, especially concerning the causes and consequences of climate change, and the urgency to act, are broadly acknowledged. Secondly, it is recognised that it is not enough to manage the ecological crisis, as suggested in mainstream sustainability debates – "something" more profound is required. While sustainable development always carried

---

2   I do not use a clear-cut notion of strategies in this text. The relationship between degrowth and strategies are (as pointed out in Chapter 3), first, degrowth as a conflictive process and explicit strategies, second, manifold strategies that refer de facto but not explicitly to degrowth as a process towards social-ecological transformations which also might imply, third, the concrete utopia of a degrowth society (also see Chapter 4).

a kind of managerial core, such a perspective is questioned given the complexity and non-linearity of challenges. Thirdly, the economic and financial crisis, as well as the related crisis of representation and the ascent of extremist right-wing parties in many European countries, and now the COVID-19 pandemic, clarify that the ecological crisis is part of a multiple crisis; and that it needs to be dealt with in a more comprehensive, i.e., transformative, fashion. And finally, this crisis is global. The era of sustainable development emerged in a time prior to globalisation where the problems and their solutions were mainly located in the Global North; look, for instance, at the 1997 Kyoto protocol, which required action only from the industrialised countries. This is not any longer the case, as the Paris Agreement from 2015 shows.

Against the background of these shifting circumstances, I see two points of consensus in how different stakeholders use the term "transformation": The first is as a reference to the alarming warnings, for instance of the IPCC report from 2018. This report calls for "rapid, far-reaching and unprecedented changes in all aspects of society to limit global warming to 1.5 degree Celsius" (IPCC 2018), and this means overcoming the fossil-fuel dependent economy and society. The second point of consensus, as Nalau and Handmer (2015) identify in a literature review, is that transformation can be understood as a "fundamental system change" which goes beyond incremental adaptation, even as it is precisely these incremental steps that still predominate. It is about "a fundamental shift that questions and challenges values and routine practices and changes prior perspectives employed to rationalise decisions and pathways" (Nalau and Handmer 2015, 351). In short, transformation implies non-linear change and that there is no prioritisation of any temporal – i.e., short, medium or long term – or spatial scale – e.g., the national or international.

Beyond these points of consensus, the way "transformation" is interpreted reflects different worldviews and approaches, interests and estimates about potential entry and starting points (O'Brien

2012, Nalau and Handmer 2015, Brand 2016a). And, therefore, there is also no clear-cut definition of what is meant by social-ecological transformation(s). I understand it as an umbrella term that constitutes a new political-epistemic terrain. The term, social-ecological transformation(s), is not as prominent of a term as sustainable development has been since the 1990s. In contemporary discourses, the more recent version of sustainable development – the Sustainable Development Goals – similarly take prominence over the term social-ecological transformation. Terms like the green economy or the Green (New) Deal have probably also gained more political attention. However, it seems that in light of the afore-mentioned deepening of the ecological crisis, discussions about transformations do not just serve to open a terrain for more radical and hence adequate diagnoses of the problems we face, but also have a similar function as sustainable development did when it first appeared. That is, this framing aims to put the crisis into a larger context and to unite different fields of thinking and action against business-as-usual strategies.

From my perspective, the fact that definitions of social-ecological transformations remain vague has to do with a constitutive tension within most uses of the term. In many contributions to the debate, the radical diagnosis of ecological problems and crises is accompanied by a rather incremental understanding of transformation processes themselves. At first sight, this is surprising because insights into the deep-rootedness of crises should lead to radical solutions or, at least, proposals that effectively deal with root causes. However, the tension between radical diagnosis and rather docile strategies has to do with an obvious implicit or even explicit assumption that transformation processes can best be initiated and amplified with and within the current political, economic and cultural institutional system, dominant actors and related rationalities. Radical diagnosis meets Realpolitik.

One could call this usage of the concept of transformation a "new critical orthodoxy" (Brand 2016b). Its main characteristic is that it is a radical diagnosis of the problem, claiming to lead to far-reaching change, while it is combined with a rather incremental understanding of the concrete processes and steps of social change in order to cope with the problems. The current critical orthodoxy does not question dominant rationalities and institutions (Biesecker and von Winterfeld 2013) but relies on a liberal understanding of societies: "States" and "markets" are assumed to be given without problematising the bureaucratic logic of the state and the capitalist logic of the market that are intrinsically linked to the logic of economic growth. A broader understanding of the economy as a basis for other forms of well-being and social-ecological transformations is not present. The new orthodoxy presupposes that with good arguments and learning processes, all relevant actors will gain adequate insights into the required transformation. And this discourse also seems to have little understanding of the conflict-driven character of modern societies, of power and domination.

This is the reason why I propose the term *radical emancipatory social-ecological transformations*. In order to provide a good life for all, one must think beyond reform. The type of transformation required is not about prioritising the change of the energy and resource base while alleviating potential social collateral damages. Emancipatory transformations are different from more technocratic, state-centred, and green growth-oriented ones, but also from the quite dynamic "radicalism" of right-wing forces. They are about a very different remaking of society, beyond exploitation and domination. It is radical emancipatory social-ecological transformations – with their manifold strategies – that degrowth seeks, and which are the topic of this book.

On degrowth

A changing context of crisis and competing ideas about what sort of "transformation" is necessary constitute the terrain on which degrowth strategies are formulated and pursued. From my perspective, and despite many internal differences (Asara *et al.* 2015, Eversberg and Schmelzer 2018, Kallis *et al.* 2018, Schmelzer and Vetter 2019), the basic common denominator of degrowth as a critical approach is that the capitalist and industrialist growth imperative, that organises many aspects of social life, is one of the major problems of our times and needs to be overcome – in the Global North *and* in the Global South.

In other chapters of this book, a diversity of degrowth approaches are outlined (see Chapters 3 and 4). Here, I want to highlight one aspect that seems important to me when we think about strategies: the importance of looking at societies as a system of power and domination. Societies organised around the capitalist growth imperative are based on and reinforce social relations in which life opportunities and spaces of action, as well as assets and income, are distributed unevenly. It guarantees economically, politically and culturally manifold social inclusion and exclusion (Brand 2018). A society liberated from growth has to tackle various forms of social domination: class, race, gender, North–South relations, and the domination of nature.

Degrowth is then about radical emancipatory social-ecological transformations "by design" – not "by disaster" – because the latter would likely imply a brutal shifting of the burden. It would enhance inequality and would not stop destructive dynamics. Transformations by design – and this is the starting point of strategic thinking – is about choices and decisions, conflicts and alliances, expectations and desires, long-term thinking and action. It is about dealing with the root causes of problems and crises, not their symptoms, about seeing the "woods rather than the trees" (Freedman 2013, ix). To sum up, degrowth is a narrative or imaginary to change social discourse, power relations, and ways of thinking, and also to promote collective action. It is therefore also a means of thinking about, developing and communicating strategies.

To foster social-ecological transformations in this direction needs material and immaterial resources, the effective application of strategies and their appropriate sequence (Freedman 2013, ix–x). In that sense, degrowth is an integral part of emancipatory debates, strategies and real social change – and it takes place in highly dynamic contexts. Those contexts are always historically concrete and sometimes shift suddenly (e.g., in times of a pandemic). This is why I think that an understanding of strategy as "a plan of collective action intended to accomplish goals within a particular context" (see Chapter 4) might run the risk of focusing too much on the relationships between formulated goals and instruments to reach the goals and may underestimate the sometimes rapidly changing context. Long- and mid-term strategies need to consider contingencies and the need for adaptation to shifting situations. Besides strategies, the spaces and organisational forms to permanently evaluate these contexts and the actions and strategies of other actors are important.

The importance of context and some pointers for degrowth's emerging debate on strategy

Strategies and strategic thinking have the goal of creating the conditions for the mid-term transformations about which we already have some ideas. But strategies also create the conditions for future transformations by changing power relations, blocking devastating economic practices, redesigning the state and public policies, and questioning the capitalist growth imperative.

Some strategies are more oriented towards movement building (see Chapters 4–6). They should remain open to contingent moments, favourable or unfavourable change, and be adaptable. Strategies require strategic actors, and they are also not just there but emerge, develop, change, gain strength, become weaker, even disappear.

When we understand degrowth strategies as thought constructs that somehow bind ends, ways and means together (see Introduction to this volume), we should not forget that many important strategic actions are rather defensive, in the sense that they try to block immediate harm and further expansion of capitalism. An example of this is when pipelines, airport expansion, coal or oil extraction or the introduction of GMOs are contested. The "end" here may appear very concrete, but defensive strategies are an integral part of the creation of emancipatory horizons and concrete alternatives.

Much analytical and political trouble starts when we consider strategies at a scale where the "object" that should be transformed is global society and its relations to nature, which is mediated by disastrous systems featuring powerful actors. This refers to a transformation of complex societal conditions, for example within the existing mobility or food systems and related relationships of forces. But my main point concerning strategies is this: If we focus on strategies (and not just on actions), we need to consider them from a relational perspective. A strategy is not a property of an organisation and should not be reduced to effects or reached goals (Golsorkhi et al. 2010, 8). Freeman (2015, xi) further argues that, in practice, strategy is rarely an orderly movement towards goals set in advance. Instead, the process evolves through a "series of states, each one not quite what was anticipated or hoped for, requiring a reappraisal and modification of the original strategy, including ultimate objectives." Strategies are fluid and flexible, "governed by the starting point and not the end point" (*Ibid.*).

To emphasise different ways to understand social-ecological transformations – as I did in the first section of this chapter – is not just a thought experiment. It mirrors different social and political projects for dealing with the deepening social-ecological crisis. This is, in a way, the playing field in relation to which degrowth strategies are defined.

I think that this is important because, without any doubt, the overall *project* of an emancipatory social-ecological transformation through manifold concrete transformations – where degrowth strategies play an important role – is in opposition to many other projects. Other actors and alliances pursue more or less liberal projects of social-ecological transformation to cope with the multiple crisis of capitalism. Many of them are in favour of "green growth", competitiveness and the role of private capital to deal with the social-ecological crisis. The terrain of struggle for degrowth perspectives and initiatives is structured by dominant approaches that intend to install green capitalism under the header of social-ecological transformations (Tanuro and Ennis 2013, Smith 2016, Brand and Wissen 2021, Chapter 7). This is sometimes framed by what was described above as a new critical orthodoxy – a more or less radical change of the resource base of capitalism without transforming its cultural political economy and related logics of growth and power relations.

Other projects openly accept the humanitarian consequences of climate change as a given – (e.g., through climate change denialism or fatalism) – and have shifted towards defending the current mode of living for some defined in-group – by force if necessary. This can be called an authoritarian stabilisation of the imperial mode of production and living (Brand and Wissen 2021).

Viewed against this backdrop, the debate on strategy within degrowth is important for several reasons: First, dominant social dynamics are not favourable: Given the increasingly intense multiple crises and the rise of right-wing forces with strategies that are obviously quite successful, radical emancipatory change is the top priority of our times – and it must be quite fast given the potential and already-occurring ecological devastation. Emancipatory forces need to be more effective in formulating goals, thinking concrete steps in advance and applying them, building alliances, and using manifold material and immaterial resources effectively.

Second, degrowth as an explicit social movement is and will remain too weak to achieve such radical changes (this weakness might also be a reason why strategic questions have not played as central of a role in the degrowth debate). Even the understandable desire to strengthen it via a *Degrowth International* will be not sufficient. This makes questions of strategy even more important because fighting for emancipation implies using "underdog strategies" (Freedman 2013, xii) in light of powerful opponents and existing un-sustainability. Strategies for emancipatory social-ecological transformations are about "the art of creating power" (*Ibid.*) not in the sense of a "duel" or a "final struggle", but as a diverse and creative process to block the destructive components of existing social life and related interests. For this, degrowth needs allies that may not use the term degrowth but might nevertheless be open to its aims and strategies for emancipatory social-ecological transformations. To put it differently, emancipatory demands (e.g., to realise better social-ecological living conditions for all, to block and shape existing power relations and dominant societal logics) necessarily evolve in many different spaces and should be linked to each other – but probably not under the header of degrowth. As an example, anti-racist, feminist and housing struggles fight power and domination but often do not deal with ecological issues. But they are key for emancipatory social-ecological transformations (see Chapter 9).

This is why I prefer to speak of social-ecological transformations rather than of degrowth transformation(s) because it is broader. An actor such as Greenpeace constantly formulates strategies but might not refer explicitly to degrowth, even if it may play a role in the transformation to a degrowth society. Similarly, in many trade unions, uneasiness with the capitalist or, at least, neoliberal growth imperative and discussions about alternative models of well-being might gain prominence. But given that workers and trade unions have historically experienced growth as a precondition of distributional policies, the term "degrowth" itself is not used by most trade unions.

Third, and relatedly, degrowth is not just a question of actors and alliances (even though this is important) but also of changing institutions – or more explicitly, organisations – and practices of public, political, economic and cultural organisations, private firms and everyday working and living practices of people that are currently in many respects destructive. In that sense, besides changing the socio-political conditions and power relations (usually the aim of social movements and a condition for this is a collective identity) social-ecological transformations imply transforming everyday subjectivities and imaginaries, and very different forms of material reproduction (the "economy"). It is also about learning and education, changing lifestyles and practices (which are often only indirectly the object of strategies), not being afraid to make mistakes, and being open to things that we cannot yet imagine. Degrowth strategies need to be "translated" into dominant institutional paradigms, through concrete micro-strategies and struggles. For instance, to shift the growth dynamics of a state bureaucracy (be it a ministry, a university or a public enterprise) also requires the action of many people and groups within the apparatus. What became clear at the *Degrowth Vienna 2020 Conference: Strategies for Social-ecological Transformation* (and even before) is that radical social-ecological transformations should go beyond being a niche movement while still avoiding the replication of a form of statism. Emancipatory transformations need to take place in many spheres.

Fourth, given existing complexities and uncertainties, I see degrowth as an important approach, but I would hesitate to look for an "overarching degrowth strategy" as a more or less coherent meta-vision. I think that strategies and their coordination are of utmost importance, but not as "grand strategies", nor should we try to coordinate all or most of them. Moreover, from my perspective, it is not necessary – and it does even not make sense – to prioritise particular strategies (activism *or* research *or* nowtopias; and this does not go hand in hand with "strategic indeterminance" as Herbert *et al.* 2018 argue). Radical social change needs good and emancipatory strategising in all spheres. In light of the required radical transformation processes, efforts and dynamics to promote them must be massively enhanced. The question of priorities might come up when, for instance, personal or financial resources are scarce, and decisions must be taken (here some evaluation criteria might help; see Chapter 7). But it cannot be answered in an abstract sense beforehand.

Finally, the role of degrowth research in the process of building, contestation, and implementation of strategies is manifold. It helps to get a better understanding of contexts, to make implicit ontological assumptions explicit and discussable. Those assumptions are highly relevant for strategy-building. Research can systematise historical experiences, or experiences in other regions or terrains of conflict (i.e., comparative perspectives), which might help sharpen strategies. It can look through in-depth case studies at successful or failed strategies – those that became part of centrist compromises.

The "question of the state"

We can learn from debates on social-ecological transformation(s) that the massive changes that are envisioned will be highly conflictive and confronted by the enormous powers and interests of those who benefit from the status quo. This is why the "question of the state" is of utmost importance. The contribution by Max Koch (Chapter 8) later in this book will deal at greater length with this issue (see also Chapter 3). But let me just briefly explain why I perceive this topic to be very important.

Degrowth emerged in the last decades as a movement-based approach or, as it is sometimes said, as "activist-led science" and often focuses on concrete alternatives in niches and on the everyday level (what Erik Olin Wright calls *interstitial strategies*). Conversely, by and large in degrowth research, little work has been done with respect to the state. However, this is changing (see D'Alisa and Kallis 2020, Koch 2020) and some contributions in this book are an expression of the increasing attention paid to the state. The state is not any longer per se seen as a barrier to emancipatory social-ecological transformations – which it still is in many respects.

Certainly, the actually-existing state has to be theorised critically as part of the dominant capitalist growth regime, which enacts class-based, gendered and racialised as well as global forms of domination and exploitation. And yet, in the tradition of critical state theory, the state can also be understood as an asymmetric terrain of struggles and as a system that can possibly block powerful interests and give emancipatory demands and achievements certain durability (Poulantzas 1978, Jessop 2007, Bretthauer et al. 2011, Lang and Brand 2015): Leaving the oil in the soil, stopping the operation of nuclear power plants and the use of GMOs, enabling the expansion of sustainable public transport and democratic energy transitions, creating an education system that is part of the transformations we are talking about, introducing a tax system that supports them, and so on. This can be promoted by creating binding rules, limiting destructive dynamics driven by existing power structures, and dedicating resources to promote social-ecological processes, such as the establishing of social-ecological provisioning systems and infrastructures that are not guided by profit.

This implies that the very structure of the capitalist, imperial, patriarchal and racist state needs to be entirely transformed and that this struggle will also happen within the state. But this will only happen in conjuncture with social movements, conscious and engaged people, a critical public and progressive businesses. An anarchist position would argue that the state needs to be abolished. I agree that this applies to the capitalist state, but I think that some form of apparatuses to administer things, to give social life certain rules and a certain level of stability will remain important. This is particularly the case if we also consider the global scale, i.e., the need for some kind of democratic and transparent mechanisms of coordination. In that sense, in a social-ecologically transformed society, a "state" also remains important as a label for a system that is an important part of emancipatory social-ecological transformations and – as a result of social struggles – secures them.

We have seen in the current COVID-19 pandemic, that the state is the crisis manager that secures certain, though unequal, forms of public interest and coherence that private capital cannot do and is not willing to do. But probably the most important argument for making use of the state is the need for massive investment, which in large parts will be public (or private investment with strong rules) and with strong involvement of the wage earners and the public (see, for example, Lehndorff 2020 on the historical New Deal, and proposals in Riexinger *et al.* 2021). Many people who see the deep problems and might be willing to actively contribute or have at least passively accepted the need for far-reaching changes expect a form of leadership from the state – at least in many countries of the Global North where we still have the experience that the state does not act exclusively in favour of the oligarchy and transnational capital.

In that sense, a transformed state that provides structure, personnel and policies is necessarily part of changing societal power relations and orientations sought by a successful broad movement towards social-ecological transformations. The debate about degrowth's strategic orientation thus needs a strategy for the state.

Conclusion

It is remarkable how social-ecological transformation processes towards an emancipated society always took and still take place in many spheres. This book gives an excellent overview of ongoing and potential processes of change in various areas, which should be amplified. Some transformative activities are formulated and realised under the header of degrowth, others refer more implicitly to degrowth ideas. In that sense, degrowth is a "vantage point" for a mosaic of alternatives (Chapter 6) – but, as I argued, in my view degrowth even goes beyond social movements. Social-ecological transformations are urgently needed in many spheres where destructive growth dynamics, related interests, and power relations still prevail. Therefore, a crucial challenge is that those alternatives do not remain in niches (which are important enough) but can be universalised at a global macro scale, i.e., can be lived in principle by all people and not at the cost of destroying the very biophysical conditions of social life on earth. To become more effective in bringing about societal change, strategies are needed.

Some authors fear that degrowth strategies might run the danger of not being anti-capitalist enough and contributing to taming capitalism, i.e., to soften its worst social and ecological impacts or to promote its greening (see Chapter 2). However, and despite the fact that we do not like it, if we consider the existing capitalist, patriarchal, racist and imperial context and related power relations, it is very likely that, for some time, anti-capitalist strategies will – not as their formulated aims but in fact – contribute to such a taming.

Indeed, one core contention of mine in this chapter has been that transformations need to take place today, under existing capitalist conditions and in the context of competing projects and visions. I argued in this chapter in favour of thinking strategies in a relational manner, particularly during periods of crisis and through policies implemented during those periods. The project of greening capitalism as well as authoritarian strategies to stabilise it might gain force and therefore shape degrowth strategies.

Meanwhile, there is a tension in the fact that some demands and initiatives need to be radical (to change the existing imaginaries and power relations) and other demands and initiatives should seek to mobilise the largest possible amount of people – for example, demands should be related to people's material interests (e.g., stop rising rents). Such a "strategic division of labour" within particular movements and among various actors might be useful: some parts are more radical and others more reformist, but they are conscious of this necessary division of labour.

I have also highlighted that alliances and engagement with institutions should not be seen from a tactical perspective ("to gain power for our project which we more or less know") but as a necessary condition of such a broad change. Many other actors and changes within organisations do not run under the header of degrowth yet might share many of its aims. Explicit degrowth actors should engage with others and build alliances.

The strength of the degrowth perspective is that it insists on the necessity to have a general idea of a society that enables a good living for all. There are important principles, such as collectively defined forms of self-limitation (Kallis 2019, Muraca 2013, Brand *et al.* 2021), but we do not know a clear "end" to our struggles beyond visions that manifest the positive experiences today (Konzeptwerk Neue Ökonomie 2020). What might be needed instead is an overall *dispositif* or orientation of emancipation, which, even now, might not have a name – a social atmosphere of acting and fighting, of saying "no" and of starting something radically different and with emancipatory principles, purposes and strategies.

But there are many open questions: How do we mobilise people to engage in political organisations and social movements, but also, how do we rethink and shape their everyday practices? Which roles do workers play and other progressive factions within capitalism? When it comes to the creation of collective identities or concrete campaigns, what is the role of (social) media?

We are also talking about degrowth research as a scientific practice. What kind of research (and development) is needed, which role will technologies and technological knowledge play? How do we change existing and powerful "sociotechnical imaginaries"?[3] How do we change the scientific and economic core of current (largely unsustainable) transformation processes? What kinds of knowledge and qualifications do we need in such a society? What role will science and experts play? What is the feasibility of different proposals and means for transformations? What is the role of social-ecological experimentation, and that of the "pioneers of change", such as inventors, companies, political activists, consumers, and non-governmental organisations – in various fields such as urban development, energy, and agriculture?

So many questions, and many more. I hope that this chapter will serve its purpose, i.e., to be a kind of extended introduction to a book in which many of these questions are dealt with and some even tentatively or concretely answered.

But most answers to those pressing questions will not be given

---

3   Jasanoff and Kim (2015, 19) define sociotechnical imaginaries as "collectively held, institutionally stabilised and publicly performed visions of desirable futures, animated by shared understandings of forms of social life and social order attainable through, and supportive of, advances in science and technology."

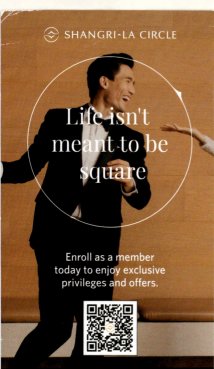

fold social practices that foster radical
al transformations. Theoretical and
the sharing and systematisation of
ented research, can help to reflect on
difficult and contradictory realisation.
e them.

Demaria, and Esteve Corbera. 2015. "Socially
ecological Transformation: Repoliticizing Sus-
, no. 3: 375–384.

interfeld. 2013. „Alte Rationalitätsmuster und
blinden Flecken der Transformationsdebat-

021. *The Imperial Mode of Living: Everyday Life
m*. London: Verso.

Brand, Ulrich, Barbara Muraca, Éric Pineault, Marlyne Sahakian, Anke Schaffartzik, Andreas Novy, Christoph Streissler *et al*. 2021. "From Planetary to Societal
Boundaries: An Argument for Collectively Defined Self-Limitation." *Sustainability: Science, Practice and Policy* 17, no. 1: 265–292.

Brand, Ulrich. 2016a. "How to Get Out of the Multiple Crisis? Contours of a Critical Theory of Social-Ecological Transformation." *Environmental Values* 25, no. 5:
503–525.

Brand, Ulrich. 2016b. 'Transformation' as a New Critical Orthodoxy: The Strategic
Use of the Term 'Transformation' Does Not Prevent Multiple Crises." *GAIA –
Ecological Perspectives for Science and Society* 25, no. 1: 23–27.

Brand, Ulrich. 2018. "Growth and Domination. Shortcomings of the (De-) Growth
Debate." In *Climate Justice and the Economy: Social Mobilization, Knowledge and
the Political*, edited by Jacobsen, and Stefan Gaarsmand, 148–167. London: Routledge.

Bretthauer, Lars, Alexander Gallas, John Kannankulam, and Ingo Stützle. 2011.
Reading Poulantzas: Towards a Contemporary Marxist State Theory. London: Merlin Press.

Golsorkhi, Damon, Linda Rouleau, David Seidl, and Eero Vaara. 2010. "Introduction: What Is Strategy as Practice?" In *Cambridge Handbook of Strategy as Practice*,

edited by Golsorkhi, Damon, Linda Rouleau, David Seidl, and Eero Vaara, 1–20. Cambridge: Cambridge University Press.

D'Alisa, Giacomo, and Giorgos Kallis. 2020. "Degrowth and the State." *Ecological Economics* 169, 106486.

Eversberg, Dennis, and Matthias Schmelzer. 2018. "The Degrowth Spectrum: Convergence and Divergence within a Diverse and Conflictual Alliance." *Environmental Values* 27, no. 3: 245–267.

Freedman, Lawrence. 2013. *Strategy: A History.* Oxford: Oxford University Press.

Herbert, Joe, Nathan Barlow, Iris Frey, Christoph Ambach, and Pietro Cigna. 2018. "Beyond Visions and Projects: The Need for a Debate on Strategy in the Degrowth Movement." *Resilience*, Degroth.info, October 3, 2018. https://degrowth.info/blog/beyond-visions-and-projects-the-need-for-a-debate-on-strategy-in-the-degrowth-movement.

IPCC. 2018. "Summary for policymakers." In *Global Warming of 1.5. An IPCC Special Report on the Impacts of Global Warming of 1.5 C above Pre-Industrial Levels and Related Global Greenhouse Gas Emission Pathways, in the Context of Strengthening the Global Response to the Threat of Climate Change, Sustainable Development, and Efforts to Eradicate Poverty,* Katowice. https://www.ipcc.ch/sr15/chapter/spm/.

Jasanoff, Sheila, and Sang-Hyun Kim, eds. 2015. *Dreamscapes of Modernity: Sociotechnical Imaginaries and the Fabrication of Power.* Chicago/London: The University of Chicago Press.

Jessop, Bob. 2007. *State Power.* London: Polity.

Kallis, Giorgos. 2019. *Limits: Why Malthus Was Wrong and Why Environmentalists Should Care.* Palo Alto, CA: Stanford University Press.

Kallis, Giorgos, Vasilis Kostakis, Steffen Lange, Barbara Muraca, Susan Paulson, and Matthias Schmelzer. 2018. "Research on Degrowth." *Annual Review of Environment and Resources* 43: 291–316.

Koch, Max. 2020. "The State in the Transformation to a Sustainable Postgrowth Economy." *Environmental Politics* 29, no. 1: 115–133.

Konzeptwerk Neue Ökonomie eds. 2020. *Zukunft für alle. Eine Vision für 2048. Gerecht. Ökologisch. Machbar.* Munich: oekom.

Kothari, Ashish, Ariel Salleh, Arturo Escobar, Federico Demaria, and Alberto Acosta, eds. 2019. *Pluriverse: A Post-Development Dictionary.* Delhi: Tulika Books and Authors Upfront.

Lang, Miriam, and Ulrich Brand. 2015. «Dimensiones de la transformación social y in this book but in the manifold social practices that foster radical emancipatory social-ecological transformations. Theoretical and conceptual work, as well as the sharing and systematisation of experiences in empirically oriented research, can help to reflect on those practices and their often difficult and contradictory realisation. But, of course, it cannot replace them.

References

Asara, Viviana, Iago Otero, Federico Demaria, and Esteve Corbera. 2015. "Socially Sustainable Degrowth as a Social-ecological Transformation: Repoliticizing Sustainability." *Sustainability Science* 10, no. 3: 375–384.

Biesecker, Adelheid, and Uta von Winterfeld. 2013. „Alte Rationalitätsmuster und neue Beharrlichkeiten: Impulse zu blinden Flecken der Transformationsdebatte." *GAIA* 22, no. 3: 160–165.

Brand, Ulrich, and Markus Wissen. 2021. *The Imperial Mode of Living: Everyday Life and the Ecological Crisis of Capitalism*. London: Verso.

Brand, Ulrich, Barbara Muraca, Éric Pineault, Marlyne Sahakian, Anke Schaffartzik, Andreas Novy, Christoph Streissler *et al.* 2021. "From Planetary to Societal Boundaries: An Argument for Collectively Defined Self-Limitation." *Sustainability: Science, Practice and Policy* 17, no. 1: 265–292.

Brand, Ulrich. 2016a. "How to Get Out of the Multiple Crisis? Contours of a Critical Theory of Social-Ecological Transformation." *Environmental Values* 25, no. 5: 503–525.

Brand, Ulrich. 2016b. 'Transformation' as a New Critical Orthodoxy: The Strategic Use of the Term 'Transformation' Does Not Prevent Multiple Crises." *GAIA – Ecological Perspectives for Science and Society* 25, no. 1: 23–27.

Brand, Ulrich. 2018. "Growth and Domination. Shortcomings of the (De-) Growth Debate." In *Climate Justice and the Economy: Social Mobilization, Knowledge and the Political*, edited by Jacobsen, and Stefan Gaarsmand, 148–167. London: Routledge.

Bretthauer, Lars, Alexander Gallas, John Kannankulam, and Ingo Stützle. 2011. *Reading Poulantzas: Towards a Contemporary Marxist State Theory.* London: Merlin Press.

Golsorkhi, Damon, Linda Rouleau, David Seidl, and Eero Vaara. 2010. "Introduction: What Is Strategy as Practice?" In *Cambridge Handbook of Strategy as Practice*, edited by Golsorkhi, Damon, Linda Rouleau, David Seidl, and Eero Vaara, 1–20. Cambridge: Cambridge University Press.

D'Alisa, Giacomo, and Giorgos Kallis. 2020. "Degrowth and the State." *Ecological Economics* 169, 106486.

Eversberg, Dennis, and Matthias Schmelzer. 2018. "The Degrowth Spectrum: Convergence and Divergence within a Diverse and Conflictual Alliance." *Environmental Values* 27, no. 3: 245–267.

Freedman, Lawrence. 2013. *Strategy: A History.* Oxford: Oxford University Press.

Herbert, Joe, Nathan Barlow, Iris Frey, Christoph Ambach, and Pietro Cigna. 2018. "Beyond Visions and Projects: The Need for a Debate on Strategy in the Degrowth Movement." *Resilience*, Degroth.info, October 3, 2018. https://degrowth.info/blog/beyond-visions-and-projects-the-need-for-a-debate-on-strategy-in-the-degrowth-movement.

IPCC. 2018. "Summary for policymakers." In *Global Warming of 1.5. An IPCC Special Report on the Impacts of Global Warming of 1.5 C above Pre-Industrial Levels and Related Global Greenhouse Gas Emission Pathways, in the Context of Strengthening the Global Response to the Threat of Climate Change, Sustainable Development, and Efforts to Eradicate Poverty*, Katowice. https://www.ipcc.ch/sr15/chapter/spm/.

Jasanoff, Sheila, and Sang-Hyun Kim, eds. 2015. *Dreamscapes of Modernity: Sociotechnical Imaginaries and the Fabrication of Power.* Chicago/London: The University of Chicago Press.

Jessop, Bob. 2007. *State Power.* London: Polity.

Kallis, Giorgos. 2019. *Limits: Why Malthus Was Wrong and Why Environmentalists Should Care.* Palo Alto, CA: Stanford University Press.

Kallis, Giorgos, Vasilis Kostakis, Steffen Lange, Barbara Muraca, Susan Paulson, and Matthias Schmelzer. 2018. "Research on Degrowth." *Annual Review of Environment and Resources* 43: 291–316.

Koch, Max. 2020. "The State in the Transformation to a Sustainable Postgrowth Economy." *Environmental Politics* 29, no. 1: 115–133.

Konzeptwerk Neue Ökonomie eds. 2020. *Zukunft für alle. Eine Vision für 2048. Gerecht. Ökologisch. Machbar.* Munich: oekom.

Kothari, Ashish, Ariel Salleh, Arturo Escobar, Federico Demaria, and Alberto Acosta, eds. 2019. *Pluriverse: A Post-Development Dictionary.* Delhi: Tulika Books and Authors Upfront.

Lang, Miriam, and Ulrich Brand. 2015. «Dimensiones de la transformación social y el rol de las instituciones.» In ¿ *Cómo transformar? Instituciones y cambio social en América Latina y Europa,* edited by Lang, Miriam, Cevallos, Belén, and Claudia López, 7–32. Quito: Abya Yala, Fundación Rosa Luxemburg.

Lehndorff, Steffen. 2020. *New Deal heißt Mut zum Konflikt. Was wir von Roosevelts Reformpolitik der 1930er Jahre heute lernen können. Eine Flugschrift.* Hamburg: VSA Verlag.

Muraca, Barbara. 2013. "Décroissance: A Project for a Radical Transformation of Society." *Environmental Values* 22, no. 2: 147–169.

Nalau, Johanna, and John Handmer. 2015. "When is Transformation a Viable Policy Alternative?" *Environmental Science & Policy,* no. 54: 349–356.

O'Brien, Karen. 2012. "Global Environmental Change II: From Adaptation to Deliberate Transformation." *Progress in Human Geography* 36, no. 5: 667–676.

Poulantzas, Nicos. 2013 (1978). *State, Power, Socialism.* London: Verso.

Riexinger, Becker, Lia Becker, Katharina Dahme, and Christina Kaindl. 2021. *A Left Green New Deal: An Internationalist Blueprint.* New York: Monthly Review Press.

Schmelzer, Matthias, and Andrea Vetter. 2019. *Degrowth/Postwachstum zur Einführung.* Hamburg: Junius Verlag.

Smith, Richard, and World Economics Association. 2016. *Green Capitalism: The God that Failed.* London: College Publications.

Tanuro, Daniel, and Jane Susanna Ennis. 2013. *Green Capitalism: Why It Can't Work.* London: Merlin Press.

Chapter 2:

A strategic canvas for degrowth: in dialogue with Erik Olin Wright

By Ekaterina Chertkovskaya

Introduction

In order to build strategies for social-ecological transformation, we need to think about them analytically, in relation to the goals of concrete organisations and social movements we are part of. In this chapter, I set out a strategic canvas that degrowthers and allies can engage with, in order to identify priorities, tensions, and think about how to avoid co-optation in building their strategies. How are you pursuing social-ecological transformation? What kind of strategy would help you in doing this? What are its potentials, and limitations? How can you keep developing your strategy to amplify collective efforts for social-ecological transformation? These are some of the questions that this chapter helps to think about.

In what follows I will argue that degrowth strategies for social-ecological transformation (see Chapter 3) need to combine several strategic approaches, reflecting the plurality of degrowth as a movement. To support the myriad of bottom-up alternatives that are already out there, degrowth actors should put a special emphasis on strategies that build power outside of the capitalist system and be very cautious of those which merely seek to tame capitalism. At the same time, the degrowth movement should also integrate the strategic logic of overthrowing capitalism altogether. Concrete initiatives would benefit from being more focused when strategising, whilst critically reflecting on the choices made. This argument comes from a dialogue with the work of the late Erik Olin Wright. I build on his helpful analytical vocabulary on transformation and strategy but diverge from the strategic configuration he calls for, primarily by seeing ruptures from the capitalist system as an important direction for pursuing transformation.

The chapter will proceed as follows. First, I introduce three modes of transformation. Second, I outline the strategic logics associated with each of them. I engage with Wright in both sections, in relation to degrowth, furthering his analytical framework and showing where I diverge from his argument. I then suggest how the strategic canvas shaped through this critical dialogue can help grassroots groups to think about their strategies.

Modes of transformation

Wright (2009, 2019) identified three modes of transformation: ruptural, interstitial and symbiotic.[4] *Ruptural transformations* seek a direct confrontation or break with existing institutions and social structures. *Interstitial transformations* involve building new forms of social empowerment on the margins of capitalist society, usually outside of spaces dominated by those in power. *Symbiotic transformations*, in turn, are aimed at changing the existing institutions, and growing power within the current system so as to ultimately transform it. For Wright, these modes of transformation are closely associated with the revolutionary socialist, anarchist and social democratic traditions respectively. Using a game metaphor, he connects symbiotic transformations to changing the rules of the game, interstitial transformations to particular moves in the game, and ruptural transformations to changing the game itself (Wright 2019).

When we talk about degrowth, we are talking about socialecological transformation, i.e., a transformation that aims to bring about two entangled outcomes – ecological sustainability and

---

4   Wright himself used different vocabularies to describe ruptural/interstitial/symbiotic transformations, such as "logics of transformation" (Wright 2019) or "strategies" (Wright 2009). In this book, when referring to Wright's work, we in the editorial team have opted for yet another term he used – "modes of transformation." It helps to describe how transformations happen, but does not equate them to strategies. Rather, particular and distinct "strategic logics" are needed to foster each mode of transformation.

social equity (see Chapters 1 and 7). This is something to keep in mind when thinking about the modes of transformation and accompanying strategic logics. Let me unpack how each of these modes of transformation connects to degrowth in more detail.

The *interstitial transformation* is crucial for degrowth as a movement and might be seen as its basis. Indeed, degrowth is about resistance to the capitalist and growth-centric system, and building directly democratic bottom-up alternatives is one of the key principles for the politics of degrowth (Asara *et al.* 2013). This is also where many movements that degrowth connects to and can learn from are located (see Chapter 6). Climate and environmental justice movements, for example, express frustration with inaction on climate change or fight against the harmful industrial expansion. As such, these movements are locally embedded and horizontally organised interstices opposed to the business-as-usual approach that puts growth and capital accumulation first. The organising practices we consider degrowthian – which work for open relocalisation and repoliticisation, such as cooperatives and commoning – operate within the interstitial mode, too. Renewable energy cooperatives, for instance, offer a community-driven approach to producing energy. Democratically run and serving the needs of a community, they are interstices between the spaces occupied by fossil energy or destructive ways to bring in renewables.

Multiple interstitial actors are already engaged in social-ecological transformation and can be said to be paving the way for rupture from capitalism (Wright 2009). However, they have little capacity to fully address the problems they raise, such as climate change; while the alternatives they embody are on the margins of the economy, often dismissed as "niche" or "unscaleable". Continuing growth and capital accumulation by all means, in turn, are supported by powerful agents such as corporations and governments, and the institutional settings created by them.

In view of this, the *symbiotic transformation* becomes important. Whether we want it or not, this is something we as a degrowth movement have to engage with in order to expand the spaces for alternatives, limit ecologically and socially harmful activities, and change the very systems that shape social institutions. Degrowth, as a movement, has been consistent in arguing for systemic change from below whilst making use of available governance and institutional mechanisms. Symbiotic transformation has already been flagged as something to engage with for degrowth, complementing and supporting interstitial transformation (e.g., D'Alisa 2019). The state and its institutions have been identified as key spaces through which symbiotic transformation in line with degrowth can be pursued (see Chapter 9). This can be done, for example, by attempting to influence policies and practices at different levels of governance (e.g., municipal, national, supranational).

To this end, various degrowth policy proposals have been formulated (e.g., Kallis 2018, Buch-Hansen and Koch 2019), and degrowthers have been part of collective calls to reorient policies away from growth. For instance, in a letter co-signed by many degrowth scholars, 238 academics called on the European Union, its institutions and member states to reorient themselves away from the logic of growth towards the aims of ecological sustainability and well-being (see *the Guardian* 2018). While this call fell on deaf ears, continuing efforts towards symbiotic transformation is important to transform the system from within. However, due to engagement with powerful actors and on terrains shaped by them, there is also a risk of critical voices being co-opted. Even if symbiotic transformation pushes the change of institutional logics, corporate actors could still remain powerful in shaping the new agenda, watering down the radical demands.

The role of the *ruptural transformation* has so far not been engaged with explicitly in the work on degrowth. This is in line with Wright himself (2009, 2019), who analytically describes what this mode of transformation entails, but is sceptical of it. Wright refers to rupture as a complete and sharp overhaul of the capitalist system, and as a direct attack on the state. According to him, the twentieth-century examples of revolutionary seizures of power did not result in truly democratic, egalitarian and emancipatory alternatives to capitalism, which makes system-level rupture implausible for overcoming capitalism (Wright 2019, 42). While ruptures are to be cautious about, making sure that the means are in line with the ends, I would not dismiss rupture as a mode of transformation. Instead, I suggest recognising different scales at which ruptures can take place – so that they refer not only to system-level break of nation-states, but also to small-scale and temporary overhauls of capitalism. Wright (2009, 309) acknowledged the possibility of reading ruptures in this way rather than as totalising and concerning the whole system, though without elaborating on it further.

Understanding of ruptures as small-scale and temporary, I argue, opens an important direction for pursuing social-ecological transformation. An act of disobedience like blocking a coal mine – something that is endorsed by degrowthers – can be seen as an example of a temporary rupture that empowers and encourages other forms of action. It includes resistance, too, but goes beyond it by disrupting, even if only temporarily, the rhythm of extractive capitalism. Another concrete example of rupture consists of workers overtaking a factory and converting it into a cooperative, as has been the case in the occupied factories in Argentina (e.g., Atzeni and Ghigliani, 2007). Such ruptures can be used to support and stimulate interstitial and symbiotic modes of transformation, and possibly create momentum for transformative change.

The three modes of transformation, as the illustrations in this section already demonstrate, are not mutually exclusive. For example, a network of small-scale renewable energy cooperatives can act politically by articulating and calling for the kinds of changes it wants to see in policies, thus combining interstitial and symbiotic transformation. Or, an occupation of a space can combine a rupture from business-as-usual with the enactment of interstitial alternatives (Aitchison 2011). Thus, these modes of transformation are not only compatible, but the different knots that are created when their entanglements are acted on are also key for pursuing social-ecological transformation (see Chapter 10).

Having connected the three modes of transformation, as identified by Wright, to degrowth, I next argue that degrowth, as a movement, needs to engage with all of them; with interstitial transformation at the core of degrowth practice, symbiotic transformation helping to expand the horizons for radical possibilities, and temporal and localised ruptures enabling radical change by taking power. Care needs to be taken that symbiotic transformations are not co-opted, and that ruptures are pursued cautiously, aligning the means with the ends.

Strategic logics

In his last book, Wright (2019) connected the three modes of transformation to specific anti-capitalist strategic logics, aimed at either neutralising harms or transcending structures: *resisting* and *escaping*; *taming* and *dismantling*; and *smashing*. In order to visualise the potential of interstitial transformations and the different ways in which ruptural transformations can happen, I complement these with two additional categories – *building alternatives* and *halting*. By introducing each strategic logic and connecting it to degrowth, in this section, I set out a strategic canvas that gives a lens for thinking about *how to act* strategically (see Table 2.1). It is important to keep in mind that degrowth is not only anti-capitalist, but also anti-productivist, which will have implications for building strategies.

Modes of transformation \ Strategic logics	Reducing harms	Transcending structures
Interstitial transformations involve building new forms of social empowerment on the margins of capitalist society, usually outside of spaces dominated by those in power.	Resisting E.g. a climate justice demonstration	Escaping / Building alternatives E.g. running an ecovillage without broader political engagement / building a network with others
Symbiotic transformations are aimed at changing existing institutional forms and deepening popular social empowerment within the current system so as to ultimately transform it.	Taming E.g. a policy that establishes absolute caps on national CO_2 emissions	Dismantling E.g. a policy that turns big companies into cooperatives in the long-term
Ruptural transformations seek a sharp confrontation or break with existing institutions and social structures (these can be short-term or done in a particular place).	Halting E.g. a disobedience action	Smashing E.g. a factory occupation by workers

Table 2.1. A strategic canvas for degrowth (building on but diverging from Wright 2019, 122, 124)

Resisting, escaping and building alternatives

Resisting and escaping are, for Wright (2019), the strategic logics of interstitial transformation. Resisting is about raising a particular problem in one way or the other and trying to bring it to the attention of decision-makers, employers, organisations, or the broader public. Climate demonstrations can be seen as in tune with the strategic logic of resisting. While undoubtedly important, resisting does not in itself transcend structures and risks staying with the diagnosis of the problem without making the next step towards transformation (Herbert 2021). However, resistance, say, in environmental justice movements, can also create spaces for reflection on the meaning of a particular protest for the groups mobilising around it, thus going beyond just reducing harms (Akbulut *et al.* 2019, Singh 2019).

Escaping, in turn, is the strategic logic of interstitial transformation that transcends structures. Here Wright (2019) distinguishes between escaping as an individualistic choice – often based on prior privileges and the initiatives that escape capitalism for more collective and egalitarian living. It is only the latter that is part of his strategic logic of anti-capitalism, with intentional communities and cooperatives being possible examples. For him, the strategic logic of escaping "typically involves avoiding political engagement and certainly collectively organised efforts at changing the world" (*Ibid.*, 177). In other words, while giving inspiring examples of living differently, initiatives that embrace this logic may be focused primarily on running their own community or organisation, while distancing themselves from wider collective action for change.

While I agree with Wright that simply escaping capitalism is not enough for bringing about transformation, I find labelling all interstitial efforts that transcend capitalist structures as only escaping capitalism problematic, as this downplays their transformative potential. Indeed, Wright acknowledges that interstitial initiatives can be building blocks of an alternative society, and it is this point that I would like to push further. By introducing the strategic logic of *building alternatives*, I argue that interstitial alternatives can go beyond escaping capitalism or the economy (see Fournier 2008), into actively and collectively building power outside of the capitalist system. For example, workers' collectives or community initiatives, apart from setting an example by their own organisations, can be building relations and networks with other like-minded groups, and supporting them in various ways (e.g., Kokkinidis 2015; Sekulova *et al.* 2017). The strategic logic of building alternatives denotes politicised engagement within and beyond a particular alternative and can be seen as key for degrowth. The distinction between escaping and building alternatives also suggests strategic directions for degrowth as a movement, pointing to the importance of encouraging and creating spaces for the politicisation and engagement of those who are already following the strategic logic of escaping.

Taming and dismantling

Taming and dismantling are the strategic logics that are part of a symbiotic transformation. Both are arguably needed for transformation and can be mutually reinforcing. The reduction of working hours – a policy proposal that is often discussed in degrowth – can be seen as an example of taming. It would liberate the time from work, without immediately changing this work itself, nor how it is organised and controlled. However, the time released can be channelled towards activities aimed at interstitial transformation, and possibly towards demanding actions that would support them, helping to dismantle the current system. Without taming, dismantling might not be enough. For example, dismantling practices, such as supporting cooperatives or locally anchored organisations institutionally, may be a drop in the ocean when powerful corporations are not tamed and existing institutions are still oriented towards growth. Thus, policy proposals such as those discussed within degrowth (e.g., Kallis 2018) or allied proposals like the Green New Deal for Europe (GNDE 2019) combine taming and dismantling. However, the balance between these strategic logic is something we as the degrowth movement should be careful about, making dismantling rather than taming key to our efforts. In other words, it is important that taming does not become a less radical compromise in the struggle for transformation.

The distinction between taming and dismantling is helpful to analytically discern how symbiotic transformation can be pursued, as well as to identify where the risk of co-optation can emerge when doing this. While dismantling without taming can be insufficient to bring about social-ecological transformation, it is possible to imagine taming being pursued without leading to dismantling, thus co-opting the efforts for symbiotic transformation. For example, in the socialist movements of the twentieth century, the more radical demands were often overtaken by those just taming capitalism. Wright (2019, 57) gives an example of Sweden in the early 1970s, where the left wing of social democrats wanted to put forward a policy that would enable labour unions to become the majority share owners of Swedish corporations in the long-term, which never happened in the end. Thus, the strategic logic of dismantling should be seen as key, with a bold vision for policies and alternative institutions that we would like to see. Taming, in turn, should be used to support and further argue for dismantling. For instance, in times of crisis like the COVID-19 pandemic, the strategic logic of taming would consist of arguing for connecting rescue packages for companies to their future environmental performance. Adopting the strategic logic of dismantling would consist of demanding the kinds of changes that would alter the power relations in society, like support for workers to turn bankrupt companies into collective and not-for-profit ownership models such as cooperatives.

Smashing and halting

The strategic logic of smashing capitalism – associated with ruptural transformation – is not part of Wright's (2019) vision for how to overcome capitalism. However, waiting for symbiotic transformation to bring the legislation and institutional changes that would support the transition of power from capital might mean that such transformation would never materialise, as was the case with the example from Sweden. Or, there would be no pioneering examples of occupied factories today had the workers not activated the strategic logic of smashing and organised to take power. Such ruptural transformations enacted by the workers in the case of factory occupations have allowed for something different than what is done by alternatives operating within interstitial transformation: overtaking a space, sometimes huge, with infrastructure that can be used and repurposing this space through collective deliberation. Without rupture, the workers would most likely not have had sufficient resources to get hold of and equip such a site in the first place.

Once the strategic logic of smashing capitalism has resulted in a ruptural transformation and a space has been repurposed, it can become a building block for interstitial transformation, enacting the strategic logic of building alternatives. For example, occupying in an urban landscape – whether a house or a plot of land – as done by squatters (see e.g., Cattaneo and Gavaldá 2010), enables its reclamation from capital, whilst also opening the possibility of converting the occupied space into a commons. Small-scale ruptures can encourage others in similar situations to take power in the spaces where they operate. Moreover, having such examples in place and demanding their recognition can ultimately push for symbiotic transformation towards cooperativisation and commoning. Despite such potentialities, it is important to be aware that actions within the strategic logic of smashing can also be criminalised, punished or delegitimised by authorities.

The understanding of ruptures as small-scale and temporal adopted in this chapter means acting towards ruptural transformations does not necessarily lead to transcending structures, but can also be about reducing harms. This is why I introduce the strategic logic of *halting capitalism*, i.e., stopping destructive activities, even if for a short time, aiming to break the rhythms of capitalism, productivism and extractivism. An act of disobedience like blocking a coal mine can be said to be following the strategic logic of halting. It manifests a sharp confrontation with existing structures, while not transcending them. Actions within this strategic logic are in tune with degrowth (D'Alisa *et al.* 2013) and movements close to it, such as the climate justice movement. An occupation of a university to protest neoliberalisation is another example (Aitchison 2011). While being a temporary act and likely not leading to a longer-term occupation, it aims to halt unjust actions. The strategic logics within ruptural transformation are most likely to be enacted in particular contexts when certain tipping points are crossed – for example, when destructive expansion continues despite the severity of climate change, when workers are not paid by their bankrupt companies, or when common people have to deal with austerity measures as a result of problems they had not created.

A degrowth strategy needs to combine several strategic approaches, reflecting the plurality of degrowth as a movement. First and foremost, it needs to support the myriad of interstitial alternatives that are not only resisting and escaping the logic of growth and capitalism, but are already building alternatives in the present. To do this, it should put a special emphasis on the strategic logic of dismantling but be very cautious about taming when pursuing symbiotic transformation. Furthermore, degrowth as a movement should integrate the strategic logics of halting and smashing capitalism, by disturbing the rhythms of business-as-usual, and by daring to take power when it is possible to do so. Pursuing ruptural transformation is particularly important and more likely to be ethically justified in times of capitalist crisis (Bond 2019), when the absurdity and violence to keep the current system going become more evident, and when cracks in this system may open spaces for expanding alternatives.

A strategic canvas for degrowth and how to take it forward

The discussion of the modes of transformation and strategic logics elaborated by Erik Olin Wright (2009, 2019) and further developed in this chapter offers a comprehensive strategic canvas that degrowthers and allied movements can relate to (see Table 2.1). So far, I have argued for degrowth as a movement – characterised by a multiplicity of actors and voices (see Chapters 4 and 5, see also Barca et al. 2019 and Paulson 2017) – to embrace the plurality of modes of transformation and strategic logics offered by this canvas, emphasising where priorities lie and where it is important to be cautious.

Specific organisations that are part of or connected to degrowth, however, can be more focused on locating themselves on this strategic canvas. If you are an environmental organisation that calls for systemic change while working close to the institutions of the European Union, symbiotic transformation may be your priority. For example, you can be aiming at reshaping the EU politics away from growth through impactful reports and by shaping discussion in the EU spaces, drawing on and helping to render visible the grassroots voices calling for social-ecological transformation, as well as promoting the policy agenda that would make dismantling possible. If you are a grassroots organisation, say, running a cooperative in an urban space, pursuing interstitial transformation via building alternatives might be key to your strategy. Depending on the context, you may decide whether you want to also pursue symbiotic transformation. For example, if operating in a municipality sympathetic to your goals, you might want to find ways to push for policy changes that would help alternatives like yours to flourish. Or, if operating in a hostile environment or under an oppressive political regime, you may decide to focus on building alternatives parallel to existing institutions and get engaged in building counter-institutions with allied groups. And yet another example – if you are an environmental justice group seeing a forest at the risk of being cut for industrial expansion, engaging in the strategic logic of halting might feel like the only right thing to do, out of which longer-term ruptures and building of alternatives may also emerge.

Having identified your terrain within this strategic canvas, you can keep thinking deeper about your strategies, putting them into the context you operate in, in relation to your goals, and the broader aspirations of social-ecological transformation. While there is an ongoing multidimensional crisis (Brand and Wissen 2012), and degrowth presents an alternative political project, there is so far little public support of it and no unity of different political forces calling for social-ecological transformation, which prevents a paradigm shift from happening (Buch-Hansen 2018). Thus, when crafting your strategy, you might go in the direction of building up popular support for degrowth, or into building alliances with other politically engaged actors. The primary purpose of some groups might be precisely to help forge these alliances and to connect and coordinate different modes of transformation within the larger movement.

As an actor within the degrowth movement, you may need to keep thinking about how you relate to institutions of the state, and the potential to push them from the bottom-up (see Chapter 9). Importantly, acting for social-ecological transformation, including devising your strategies, is not something static that is decided on once and for all. It is a process to keep engaging in, evaluating (see Chapter 8), and amending. Finally, in acting for change and strategically, it is important to stay true to degrowth principles, its spirit and multiplicity. To do this involves a particular approach: critically reflecting on actions for alternatives, being alert to possible closures and co-optations that might arise in the process, and being ready to address them while also finding inspiration and knowledge in different spaces – which has been articulated as nomadic utopianism (Barca *et al.* 2019).

To conclude, I hope that this chapter can help both degrowth and allied movements, as well as different grassroots groups, to think analytically about the mode(s) of transformation they pursue, and which strategic logics to mobilise. Many questions about the *how* of building and enacting these strategies remain, which this book will help you to think through, via theoretical reflections in Part I and concrete examples from different spheres of life in Part II.

References

Aitchison, Guy. 2011. "Reform, Rupture or Re-imagination: Understanding the Purpose of an Occupation." *Social Movement Studies* 10, no. 4: 431–439.

Akbulut, Bengi, Federico Demaria, Julien-François Gerber, and Joan Martínez-Alier. 2019. "Who Promotes Sustainability? Five Theses on the Relationships between the Degrowth and the Environmental Justice Movements." *Ecological Economics* 165 (November), 106418.

Asara, Viviana, Emanuele Profumi, and Giorgos Kallis. 2013. "Degrowth, Democracy and Autonomy." *Environmental Values* 22 no. 2 (April): 217–239.

Atzeni, Maurizio, and Pablo Ghigliani. "Labour Process and Decision-Making in

Factories under Workers' Self-Management: Empirical Evidence from Argentina." *Work, Employment and Society* 21, no. 4 (December 2007): 653–671.

Barca, Stefania, Ekaterina Chertkovskaya, and Alexander Paulsson. 2019. "The End of Growth as We Know It: From Growth Realism to Nomadic Utopianism." In *Towards a Political Economy of Degrowth*, edited by Ekaterina Chertkovskaya, Alexander Paulsson and Stefania Barca, 1–17. London: Rowman & Littlefield.

Bond, Patrick. 2019. "Degrowth, Devaluation and Uneven Development from North to South." In *Towards a Political Economy of Degrowth*, edited by Ekaterina Chertkovskaya, Alexander Paulsson and Stefania Barca, 137–156. London: Rowman & Littlefield.

Brand, Ulrich, and Markus Wissen. 2012. "Global Environmental Politics and the Imperial Mode of Living: Articulations of State-Capital Relations in the Multiple Crisis." *Globalizations* 9, no. 4: 547–560.

Buch-Hansen, Hubert. 2018. "The Prerequisites for a Degrowth Paradigm Shift: Insights from Critical Political Economy." *Ecological Economics* 146 (April): 157–163.

Buch-Hansen, Hubert, and Max Koch. 2019. "Degrowth through Income and Wealth Caps?" *Ecological Economics* 160 (June): 264–271.

Cattaneo, Claudio, and Marc Gavaldà. 2010. "The Experience of Rurban Squats in Collserola, Barcelona: What Kind of Degrowth?" *Journal of Cleaner Production* 18, no. 6: 581–589.

D'Alisa, Giacomo. 2019. "The State of Degrowth." In *Towards a Political Economy of Degrowth*, edited by Ekaterina Chertkovskaya, Alexander Paulsson and Stefania Barca, 243–257. London: Rowman & Littlefield.

D'Alisa, Giacomo, Federico Demaria and Claudio Cattaneo. 2013. "Civil and Uncivil Actors for a Degrowth Society." *Journal of Civil Society* 9, no. 2: 212–224.

Fournier, Valérie. 2008. "Escaping from the Economy: The Politics of Degrowth." *International Journal of Sociology and Social Policy* 28, no. 11/12: 528–545.

GNDE (Green New Deal for Europe). 2019. "Blueprint for Europe's Just Transition." Edition II. December 2019. https://report.gndforeurope.com.

The Guardian. 2018. "The EU Needs a Stability and Wellbeing Pact, Not More Growth." *Letters*, September 16, 2018. Please enter this link: https://www.theguardian.com/politics/2018/sep/16/the-eu-needs-a-stability-and-wellbeing-pact-not-more-growth

Herbert, Joe. 2021. "The Socio-Ecological Imagination: Young Environmental Activists Constructing Transformation in an Era of Crisis." *Area* 53, no. 2 (June): 373–380.

Kallis, Giorgos. 2018. *Degrowth*. Newcastle-Upon-Tyne: Agenda Publishing.

Kokkinidis, George. 2015. "Spaces of Possibilities: Workers' Self-management in Greece." *Organisation* 22, no. 6: 847–871.

Paulson, Susan. 2017. "Degrowth: Culture, Power and Change." *Journal of Political Ecology* 24, no. 1: 425–448.

Sekulova, Filka, Isabelle Anguelovski, Lucia Argüelles, and Joana Conill. 2017. "A 'Fertile Soil' for Sustainability-Related Community Initiatives: A New Analytical Framework." *Environment and Planning A* 49, no. 19: 2362–2382.

Singh, Neera M. 2019. "Environmental Justice, Degrowth and Post-Capitalist Futures." *Ecological Economics* 163 (September): 138–142.

Wright, Erik O. 2009. *Envisioning Real Utopias*. London: Verso.

Wright, Erik O. 2019. *How to Be an Anti-Capitalist in the 21st Century*. London: Verso.

Chapter 3:

Taking stock: degrowth and strategy so far

By Nathan Barlow[5]

As I write this chapter, one of the biggest developments in the debate on strategy within degrowth is happening: this book! In this chapter, I will attempt to summarise what has been said thus far on the topic of degrowth and strategy. Notably, this book marks an important step in bringing forward the discussion about *how* to achieve social-ecological transformation. My task will be to provide the reader with some background context underlying these discussions.

Thus far, advocates of degrowth have focused predominantly on the *what* and *why* questions of social-ecological transformation. By this, I mean degrowth proponents have developed a nuanced critique of *why* the current political-economic system is failing in myriad social and ecological ways, as well as concrete utopias and visions of *what* a different society could look like. Research, communication and public mobilisation around these questions have elevated degrowth to becoming one prominent critique in academia of the current political-economic system, which is an important and impressive feat. Degrowth is also increasingly mentioned in the mainstream media, albeit not always in the most honest or favourable way (Pringle 2021). Additionally, the degrowth vision of an alternative way to organise society, structure the economy, and re-embed human activities within ecological boundaries in a convivial

---

5   I am highly appreciative for the insights of Joe Herbert who I have worked together with on the topic of strategy for the last few years, and he provided invaluable comments on this chapter. Additionally, many informal conversations amongst the editorial team of this book as well as the web team of degrowth.info were of immense inspiration. My supervisor Andreas Novy also contributed to developing my perspective of the importance of thinking seriously about the *how* of transformation, and some of degrowth's deficits in this regard. Lastly, one shortcoming of this chapter is the focus on text and discussion in English, and overlooks debates on strategy in degrowth in languages other than English – like those in the journal Entropia – a point highlighted by Federico Demaria.

and equitable way has been inspiring for many in a moment when few political projects dare to imagine another world (Herbert 2021).

Central to this project is the need to overcome various institutions of capitalist society and the dynamics they create, including growth, profit maximisation, neoimperialism, extractivism, productivism, patriarchy, inequality and consumerism. Given these ambitions, the *how*-question is a crucial and long under-considered aspect (Demaria 2018, Kallis 2018). The degrowth movement has yet to provide a detailed and nuanced articulation of *how* to get from our current destructive mode of living to a radically changed society, an important yet challenging task. In the last few years, there have been many exciting developments within the degrowth discourse on the topic of strategy. Specifically, there has been work done to better understand pathways and barriers to transformation while considering important questions such as those of process, political action, plurality, openness and decision-making in the face of complexity.

This chapter will firstly show some of the different ways strategy has been conceptualised in relation to degrowth, which will capture the diversity of its usage and the implications this has. Secondly, I will sketch the evolution of the degrowth movement's consideration of strategy, to capture the flow and development of ideas, showing how strategy has always been a present topic in degrowth debates, but is now becoming one of increasing importance. In particular, I will highlight the work of Erik Olin Wright, the question of the state and contending theories of change. Finally, the chapter concludes with a suggestion, of a promising next step in the discussion. I adhere in this chapter to the definition of "strategy" developed by the editorial team of this book, which was created when putting the book together to clarify how we collectively understood "strategy." That definition can be found in full in the book's introduction. This brings us to the first central question of degrowth's discussion of strategy – what is strategy and how does it relate to degrowth?

Is degrowth a strategy, a goal or a quality?

One challenge for providing an overview of the debate about strategy within the degrowth discourse is the need to first recognise that the usage and implied meaning of the term varies widely. The way strategy is used in relation to degrowth often reflects one of the following understandings: (i) degrowth is itself a strategy, (ii) degrowth is a goal or (iii) degrowth is a specific quality of a strategy. While these different applications of strategy do not need to be contradictory or mutually exclusive, they reflect the disjointed nature of prior discussions of strategy within degrowth and the need for more conceptual clarity. This would imply consistent use of terms, commonly accepted definitions, and more specificity on the relationship between degrowth and strategy.

In some texts, degrowth itself is the strategy, e.g., "degrowth as a transition strategy" (Perey 2016) and "degrowth as a social movement and an economic strategy" (Murphy 2013). In these usages, degrowth's provocative problematisation of the economy can be understood as a strategy in itself, which echoes its origins as a "missile word". Through this understanding of degrowth as a strategy in itself, the degrowth critique of the current political-economic system may open up pathways for other concepts and movements to become hegemonic, e.g. environmental justice struggles. This usage is echoed clearly in the statement, "ecosocialism is the horizon, degrowth is the way" (Miller-McDonald 2021). However, this usage can be blurry because what exactly "degrowth" is remains unclear, does it imply just the concept, an economic programme, or something else?

Elsewhere, degrowth is positioned as a goal and different practices like commoning (Sato and María Soto Alarcón 2018) or civil disobedience (Fromm and Schöning 2020) are described as strategies to achieve this goal. In these usages, degrowth is an end-point that strategies take us towards. This usage reflects a commonly held understanding in the degrowth community, that degrowth is not just a process but also a *concrete utopia* (Muraca 2017). This second usage

– degrowth as a goal – is clear on the relation between the two terms. It positions degrowth on one side and strategies as the way to get there. However, the term "strategies" is left as an open container to be filled according to one's understanding.

Finally, in a third case, degrowth is used as an adjective, to describe a characteristic of a strategy, e.g., "the slow city approach as a degrowth strategy" (Chang 2016). Often implicit in this type of usage is that a degrowth strategy has distinct characteristics different from non-degrowth strategies, likely reflecting degrowth principles and values. In this usage, the goal is vague, one implicit horizon of degrowth strategies is a "degrowth future", but we can also imagine that degrowth strategies contribute to achieving other utopias. On the other hand, in this usage, the means is rather clear, but it again depends on how one understands degrowth and what this descriptor implies for the strategies it describes.

This exercise of disentangling the different usages of degrowth and strategy can sharpen our understanding of how these terms are employed, but it also obscures the inter-linkages. These different usages are not mutually exclusive and it can easily be imagined how two of them can co-exist in a single theory of change. The various usages are also important as they can imply a focus on different processes and aims. Namely, the usage of (ii) degrowth as a goal and (iii) degrowth as a characteristic of a strategy are often inter-linked. Specifically, a common argument in the degrowth community, and social movements more broadly, is that strategies for degrowth (as a goal) must follow degrowth principles, or else the strategy will undermine the goal (Schmid 2020). In other words, degrowth strategies *for* a degrowth future. Yet we should ask, is it possible that degrowth futures could be achieved through means not identified by or with degrowth principles? These two usages, *degrowth as a goal* and *a characteristic of a strategy* are the two most often used and relevant for the debate, whereas the third usage, *degrowth as a strategy*, is seldom used and most blurry in its meaning.

It is important then to draw out the implicit assumptions in the various usages of strategy as a term and concept in degrowth debates, and attempt to make explicit: what is the strategy, what is the goal, who is the agent of change, and where degrowth is situated. Relatedly, the multiplicity of meanings of degrowth often adds confusion or ambiguity when using it alongside strategy, since degrowth can be understood as a loose movement (with some agency), an umbrella term uniting a diversity of critical social-ecological academic disciplines, a concrete utopia, and so on. Thus, it is not always clear what "degrowth" means when used in relation to strategy, so specificity would help, e.g., "the degrowth movement" can pursue strategies, "the degrowth concept" is an effective strategy for many social-ecological utopias, or "degrowth is a utopia" to orient strategic action. Another recurring ambiguity in the usage of strategy in relation to degrowth is the agent of change, does the loose degrowth network enact these strategies, allied groups or some other actors? Lastly, often it is unclear what the relationship is between strategies, if any. In summary, there has been a lack of both consistency and clarity in the application of strategy as a term and concept. Degrowth scholarship would, in turn, benefit from conceptual sharpening and further dialogue. This chapter will later explore a fourth usage of relating degrowth and strategy, which hopefully points towards a useful next-step in degrowth's discussion of strategy.

The importance of strategy for degrowth

The question of *how* to make degrowth possible was already clearly raised at the 2nd *International Degrowth Conference in Barcelona* (2010). The final sentence of the one-page declaration from that conference reads, "The challenge now is *how* to transform, and the debate has just begun." For those who were not there, Demaria *et al.* (2013) describe the conference and the discussion on strategy, "[it] resulted in some differences and even frictions, but ultimately dialogue was established" (*Ibid.*, 208). Interestingly, they begin a section of their article titled "Degrowth Strategies" by writing, "The debates and controversies over strategies employed within each source of the degrowth movement have been most intense" (*Ibid.*, 207). However, the authors aim to reconcile this, arguing for "the potential for compatibility among the strategies", since "diversity is an indispensable source of richness – so long as participants are conscious of the limitations of their activities and humble enough to remain open to constructive criticism and improvements" (*Ibid.*). In 2012, a special issue titled, "Degrowth futures and democracy" (Cattaneo *et al.* 2012) outlined the contours of key questions related to strategy – who is the political subject of a degrowth transformation, what is the role of democracy, and what scale is most effective for intervention. The introduction to the special issue concludes, "What are the implications of different understandings of how change happens for degrowth, e.g., in terms of strategies available for degrowth transitions?" (*Ibid.*, 522). So the questions that this book raises are nothing new per se, however, since these important questions were raised, there was little direct engagement with the topic of degrowth and strategy. Instead, the community focused on other important things: different theoretical perspectives that inform degrowth (e.g., feminism, environmental justice, etc.), digging deeper into specific fields (e.g., technology), establishing degrowth as an emerging academic field as well as placing it in new forums (media, politics, etc.) and expanding its network of researchers and activists. While these were and are valuable endeavours, comprehensively addressing the question of strategy was postponed.

In 2018 a *degrowth.info* blog post titled, "Beyond visions and projects – the need for a debate on strategy in the degrowth movement" (Herbert *et al.* 2018) called on the degrowth community to further develop its consideration of the role of strategy in degrowth. Given the seemingly insurmountable barriers to transformation, the authors argued more attention to the *how* was necessary. They argued that degrowth scholars had until then been hesitant to recognise certain approaches as more appropriate in certain contexts, and that some strategies could be incompatible with each other. The blog post identified what it saw as *strategic indeterminism* in the degrowth community (*Ibid.*). This post then sparked a ten-part series on strategy at degrowth.info (Barlow 2019). A diversity of authors articulated important considerations, including the role of complexity and challenges of strategic planning (Zografos 2019), the importance of considering *who* is strategising (Sze and Saif 2019), the danger of prioritising certain strategies (Foramitti 2020), the usefulness of history (Feola 2019), the applicability of Erik Olin Wright's framework on strategies (Chertkovskaya 2020; Petridis 2019), identifying strategic entry points for transformative politics (Krüger 2020), and the need to distinguish between strategy in degrowth research versus degrowth movement organising (Barlow and Herbert 2020).

Since 2018, there has been visibly much more engagement with strategy in degrowth debates, which culminated in the most explicit manifestation engagement by degrowth with strategy thus far: the *Degrowth Vienna 2020 Conference: Strategies for Social-ecological Transformation*. The conference put the topic in the spotlight in a way that had not occurred previously. The conference drew on threads of discussion in the degrowth community over the previous ten years (or more), which had addressed the topic of strategy to varying degrees. The importance of strategy for degrowth has ebbed and flowed but the question of strategy is again getting attention, and still creating friction but also dialogue. Thus, strategy has clearly been a hot topic before, which lay dormant while the community focused on other endeavours, but is now resurfacing as a key question amongst many scholars and activists. Let us further consider some other points in the degrowth and strategy discussion – namely the role of Erik Olin Wright's framework.

The work of Erik Olin Wright (and beyond)

In 2013 Demaria *et al.* used the classification of *opposition, reformism* and *alternatives* to distinguish different ways of transforming society towards degrowth, echoing the modes of transformation outlined by Erik Olin Wright in *Envisioning Real Utopias* (2010) (see Chapter 2 for more detail on Wright's work). Reviving the work of Wright after some dormancy, Petridis at the 5th *International Degrowth Conference in Budapest* outlined the usefulness of Wright's strategic approaches for degrowth (Petridis 2016). Four years after Petridis' presentation in Budapest, Wright's typology of strategy was also at the centre of a panel discussion at the *Degrowth Vienna 2020 Conference*, titled *Strategic Approaches: an overview* where the panellists explored the potential and limits of Wright's work for degrowth. Wright's framework was again employed by Tim Parrique in his thesis on *The Political Economy of Degrowth* (2019) with a strong focus on how different degrowth demands (often policies) can be brought forward together from a strategic-political perspective. Limits of Wright's work for degrowth, such as its downplaying of ruptural approaches (Chapter 2), limited incorporation of the ecological crises (Bardi *et al.* 2021), among others, make clear the need for degrowth proponents to further develop a framework for transformation that is adequate for its vision of social-ecological transformation. This collected volume also employed Wright's work to aid in the editorial team's and authors' understanding of strategy, while also being aware of the limits of Wright's work.

Talking about strategies (their strengths, weaknesses, appropriateness, synergies, etc.) necessarily requires a preliminary conversation about what kind of strategies exist, as well as some kind of common ontological understanding, which is why Wright's typology of strategies has been a useful starting point for degrowth scholars. It has helped to provide a common language and a basis for deeper discussions. It can be beneficial to first establish this basis of discussion and understanding before entering into heated discussions about which strategy is most in line with degrowth principles, which may be most effective and which are untenable for degrowth. The work of Wright is also useful for the discussion of strategy in the degrowth movement because it outlines a diversity of strategic approaches, which is compatible with degrowth's own plurality and provides a basic vocabulary (interstitial, symbiotic and ruptural) for talking about strategy.

Degrowth, being an umbrella term (Barca 2018) composed of diverse approaches, lends itself to a diversity of strategies being put forth. Thus, strategy is a key consideration for not only advancing degrowth, but also reflecting on its internal diversity; a consideration which is elaborated further by Viviana Asara (see Chapter 4). Related, Dennis Eversberg and Matthias Schmelzer (2018) surveyed the degrowth community and identified a "spectrum" of "currents" within degrowth. Eversberg later connected this research to the typology of Erik Olin Wright at the *Degrowth Vienna 2020 Conference*, describing the different currents of the degrowth movement according to their strategic orientation. This research echoed Demaria *et al.* (2013), who linked the different sources of degrowth to a diversity of strategies. Importantly, it is this diversity within degrowth that is sometimes underpinned by differences in the understanding of what strategies should be pursued for a degrowth transformation. One such difference appears with regards to theories of change and in particular the contested role of the state, which will be considered next.

Contested theories of change

To start, let us consider the challenges of a social-ecological transformation. Blühdorn (2007) argues society has an immense capacity for and tendency to sustain the unsustainable and the subsequent politics of unsustainability. Others have written about the challenges of transformative social-ecological politics due to the resilience of the rich Western way of living, which is simultaneously defended politically and made possible through externalising costs to the periphery – aptly named *the imperial mode of living* (Brand

and Wissen 2017). In the context of massive challenges to social-ecological transformation, Blühdorn *et al.* (2018) argue that degrowth lacks a theory of social change, and therefore cannot account for why a degrowth transformation is not happening and is unlikely to happen. Given this bleak landscape, how can a degrowth transformation be understood?

In response to the challenges of realising a social-ecological transformation, degrowth scholars have explored the usefulness of causal models to identify leverage points for increasing the viability of certain degrowth proposals (Videira *et al.* 2014). Related, the political economist and degrowth scholar Hubert Buch-Hansen has written an article that is highly relevant for degrowth's thinking about strategy (2018). It outlines the key factors that are necessary for degrowth to be realised as a political project. Additionally, the collected volume *Towards a Political Economy of Degrowth* highlights central questions on this topic and flags the need for degrowth to devote more attention to "political subjectivity and strategy" due to "the lack of a clear political strategy" (Chertkovskaya *et al.*, 2020). More recently, in March 2021, a panel with leading degrowth scholars entitled *How do we get out of this mess? Degrowth strategies for change* focused on strategies and theories of change for degrowth. Bringing together the work of Wright and the perspectives of critical transformation scholars, Schoppek and Krams (2021) further develop an understanding of pathways and barriers for transformation, which offers much for thinking about degrowth and strategy. At the Vienna Degrowth Days in 2020, Jefim Vogel presented the two-loops model for thinking about how systemic change can happen, and its usefulness for degrowth scholars reflecting on strategy. It is clear that degrowth scholars and scholars of transformation are increasingly engaging with the tricky question of why a *desired* social-ecological transformation may not happen, how to make it more likely, and what the strategic entry-points, pathways and selectivities (Sum and Jessop 2013) are that should be pursued in this specific conjuncture (Eckersley 2021).

Following from the emerging discussion on theories of change in degrowth, one of the key questions is the role of the state. Before considering specifically how (or if) a degrowth strategy should engage with the state, a conceptualisation of the state from a degrowth perspective is necessary. D'Alisa (2019) makes an important contribution by first outlining degrowth's lack of a theory of the state mentioned earlier. D'Alisa (*Ibid*), and then later D'Alisa and Kallis (2020), suggested that degrowth should adopt a Gramscian understanding of the state and approach its own transformative ambitions as a counter-hegemonic struggle. They also employ Wright's typology of strategic approaches, solidifying its usefulness for degrowth and its conceptualisation of strategies. Further drawing on Wright, they argue that rupture (a total break from capitalism) is unfeasible for achieving degrowth and instead identify interstitial and symbiotic strategies as the two key modes of transformation to be pursued. In this, D'Alisa and Kallis echo Wright's own position, dismissing ruptural approaches in favour of symbiotic and interstitial strategies.

Another event that sparked debate on strategy and the role of the state was the *6th International Degrowth Conference in Malmö* (2018), where a panel discussion intensified over questions of how to achieve social-ecological transformation, from the perspectives of scholars outside degrowth but sympathetic to it (Degrowth.info Editorial Team 2018). While degrowth is a uniting term for many diverse academic fields and political traditions, this panel revealed the potential for real divisions within degrowth (see Chapter 2, for more detail).

These differences within the degrowth community also surfaced at the *Degrowth Vienna 2020 Conference*. For example, Miriam Lang cautioned about the role of the state in a degrowth transformation. She has written elsewhere (2017) that the state perpetuates domination and stabilises capital accumulation, a process that morphs agents for transformative change into upholders of rules, norms and institutions they aimed to transform. On the same panel, Andreas Novy, drawing on the work of Karl Polanyi, argued that coercion, rules/regulation, and collectively defined (as well as enforced) limits are necessary to achieve a good life for all within planetary boundaries, which necessitates "another statehood" (Novy 2020). Related, Koch (2020) argues the state has the potential to overcome its growth imperative and transition to a post-growth green state.

During a session on theories of change at the *Degrowth Vienna 2020 Conference*, Andro Rilovic (2020) argued in his presentation *Anarchism and Degrowth, two sides of the same coin*, that eco-anarchism is most compatible with degrowth principles and that interstitial transformations should be pursued instead of symbiotic approaches. Similarly, Ted Trainer (2021) has argued for a community-based approach to degrowth that excludes, bypasses, or radically reduces the role of the state in a process of transformation. At the *8th International Degrowth Conference in The Hague* (2021), a thematic stream was dedicated to anarchism and degrowth, highlighting the compatibilities between these two approaches and the potential for mutual learning. On the one hand there are voices within degrowth arguing that the state is not a viable agent of change towards degrowth, and on the other hand, many degrowth scholars have written extensively on policy proposals, which often implicitly require the state apparatus (Cosme *et al.* 2017)(Cattaneo and Vansintjan 2016) e.g., universal basic income or a Green New Deal (Mastini *et al.* 2021). Thus, the analysis within degrowth on the role of the state is varied and at times contested.

Clearly, the contradictions and compatibilities of the state in a transformation towards degrowth is one of the key conversations around strategy in degrowth at the moment. These differences do not *per se* imply incompatibly or conflicting approaches, but surely there are some real differences between these approaches in how they come to terms with the likelihood of degrowth actually happening *or*, more consequentially, what it implies about whether degrowth *cannot* happen (due to incompatibilities between means and goals).

This makes it increasingly clear that "degrowth's strategic orientation (...) needs a strategy for the state" (Chapter 1).

Considering viable and desirable pathways to creating degrowth societies is a key point for the degrowth community's discussion of strategy. The next section will try to bring together some of the learnings from degrowth's consideration of strategy so far and link it to a possible next step in the discussion.

A strategic assemblage for degrowth

This chapter has so far considered how strategy as a term has been used differently in degrowth, the relevance of Wright's transformative strategies, the internal diversity and plurality of degrowth approaches, the ongoing work to better understand degrowth's theory of change, and the contentious question of the role of the state in a degrowth transformation. Degrowth scholars are engaging more and more with degrowth's relationship to strategy, but still, there are under-explored aspects, and this final section will explore one – which mix of actions and strategies degrowthers finds desirable and necessary for transformation and what its own role in this transformation can be. Brand and Wissen write, with regards to research on social-ecological transformation, the urgent need to "consider and evaluate the various strategies and possibilities for dealing with the multiple crises" (2017, 7). So what does that process look like for degrowth?

We can separate the process into two nested questions, the first is a broader question, and the second is a more specific question: (1) what mix of strategies does the degrowth community find appropriate and necessary for a process of social-ecological transformation?; and (2) what is the degrowth community's role in this process? The considerations necessary for each of these two questions are distinct. The former requires new methods, criteria for analysis, and evaluation, which would be underpinned by a theory of change. Whereas the latter requires internal deliberation, decision-making and possibly action.

To help answer the second, and more specific question, we can return to the three usages of degrowth and strategy described at the start of this chapter. To repeat, references to "strategy" in the degrowth literature so far fall roughly into three overlapping categories: (i) *degrowth as a strategy*: degrowth is itself a strategy for achieving a goal of just and sustainable futures; (ii) *strategies for degrowth*: degrowth is a goal and otherwise defined practices or actions are the strategies to realise it; and (iii) *degrowth strategies*: degrowth is a descriptor and characteristic of certain strategies. Here, the usage *strategies for degrowth*, and qualified to those strategies pursued *by the degrowth movement*, specify clearly the relationship between strategy and degrowth (as a movement) that would need to be investigated to answer the question (2) above. The contribution of members of the *degrowth.info* editorial team (see Chapter 5) and Asara (see Chapter 4) are invaluable in addressing this topic. They suggest possible forums for such discussions, hinting at the potential for the degrowth movement to make decisions and prioritisations if it so desires, but also reflecting the tensions in a diverse movement making common decisions.

To answer the first and broader question, (1) *what mix of strategies does the degrowth community find appropriate and necessary?* the usages of strategy which have been used thus far in degrowth literature are not enough. Since few scholars have attempted to articulate which mix, collection, or *assemblage* of strategies are necessary for a social-ecological transformation. Here I will introduce a fourth usage mentioned earlier in this chapter to assist in answering this question – a *strategic assemblage for degrowth*. A strategic assemblage for degrowth is an understanding of how an intentional mix[6] of strategies could fit together for reflexive action towards a degrowth society, with an understanding of where the degrowth movement's own humble actions fit into this broad, complex and interlinking mix.

---

6   An assemblage implies multiplicity rather than unity, but it is not just a random mix of multiple elements, but a particular arrangement. This definition draws on the work of Nail (2017), which Ekaterina Chertkovskaya pointed me to.

The word assemblage is important for degrowth's approach to strategy because it is rooted in the need for intentionality but also diversity. Intenionality acknowledges the massive barriers that an ambitious project like degrowth faces, but also the need to act in the here and now towards a desired social-ecological transformation. This therefore requires coordinated and meaningfully inter-linked actions, since plurality alone is not a strategy. On the other hand, a key feature of using strategic assemblage as a term is that it acknowledges the diversity of degrowth, and the multitude of actions and approaches associated with it. Therefore, such an assemblage would accommodate plurality but also necessitate prioritization[7] and an intentional consideration of how strategic actions can (or in some instances cannot) inter-relate and the role of coordination towards such an assemblage.

Adhering to the definition that strategy is a thought construct (see the Introduction), this means that a strategic assemblage is a self-understanding and articulation by the degrowth community of activists and scholars. Thus, a strategic assemblage is not a static plan nor a specific action, but rather a "flexible mental map" (Introduction, 21) of desired strategies. Flexibilty is key, because it ensures space for feedback, learning, experimentation and adaptation. An understanding of desired strategies would be empirically and theoretically informed, comprised of strategies in line with degrowth principles (self-organised, rooted in principles of justice, feminism, anti-racism, etc.). This would require further deliberation on where to draw the difficult lines between what is/isn't a strategy rooted in degrowth principles. Thus, a strategic assemblage is a constantly evolving orientation, balancing between an arbitrary direction and a fixed course.

In terms of agency, a strategic assemblage must include a diversity of actors for a social-ecological transformation, with the degrowth

---

7   Gabriel Trettel Silva encouraged me to preserve the term assemblage rather than assemblages to emphasise the need for greater coordination, prioritization, and a further problematisation of strategic indeterminism.

movement itself being only one of a plethora of actors. Implying that while a degrowth society may be the strategic horizon for the degrowth movement of scholars and activists, there are other related and allied visions of a desired social-ecological transformation. Additionally, such an imagined degrowth transfomartion cannot be achieved alone by the degrowth movement, but necessarily requires allies.

In summary, articulating a strategic assemblage for degrowth is one of the most challenging tasks for degrowth's debate around strategy as it will require embracing plurality while acknowledging that not all strategies are equally useful for achieving degrowth in a given context. Much work has already been done in preparing the foundation for the degrowth community, if it so chooses, to collectively enhance a common understanding of a strategic assemblage for degrowth and situating its own agency within this canvas of actions.

This chapter has argued that engagement with the topic of strategy has ebbed and flowed since 2010, but there has undoubtedly been a growing consensus in recent years around the need for more rigorous debates on strategy within the degrowth community. This has been reflected in informal talks and blog posts, panel discussions and scientific papers. The uptick of interest has drawn together diffuse threads of discussion throughout the history of the degrowth movement that had not yet consolidated into a coherent debate. There are still many open questions around this topic, of which the usefulness of thinking about a *strategic assemblage* is just one. The rest of this book aims to continue to enhance the knowledge on degrowth and strategy while also pointing towards promising areas of further development.

References

Barca, Stefania. 2018. "In Defense of Degrowth. Opinions and Minifestos/Doughnut Economics. Seven Ways to Think Like a 21st Century Economist." *Local Environment* 23, no. 3: 378–381.

Bardi, Carol, Nathan Barlow, Joe Herbert, and Jacob Smessaert. 2021. "Degrowth Strategies: Thinking with and beyond Erik Olin Wright." *Degrowth.info* Resilience, October 25, 2021. https://www.resilience.org/stories/2021-10-25/degrowth-strategies-thinking-with-and-beyond-erik-olin-wright/

Barlow, Nathan. 2019. "A Blog Series on Strategy in the Degrowth Movement." *Degrowth.info* (blog), January 9, 2019. https://degrowth.info/blog/a-blog-series-on-strategy-in-the-degrowth-movement

Barlow, Nathan, and Joe Herbert. 2020. "Reflecting on the Emerging Strategy Debate in the Degrowth Movement." *Degrowth.info* (blog), October 12, 2020. https://degrowth.info/de/blog/reflecting-on-the-emerging-strategy-debate-in-the-degrowth-movement

Blühdorn, Ingolfur. 2007. "Sustaining the Unsustainable: Symbolic Politics and the Politics of Simulation." *Environmental Politics* 16, no. 2: 251–275.

Blühdorn, Ingolfur, Felix Butzlaff, Michael Deflorian, and Daniel Hausknost. 2018. *Transformation Research and Academic Responsibility. The Social Theory Gap in Narratives of Radical Change*. Institute for Social Change and Sustainability (IGN), Wien Universität.

Brand, Ulrich, and Markus Wissen. 2017. "Social-EcologicalTransformation." In *International Encyclopedia of Geography: People, the Earth, Environment and Technology*, edited by Douglas Richardson, Noel Castree, Michael F. Goodchild, Audrey Kobayashi, Weidong Liu, and Richard A. Marston, 1–9. Oxford, UK: John Wiley & Sons, Ltd.

Buch-Hansen, Hubert. 2018. "The Prerequisites for a Degrowth Paradigm Shift: Insights from Critical Political Economy." *Ecological Economics* 146 (April): 157–163.

Cattaneo, Claudio, Giacomo D'Alisa, Giorgos Kallis, and Christos Zografos. 2012. "Degrowth Futures and Democracy." *Special Issue: Politics, Democracy and Degrowth* 44, no. 6: 515–523.

Cattaneo, Claudio, and Aaron Vansintjan. 2016. "A Wealth of Possibilities: Alternatives to Growth." *Green European Foundation*.

Chang, Heuishilja. 2016. "Evaluation of the Slow City Approach as a Degrowth Strategy for Shrinking Communities." *5th International Conference on Degrowth for Ecological Sustainability and Social Equity*, Budapest, 30 August – 3 September.

Chertkovskaya, Ekaterina. 2020. "From Taming to Dismantling: Degrowth and Anti-Capitalist Strategy." *Degrowth.info* (blog), September 21, 2020. https://degrowth.info/en/blog/from-taming-to-dismantling-degrowth-and-anti-capitalist-strategy

Cosme, Inês, Rui Santos, and Daniel W. O'Neill. 2017. "Assessing the Degrowth Discourse: A Review and Analysis of Academic Degrowth Policy Proposals." *Journal of Cleaner Production* 149 (April): 321–334.

D'Alisa, Giacomo. 2019. "Towards a Political Economy of Degrowth." In *Transforming Capitalism*, edited by Ekaterina Chertkovskaya, Alexander Paulsson, and Stefania Barca. London: Rowman & Littlefield International.

D'Alisa, Giacomo, and Giorgos Kallis. 2020. "Degrowth and the State." *Ecological Economics* 169 (March): 106486.

Demaria, Federico. 2018. "The Rise– and Future- of the Degrowth Movement." *Ecologist Informed by Nature*. https://theecologist.org/2018/mar/27/rise-and-future-degrowth-movement

Demaria, Federico, Francois Schneider, Filka Sekulova, and Joan Martinez–Alier. 2013. "What Is Degrowth? From an Activist Slogan to a Social Movement."*Environmental Values* 22, no. 2: 191–215.

Eckersley, Robyn. 2021. "Greening States and Societies: From Transitions to Great Transformations." *Environmental Politics* 30, no. 1–2: 245–265.

Editorial Team, *Degrowth.info*. 2018. "Looking Back on the 6th International Degrowth Conference for Ecological Sustainability and Social Equity." *Degrowth.info* (blog), August 31, 2018. https://degrowth.info/blog/looking-back-on-the-6th-international-degrowth-conference-for-ecological-sustainability-and-social-equity

Eversberg, Dennis, and Matthias Schmelzer. 2018. "The Degrowth Spectrum: Convergence and Divergence Within a Diverse and Conflictual Alliance." *Environmental Values* 27, no. 3: 245–267.

Feola, Giuseppe. 2019. "Strategies for a Degrowth Transformation: How Useful Are Historical Analogies?" *Degrowth.info* (blog), October 9, 2019. https://degrowth.info/en/blog/strategies-for-a-degrowth-transformation-how-useful-are-historical-analogies.

Foramitti, Joël. 2020. "Building Counter–Institutions: A Call for Activism beyond Raising Awareness." *Degrowth.info* (blog), May 27, 2020. https://degrowth.info/blog/building-counter-institutions-a-call-for-activism-beyond-raising-awareness.

Freedman, Lawrence. 2013. *Strategy: A History*. Oxford: Oxford University Press, USA.

Fromm, Sarah, and Simon Schöning. 2020. "Civil Disobedience as a Strategy for Degrowth." *Degrowth.info* (library). https://degrowth.info/en/library/degrowth-vienna-2020-civil-disobedience-as-a-strategy-for-degrowth.

Herbert, Joe. 2021. "The Socio-ecological Imagination: Young Environmental Activists Constructing Transformation in an Era of Crisis." *Area* 53, no.2: 373–380.

Herbert, Joe, Nathan Barlow, Christoph Ambach, Iris Frey, and Pietro Cigna. 2018. "Beyond Visions and Projects – the Need for a Debate on Strategy in the Degrowth Movement." *Degrowth.info* (blog), October 3, 2018. https://degrowth.info/blog/beyond-visions-and-projects-the-need-for-a-debate-on-strategy-in-the-degrowth-movement.

Kallis, Giorgos. 2018. *Degrowth.* The Economy Key Ideas. Newcastle upon Tyne: Agenda Publishing.

Koch, Max. 2020. "The State in the Transformation to a Sustainable Postgrowth Economy." *Environmental Politics* 29, no. 1: 115–133.

Krüger, Timmo. 2020. "Entry Points for Transformative Politics: The Power of Unstated Premises." *Degrowth.info* (blog), March 5, 2020. https://degrowth.info/blog/entry-points-for-transformative-politics-the-power-of-unstated-premises.

Lang, Miriam. 2017. "Degrowth: Unsuited for the Global South?" *Alternautas* (blog), July 17, 2017. https://journals.warwick.ac.uk/index.php/alternautas/article/view/1057.

Mastini, Riccardo, Giorgos Kallis, and Jason Hickel. 2021. "A Green New Deal without Growth?" *Ecological Economics* 179 (January), 106832.

Miller-McDonald, Samuel. 2021. "Ecosocialism Is the Horizon, Degrowth Is the Way: A Review of Less Is More and Interview with Jason Hickel." *The Trouble*, February 11, 2021. https://www.the-trouble.com/content/2021/2/11/ecosocialism-is-the-horizon-degrowth-is-the-way.

Muraca, Barbara. 2017. "Against the Insanity of Growth: Degrowth as Concrete Utopia." *Socialism in Process*: 183–187.

Murphy, Mary P. 2013. "Translating Degrowth into Contemporary Policy Challenges: A Symbiotic Social Transformation Strategy." *Irish Journal of Sociology* 21, no. 2: 76–89.

Nail, Thomas. 2017. "What Is an Assemblage?" *SubStance* 46, no. 1: 21–37.

Novy, Andreas. 2020. "Effective Strategies for Degrowth." *Karl Polanyi Society*, May 29, 2020. https://www.karlpolanyisociety.com/2020/05/29/effective-strategies-for-degrowth/.

Parrique, Timothée. 2019. "The Political Economy of Degrowth." PhD thesis, Université Clermont Auvergne; Stockholms universitet.

Perey, Robert. 2016. "Degrowth as a Transition Strategy." In *A Future beyond Growth: towards a Steady State Economy*, edited by Haydn Washington, and Paul Twomey. London; New York, NY: Routledge.

Petridis, Panos. 2016. "Strategies for Purposive Degrowth Transformations." *Proceedings of the 5th International Degrowth Conference, Budapest, 2016.* https://degrowth.

info/es/library/strategies-for-purposive-degrowth-transformations.

Petridis, Panos. 2019. "On Strategies for Social-Ecological Transformation." *Degrowth.info* (blog), January 9, 2019. Resilience, January 11, 2019. https://www.resilience.org/stories/2019-01-11/on-strategies-for-socioecological-transformation/.

Pringle, Anna. 2021. "Portrayals of Degrowth in the Press: "Free Market Magic" vs "Radical Doomsayers." *Degrowth.info* (blog), June 4, 2021. https://degrowth.info/en/blog/portrayals-of-degrowth-in-the-press-free-market-magic-vs-radical-doomsayers.

Rilovic, Andro. 2020. "Degrowth Vienna 2020–Anarchism and Degrowth: Two Sides of the Same Coin." *Degrowth.info* (library). https://degrowth.info/de/library/degrowth-vienna-2020-anarchism-and-degrowth-two-sides-of-the-same-coin.

Sato, Chizu, and Jozelin María Soto Alarcón. 2018. "Towards a Postcapitalist Feminist Political Ecology Approach to Commoning." *International Journal of the Commons* 13, no. 1: 36–61.

Schmid, Benedikt. 2020. "Sketching a Degrowth Transition." In *Making Transformative Geographies: Lessons from Stuttgart's Community Economy*, 235–252.

Schoppek, Dorothea Elena, and Mathias Krams. 2021. "Challenging Change: Understanding the Role of Strategic Selectivities in Transformative Dynamics." *Interface* 13, no. 1: 104–128.

Sum, Ngai–Ling, and Bob Jessop. 2013. *Towards a Cultural Political Economy: Putting Culture in Its Place in Political Economy*. Cheltenham, UK, Northampton, MA: Elgar.

Sze, Jocelyne, and Omar Saif. 2019. "Before Strategy, Who Is Strategising?" *Degrowth.info* (blog), January 30, 2019. https://degrowth.info/en/blog/before-strategy-who-is-strategising.

Trainer, Ted. 2021. "Degrowth: How Much Is Needed?" *Biophysical Economics and Sustainability* 6, no. 2: 5.

Videira, Nuno, François Schneider, Filka Sekulova, and Giorgos Kallis. 2014. "Improving Understanding on Degrowth Pathways: An Exploratory Study Using Collaborative Causal Models." *Futures* 55 (January): 58–77.

Wright, Erik Olin. 2010. *Envisioning Real Utopias*. London; New York: Verso.

Zografos, Christos. 2019. "Degrowth and Transformation: A Reflection." Resilience, February 8, 2019. https://www.resilience.org/stories/2019-02-08/degrowth-and-transformation-a-reflection/

Degrowth movement(s): strategising and plurality

Chapter 4:

Strategising within diversity: the challenge of structuring

By Viviana Asara

Introduction

The concept of degrowth refers to at least three interconnected analytical objects or levels of meaning[8]. First, degrowth is a political project and a (concrete) utopia (Muraca 2013) with a set of ideas and imaginaries about what an alternative society is to be, and a critique of current (growth-centred, capitalist) societies. Second, degrowth has a movement dimension: while for some it is itself an emerging social movement (Burkhart, Schmelzer, and Treu 2020; Eversberg and Schmelzer 2018, 246; Martínez-Alier *et al*. 2010), for others it is rather "an interpretative frame" (Demaria *et al*. 2013) or even an "archipelago" (Muraca 2020, 4–5) for the convergence of different movements. Here, two similar concepts borrowed from social movement studies can help us understand this movement dimension. One is the concept of the "movement area" introduced by sociologist Alberto Melucci back in the 1980s[9], namely "networks composed of a multiplicity of groups that are dispersed, fragmented, and submerged in everyday life, and which act as cultural laboratories" (Melucci 1989, 60). This concept emphasises collective action that is mainly engaged in *latent* movement activities – such as the experimentation and practice of new cultural models, forms of relationships, and meanings of the world – characterised by multiple forms of memberships and only periodical contentious

---

8   I thank Emanuele Leonardi for suggesting this threefold distinction during our conversations. Furthermore, this distinction is similar to the one highlighted by Chertkovskaya 2022.

9   I thank Laura Centemeri for having raised this point during our conversations.

mobilisation (Melucci 1984). The concept of "social movement community"(Staggenborg 1998) is also useful in that it stresses that "community" is forged through social networks and a movement culture created through the overlapping participation of individuals in diverse movements with similar values (i.e., the alter/anti-globalization movement, feminist movement, environmental and climate justice movements, solidarity economy movements etc.).

Finally, born at the intersection between a culturalist and ecological critique of economics (Latouche 2011), degrowth's third level of meaning has increasingly involved the development of an interdisciplinary field of investigation and can now be considered to be a research paradigm, interlacing disciplines from ecological economics, social ecology, and political ecology to anthropology, sociology, and political science and economy, among others (Kallis *et al.* 2018; Weiss and Cattaneo 2017).

This multi-perspectival approach suggests that the degrowth community and worldviews hold some substantial degree of heterogeneity and diversity, as is often remarked by degrowth authors. For example, Barca *et al.* (2019, 5) argue that degrowth's key strength is its multiplicity of ideas and movements, and that it should further embrace a "nomadic utopianism" which, by proceeding through a non-hierarchical organisation, maximises difference and benefits from a pluriverse of possible worlds and self-critiques. But how is such a difference articulated? And, more importantly, if the degrowth movement aims to have any impact on social and political systems, how can a strategic plan be devised in the face of plurality?

In this chapter, I will scrutinise the range and features of degrowth's plurality and, using a lens of social movement theory, discuss what movements' internal diversity and intersectionality might involve in terms of collective identity and transformative potential. Furthermore, I will delve into the multi-dimensionality of strategy, arguing that the fostering of strategic thinking and decision-making cannot prescind from dealing with the movement's *organisational structure*. I will situate this argument within the degrowth movement's recent history, and show that the movement is facing a critical juncture, reflecting on some weaknesses and potential ways forward.

This chapter's findings draw, first, on my own experience as a participant in the degrowth movement as both an "activist" – as a member of the association Research & Degrowth since 2011, of the Support Group for only a few months in 2013, and of the Advisory Board of the *Degrowth Vienna 2020 Conference: Strategies for Social-ecological Transformation* – as well as an academic that has participated in six international degrowth conferences. Second, the findings have been substantially enriched by an interview carried out with an activist, Jean-Louis Aillon, deeply involved in the degrowth movement at both the national (in the Italian *Movimento per la Decrescita Felice*) and international scale (as a member of the Support Group).

Plurality in degrowth

The degrowth movement's diversity has been investigated empirically. Eversberg and Schmelzer (2018) conducted a survey at the 4th *International Degrowth Conference in Leipzig* (2014), drawing on a sample of 814 respondents out of more than 3000 conference participants. While the sample is not representative of the entire degrowth community, it provides an idea of the diversity inherent in the movement and I believe is useful for grasping some main cleavages and tensions cutting across the degrowth community. The survey identified five different and even conflicting currents within the movement : 1) a group of Critics of Civilisation, who have a radical ecological and sufficiency-oriented approach, and hold a very negative view of industrial contemporary society as incapable of being reformed, thus focusing on building small-scale and frugal alternative local community projects; 2) a pragmatic and moderate group of Immanent Reformers, with an optimistic stance on technology and progress and a pragmatic take on politics, believing that changes should be pursued within existing institutions rather than by means of individual behaviour; 3) a younger and weakly politicised cluster of voluntarist-pacifist idealists, probably transitory due to their young age, who see degrowth as a peaceful and voluntary process; 4) a group of classical Modernist-Rationalist Leftists, privileging just distribution rather than ecological issues, and oriented towards an understanding of transformative change based on strategic considerations (rather than on ethical grounds) by means of classical mass organisations and socialist policies; 5) a particularly militant Alternative Practical Left group displaying a fierce critique of capitalism and industrial civilisation, with the belief that the necessary transformation will require a decisive rupture with existing societal structures. This latter group combines a radical critique of society with a practice of experimenting with possible alternatives, inspired by anarchist thought. Based on their cluster analysis, the authors note that while the two most ideologically divided positions are clusters 1 and 4, the fifth group seems to occupy a mediating position between them because its "radical views criss-cross the divide between a wholesale critique of civilisation on the one hand and a rationalist-progressive position on the other" (*Ibid.*, 263).

The tension between more classical left/Marxist currents and more anarchic strands seems indeed to be one that is cutting across the degrowth community. On the one hand, degrowth is conspicuously inspired by an anarchist subculture and tradition that "rely on self-organisation from the bottom-up" (Burkhart *et al.* 2019, 10) and stresses "the need for a voluntary and democratic downshift" (Cosme *et al.* 2017, 327). Often this influence is explicit at international conferences. For example, anarchism was one of the thematic strands of the *8th International Degrowth Conference in The Hague* (2021). On the other hand, as shown by a review of academic works published in peer-reviewed journals (Cosme *et al.* 2017), the majority of degrowth proposals "require direct control by governments (e.g., caps, taxes, and regulations), which suggests the need for a high level of state intervention to pursue a degrowth transition" (*Ibid.*, 327). D'Alisa (2019) sees in this paradox a bifurcation between two approaches that are currently bringing life into the degrowth camp, one dedicated to practice (such as alternative economies) and the other to policies (such as basic income, work-sharing etc.), and reads these two factions as embodying Erik Olin Wright's interstitial and symbiotic strategies for transformation beyond capitalism (see also Chapter 8).

Other degrowth authors have drawn on Wright's categories (see e.g., Chapter 2 this volume; Asara 2020a) to stress that complementarity between different ideological positions can be found. Indeed, for Wright, interstitial transformations are associated with some strands of anarchism, ruptural strategies with Leninism and, more generally, revolutionary communism and socialism, and symbiotic strategies are associated with social democracy (Wright 2010). However, this complementarity cannot be taken for granted. It is noteworthy, for example, that the meaning of "ruptural" strategies becomes quite different when read through an anarchist-inspired lens (see Chapter 2) or from the perspective of Marxist/classical left tradition, which is more consonant with Wright's (2019, 2010) meaning of "ruptural" as the Leninist strategic logic of "smashing capitalism" that Wright attributes to revolutionaries.

At the *6th International Degrowth Conference in Malmö* (2018), this tension between different ideological positions was manifested in a heated plenary (MalmoDegrowth 2018) where the discussion increasingly drifted from the planned topic of a dialogue between different knowledges to the "hot" topics of political strategies and ideologies not heretofore debated at previous degrowth conferences (see Table 5.1 in Chapter 5). One of the panellists, Andreas Malm – in his first participation in a degrowth conference – advocated for a politics of vanguardism and what he called "ecological Leninism" and "war communism", with a strong role of the state forcing through unpopular policies such as mandatory veganism. This created some strong reactions from the audience – with some people clapping and several protesting – including the intervention of Miriam Lang, which pointed to the limits of "Leninist" progressive governments during the Latin American pink tide. Malm responded that these governments were akin to social democracy rather than revolutionary socialism or oppositional communism. In his latest book (Malm 2020), he deepened these arguments, arguing that in today's chronic (climate) emergency hard state power is required, starting with "draconian restraints and cuts", including economic plans, covering all branches of economic activities, and nothing less than ecological war communism (*Ibid.*, 46). An ecological Leninism for Malm is the "only one that can point to an emergency exit", foregrounding "speed as paramount virtue" (*Ibid.*, 47), and imposing, in a way that resounds with the Marxist dictatorship of the proletariat, the will of one part of the population upon the other.

Malm's position seems to be poles apart from other degrowth authors' invocation of the deepening of democracy as part and parcel of the degrowth transformation, or visions of a bottom-up constitution of local communities or *demoi* federated at different levels (Demaria *et al.* 2013; Asara *et al.* 2013; Deriu 2012; Chertkovskaya forthcoming). While it is uncertain whether Malm can be depicted as a degrowth supporter himself (i.e., in his publications he does not use the term), bringing Leninism and in general communism together with degrowth has not been solely Malm's pursuit. A mailing list and forum for discussion called "degrowth communism" was born in recent years, aiming to bring together and establish a dialogue between communism and the tradition of historical materialism, on one hand, and degrowth, on the other, as "traditions of thinking and practising the social-ecological transformation and the system change needed to achieve an environmentally safe and socially just life for all" (Beuret *et al.* 2020). This led to the setting up of a workshop session at the *Degrowth Vienna 2020 Conference* (*Ibid*). Malm's book has stimulated some vibrant discussions within the degrowth communism mailing list, with diverse positions, from critical to sympathetic[10], and some

---

10 I thank Emanuele Leonardi for this insight.

of these reflections have reached an external public. Bue Rübner Hansen (2021), for example, interestingly notes that Malm's framing of the key choice to be made "in terms of the old debate between anarchism and a politics aimed at seizing state power" introduces a "strategic blindspot": while there is "plenty of Leninist will" (take state power), there is "little to say about the processes of class composition which allowed Lenin's rise", thus relying on a "popular power it cannot bring into being, and that it does not respect, even as it mythologises it".

These discussions reveal how nuanced the ideological landscape is, yet ideological divergences are not the only forms of differences. In terms of members' background, while there is a heterogeneity of profiles from practitioners to artists, and researchers – and while activists have played an important role in the genealogy of degrowth (Muraca 2013; Parrique 2019) – academics seem to have played a leading role as "movement intellectuals" (Eyerman and Jamison 1991), crucial for the construction of the movement's collective identity, since at least 2010. As my interviewee stated: "what defines us the most is our theoretical frame, rather than a profile of action or practical activism (…) and those who define our identity are mainly academics." Not only have international conferences, partly due to their very format, seen academics as protagonists of most sessions and plenaries, researchers have also played a prominent role in collectives that act as central nodes for the movement, such as Research & Degrowth in Barcelona, Konzeptwerk Neue Ökonomie in Germany, Associazione per la Decrescita in Italy, or the Institute of Political Ecology in Croatia. Indeed, around 65% of all degrowth groups are involved in research, as identified by an online survey and mapping exercise organised by degrowth activists and advertised across degrowth mailing lists and networks. Relatedly, while another form of diversity has to do with the various foci and practices of degrowth activism (see Chapter 6), probably the most important repertoire of action of the degrowth movement area so far has been the gathering of researchers, activists, practitioners, and artists around international and regional degrowth conferences that take place (almost) annually (see Chapter 5).

There is also not much diversity in activists' class and ethnic background, as supporters seem to mainly come from the ranks of the white and academically-educated middle class and students (Eversberg and Schmelzer 2018), a point also discussed extensively during the 2020 degrowth conference in Vienna. While degrowth conferences have fostered a dialogue and built alliances with alternatives and movements from the Global South, increasingly foregrounding the need for a decolonial and pluriversal approach, degrowth has so far been mostly a debate and movement developed in the Global North, as visible in the "degrowth map" (Karte von morgen n.d.) which found 372 groups/collectives across the world that define themselves as part of the degrowth movement, based however mostly in the Global North, and, most of all, in Europe.

Having ascertained that the degree of diversity is substantial in some respects (ideologies and strategic logics) but more limited in others, the question is whether this degree of diversity is unique or exceptional in social movements, and how such diversity can be integrated into a common narrative.

It is important to point out that plurality has been a key feature of movements that can be considered as "sister" and even "mother" movements of degrowth. The valorisation of difference has been at the heart of the global justice movement, not by chance referred to as the "movement of movements". The World Social Forum has been a prominent space for encountering and cross-pollinating differences. However, the movement was not simply a collection of heterogenous groups, rather, its collective identity was characterised by "a common construction" of an "alter-global subjectivity" (Toscano 2012, 79), displaying an ideological coherency around "justice globalism" (Steger and Wilson 2012). Similarly, environmental movements at both the international scale and in diverse countries such as the United Kingdom and Italy have been referred to as a "very broad church" (Berny and Rootes 2018, 947), an "archipelago" (Diani 1988), or a "phenomenon that is highly diverse in its forms of organisation and action (Doherty 2002). The family of environmental justice movements is particularly diverse, including, more prominently, the poor and marginalised – also due to their embeddedness in other social movements, from Indigenous movements and those for racial equality to movements for occupational health (Asara 2022; Sicotte and Brulle 2017).

Such entanglements have been found to have the potential of reaching a more heterogenous constituency (Heaney and Rojas 2014) and of increasing a movement's transformative potential thanks to the intersectionality of struggles that allows to integrate social justice and ecological concerns (see Asara 2020b; Gottlieb 2005). What plays a fundamental role are movements' efforts to integrate the different dimensions of their collective identity (Melucci 1989; Toscano 2012; Asara 2016), i.e., the sense of a "we" negotiated through evolving tensions within movements, developed interactively through connections within a group at three interwoven levels: a cognitive and moral framework, relational, and emotional investments (Calhoun 1993; Polletta and Jasper 2001).

In the degrowth movement, despite its internal diversity, empirical research has found that two main cognitive pillars of collective identity involve the insistence on the destructiveness of economic growth. This entails the need for a reduction of material throughput and consumption in the Global North and a vision of a transformation that is pro-feminist, peaceful, democratic, bottom-up, and critical of capitalism (Eversberg and Schmelzer 2018). However, the capitalist and industrial growth imperative would also need to be overcome in the Global South (see Chapter 1).

In the next and final section, I will turn to the issue of strategy, trying to grapple with the following question: how can or should such a heterogenous and multiple transnational movement try to set up and enact a "common strategy" (Barca *et al.* 2019, 7)? This requires first defining what we mean by strategy in social movements.

Movement strategies and structure: the degrowth movement at a critical juncture

Social movement scholars define strategy as:

> "A plan of collective action intended to accomplish goals within a particular context. Social movement strategy is located at the intersection between structure and agency, and it entails defining, interpreting, communicating, and implementing a plan of collective action that is believed to be a promising way to achieve a desired alternative future in light of circumstances." (Maney *et al.* 2012, xviii).

Strategy is a multi-level process, as plans of action, contexts and goals can be distinguished based on the level of social aggregation (micro, e.g., individual level; meso, e.g., groups or organisational level; or macro, e.g., movement or coalition level), type of institution, geographic scope, duration (short term or long term), cultural and structural characteristics, and multiple strategies can be in place in the same movement (Maney *et al.* 2012).

This clarifies that there is not a single, common strategy that should be devised by the degrowth movement, but manifold, overlapping, and embedded types of strategic decisions, depending for instance on the scale of consideration (transnational movement or local), on the temporal timeframe, or arena of action. This is especially the case for degrowth activism which is, similarly to other environmental movements, diffuse and wide-ranging and involves a complex web of actors and a range of spaces and scales (North 2011; Porta and Rucht 2002).

Moreover, following Meyer and Staggenborg (2012) we can identify (at least) three major elements of strategic decision-making: the goals and demands made by a social movement; the tactics or forms of collective action (that is, the specific means of implementing strategy, such as demonstrations, lawsuits, direct action tactics and institutionalised tactics such as lobbying etc.); and arenas (i.e., venues in which to press movement claims, e.g., legislatures, courts, the public, mass media, electoral politics). However, it is noteworthy that while for Meyer and Staggenborg a movement's internal organisation only counts as an influence for strategies, according to a prefigurative understanding of social movements, a movement's internal organisation counts as one main dimension of a movement strategy, because means and ends should not be overly detached and a movement's internal practices and organisations are themselves strategic (Maeckelbergh 2011). Indeed, internal strategy (movement building) and external strategy (projected outward towards achieving goals beyond the movement) are intimately linked, not only because the latter depends on the way the movement (and social movement organisations within it) is organised, but also because the former is also subject to strategic decision-making. Organisational variation includes various issues such as the extent and type of formalisation or bureaucratisation, professionalisation, grassroots participation, centralisation and hierarchy in decision-making structures, links among various levels such as national, local and, international levels, and forums available for decision-making and deliberation (Meyer and Staggenborg 2012).

How has the degrowth movement fared against such a backdrop, and evolved over time? One of the outcomes of the first two international conferences in Paris (2008) and Barcelona (2010) was the creation of the association Research & Degrowth in France and then in Spain. The latter, with its Barcelona group of ICTA (Institute of Environmental Science and Technology) researchers, acted as a supervising actor for the organisation of the following conferences, starting with the 2012 Venice and Montreal conferences. Following some accusations of over-directing the conference organisation process, the Support Group – composed of delegates of organisational groups of previous conferences – was created after the 3rd *International Degrowth Conference in Venice* (2012) to facilitate the organisation of each conference in a more collegial way. At the 5th *International Degrowth Conference in Leipzig* (2014), a Group Assembly Process called "Building Collective Actions" was set up to "understand who we are, what we do, whom we want to collaborate with" (interview). As mentioned by the interviewee, from the Leipzig Group Assembly Process "emerges the need to structure ourselves a bit better, also in order to provide people with the possibility to participate in this international network". This led to the first mapping exercise, and to the first assembly of the international degrowth movement, which took place in Christiania just before the *6th International Degrowth Conference in Malmö* (2018), as a pre-conference. This first assembly was facilitated by an informal ad-hoc Network Coordination Group that sprouted from the Support Group. The assembly included around 70 people as part of 40 collectives, and "took a very basic decision, that is to create a loose network and stay in contact through a movement's mailing list" (interview). Moreover, in the Christiania assembly, several working groups were created, such as the Activists and Practitioners group – which among other things has been organising the Global Degrowth Day since 2019 – and the *degrowth.info* editorial team was formalised (see Chapter 5), becoming the media arm of the degrowth movement (Degrowth.info n.d.).

During this period the need emerged to "give us a more representative bottom-up structure than the SG" (interview). Indeed, while the SG is perceived as a horizontal structure, it is not an open body representative of the movement (as mentioned above, it is constituted of organisers of previous conferences) or a body endowed with the task of coordinating or catalysing specific initiatives outside of the conference realm. Due to the lack of other representative bodies, the Support Group has however increasingly assumed several tasks beyond conference organisation such as managing funds from foundations. This happened after the granting of the first substantial funding in 2018 from the *Fondation Charles Léopold Mayer pour le Progrès de l'Homme*, and a Support Group meeting in Paris. Here "there has been a debate: 'do we want to take responsibility only for the conferences or for the movement?' – 'But we don't have the mandate to take care of the movement.' – 'But no one does it'..."

(interview). Ultimately, it was decided that in a 2-year-transition period the Support Group would try to bring about a structuring of the network, and a network coordination group was formally established to organise and facilitate the assemblies. The funding fed into conference expenses, the *degrowth.info* media platform, summer schools, a scholarship for the ICTA Master programme on degrowth, IT support, expenses for the Support Group and the Activist Group meetings, and so on. As expectable, decisions over funding allocation, however, generated some tensions in the Support Group. In addition, insufficient coordination between the autonomous groups resulted in some "misunderstandings" or "tensions" between them. This has somewhat improved in the last year with the constitution of the "Coordination of the nodes of degrowth", a (virtual) space of encounter and information exchange between the diverse groups that compose its network.

The second assembly took place right before the *8th International Degrowth Conference in The Hague* (2021), where a potential two-level structure was discussed: the assembly, and a group that will represent it and constitute the "political steering" of the international degrowth movement – potentially endowed with the tasks of organising international initiatives, managing the funds, and coordinating the various autonomous groups. However, a decision on this issue was postponed to a later meeting to take place in Spring 2022.

As this short historical excursus demonstrates, the degrowth movement has mostly had a very loose organisational structure (also referred to as "an unstructured (…) way of organising" in Chapter 5) but steps are slowly being taken, in dribs and drabs, to endow it with more structure and coordination following increasing recognition that this structurelessness is greatly limiting the movement's potential.

In the 1970s, Jo Freeman (1972) referring to the women's liberation movement, famously argued that structurelessness led to the production of elites not accountable to the rest of the movement and to a weakened capability to control the directions in which it develops and the political actions in which it engages. I believe that this loose organisation may have indeed hampered the political actions and efficacy of the movement as well as kept it in a sort of limbo, for instance with respect to the role of the Support Group, or the capability of making political declarations about degrowth (accomplished only at the first two conferences). Furthermore, it seems to have created "some underlying tensions between the different groups – which however have never been revealed in a clear-cut manner – which have to do with *legitimacy* and with *what degrowth is*" (interview). Finally, this structurelessness has probably also contributed to the heightened visibility of academics' contribution to the movement's collective identity. However, according to my interviewee, there are some countervailing fears linked with advancing towards structuring, because "structures" are paradoxically associated with "granting power" (interview).

The two-level structure discussed at the pre-conference in The Hague could be a nice starting point. Following Freeman (1972), its institution would need to take into consideration the following basic issues (the same goes with the *Degrowth International*, see Chapter 5): procedures for the selection of delegates and their rotation, accountability mechanisms, allocation of tasks/distribution of labour and type of relationships among the nodes of the network, distribution of authority and of resources, and diffusion of information to everyone. Whether the opportunity will be seized or whether the state of limbo will be protracted due to some underlying fears or failure to reach a consensus cannot be anticipated now. What is certain is that time has come for the degrowth movement to evolve into a space where not only political debates are made in academic journals, in the media or at conferences – thus spreading its ideas – but wherein strategic decisions are made to reach specific goals.

References

Asara, Viviana. 2016. "The Indignados as a Socio-Environmental Movement: Framing the Crisis and Democracy." *Environmental Policy and Governance* 26, no. 6: 527–542.

Asara, Viviana. 2020a. *Democrazia Senza Crescita*. Rome: Aracne Edizioni.

Asara, Viviana. 2020b. Untangling the radical imaginaries of the Indignados' movement: Commons, autonomy and ecologism. *Environmental Politics*. http://doi.org/10.1080/09644016.2020.1773176

Asara, Viviana. 2022. "Socio-environmental movements as democratizing agents". In Routledge Handbook of Democracy and Sustainability, edited by B. Borneman, H. Knappe and P. Nanz. Abingdon (UK): Routledge, ISBN 9780367109585

Asara, Viviana, Emanuele Profumi, and Giorgos Kallis. 2013. "Degrowth, Democracy and Autonomy." *Environmental Values* 22, no. 2: 217–239.

Barca, Stefania, Ekaterina Chertkovskaya, and Alexander Paulsson. 2019. "Introduction: The End of Political Economy as We Knew It? From Growth Realism to Nomadic Utopianism." In *towards a Political Economy of Degrowth*, edited by Ekaterina Chertkovskaya, Alexander Paulsson, and Stefania Barca, 1–18. London: Rowman & Littlefield.

Berny, Nathalie, and Christopher Rootes. 2018. "Environmental NGOs at a Crossroads?"*Environmental Politics* 27, no. 6: 947–972.

Beuret, Nicholas, Emanuele Leonardi, Tomislav Medak, Manuela Rübner Hansen, and Bue Zechner. 2020. "Degrowth Communism: towards a Convergence of Strategies." *Workshop Session at the Degrowth Vienna 2020 Conference.*

Burkhart, Corinna, Matthias Schmelzer, and Nina Treu. 2020. *Degrowth in Movement(s): Exploring Pathways for Transformation*. Winchester, UK: Zero.

Calhoun, Craig. 1993. "New Social Movements of the Early Nineteenth Century." *Social Science History* 17, no. 3: 385–427.

Chertkovskaya, Ekaterina. 2022. "Degrowth." In *Handbook of Critical Environmental Politics*, edited by Luigi Pellizzoni, Emanuele Leonardi, and Viviana Asara. Edward Elgar Publishing.

Cosme, Inês, Rui Santos, and Daniel W. O'Neill. 2017. "Assessing the Degrowth Discourse: A Review and Analysis of Academic Degrowth Policy Proposals." *Journal of Cleaner Production* 149 (April): 321–334.

D'Alisa, Giacomo. 2019. "The State of Degrowth." In *towards a Political Economy of Degrowth*, edited by Ekaterina Chertkovskaya, Alexander Paulsson, and Stefania Barca, 243–258. London: Rowman & Littlefield.

Degrowth.info. n.d. *International working groups*. shorturl.at/czZo2.

Deriu, Marco. 2012. "Democracies with a Future: Degrowth and the Democratic Tradition." *Futures* 44, no. 6: 553–561.

Diani, Mario. 1988. *Isole Nell'arcipelago. Il Movimento Ecologista in Italia*. Il Mulino.

Doherty, Brian. 2002. *Ideas and Actions in the Green Movement*. Routledge.

Eversberg, Dennis, and Matthias Schmelzer. 2018. "The Degrowth Spectrum: Convergence and Divergence within a Diverse and Conflictual Alliance." *Environmental Values* 27, no. 3: 245–267.

Freeman, Jo. 1972. "The Tyranny of Structurelessness." *Berkeley Journal of Sociology* 17: 151–164.

Heaney, Michael T., and Fabio Rojas. 2014. "Hybrid Activism: Social Movement Mobilization in a Multimovement Environment." *American Journal of Sociology* 119, no. 4: 1047–1103.

Kallis, Giorgos, Vasilis Kostakis, Steffen Lange, Barbara Muraca, Susan Paulson, and Matthias Schmelzer. 2018. "Research on Degrowth." *Annual Review of Environment and Resources* 43: 291–316.

Karte von morgen. n.d. *Karte von morgen#degrowth*. https://kartevonmorgen.org/#/?center=37.719,13.359&zoom=3.00&categories=initiative&search=%23degrowth&dropdowns=kvm.

Latouche, Serge. 2011. *Come Si Esce Dalla Societa' Dei Consumi. Corsi e Percorsi Della Decrescita*. Torino: Bollati Boringhieri.

Maeckelbergh, Marianne. 2011. "Doing Is Believing: Prefiguration as Strategic Practice in the Alterglobalization Movement." *Social Movement Studies* 10, no. 1: 1–20.

Malm, Andreas. 2020. *Corona, Climate, Chronic Emergency: War Communism in the Twenty-First Century*. London: Verso.

MalmoDegrowth. 2018. "Plenary – Dialogues between critical social theories, science and degrowth." Uploaded on August, 27, 2018. YouTube video, 1:48:20 min. https://www.youtube.com/watch?v=2GBkJVHx6mM.

Maney, Gregory M., Rachel V. Kutz-Flamenbaum, Deana A. Rohlinger, and Jeff Goodwin. 2012. *Strategies for Social Change*. Minneapolis: University of Minnesota Press.

Martínez-Alier, Joan, Unai Pascual, Franck Dominique Vivien, and Edwin Zaccai. 2010. "Sustainable De-Growth: Mapping the Context, Criticisms and Future Prospects of an Emergent Paradigm." *Ecological Economics* 69, no. 9: 1741–1747.

Melucci, Alberto. 1989. *Nomads of the Present*. London: Hutchinson Radius.

Melucci, Alberto, ed. 1984. *Altri Codici. Aree Di Movimento Nella Metropoli*. Bologna: Il Mulino.

Meyer, David S., and Suzanne Staggenborg. 2012. "Thinking about Strategy." In *Strategies for Social Change*, edited by Gregory M. Maney, Rachel V. Kutz-Flamenbaum, Deana A. Rohlinger, and Jeff Goodwin, n.a. Minneapolis: University of Minnesota Press.

Muraca, Barbara. 2013. "Décroissance: A Project for a Radical Transformation of Society." *Environmental Values* 22, no. 2: 147–169.

Muraca, Barbara. 2020. "Foreword." In *Degrowth in Movement(s): Exploring Pathways for Transformation*, edited by Corinna Burkhart, Matthias Schmelzer, and Nina Treu, 4–8. Winchester, UK: Zero.

North, Peter. 2011. "The Politics of Climate Activism in the UK: A Social Movement Analysis." *Environment and Planning A* 43, no. 7: 1581–1598.

Parrique, Timothée. 2019. "The Political Economy of Degrowth." PhD thesis, Université Clermont Auvergne & Stockholm University.

Polletta, Francesca, and James M. Jasper. 2001. "Collective Identity and Social Movements." *Annual Review of Sociology* 27: 283–305.

Porta, Donatella, and Dieter Rucht. 2002. "The Dynamics of Environmental Campaigns." *Mobilization: An International Quarterly* 7, no. 1: 1–14.

Rübner Hansen, Bue. 2021. "The Kaleidoscope of Catastrophe: On the Clarities and Blind Spots of Andreas Malm." *Viewpoint Magazine*, April 14, 2021. https://viewpointmag.com/2021/04/14/the-kaleidoscope-of-catastrophe-on-the-clarities-and-blind-spots-of-andreas-malm/

Sicotte, Diane M., and Robert J. Brulle. 2017. "Social Movements for Environmental Justice through the Lens of Social Movement Theory." In *The Routledge Handbook of Environmental Justice*, edited by Ryan Holifield, Jayajit Chakraborty, and Gordon Walker. Routledge.

Staggenborg, Suzanne. 1998. "Social Movement Communities and Cycles of Protest: The Emergence and Maintenance of a Local Women's Movement." *Social Problems* 45, no. 2: 180–204.

Steger, Manfred B., and Erin K. Wilson. 2012. "Anti-Globalization or Alter-Globalization? Mapping the Political Ideology of the Global Justice Movement." *International Studies Quarterly* 56, no. 3: 439–454.

Weiss, Martin, and Claudio Cattaneo. 2017. "Degrowth – Taking Stock and Reviewing an Emerging Academic Paradigm." *Ecological Economics* 137: 220–230.

Wright, Erik Olin. 2010. *Envisioning Real Utopias*. Verso.

Chapter 5:

Degrowth actors and their strategies: towards a *Degrowth International*

By Andro Rilović, Constanza Hepp, Joëlle Saey-Volckrick, Joe Herbert and Carol Bardi[11]

> *En el mundo que queremos nosotros caben todos.*
> *El mundo que queremos es uno donde quepan muchos mundos.*
> *In the world we want everyone fits.*
> *The world we want is one where many worlds fit.*
> —EZLN *(1996)*

Introduction

The degrowth movement is complex and diffuse. There is no one specific entity or gathering space from which to collect concrete and definitive information about it; the international degrowth conferences perhaps come closest. Nevertheless, in this chapter, we offer an analysis of the current landscape of key degrowth actors and their strategies, as seen from our position within one of the nodes of international degrowth networks: the *degrowth.info* webportal.

The webportal provides information on degrowth as both an academic concept and a growing movement comprised of activists, practitioners and researchers. Our contribution towards social-ecological transformation lies in the provision of degrowth information and resources, acting as an important organisational node and platform within wider degrowth networks. The current *degrowth.info* team came together after an effort was made in 2018 to give the web portal a more international outlook and reach,

---

11 The order of authors has been randomised

building from its German origins as the website for the *International Degrowth Conference in Leipzig* (2014). During our time within the *degrowth.info* collective, each of us has also participated in various other degrowth groups, campaigns and research, mainly within European degrowth networks. The perspective we offer in this chapter emerges from these experiences and contexts.

In the language we will use to describe current degrowth actors, there are many nuances, and we can start by considering the characterisation of degrowth as a *movement*. With plurality, self-determination and decolonisation as core principles, it would be imprecise – and some would argue undesirable – to describe degrowth as *a* movement, in the singular form. In fact, it is more of a network, or movement of movements, and an overarching discourse that touches upon and intertwines with a myriad of social movements striving for social-ecological transformation – as described, for example, in the book *Degrowth in Movement(s)* (Burkhart *et al.* 2020) – which makes for a challenging terrain to navigate in an organisational and strategic sense. Boundaries of degrowth networks are permeable since definitions are either loose or non-existent and depend on who is observing or describing these networks and for what purpose.

This degrowth network of networks remains largely unstructured and functions mainly through personal connections, with loose arrangements for communication, and virtually no overarching coordination. While some of this flexibility is intentional, we argue that the current lack of organisational structure increasingly appears more limiting than beneficial for degrowth strategising. In this chapter, we identify key existing degrowth actors and their strategies based on our perception of their agency, which emerges from either the respect they hold within the wider degrowth networks, their resources (intellectual and/or financial), or evidence that they have played an important role in shaping the degrowth discourse and movement(s). Based on our analysis, we propose moving forward with the creation of an intentional organisational structure that can facilitate more effective strategising amongst degrowth actors, while also addressing problematic power dynamics, colonial attitudes, and patriarchal biases.

Before moving on to the more concrete description of current degrowth actors, networks and their strategies, we start by providing some important historical context of their development.

The academic-centred development of degrowth actors and strategies

Degrowth as a concept has its roots in the 1970s (Gorz 1972), or arguably even before that. However, modern degrowth networks emerged at the beginning of the 21st century. From our perspective, the most clear and consistent strategy of degrowth actors so far has been knowledge building, engaging in dialogue, and diffusing ideas. One prominent tool for accomplishing this strategy has been the organisation of international conferences where all those interested in degrowth ideas – activists, practitioners, artists, academics and so on – can come together and build connections to work towards social-ecological transformation(s). Accordingly, the actors that have so far become important and visible nodes in degrowth networks have – in one way or another – been associated with one of the international degrowth conferences. Our collective at *degrowth.info* is one such group. After attracting much interest as the website of the International Degrowth Conference in Leipzig (2014) (as *degrowth.de*), the idea emerged to transform the domain into an international degrowth webportal in order to proliferate the dissemination of degrowth ideas and information.

From the very beginning, international degrowth conferences were envisioned as more than purely academic gatherings. For example, an early degrowth symposium in Lyon in 2003 included "protests for a car- and ad-free city, the foundation of food cooperatives, as well as communal meals in the streets" (Degrowth.info 2021a). The *International Degrowth Conferences for Ecological Sustainability and*

Social Equity – which started in Paris in 2008 – have continued in this spirit, providing a space and time in which to engage with key theoretical debates as well as to live a degrowth life for a week and enact degrowth practices.

In a similar vein, since 2014, the *Research and Degrowth* collective, which is largely based at the Institute of Environmental Sciences and Technologies (ICTA) in the Universidad Autónoma de Barcelona (UAB), has hosted a popular annual *Degrowth and Environmental Justice Summer School* (R&D 2021a), that brings together international participants to engage with degrowth research *and* practices. Building from this, ICTA has launched the first master's degree programme on the explicit topic of degrowth, which incorporates dialogues and engagement with activist projects (R&D 2021b).

While the issue of strategy has been present in degrowth debates from the very early days of the movement's emergence at the beginning of the 21st century (see e.g., Videira *et al.* 2014), it was not until the online conference in 2020 organised from Vienna that *strategy* became a focused theme of any degrowth meeting. Yet, organisers of other degrowth conferences have themselves adopted different strategic orientations depending on the contexts in which they operate, and their judgements regarding the most effective ways for advancing a degrowth agenda. For example, broadly speaking, the Budapest conference (2016) foregrounded the academic rigour of degrowth research, which would mark degrowth as a serious concept in the eyes of policy-makers, whereas the Leipzig conference (2014) aimed to draw links to social movements (e.g., climate justice) by adopting a more activist tone (Brand 2014).

The above exposition could lead to the conclusion that degrowth's development is centred in academia. However, this academic work should not be seen as separate from broader action for social and political change. After all, academic and social/political engagement are not binary and exclusive categories – and much of the work in degrowth has indeed blurred the boundaries between the two.

Actors in the degrowth networks

Having provided some background context of degrowth's development, we now introduce the current landscape of degrowth actors as we see it, whilst acknowledging that there may be more relevant actors than can possibly be mentioned in this short contribution. In line with our discussion of the key role of the international conferences in degrowth's evolution, in Table 5.1. we present a selection of notable actors that are active (albeit to varying extents) in *international* degrowth networks, displayed in relation to the conference they emerged from/around. Importantly, the table does not suggest a specific sequence of causality. Some of the groups existed prior to their respective conference or were set up to organise it, while others emerged as outcomes of the conferences. It also must be acknowledged that the "international" degrowth conferences have so far reflected closely degrowth's European-centred development, with only two conferences to date taking place on other continents: one in Montreal, Canada in 2012, and one in Mexico City, Mexico, in 2018.

Year	Conference location	Groups/organisations/initiatives	Websites
2008	Paris, France	Research and Degrowth	degrowth.org
2010	Barcelona, Spain	Research and Degrowth	degrowth.org
2012	Montreal, Canada	Mouvement Québécois pour une décroissance conviviale, now transformed into Décroissance conviviale au Québec	decroissance.qc.ca/ facebook.com/groups/ decroissanceconvivialeQC
2012	Venice, Italy	La decrescita, MDF	decrescita.it decrescitafelice.it
2014	Leipzig, Germany	Konzeptwerk Neue Ökonomie, Forderverein Wachstumswende	konzeptwerk–neue– oekonomie.org wachstumswende.org/ verein.htm
2016	Budapest, Hungary	Cargomania, Ena banda, Institute for Political Ecology	cargonomia.hu enabanda.si ipe.hr
2018	Malmö, Sweden	Institute for Degrowth Studies	degrowth.se

2018	Mexico City, Mexico	Descrecimiento Mexico, Ecomunidades	descrecimiento.org
2020	Vienna, Austria	Degrowth Vienna Association	degrowthvienna2020.org
2021	Manchester, UK	The University of Manchester, Steady-State Manchester	steadystatemanchester.net
2021	The Hague, Netherlands	Ontgroei, International Institute of Social Studies (ISS)	degrowth.nl ontgroei.degrowth.net iss.nl

Table 5.1.: International Conferences and the groups or organisations associated

Beyond those degrowth actors linked closely to conferences, a selection of further groups active within international degrowth networks is displayed in Table 5.2. This is a non-exhaustive list, considering the evolving character of the networks and the limits of our knowledge. Because of its international scope, this list does not involve the many groups active at national and regional levels (for those, see sections "map" and "regional groups" on *degrowth.info*).

Name	Description	Website/Contact
Support Group	Official promoter of international conferences composed of organisers of the previous conferences	supportgroup@degrowth.org
Degrowth movement	Connects people active in local degrowth groups and people engaged in international working groups	movement@lists.degrowth.net
Feminisms and Degrowth Alliance (FaDA)	Academic/activist network	fada-subscribe@lists.riseup.net
Latin American Degrowth Forum	Self-organised online forums	www.centrosocioambiental.cl/iniciativas
Degrowth.net	Networking platform	www.degrowth.net
Degrowth World	Open mailing list	Degrowth-world-subscribre@lists.riseup.net
Degrowth.info	Web portal run by an international volunteer group	contact@degrowth.info, www.degrowth.info

Table 5.2.: Other groups and relevant actors within international degrowth networks

While detailed descriptions of each of these actors and their respective strategies go beyond the scope of this chapter (and our knowledge), we will briefly reflect on a few of those listed in Table 5.2. The Support Group is the official promoter of the

International Conferences and is composed of representatives of the Local Organising Committees of the previous international conferences (Degrowth.info 2021d). Its primary aim is to facilitate the organisation of future international degrowth conferences, and thereby the advancement and promotion of degrowth, both as a concept and as a movement. The Feminisms and Degrowth Alliance (FaDA) was launched at the Budapest International Degrowth Conference (2016) – it is an inclusive network of academics, activists, and practitioners that aims to foster dialogue between feminists and degrowth proponents, and integrate gender analysis and ideas into degrowth activism and scholarship (Degrowth.info 2021e). Our own collective, *degrowth.info*, has its roots in the Leipzig conference, and some members of our collective have been involved in the Local Organising Committees of the degrowth conferences in Vienna (2020) and in The Hague (2021). As already mentioned above, we see our contribution mostly in the provisioning of degrowth information and resources, as well as serving as a platform for bringing together the wider degrowth networks. Clearly, even the groups which are not directly linked to the organisation of any particular international degrowth conference (those listed in Table 5.2.) are nevertheless, in one way or another, closely tied to these conferences. Hence our claim of the central role that the international degrowth conferences play in degrowth's strategic orientations.

Additional to groups such as those listed in the tables, there are also several open mailing lists that act as nodes in degrowth networks. The "degrowth movement" mailing list, for example, focuses on connecting activists, particularly around the annual *Global Degrowth Day* (Degrowth.info 2021b), but is also used to organise the movement's assemblies: in-person meetings dedicated to organising the degrowth movement beyond academia, which coincide with the international conferences. Ahead of the Malmö conference in 2018, the movement assembly gathered in Christiania, Copenhagen, and established several international working groups (also called *nodes*), that were meant to foster the connections between degrowthers around the world on interests such as activists and practitioners, research, external and internal communications, artists and designers (see Degrowth.info 2021c). Throughout the pandemic, we perceived little traction within these nodes and no concrete strategy beyond the fact of being in contact. This might change after the assembly that took place before the conference in The Hague in August 2021, where some members of the *degrowth. info* collective proposed the creation of a coordination or facilitation body (terminology is being discussed). This idea is presently up for debate, and the assembly concluded with the intention of meeting more regularly.

Dynamics and structure of international degrowth networks

We have described degrowth actors as hard to pin down because of the intangible nature of the networks, which exist through diverse and often informal connections, without an overarching structure of communication, coordination or cooperation. The Support Group seems to be commonly perceived as being at the core of the degrowth networks, although it is not intended – or willing – to have an overarching coordinating role beyond the conferences. The ambiguity of this position lies in the fact that we have described before: so far degrowth's development has been academically centred, following a strategy based on the organisation of international conferences. Therefore the Support Group, albeit as a non-central body, does control the most visible and substantial strategy within degrowth networks and has a *de facto* leadership position.

Keeping the network diffuse has often been perceived as a way of maintaining decentralisation – a core value of degrowth – and some have feared that pursuing greater structure might wither the diversity of degrowth actors and lead to hierarchical dynamics. Nonetheless, in recent years some efforts were made to establish a more overarching structure and coordination, as is the case with the international degrowth "movement assembly" we mentioned before.

Yet, the fundamentally unstructured character of the degrowth networks has largely prevailed. This means that emerging initiatives sprout spontaneously and self-define as degrowth actors. Two recent examples are the Latin American degrowth forum which brought people together to exchange ideas, knowledge and experience to reflect on what degrowth means in the Latin American context (Arahuetés *et al.* 2021), and the "New Roots" open letter (Barlow *et al.* 2020) written by a group of self-organised degrowthers to highlight the failures of current economies in responding to the COVID-19 crisis, subsequently signed by over 2,000 people and 60 organisations and translated into 20 languages.

While it is important to celebrate and encourage the spontaneity and autonomy of such initiatives, the lack of structured communication and coordination also means that a lot of energy is lost in setting up each of these activities. Similarly to the global financial crisis in 2008, when the degrowth movement spoke out to say "this recession is not our degrowth", the "New Roots" open letter argued that the slowdown triggered by the pandemic was also not our degrowth. But despite all the increasing interest in the concept of degrowth since, the degrowth networks did not seem more prepared and organised to respond to a crisis in 2020 than they were in 2008. Connections, strategies, working groups, mailing lists and more had to be created on the spot. With poor communication across degrowth actors, similar statements were written many times by different people in different places (to name a few: *degrowth.info* 2020; Chassagne 2020; Kallis *et al.* 2020), and there was little reflection on how to be inclusive, whose voices get the most visibility, and what decision-making processes to use.

When we do not pay attention to such dynamics and we organise hastily – with limited existing structures to rely on – it is easy to end up subconsciously replicating patterns of exclusion, dominance and patriarchy. We connect with those that we are already in contact with and we refer and give voice to those who already occupy privileged and high-profile positions – often meaning white European middle-aged cis men.

The meetings of the "nodes" or the "New Roots" open letter, which involved a predominantly white Western demographic, are examples of activities that must prompt reflection on the degree to which engaging actively in the international degrowth networks demands a *privileged position*. Several requirements for participation came together in this instance to create barriers to entry: free time during European daytime hours, a computer or smartphone with a decent internet connection, and contacts with meeting organisers or being up-to-date with information flowing through international degrowth networks. Another crucial point is that the vast majority of degrowth organising is done on a voluntary basis, which makes it less accessible to those with little financial security. While the international degrowth networks aim to be decentralised and non-hierarchical, the reality is then a lot messier. We have witnessed little collective reflection on these important points and hence there are no real strategies for inclusion.

In emergency situations, considerations of how to create safe spaces and non-hierarchical, decolonial, anti-patriarchal, participative structures are easily lost. Creating such dynamics requires more considered processes contingent on unlearning and deconstructing internal biases. Ever since the creation of *degrowth. info*'s international team in 2018, we have been working on our internal dynamics and organisational structure. In our operation, we strive to bring to life the kinds of collective processes we would like to see proliferated throughout society more broadly: consensus decision-making mechanisms, transparent processes and horizontal structures. These kinds of democratic and inclusive structures could be nurtured throughout the wider international degrowth networks, if there is the will to devote time and energies to this task. They will not simply appear by themselves.

To ensure that we create a movement that embodies the values that we care about in degrowth and nourishes dynamics that make every degrowther feel included, we need to be more intentional in our actions. Establishing this greater intentionality will require better communication across and between degrowth networks. This raises another downside of the current diffuse and uncoordinated nature of the networks: the absence of dedicated structures through which to engage in dialogue. This hinders not only communication and strategising within degrowth networks, but also coalition building with other movements and actors.

Whilst most degrowthers probably agree on the principle that the networks remain decentralised, there is a difference between being centralised and being better *coordinated,* whilst still allowing for the spontaneous emergence of local groups and being respectful of autonomy. It is our understanding that the pitfalls of an unstructured, strategically vague, and improvised way of organising are now outweighing the benefits and hindering the further flourishing of degrowth networks by *unintentionally* reproducing detrimental dynamics. To put it differently, elements of greater autonomy that could be provided by this *laissez-faire* approach are – in our experience – often being obscured by unhealthy reproductions of hegemonic structures that need to be *intentionally countered.*

Next, we move the focus from internal dynamics within the degrowth movements to questions of its wider strategies for transformation. Finally, we outline a proposal for a *Degrowth International,* which would incorporate both *intentional* internal dynamics described above and the strategic direction we now present.

Strategy as a consideration in degrowth

As mentioned earlier, the issue of strategy has been present in degrowth debates from the very early days of the movement's emergence at the beginning of the 21st century. By way of example, we highlight one prominent, polemical, and controversial question with regards to degrowth's strategic orientation – the issue of how to engage with existing structures of the nation-state. This question has been (and is being) debated throughout degrowth's short history, particularly so in the Francophone degrowth literature, and more recently in the English one as well (for an overview of this debate, as well as a particular position within it, see D'Alisa and Kallis 2020).

However, notwithstanding all of the debates that in one way or another pertain to degrowth's strategic orientation, we point to two very recent processes that have, in our view, centred the issue of strategy as a whole on the degrowth agenda.

First, from January 2019 to October 2020, *degrowth.info* coordinated and published a ten-part blog series focusing specifically on the question of strategy in degrowth debates (Barlow 2019). The series emerged from a sense amongst members of the *degrowth.info* collective that considerations of strategy, or the *how* of bringing about degrowth-oriented transformations of society, had so far not been subject to systematic and substantive debate at a movement-wide level. The strategy series thus aimed to foreground such discussions and provide an initial forum to address degrowth's lack of clarity around strategy, as well as lingering tensions around different strategic perspectives within the networks.

The enthusiastic response to the blog series at *degrowth.info* provided evidence that concerns around the lack of debate on strategy were shared throughout much of the wider degrowth networks. It became clear across many of the contributions to the series that there existed a large appetite for more concentrated and systematic consideration of strategies, in order to enhance the capacities of the degrowth networks to effect material societal change. One notable contribution on this point came from Panos Petridis (2019), who argued the need to develop a means for evaluating different degrowth strategies for their emancipatory potential, and that this could help address tensions within the degrowth networks between those advocating more top-down and bottom-up strategies respectively (see Chapter 8).

Building on Petridis' arguments, Ekaterina Chertkovskaya's (2020) article in the series considered how the sociologist Erik Olin Wright's framework of anti-capitalist political strategies could shape degrowth thinking around strategies for social-ecological transformation. Chertkovskaya argued that – while intertwining multiple strategic approaches – degrowthers should give particular emphasis to strategies that build power *outside* the capitalist system, and approach with caution those that seek reform within existing systems and can thus end up stabilising the status quo (see Chapter 2).

Across the wide-ranging contributions, a key point revealed by the series was the perceived importance of structures and mechanisms that can facilitate the discussion, evaluation and coordination of different strategies for degrowth transformations. Such movement-level structures have so far been lacking in degrowth networks. It should be noted, however, that the "movement assemblies" described above, facilitated by the Support Group, have tried to move precisely in the direction of building more coherent organisational structures for the movement as a whole.

This issue also became a point of lively discussion at the 2020 (online) Vienna conference on degrowth and strategy. Following many conversations within the *degrowth.info* collective and wider degrowth networks, one of our members proposed the establishment of a *Degrowth International* during the panel "Advancing a Degrowth Agenda in the Corona Crisis" (Rilović 2020; see also Asara 2020). Envisaged as a more defined and transparent overarching structure for global degrowth networks (perhaps taking the form of decentralised local chapters that feed delegates into national and international assemblies), such a *Degrowth International* represents one possible means for facilitating the more focused consideration and coordination of transformative strategies that many degrowthers are increasingly recognising as necessary.

It remains to be seen, however, whether a critical mass of the degrowth community desires such a development. Some will prefer to retain degrowth's current centre of gravity in academia. In this case, the predominant strategic orientation is to influence the actions of policy-makers and grassroots activists through degrowth research and writing, and so a more concentrated consideration of strategy may be deemed unnecessary.

Alternatively, degrowth networks could choose to pursue pathways oriented to social movements, which could themselves take various forms. On the one hand, degrowth networks could seek to proliferate degrowth as a frame for action, bringing in ever more people and projects to take action under the degrowth banner. This would require expanding considerations of strategy, in terms of how to build the size of the degrowth networks and which actions should be taken in the name of degrowth. Alternatively, it could be accepted that the degrowth banner remains relatively niche whilst the movement carves out a more agile approach, seeking to connect with and influence the direction of more high profile social movements and political projects (e.g., Extinction Rebellion, Climate Justice, Green New Deal(s)). Considerations of strategy are again vital in this pathway, in terms of deliberating which movements, projects and institutions degrowth should seek to influence and how in order to further its ultimate aim of social-ecological transformation. Accordingly, if the degrowth community wishes to solidify itself in a social movement form (on top of its academic stream), something akin to a *Degrowth International* would undoubtedly be required. In the next section, we outline some key considerations that the construction of a *Degrowth International* would necessitate.

A Degrowth International

If a *Degrowth International* were to be developed, one of its primary objectives would be to facilitate effective communication and strategising amongst far-spread degrowth actors and networks. Importantly, as argued above, this communication would need to be conscious of and seek to address biases and power dynamics which exist in society at large and also in progressive social movements. As we have laid out in this contribution, thinking intentionally about strategy and organisation in degrowth networks is not only desirable but *required*, if we are to avoid the perpetuation of patriarchal, colonial and hierarchical dynamics within our discursive practices and organisational structures.

As a point of departure for this emerging conversation around the idea of a *Degrowth International*, we offer a few key points of consideration:

1. A *Degrowth International* can provide the structures necessary for the degrowth community to communicate, co-create multi-scalar strategies, understand each other's strategies, set priorities for the networks, and address tensions as they emerge. The *extent* of decision-making powers granted to such structures, or whether they would simply act as a forum for communication, however, is something that must be debated.

2. Acosta and Brand (2019) have explained that economies beyond the growth imaginary require different characteristics for Global South and Global North countries. Therefore, different degrowth strategies need to be debated and prioritised as appropriate for different contexts. There is a real danger that social-ecological transformations in the Global North could perpetuate colonial and extractivist relations with the Global South. Some authors already point to an intensification of mining for lithium in Latin American countries as the race to offer electric cars and lower-carbon mobility options become more prevalent in Europe, China and the US (Götze 2019). As such, even if successfully influenced by degrowth thinking, a Green New Deal in Europe could mean worse living conditions for Global South communities (Zografos and Robbins 2020). Therefore, a *Degrowth International* would need to include different actors from the Global South aligned with degrowth principles, even if they do not explicitly label themselves "degrowth" movements, in order to move beyond the current Eurocentrism of degrowth debates. There is a correspondence between degrowth and post-extractivist ideals and notions of

the *pluriverse*[12] (Kothari *et al.* 2019). A *Degrowth International* should strive to engage in discussions and actions that not only consider problems of post-industrialisation, but also more sustainable modes of living that do not mimic a minimalist version of Western/Northern lifestyles.

3. A *Degrowth International*, if created, could fall into the trap of containing an over-representation of academia. This could deepen our community's current asymmetry and reinforce (whether intentionally or not) an academic focus. A concerted effort would need to be made to balance the representation of academic with non-academic voices, strategic perspectives and lived experiences.

4. We stress that *intentionality* is a crucial concept to keep in mind if the degrowth networks – and a possible *Degrowth International* – are to counter dominant power structures within the behaviours and discourse of actors. The predominance of cis-gender, white, and Western voices is still a reality in the academically-centred degrowth community. A *Degrowth International* would need to be carefully and conscientiously constructed in order to prefigure the more just and egalitarian degrowth society we wish to create.

Conclusion

After reviewing the current landscape of actors in the international degrowth networks and laying out the lack of strategic clarity, we have argued that the creation of a *Degrowth International* would be beneficial, and must be centred on an intentional effort to unlearn patriarchal and hierarchical patterns of behaviour and organisation.

We have also raised questions of inclusion, privilege and,

---

12 The pluriverse is a term that evokes a deep diversity of world-views. It refers to possible co-existence of diverse ontologies, epistemologies and non-Western approaches. It was first described by the Zapatista movement (EZLN 1996) as a liberating alternative to the homogenizing discourse of western capitalist development.

thresholds for participation in the degrowth movement. Underlying the analysis and proposals detailed here, our core interest is: how can we generate truly transformative degrowth networks and strategies that are radical, decolonial, inclusive, and embody all the other dynamics we want to see in our societies at large, where autonomy is respected and cherished but communication and collaboration are also strong?

We envision a *Degrowth International* as a global degrowth network that would provide dedicated structures for all smaller-scale degrowth networks to connect together and collaborate around strategies for social-ecological transformation and would help participants to consciously and intentionally unlearn internal biases. A *Degrowth International* would bring to life a diverse global network of networks through creative collaboration and communication flows that would help to nourish and sustain a pluriverse of movements and actors striving for a good life for all.

References

Acosta, Alberto, and Ulrich Brand. 2019. *Pós-extrativismo e decrescimento: saídas do labirinto capitalista*. São Paulo: Editora Elefante.

Arahuetés, Diego, Cabaña, Gabriela, Calcagni, Mariana, and María P. Aedo. 2021. "Collective Learnings from the 2020 Latin American Degrowth Forum." *degrowth.info* (blog), March 5, 2021. https://viewpointmag.com/2021/04/14/the-kaleidoscope-of-catastrophe-on-the-clarities-and-blind-spots-of-andreas-malm/.

Asara, Viviana. 2020. "Degrowth Vienna 2020: Reflections upon the Conference and How to Move Forward – Part II." *degrowth.info* (blog), August 3, 2020. https://viewpointmag.com/2021/04/14/the-kaleidoscope-of-catastrophe-on-the-clarities-and-blind-spots-of-andreas-malm/.

Barlow, Nathan. 2019. "A Blog Series on Strategy in the Degrowth Movement." *degrowth.info* (blog), January 9, 2019. http://degrowth.info/blog/a-blog-series-on-strategy-in-the-degrowth-movement.

Barlow, Nathan, Ekaterina Chertkovskaya, Manuel Grebenjak, Vincent Liegey, François Schneider, Tone Smith, Sam Bliss, Constanza Hepp, Max Hollweg, Christian Kerschner, Andro Rilović, Pierre Smith Khanna, and Joëlle Saey-Volckrick. 2020. "Degrowth: New Roots for the Economy." *degrowth.info* (blog).

http://degrowth.info/en/open-letter.

Brand, Ulrich. 2014. „Degrowth: Der Beginn einer Bewegung?, Blätter für Deutsche und Internationale Politik." *Eurozine*, October 29, 2014. http://www.eurozine.com/degrowth-der-beginn-einer-bewegung/.

Burkhart, Corinna, Schmelzer, Matthias and Nina Treu. 2020. *Degrowth in Movement(s): Exploring Pathways for Transformation*. London: Zero Books.

Chassagne, Natasha. 2020. "Here's What the Coronavirus Pandemic Can Teach Us about Tackling Climate Change." *The Conversation*, March 26, 2020. http://theconversation.com/heres-what-the-coronavirus-pandemic-can-teach-us-about-tackling-climate-change-134399.

Chertkovskaya, Ekaterina. 2020. "From Taming to Dismantling: Degrowth and Anti-Capitalist Strategy." *degrowth.info* (blog), September 21, 2020. http://theconversation.com/heres-what-the-coronavirus-pandemic-can-teach-us-about-tackling-climate-change-134399.

D'Alisa, Giacomo, and Giorgos Kallis. 2020. "Degrowth and the State." *Ecological Economics* 169, 106486.

Degrowth.info international team. 2020. "A Degrowth Perspective on the Coronavirus Crisis." *degrowth.info* (blog), March 19, 2020. http://degrowth.info/blog/a-degrowth-perspective-on-the-coronavirus-crisis.

Degrowth.info. 2021a. *A History of Degrowth*. https://www.degrowth.info/en/history.

Degrowth.info. 2021b. *Global Degrowth Day – Good Life for All*. http://degrowth.info/en/gdd-good-life-for-all.

Degrowth.info. 2021c. *Want to Become Active? Join an International Working Group*. shorturl.at/czZo2.

Degrowth.info. 2021d. *Support Group*. http://degrowth.info/en/conference/support-group.

Degrowth.info. 2021e. *Feminism(s) and Degrowth Alliance*. https://www.degrowth.info/en/fada.

EZLN (Ejército Zapatista de Liberación Nacional). 1996. *Fourth Declaration of the Lacandona Jungle*. http://enlacezapatista.ezln.org.mx/1996/01/01/cuarta-declaracion-de-la-selva-lacandona/.

Gorz, André. 1972. "The Global Equilibrium, for Which No-Growth – or even Degrowth – of Material Production Is a Necessary Condition, Is It Compatible With the Survival of the (Capitalist) System?" *Nouvel Observateur*, June, 1972, IV.

Götze, Susanne. 2019. „Lithium–Abbau in Südamerika. Kehrseite der Energiewende." *Deutschlandfunk*, April 30, 2019. https://www.deutschlandfunk.de/lithium-abbau-in-suedamerika-kehrseite-der-energiewende-100.html.

Kallis, Giorgos, Susan Paulson, Giacomo D'Alisa, and Federico Demaria. 2020. "The Case for Degrowth in a Time of Pandemic." *Open Democracy*, May 14, 2020. https://www.opendemocracy.net/en/oureconomy/case-degrowth-time-pandemic/.

Kothari, Ashish, Ariel Salleh, Arturo Escobar, Federico Demaria, and Alberto Acosta. 2019. *Pluriverse: A Post-Development Dictionary*. New Delhi: Tulika.

Petridis, Panos. 2019. "On Strategies for Socioecological Transformation." *degrowth. info* (blog), January 9, 2019. https://www.degrowth.info/en/2019/01/on-strategies-for-socioecological-transformation/

Rilović, Andro. 2020. *Advancing a Degrowth Agenda in the Corona Crisis*. http://degrowth.info/en/library/degrowth-vienna-2020-advancing-a-degrowth-agenda-in-the-corona-crisis.

R&D (Research & Degrowth). 2021a. *Degrowth Summer School*. http://summerschool.degrowth.org/.

R&D (Research & Degrowth). 2021b. *Master on Degrowth*. https://master.degrowth.org/.

Zografos, Christos, and Paul F. Robbins. 2020. "Green Sacrifice Zones, or Why a Green New Deal Cannot Ignore the Cost Shifts of Just Transitions." *One Earth* 3, no. 5: 543–546.

Chapter 6:

Who shut shit down? What degrowth can learn from other social-ecological movements

By Corinna Burkhart, Tonny Nowshin, Matthias Schmelzer and Nina Treu

"Who shut shit down? We shut shit down!" This slogan has become a common cry amongst activists doing direct actions of civil disobedience, blocking fossil infrastructures such as lignite mines, gas terminals, or the construction of new highways. These actions, which Naomi Klein (2014) called "blockadia", are not only effective in raising awareness around issues of climate justice but have helped to actually shut down fossil infrastructure or effectively prevented the construction of new projects. In this chapter, we discuss what degrowth can learn from existing social-ecological movements – such as those who engage in direct actions around climate justice – and their strategies for systemic change. Similarly, we delve into how degrowth should orient strategically.

We understand degrowth as an emerging social movement that overlaps with proposals for systemic change such as alter-globalisation and climate justice, the commons and Transition Towns – a mosaic of initiatives for social-ecological transformation. Degrowth is one strategic vantage point for movements that explicitly aim at a society and economy beyond growth, industrialism and capitalism – not because it is or should be a key term for all movements in the mosaic, but because degrowth symbolises the most radical rejection of the eco-modernist mainstream of growth-centredness, extractivism, and industrialism. Similarly, degrowth has in recent years developed into a framework for many movements, initiatives, and projects that provides a set of theories, arguments, and visions that give meaning to prefigurative "nowtopias" (for more on this, c.f. Burkhart *et al.* 2020, Schmelzer *et al.* 2022).

In the following, we will discuss what the degrowth movement in the narrow sense – the community of activists, scholars, practitioners, and politicians involved in degrowth-related projects – can learn from other social-ecological movements that are part of the mosaic in terms of strategising. In focusing on those movements with already existing links to degrowth as explored in *Degrowth in Movement(s)* (Burkhart et al. 2020), we discuss the following questions: Which strategies do other movements employ to reach their goals and to expand their movements? To what degree should the degrowth movement consider these? (How) should the degrowth movement act strategically towards related social-ecological movements?

We argue that in thinking through strategies for the transformation of the current economic organisation to a degrowth society, there is much to learn from ongoing struggles and other social-ecological movements. We highlight four different strategies, which can be found within the larger spectrum of movements of this emerging mosaic of alternatives: Opposing, communicating, reforming, and practising. The degrowth community, we argue, should embrace, actively relate to, and support *all* these strategies and a diversity of strategic actions.

Strategies within the mosaic of alternatives

The question of whether degrowth is itself a social movement, an interpretative frame for movements, or whether it is more adequate to talk of the degrowth spectrum is much debated (Demaria *et al.* 2013; Eversberg and Schmelzer 2018). However, one thing is certain: the degrowth community, with its critiques, proposals, and practices, has diverse intellectual, social, and political links to many other social movements (Burkhart *et al.* 2020).

Degrowth can learn from the various strategies these social-ecological movements employ. Building on the many examples discussed in *Degrowth in Movement(s)* (Burkhart *et al.* 2020), ranging from the alter-globalisation or climate justice movements to movements and alternatives such as the commons, Buen Vivir, food sovereignty, non-profit cooperatives, the care revolution, free software, basic income, or Transition Towns, four strategies emerge as particularly relevant. In discussing these, we provide examples of movements that are particularly strong with regard to specific strategies, while keeping in mind that this is an idealised systematisation and, in reality, strategies often overlap. Indeed, the fact that so many movements deploy a mix of strategies might already be an indication of the importance of combining different strategic approaches for a successful interaction with – or confrontation of – the status quo.

Our typology builds on the work of sociologist Erik Olin Wright, which we adapted and built on for this book chapter. We distinguish between four strategies: Opposing (in Wright's terms: ruptural strategies), reforming (symbiotic strategies), practising (interstitial strategies), and believe it is key to also discuss communicating as a fourth strategy (for more on this, see Wright 2010; Chapter 2, for an adaptation to degrowth strategies, see Schmelzer *et al.* 2022). The four categories identified can be further regarded as a development of three strategies that appear in earlier degrowth publications, namely: oppositional activism, the building of alternatives, and political proposals (see for example Demaria *et al.* 2013).

Oppositional strategies create counter-hegemonic power through various forms of public mobilizations and actions. These include protests, demonstrations, strikes, direct action, civil disobedience, blockades, flash-mobs, occupations, or even insurrectionary tactics of riots and the demolition or sabotage of property. In recognising that not all of these actions are legal, it is key to understand that almost all the rights movements have struggled for throughout modern history, including the end of colonialism, women's and workers' rights were also achieved by acts of resistance and civil disobedience (Federici 2004; Harman 2008).

	Opposing	Communicating	Reforming	Practising
Key actors	Activists, citizens	Academics, NGOs, journalists, activists	Parties, NGOs, thinktanks	Practitioners, activists
What it is about	Opposing destruction, creating counter-hegemonic power	Changing paradigms, creating narratives of transformation, connecting topics and movements	Transforming institutions and changing rules	Building alternative structures, creating post-capitalist nowtopias
Activities	Demonstrations, strikes, direct action, civil disobedience, blockades, riots, sabotage	Research, media articles, conferences and public events, public statements	Developing and promoting (radical) reforms, lobbying	Creating spaces, alternative infrastructure, support networks
Typical movements	Climate justice, refugee movement, care revolution, People's Global Action, artivism	Commons, demonetise, the reception of Buen Vivir in Europe, decolonise the climate movement, decolonial degrowth, post-development	Basic income, environmental and global justice NGOs, trade unions	Solidarity economy, Transition Towns, urban gardening, free software movement, open workshops
Strengths	Creating strong symbols, building up power from below	Motivating people, building alliances, shaping narratives and changing cultures inside and outside of movement spaces	Incremental steps towards social-ecological transformation, broad alliances between state and civil society organisations, enshrining social-ecological thought in law	Open and welcoming, experimenting with alternatives, learning different imaginaries, independence
Limits	Difficulties of including visionary politics and alternatives, experiences of (state) repression	Mainly discursive, lack of actors to fight for and implement narratives	Danger of appellative politics to legitimise power, creation of false solutions, dependence on hegemonic power	Difficult to connect with wider struggles and movements

Table 6.1.: Four strategic approaches of social movements

The following three examples illustrate such oppositional strategies or "blockadia" actions where people use their bodies in acts of civil disobedience (Klein 2014). First, in Germany, the degrowth movement held several summer schools at climate camps, in which hundreds of participants discussed degrowth before joining an *Ende Gelände* action and, by entering a lignite coal mine, directly stopped the burning of coal at Europe's largest site of emissions. Second, the refugee movement has not only created a network of solidarity throughout European cities, but, in the year 2015 in particular, the thousands of people that collectively entered Europe through the Balkans have effectively disrupted the border regime of Fortress Europe. Third, the 15M movement in Spain set an example with massive occupations of public spaces as a reaction to the financial crisis from 2008 onward. It created autonomous structures that demonstrated what real democracy could look like and that life beyond competition and commodification was possible.

Oppositional strategies can be highly effective: a recent study has shown that Indigenous campaigns of resistance against fossil fuel expansion across what is currently called Canada and the United States of America, which included militant actions, civil disobedience, and sabotage, have effectively stopped or delayed greenhouse gas pollution equivalent to at least 25% of annual U.S. and Canadian emissions (Indigenous Environment Network and Oil Change International 2021). Often, oppositional strategies create powerful symbols that define entire eras, motivate and transform people, and shift existing power relations in society, thus making things possible that hitherto seemed unachievable. A key limit of oppositional strategies is the difficulty of including visionary politics and alternatives in the struggles, which often focus on *opposing* the destruction of something rather than imagining or creating something new, even as they do often contain a utopian element. Actions tend to take a lot of energy and time and are afterwards often confronted with state repression that targets systemically marginalised and racialised groups in particular. Thus, there are barriers to entry for these actions, which renders the creation of long-term structures difficult.

Communication strategies are central to many academics, professionals in non-governmental organisations (NGOs), journalists, and activists that engage with and in social movements. Their aim is to change paradigms and to create narratives of transformation. This includes, among many others, activities such as research that explains, politicises, and frames key issues, and the writing of media articles or public statements to create publicity and outreach. It further entails the organisation of workshops, conferences, and public events to engage with the public, to strategise within the movement, or to involve politicians. The degrowth community has – up until now – centred its strategic energy around communication. It has pursued basically all of the actions that fall into the category of communication: an immense output in terms of research and academic teaching; growing visibility in the public discourse through statements such as the "Open Letter: Re-imagining the Future After The Corona Crisis"; (popular) scientific books and media articles; a considerable number of workshops and lectures; dozens of summer schools and large international conferences that often sparked new networks among social-ecological initiatives and some mobilisations (Kallis *et al.* 2018; Eversberg and Schmelzer 2018; *degrowth.info* 2020).

Degrowth has also contributed to an ongoing process of undermining the hegemony of growth in growing segments of related social movements, academic debates, and new fragments of society, by framing green growth as an oxymoron and presenting degrowth as a viable alternative (Hickel 2020). In recent years, activists have also included decolonial narratives in the degrowth framework and have grown awareness related to the importance of intersectional justice in degrowth visions (Tyberg 2020). However, this has only just begun and much still needs to be done. Many other movements have demonstrated the power of communicative strategies: the global commons movement, for example, has created a collective narrative and framing for the thousands of historical and currently ongoing institutions and communities that organise economies based on bottom-up non-market relationships, linking local practices with academic research and political demands (Bollier and Helfrich 2015). Further, the post-development movement has contributed to the critique of the notion of "development." Through on-the-ground knowledge generation, publications, communication strategies, and international networking, it laid the ground for and inspired many other social movements (Burkhart *et al.* 2020; Escobar 2018, Hickel 2020; Kothari *et al.* 2019).

Communicative strategies can be very powerful in motivating people by creating a narrative that clearly articulates the problems, provides solutions, and shows pathways for transforming society. A good speech, a well-articulated demand, a powerful political slogan – all of these can make a significant difference, in particular, if they are framed in a way that people perceive them as a new common sense, as can be seen throughout the history of social movements. Recent examples for this are the actions and words of youth climate activist Greta Thunberg and the Fridays for Future movements, which helped put the climate crisis on the political agenda (Fopp et al. 2021). However, standing on their own, communication strategies lack the actors and the power to fight for and implement change. They are, so to speak, the underlying work of ploughing and fertilising the soil, on which social movements grow, and with the help of which alliances and counter-hegemonic power can emerge.

Reforming politics and institutions is the key strategic terrain of politicians and professionals in NGOs that work to change the rules of societies and their systems. Strategic actions to achieve reforms could include developing and promoting laws and legal reforms, lobbying politicians and bureaucrats to adopt these laws, informing the public about reform initiatives to create a constituency, starting petitions to raise awareness, or even joining or creating parties. It is important to highlight that degrowth actors do not aim at reforming society, but at a structural and systemic change. That is why degrowth proposals are often interpreted as "non-reformist reforms" (André Gorz) or "revolutionary realpolitik" (Rosa Luxemburg) – commonsensical demands that would transform the growth-based capitalist system (for more on this, see Schmelzer et al. 2022). Still, promoting key degrowth political demands such as basic and maximum income, a cap on resource use, or radical working time reductions constitute central steps on the path towards a degrowth society.

Examples of movements that focus on such reforms are the global basic income movement, which uses a diversity of strategic actions, ranging from petitions to local experiments and demonstrations. A different example would be environmental and global justice NGOs that lobby around local, national, and international political institutions. An interesting case is trade unions, which historically have started mainly through oppositional strategies, but now – as discussed in one contribution in *Degrowth in Movement(s)* – largely focus on the reform strategy of changing laws. As a social movement strategy, reforms are important insofar as they can improve concrete situations and lives through incremental but legally secured change that cements what movements have been fighting for, and because reforms can generalise certain rights and practices that had hitherto only existed in alternative niches (or what Erik Olin Wright referred to as interstitial modes of transformation, see Chapter 2) to the entire society. A danger and limit of this strategy is that political action that strongly appeals to governments tends to legitimise power. This comes often with the problematic understanding that "demanding" solutions from politicians is in itself enough to achieve them (which in the case of degrowth demands is clearly illusionary) and tends to lead to superficial reforms that function only as symptomatic treatment and maintain the status quo.

Practice or *prefigurative strategies* through which practitioners and activists create post-capitalist nowtopias in the here and now seek to experiment with new institutions, infrastructures, or forms of organisation. They are laboratories in which new social practices are intentionally developed, tried out, and practised. They emerge within and despite the old system and prefigure post-capitalist relations on a small scale (for more, see Wright 2010; Schmelzer *et al.* 2022; Carlsson 2014; and also see Part II in this volume). Temporary interstitial practices such as the degrowth summer schools or other political camps around the world offer people an experience of a communal, self-determined and sufficient lifestyle through collective self-organisation, shared care work, and the use of, for example, exclusively renewable energies and compost toilets. More important, still, are the more permanent movements that employ prefigurative strategies: solidarity economy, Transition Towns, urban gardening, the free software movement, open workshops and repair cafes, community-supported agriculture, alternative media, collective kitchens and food recuperation, community housing projects and squats, occupations, municipal energy projects, time banks or regional currencies. Such practices that engage in bottom-up social change are particularly present in the discussion on degrowth. Reference is often made to them to show that the principles of a degrowth society are already being implemented on a small scale today. In providing an interpretative frame, degrowth has, one could argue, contributed in recent years to advancing the visibility and politicisation of these practices.

One strength of many of these initiatives is a relatively low threshold for participation. Gardening with others in the neighbourhood attracts many and does not necessarily require substantial political knowledge. Citizens with various backgrounds, who might otherwise not meet, get together, strengthen the local community, and practice alternatives to a market economy. Community organising and small-scale agriculture are practised and normalised. However, some of these have comparatively high thresholds for participation, as projects can be time-intensive and difficult to make compatible with, for example, care responsibilities. Since these projects often do not involve any political engagement or commitment, they risk remaining focused on their local situation and do not connect to wider struggles, nor do participants necessarily politicise their practices.

What should the degrowth movement do?

After presenting these four groups of strategies, we will discuss how the degrowth movement in the narrow sense should consider these. As stated above, we would like to stress again that we see a combination of strategies as the best way forward. The question is, then, how the degrowth community can widen their repertoire and combine different strategic approaches. The degrowth community is experienced in communication, but less involved in opposing, reforming, and practising. We suggest that the degrowth movement build on its strengths and collaborate with other social-ecological movements and initiatives that have different foci and areas of expertise. To be more concrete, we make the case for three tasks for the degrowth movement: firstly, to intervene in ongoing debates, struggles, and conflicts; secondly, to provide visions and narratives that are concrete; and thirdly, to actively reflect, change attitudes, and act towards intersectional justice.

Intervene into ongoing debates, struggles, and conflicts

The idea of intervening in ongoing debates, struggles, and conflicts serves the aim of bringing degrowth perspectives into new arenas and learning from the ideas and strategies of existing struggles. One example mentioned earlier is the integration of degrowth summer schools into climate camps. Here we have a concrete struggle (climate justice), a local conflict (displacement of citizens or the loss of a forest), direct action (Ende Gelände), and a camp where all is linked to degrowth ideas that are discussed, developed, and practised. Communicating, opposing, and practising come together and create various outcomes, which generate an opportunity for communication to the wider public, politicisation, and networking.

Another example for connecting different strategies and a concrete struggle to degrowth were the 15M protests in Spain mentioned earlier. Here, citizens occupied squares, organised protests and direct action, while trying out direct democracy. The protests were further joined and supported by small local projects that were promoting alternatives to capitalism and could gain momentum from the protests. Others active in the protests followed a reform strategy by joining established political institutions and later entering parliament. Throughout the protests, degrowth ideas informed political action and organisation – and the 15M protest in turn inspired the further development of degrowth ideas and practice (see the chapter by Eduard Nus in Burkhart *et al.* 2020).

What do we suggest for the near future? In a post-lockdown world, we hope to see the degrowth community continue to intervene in climate justice struggles, in particular in the Fridays for Futures movement, to connect with the refugee movement and social justice struggles – of which there will be plenty as a result of the pandemic. As the two examples above show, intervention in those and other ongoing debates, struggles, and conflicts provides a moment to make degrowth ideas concrete and to develop them further in dialogue with other experiences and realities.

Provide visions and narratives that are concrete

Degrowth has its strength in discussing and arguing for alternative economies in an academic context and increasingly in public debates around the future of economics and climate justice. Beyond that, it is, however often a struggle to explain what degrowth really is about. To make degrowth common sense, we need a language, narratives, and visions that are concrete and easy to communicate. This requires the pursuit of a well-thought-through communication strategy. Engaging communication should be targeted at various groups, including politicians who are potentially already close to some degrowth ideas but still holding on to growth politics. One example are the ten degrowth policy proposals published by Research & Degrowth in 2015 (Research & Degrowth 2015), which were directed to political left parties and concretely outline reforms that would foster a degrowth economy, including a citizen debt audit, a minimum and maximum income, and a green tax reform.

Aimed at a much wider audience is the project "Future for All", by Konzeptwerk Neue Ökonomie (Laboratory for a New Economy, based in Leipzig, Germany) and many partners, in which some of the authors of this chapter were involved. Through workshops with visionary thinkers from academia, civil society, and social movements, we developed and published ideas for a utopian society in 2048 and ways to get there. "Future for All" includes degrowth ideas but does not use the word and has a much brighter and more inviting framing (Kuhnhenn *et al.* 2020). In contrast to the many text-heavy and often abstract degrowth publications, this project has made very concrete what everyday life could look like in 2048 if degrowth proposals would be put to practice. The publication aims at communicating in an accessible language with illustrations and concrete scenarios, while also highlighting controversies and struggles within diverse fields of action such as global justice, inclusion, mobility, food, housing, and finances. These visons and narratives can serve as starting points for discussions led by the degrowth movement in circles beyond academia.

If degrowth is to reach more people, it needs to use accessible language and relatable visions. The communication of such concrete visions and narratives needs to go beyond text and purely informing formats such as documentaries, magazines, or popular science publications. This could be art, fiction, or theatre as well as hands-on actions that are engaging, enabling, and inviting.

Develop an attitude and pursue actions towards intersectional justice

As the core of degrowth is built around criticising and reversing oversized economies based on accumulation, oversized economies sustained by a complex web of (neo)colonial and intersectionally exploitative business, trade, and cultural dominance, it is fundamental for the degrowth movement to actively include intersectional justice in its agenda. The moral and ideological power of the movement is weakened unless conscious commitments to anti-racism, anti-patriarchy, and anti-classism become an inherent part of its strategy, vision, and actions. Degrowth is about global justice, and one of the main ways to ingrain this vision in the movement's thinking and narratives is to also take practical actions towards working on internalised structural biases and building up political power on intersectional issues. We see changes in recent years by more and more scholars, activists, and organisers from the Global South taking a degrowth position from a decolonial perspective, and thus shaping the predominantly Northern degrowth discourse towards a more inclusive vision (Tyberg 2019; Ituen 2021; Nowshin 2019). For the movement to reach the next level of its potential and unfold more holistically, intersectional justice needs to become a priority.

Conclusion

Degrowth – a movement in the making that is mainly academic and has so far mostly focused on creating knowledge, shifting discourses, and changing mind-sets – should learn from, embrace, and actively relate to ongoing struggles of existing social-ecological movements. As we have argued in this chapter, in doing so, the degrowth community should use and support a diversity of strategies. We have identified four core categories: opposing, communicating, reforming, and practising.

While engaging with a sorting and labelling exercise, it becomes obvious that in practice strategies are interconnected – often employed simultaneously and deeply depending on one another. It is often difficult to pinpoint where, for example, communicating ends and reforming starts or when an action becomes a practice. Thus, while categorising, it is important to remember that strategies are contingent on one another.

The notion of a "mosaic" highlights the vision of building a plural world, rooted in multiple struggles and with many different strategies – composed of different forms of economies, living worlds, and cultures, pollinating, interacting, and collaborating with each other. To differentiate it from the one-way future of capitalism and economic growth, the various alternatives to economic growth have recently been termed the "pluriverse" by a group of scholar-activists from various continents (Kothari *et al.* 2019). We should combine different strategies to build this pluriverse!

References

Blasingame, Samie. 2021. "Tools for a Post-Growth Society – an Interview with Imeh Ituen." *Ecosia* (blog), March 18, 2021. http://blog.ecosia.org/post-growth-society-imeh-ituen/.

Bollier, David, and Silke Helfrich. 2015. *Patterns of Commoning*. Commons Strategy Group and Off the Common Press.

Burkhart, Corinna, Matthias Schmelzer, and Nina Treu, eds. 2020. *Degrowth in Movement(s): Exploring Pathways for Transformation*. London: Zero.

Burkhart, Corinna, Matthias Schmelzer, and Nina Treu. 2020. "Degrowth and the Emerging Mosaic of Alternatives." In *Degrowth in Movement(s): Exploring Pathways for Transformation*, edited by Corinna Burkhart, Matthias Schmelzer, and Nina Treu, 9–28. London: Zero.

Carlsson, Chris. 2014. "Nowtopias." In *Degrowth: A Vocabulary for a New Era*, edited by Giacomo D'Alisa, Federico Demaria and Giorgos Kallis, 182–184. New York: Routledge.

Demaria, Federico, Francois Schneider, Filka Sekulova, and Joan Martinez-Alier. 2013. "What is Degrowth? From an Activist Slogan to a Social Movement." *Environmental Values* 22, no. 2: 191–215.

Degrowth.info. 2020. *Open Letter. Re-imagining the Future After the Corona Crisis*. http://degrowth.info/en/open-letter.

Escobar, Arturo. 2018. *Designs for the Pluriverse: Radical Interdependence, Autonomy, and the Making of Worlds*. Durham: Duke University Press.

Eversberg, Dennis, and Matthias Schmelzer. 2018. "The Degrowth Spectrum: Convergence and Divergence within a Diverse and Conflictual Alliance." *Environmental Values* 27, no. 3: 245–267.

Federici, Silvia. 2004. *Caliban and the Witch: Women, the Body and Primitive Accumulation*. New York: Autonomedia.

Fopp, David, Isabelle Axelsson, and Loukina Tille. 2021. *Gemeinsam für die Zukunft – Fridays For Future und Scientists For Future: Vom Stockholmer Schulstreik zur weltweiten Klimabewegung*. Bielefeld: transcript.

Harman, Chris. 2008. *A People's History of the World: From the Stone Age to the New Millennium*. London/New York: Verso.

Indigenous Environment Network and Oil Change International. 2021. *Indigenous Resistance Against Carbon*. Washington: Oil Change International. http://www.ienearth.org/indigenous-resistance-against-carbon/.

Kallis, Giorgos, Vasilis Kostakis, Steffen Lange, Barbara Muraca, Susan Paulson, and Matthias Schmelzer. 2018. "Research on Degrowth." *Annual Review of Environment and Resources* 43: 291–316.

Klein, Naomi. 2014. *This Changes Everything: Capitalism vs. the Climate*. London: Penguin UK.

Kuhnhenn, Kai, Anne Pinnow, Matthias Schmelzer, and Nina Treu. 2020. *Zukunft für alle: Eine Vision für 2048: gerecht. ökologisch. machbar.* München: oekom.

Kothari, Ashish, Ariel Salleh, Arturo Escobar, Federico Demaria, and Alberto Acosta, eds. 2019. *Pluriverse: A Post-Development Dictionary*. Delhi: Authors Up Front.

Nowshin, Tonny. 2019. *Presentation and Speech at Leipzig Degrowth Summer School 2019.*

Research & Degrowth, and Giorgos Kallis. 2015. "Prosperity without Growth: 10 Policy Proposals for the New Left." *The Ecologist*, February 28, 2015. http://theecologist.org/2015/feb/28/prosperity-without-growth-10-policy-proposals-new-left.

Schmelzer, Matthias, Andrea Vetter, and Aaron Vansintjan. 2022. *The Future Is Degrowth: A Guide to a World Beyond Capitalism*. London/New York: Verso.

Tyberg, Jamie. 2020. "Unlearning: From Degrowth to Decolonization." *Rosa Luxemburg Foundation*, July 3, 2020. http://rosalux.nyc/degrowth-to-decolonization/.

Wright, Erik O. 2010. *Envisioning Real Utopias*. London/New York: Verso.

Strategising with our eyes wide open

Chapter 7:

Social equity is the foundation of degrowth

By Samantha Mailhot and Patricia E. Perkins

Introduction

Since growth-driven capitalist economic systems rely on and exacerbate social inequities, uprooting and minimising those inequities is an essential step towards degrowth. But this implies much more than a binary replacement of growth-oriented systems by their opposite. Social equity is the key to a degrowth transformation for a range of reasons: political, theoretical, ontological, and ethical perspectives are all motivations for prioritising social equity. To be politically viable, degrowth movements must focus on supporting alliances amongst all those who are alienated or excluded by growth-driven systems due to their intersectional, discriminatory exploitation: a diverse and socially united movement is a strong movement. Theoretically, since social equity is central to social trust and wellbeing, degrowth governance processes also depend on fairness (Büchs and Koch 2019). Ontologically, non-Western understandings of relational collective sociality, pluriversity, and inter-species reciprocity are helping to envision degrowth's emergent future potentials (Nirmal and Rocheleau 2019). And ethically, social equity is a commonly recognised value and goal that instils hope and common purpose, laying a firm foundation for degrowth. Inclusivity and social equity are thus closely intertwined with degrowth; in this chapter, we explore how they undergird ethical, astute, well-grounded, and forward-oriented degrowth strategies.

In writing this chapter and discussing these interrelated perspectives, we are aware of our privilege as white middle-class cisgender women academics, living on stolen land in the territories of the Anishinaabe, Haudenosaunee, and Wendat peoples in

Montreal and Toronto; our view is necessarily partial, and we hope others will engage and enrich this discussion.

In the following section, we focus on the expansion of discriminatory structures as the basis for systemic capitalist exploitation, which, linked to colonialism, has led to appalling levels of social inequity both within and between countries. The third section looks at why and how degrowth is a pathway for achieving greater social equity. The fourth and fifth sections advance suggestions for how degrowth scholars and activists might more deeply engage with social equity as fundamental to their transformative activism: alliance-building and commons are specific strategies for the degrowth movement to advance social equity.

How do growth-oriented systems rely on and generate inequities?

Economic growth has led to an increase in the standard of living in some nations, by enabling longer and healthier human lives at very high levels of comfort (Victor 2019, Folbre 2020). However, these benefits have come with many ecological costs – such as the adverse effects of resource extraction, waste disposal, loss of species and habitats – as well as social costs including poverty, social exclusion, the breakdown of communities, alienation, crowding, crime (e.g., Victor 2019), and the exploitation of both productive and reproductive labour (Salleh 2017). These, and many other effects of relentless growth, have been disproportionately divided on local and regional scales and between countries, where economic growth in some places has largely been dependent on de-development and oppression of others (Victor 2019). This exploitation links intersectionally to class, gender, origin, clan, ethnicity, race, dis/ability, and nationality (Kallis 2018, 40). Growth–related inequities are multiplying both within and among countries, and they are enmeshed and unavoidable in growth-oriented systems (e.g., Piketty 2020, Wilkinson and Pickett 2010, Stiglitz 2016). Many degrowth scholars/activists centre their critique on illusions regarding growth's benefits, as well as its social equity implications (e.g., Kallis *et al.* 2020, Gilmore 2013, Gabriel and Bond 2019).

Industrial growth in Europe was dependent on elite accumulation by forcefully privatising land and commons, denying the "peasants" access to basic needs and forcing them to sell their labour cheaply to survive (Hickel 2021). Marx (1887) referred to this as "primitive accumulation." Class struggles were just part of the different forms of intersectional discrimination that were produced; the drive for accumulation also led to imperialism and racial discrimination. Colonisation paved the way for greater growth, bringing more land, resources, raw materials, and Indigenous slave labour to extraction and production (e.g. Marx 1887). At the same time, unequally distributed economic benefits allowed Europeans to prey on others and fuelled the expansion of the trans-Atlantic slave trade (e.g. Folbre 2020, 131). Economic growth was quite literally built on the backs of violently exploited peoples. Identifying "primitive accumulation" as an ongoing process, Harvey (2004, 75) describes the credit system and finance capital as major levers of predation, fraud, and thievery, and describes new mechanisms of "accumulation by dispossession." These include, for example, the commodification of nature and capital-intensive modes of agricultural production that have led to the depletion of global environmental commons as well as habitat destruction; the commodification of cultures, histories and intellectual creativity; and the corporatisation and privatisation of public assets (e.g. universities).

Gendered division of labour and exclusion also undergird growth-based societies. As Mies (1998) explains, for several centuries women have been "externalised, declared to be outside civilised society, pushed down, and thus made invisible as the underwater part of an iceberg is invisible, yet constitutes the base of the whole" (77). Wage labour "took a distinctly gendered form, with women restricted to the least remunerative jobs" (Folbre 2020, 15). The growth paradigm has perpetuated gender inequality by "reinforcing dualisms and devaluing care" (Dengler and Strunk 2018). Heteronormatively framed gender roles have persisted through time and have reinforced a binary logic where women still bear the brunt of domestic care work (Craig 2016), making some women/mothers responsible for both paid and unpaid work, and thus not fully available for paid work (Dengler and Strunk 2018). Because the growth paradigm rests on increasing GDP, it necessitates the valuation of wage labour over unpaid labour.

Importantly, gender and all other inequities have an intersectional dimension, meaning that they are "generally shaped by many factors in diverse and mutually influencing ways" (Hill Collins and Bilge 2016, 2), such as race, ethnicity, class, sexuality, ability, and age. The needs of African-American women were not addressed by anti-racist social movements, second-wave white feminism, or unions organising for workers' rights in the 1960s and 1970s, since each movement was solely focused on one category of analysis and action (race, gender, or class, respectively). "Because African-American women were simultaneously Black *and* female *and* workers, these single-focus lenses on social inequality left little space to address the complex social problems that they face(d)" (Hill Collins and Bilge 2016, 3). Intersectionality was first introduced as an analytical concept by Black women (Crenshaw 2017). From husbands acting as guardians or masters, to witch-hunts and torture of economically and sexually independent women, to the expropriation and exploitation of slave women/all women, to images of the "good woman", or woman as *mother* and *housewife* (to be maintained by a male "breadwinner") (Mies 1998, Federici 2004), women's struggles against these inequities seem never-ending.

In fact, growth-induced inequities have intersectionally negative impacts which exacerbate marginality for most people (Olofsson *et al.* 2014) – and focus their outrage. Ecological harms related to extraction, dispossession, and waste disposal in "sacrifice zones" spark environmental justice and land back movements (Hickel 2021, Yellowhead Institute 2020). Unjust burdens on those providing unpaid work, care, and physical and social reproduction lead to gender justice, care economy and frontline worker movements. Differential burdens of policing and incarceration related to private property, slavery and racism trigger prison abolition, defund the police, Idle No More, and Black Lives Matter movements. Use of immigrant labour for personal services, agriculture, dangerous work, and environmental and social harms embodied in product imports and exports between countries with weaker protections, also lead to movements opposing the negative effects of growth across countries and supply chains, along with divestment, tax harmonization, immigration rights and other attempts to regulate finance/capital, labour, and product movements internationally. Climate justice movements focus on the differential impacts of the growth-driven climate crisis on marginalised groups and geographic regions deprived of agency and means to address those impacts. Growth's failure to bring trickle-down benefits for the Majority World, or equitable distribution of wealth and living standards within the Minority World, is a long-standing "development" deception that continues to fuel resistance movements worldwide (Stiglitz 2016). And, set apart by their degree of criminality and impunity, are capitalism's colonial legacies of land theft, genocidal violence, and ongoing environmental and social destruction focused on Indigenous peoples – which are opposed by their continuance, resurgence, and leadership, with non-Indigenous supporters. All of these movements can be understood politically, theoretically, ontologically, and/or ethically – which offers ways of shaping alliances among them.

The cost of the inequities produced by growth is immeasurable, and there is certainly the potential for common cause among those affected, possibly leading to powerful political counterforces. The next sections discuss related challenges and potentials.

Potentials and challenges of a social equity focus within degrowth

Among those who are generally left out and discontented with various aspects of capitalist growth, degrowth may be able to spark some recognition and solidarity, as a convenor of sorts. But as Muradian (2019) notes, degrowth is not an easy sell. The degrowth community tends to be mostly white, well-educated, and middle class (Muradian 2019), representing values, concerns and interests that "create communication and emotional barriers for connecting with disadvantaged populations in other parts of the world" (257). While degrowth draws from theoretical and activist traditions, and ontologies of the Majority World (Hickel 2021, Latouche 2009), it is sometimes presented as a concept developed in and for the Minority World, with a tendency to recreate "longstanding (neo-) colonial asymmetries by setting the agenda on what ought to be done to solve problems of global relevance", where the Minority World establishes the norms, limits and strategies for degrowth proposals (Dengler and Seebacher 2019, 249). Some social and environmental justice groups feel that the term "degrowth" is not appealing or does not match the demands of poor and marginalised communities; that degrowth may not be taking into account the multiculturality and pluriversality of different countries; that degrowth is too anthropocentric; that degrowth is not even widely known in the Majority World; that degrowth is inherently Eurocentric (or Northern) in origin, so that it does not provide much space for resistance from a decolonial perspective, and puts forth a disconnected framework for those not living in rich, high-consumption societies (Rodríguez-Labajos *et al.* 2019, 177–179).

An *ethical* standpoint for degrowth, therefore, focuses on the tendency for existing power differences and dominant *ontological* standpoints to become reified even within resistance movements, which then turn on themselves in a toxic cycle. People who are culturally and ontologically alienated from and excluded by capitalism are likely to be uninterested in engaging with growth – or, possibly, with degrowth. Instead, their activism and resurgence operate along different planes and relationships altogether. As Indigenous climate scholar Kyle Whyte has explained in relation to non-Indigenous Western climate justice, "in the absence of a concern for addressing colonialism, climate justice advocates do not really propose solutions ... that are that much better for Indigenous well-being than the proposed inaction of even the most strident climate change deniers... Indigenous climate justice movements are distinct in their putting the nexus of colonialism, capitalism and industrialisation at the vanguard of their aspirations" (Whyte 2017, 1). Those degrowth activists who are able to recognise shared ideas and expand their conceptualisations and priorities may be able to build relationships across ontological divides (Singh 2019).

Indigenous ontological understandings regarding value, "goodness" or "wellth[13]" in human/society/nature relationships, as expressed in terms like "buen vivir", "sumak kawsay", "suma qamaña" and others, "displace the discussion of growth to that of social and environmental fulfilment" (Gudynas 2015, 204). "Buen Vivir is only possible within communities of extended or relational ontologies... a fulfilled life can only be achieved by deep relationships within a community" (Gudynas 2015, 203). This ontological understanding thus expands the conception of degrowth in time, space, species-relationships, and diversity/pluriversity-concepts that degrowth activists and theorists are only beginning to explore (Richter 2019). Cartesian and anthropocentric views of nature inherent to growth, and present in some degrowth thinking, separate nature from society and are anchored in Western ways of thinking (and colonising). This is a root cause of the current ecological crisis and, according to some authors, it may be perpetuated by the degrowth discourse (Richter 2019) in an emergent process that is continually shaped by ontological difference (or the pluriverse; see Escobar 2017; Nirmal and Rocheleau 2019).

Beyond ontological divides, another challenge for non-Indigenous people who want to work in solidarity with Indigenous peoples involves actively resisting rather than replicating colonial relations (Davis 2010). Rather than trying to strategise and lead in decolonial movements, this means supporting Indigenous struggles while also fighting broad settler ignorance and complacency:

---

13 The term "wellth" means "well-being expressed as paid and unpaid activities aimed at social and individual flourishing" (Mellor 2018, 125).

> "(C)olonial settler actions, even when not intended as such, can appear as greed for power and privilege, insulation from conflict or fear, and the freedom to completely ignore problematic 'others' as well as the effects of individual actions. Decolonisation, on any scale, cannot be motivated by an effort to maintain as much comfort or privilege as possible; given the nature of hierarchical oppression, confronting oppression requires that some individuals within the hierarchy will have to make significant sacrifices" (Barker 2010, 322).

Privileged degrowth activists must strive to understand the current state of injustice(s) around them and their role in the systems that perpetuate these injustices, as well as the unjust sacrifices involved in dismantling capitalism. Those seeking to build social equity-focused alliances need to actively learn about and reflect on the racism, sexism, xenophobia, homophobia, ableism and so on that currently exist locally and globally, their own privilege *vis-à-vis* these systems, and how to dismantle them. From this new self-understanding they can reach out to groups concentrating their political work on social struggles without colonising these struggles, but rather in support of them (Gobby 2020).

As different groups' struggles are situated in different economic and cultural contexts, differences in narratives, motivations, and strategies are almost inevitable (Burkhart *et al.* 2020). For example, "moral frame of reference" gaps can arise when several movements may all be seeking justice, but for different kinds of people (20). From a degrowth perspective, social equity-focused movements may not see growth or capitalism as the main cause of the injustices they are fighting, since the growth paradigm is "deeply embedded in people's minds and bodies" (Büchs and Koch 2019, 160). They may focus on the symptoms of growth rather than capitalism's fundamental need to divide and exploit.

In the next two sections, we venture some thoughts about how degrowth combined with alliance-building might address the political, theoretical, ontological and ethical distinctions noted above.

Alliance strategies for the degrowth movement

Degrowth authors have been writing for some time about the need to form alliances, given that multiple seemingly disconnected social-ecological struggles can be traced back to the growth-based economic system. Alliances among justice movements provide fertile ground for degrowth initiatives, both locally and globally. In fact, movements can build partnerships from the ground up, reaching out both locally and through social media via political networks (Lorek and Fuchs 2013). For example, Indigenous and decolonial movements to dismantle colonial violence share ontological wisdom, providing the foundation for a new approach to movement governance that builds and relies on social equity from the start. Environmental justice, feminist, LGBTQIA*, anti-racist, and anti-ableist groups, in alliance, provide strength, unity and solidarity to a cause or social movement (e.g., Davis 2010, Rodríguez-Labajos *et al.* 2019). Well-built alliances allow space to address all groups' particular needs and concerns.

Alliance formation draws from mutual support and practical, collective energy. In addition to fostering socio-political action and conceptual cross-fertilisation (Akbulut *et al.* 2019, 6), alliances invite a diversity of perspectives that can aid the development of new strategies to overcome the shared obstacles posed by the growth imperative (Scheidel and Schaffartzik 2019, 331).

Personal relationship-building and information-sharing is the only way to build alliances in such contexts. Their strength may be directly related to the depth of the relationships built over time. Hence, some of the elements needed for building alliances include respectful relationships, trust, taking time, acknowledging anger and the colonial legacy, understanding privilege and benefit, working through guilt, respecting difference, collaboration, and learning the history of Indigenous–non-Indigenous (or settler) relationships (Fitzmaurice 2010, summarising a 2005 lecture by Lynne Davis and Heather Shpuniarsky).

As Dengler and Seebacher explain, "degrowth must not be

misunderstood as a blueprint for a global transformation proposed by the Global North and imposed on the Global South, but rather as a Northern supplement to Southern ideas and movements, which already exist"[14] (Dengler and Seebacher 2019, 249). In this sense, historical economic relations, particularly inequities, should certainly remain at the forefront of the degrowth movement – an ongoing topic for discussion, deconstruction, and reassessment.

Building commons as a strategy for the degrowth movement

Another related approach is to build non-capitalist, equitable ways to provide livelihoods and wellbeing at community levels. As noted above, commons theorists have made many contributions to degrowth theory and praxis.

Commons theorists Silke Helfrich and David Bollier point out that many commons (on which billions of people already depend) are entirely outside the growth economy, and thus can be seen as cornerstones of degrowth. Their contributions to social trust, wellbeing, food and service provision of many kinds, innovations in social norms and collective governance, and skills for non-market provisioning are all part of an equitable degrowth transformation:

> "If 'the economy' is re-imagined through key commons notions like distributed production, modularity, collective ownership, and stewardship, it is possible to embrace the idea of a high-performance economic system while rejecting capitalist notions and institutions (corporations, global markets, competition, labour)" (Helfrich and Bollier 2015, 78).

Movements that focus on social equity can also foster ways to support livelihoods outside the market, consistent with degrowth. But degrowth activists should join struggles to resist the co-optation of commons through capitalist bail-outs or neoliberal remedies, e.g., when the U.S. and other universities in the Majority World

---

14   Dengler and Seebacher (2019) provide a good preliminary list of degrowth considerations in non-European contexts.

shield their research results behind secrecy and paywalls in order to commercialise the results (Caffentzis and Federici 2014), or the World Bank expels local people from forests and new "game parks" where they have lived for generations (Isla 2009), or unenclosed Swiss Alpine meadows and dairy cooperatives and Maine lobster fishery commons are driven to produce for the market (Caffentzis and Federici 2014). Commons require a community that is equitably organised and run, with transparently shared wealth that is cooperatively and socially produced in ways that strengthen and reinforce communal values. When degrowth and commons are mutually supporting, livelihoods and social equity are also reinforced (Caffentzis and Federici 2014) and inter-personal relationships also grow. The degrowth movement should thus strategically focus on the creation/restoration of commons in theoretical and practical terms, in order to help build social equity from the ground up (Brownhill *et al.* 2012).

Conclusion: social equity is central to degrowth

Since capitalist growth is grounded in and dependent on colonialism, patriarchy, and race and class discrimination, undoing and eliminating these pernicious structures is central to degrowth. In this chapter, we have attempted to show that with social equity at the forefront of the degrowth movement, social-ecological transformation becomes more ethical, politically feasible, theoretically grounded and ontologically rich. Even in the Minority World, alliances among groups with pressing social equity claims are a crucial part of the socio-political transformations that include degrowth. Globally, wellbeing for all is an urgent priority, especially in times of pandemic and climate chaos, when the marginalised are more likely than ever to find themselves underserved and exploited by growth-oriented economic systems, despite their long-standing knowledge of how to cope (Kousis and Paschou 2017). Such crises demand a social equity-oriented approach that builds structures and skills to create communities of wellbeing and trust while sustaining livelihoods outside and beyond capitalism.

References

Akbulut, Bengi, Federico Demaria, Julien-François Gerber, and Joan Martínez-Alier. 2019. "Who Promotes Sustainability? Five Theses on the Relationships Between the Degrowth and the Environmental Justice Movements." *Ecological Economics* 165, 106418.

Barker, Adam. 2010. "From Adversaries to Allies: Forging Respectful Alliances between Indigenous and Settler Peoples." In *Alliances: Re/envisioning Indigenous–non-Indigenous relationships*, edited by Lynne Davis. University of Toronto Press.

Brownhill, Leigh, Terisa Turner, and Wahu Kaara. 2012. "Degrowth? How about Some "De–Alienation"?" *Capitalism Nature Socialism* 23, no. 10: 93–104.

Büchs, Milena, and Max Koch. 2019. "Challenges for the Degrowth Transition: The Debate about Wellbeing." *Futures* 105: 155–165.

Burkhart, Corinna, Matthias Schmelzer, and Nina Treu, eds. 2020. *Degrowth in Movement(s)*. Hampshire UK: John Hunt Publishing.

Caffentzis, George, and Silvia Federici. 2014. "Commons against and beyond Capitalism." *Community Development Journal* 49, no. 1: 92–105.

Craig, Lyn. 2016. *Contemporary Motherhood: The Impact of Children on Adult Time*. Routledge.

Crenshaw, Kimberlé. 2017. "Kimberlé Crenshaw on Intersectionality, More than Two Decades Later." *Columbia Law School News*, June 8.

Davis, Lynne, ed. 2010. *Alliances: Re/Envisioning Indigenous–non-Indigenous Relationships*. University of Toronto Press.

Dengler, Corinna, and Lisa M. Seebacher. 2019. "What about the Global South? Towards a Feminist Decolonial Degrowth Approach." *Ecological Economics* 157: 246–252.

Dengler, Corinna, and Birte Strunk. 2018. "The Monetized Economy Versus Care and the Environment: Degrowth Perspectives on Reconciling an Antagonism." *Feminist Economics* 24, no. 3: 160–183.

Escobar, A. 2017. *Designs for the Pluriverse: Radical Interdependence, Autonomy, and the Making of Worlds*. Duke University Press

Federici, Sylvia. 2004. *Caliban and the Witch*. Autonomedia.

Fitzmaurice, Kevin. 2010. "Are White People Obsolete? Indigenous Knowledge and the Colonizing Ally in Canada." In *Alliances: Re/envisioning Indigenous–non-Indigenous relationships*, edited by Lynne Davis. University of Toronto Press.

Folbre, Nancy. 2020. *The Rise and Decline of Patriarchal Systems: An Intersectional Political Economy*. New York: Verso.

Gabriel, Cle-Anne, and Carol Bond. 2019. "Need, Entitlement and Desert: A Distributive Justice Framework for Consumption Degrowth." *Ecological Economics* 156: 327–336.

Gilmore, Brian. 2013. "The World is Yours: 'Degrowth', Racial Inequality and Sustainability." *Sustainability* 5, no. 3: 1282–1303.

Gobby, Jen. 2020. *More Powerful Together: Conversations with Climate Activists and Indigenous Land Defenders*. Fernwood.

Gudynas, Eduardo. 2015. "Buen Vivir." In *Degrowth: A Vocabulary for a New Era*, edited by Giacomo D'Alisa, Federico Demaria, and Giorgos Kallis. New York: Routledge.

Harvey, David. 2004. "The 'New' Imperialism: Accumulation by Dispossession." *Socialist Register* 40.

Helfrich, Silke, and David Bollier. 2015. "Commons." In *Degrowth: A Vocabulary for a New Era*, edited by Giacomo D'Alisa, Federico Demaria, and Giorgos Kallis. New York: Routledge.

Hickel, Jason. 2021. *Less is More: How Degrowth Will Save the World*. London: William Heinemann.

Hill Collins, Patricia, and Sirma Bilge. 2016. *Intersectionality*. Cambridge: Polity.

Isla, Ana. 2009. "Who Pays for the Kyoto Protocol? Selling Oxygen and Selling Sex in Costa Rica." In *Eco-Sufficiency and Global Justice: Women Write Political Economy*, edited by Ariel Salleh. London: Pluto.

Kallis, Giorgos. 2018. *Degrowth*. Newcastle UK: Agenda Publishing.

Kallis, Giogos, Susan Paulson, Giacomo D'Alisa, and Federico Demaria. 2020. *The Case for Degrowth*. Cambridge UK and Medford Massachusetts: Polity.

Kousis, Marua, and Maria Paschou. 2017. "Alternative Forms of Resilience: A Typology of Approaches for the Study of Citizen Collective Responses in Hard Economic Times." *Partecipazione e Conflitto* 10, no. 1: 136–168.

Latouche, Serge. 2009. *Farewell to Growth*. Cambridge UK and Malden Massachusetts: Polity.

Lorek, Sylvia, and Doris Fuchs. 2013. "Strong Sustainable Consumption Governance – Precondition for a Degrowth Path?" *Journal of Cleaner Production* 38: 36–43.

Marx, Karl. 1887. *Capital: A Critique of Political Economy. Volume I. Book One: The Process of Production of Capital*. Moscow: Progress Publishers.

Mellor, Mary. 2018. "Care as Wellth: Internalising Care by Democratising Money." In *Feminist Political Ecology and the Economics of Care*, edited by Christine Bauhardt and Wendy Harcourt. London: Routledge.

Mies, Maria. 1998. *Patriarchy and Accumulation on a World Scale: Women in the International Division of Labour*. London, New York: Zed Books.

Muradian, Roldan. 2019. "Frugality as a Choice vs. Frugality as a Social Condition. Is De–growth Doomed to Be a Eurocentric Project?" *Ecological Economics* 161: 257–260.

Nirmal, Padini, and Dianne Rocheleau. 2019. "Decolonizing Degrowth in the Post-Development Convergence: Questions, Experiences, and Proposals from Two Indigenous Territories." *Environment and Planning E: Nature and Space* 2, no. 3: 465–492.

Olofsson, Anna, Jens O. Zinn, Gabriele Griffin, Katarina Giritli Nygren, Andreas Cebulla, and Kelly Hannah–Moffat. 2014. "The Mutual Constitution of Risk and Inequalities: Intersectional Risk Theory." *Health, Risk & Society* 16, no. 5: 417–430.

Piketty, Thomas. 2020. *Capital and Ideology*. Cambridge, Massachusetts, Harvard University Press.

Richter, Katharina. 2019. "Struggling for Another Life: The Ontology of Degrowth." *Journal of Global Cultural Studies* 14.

Rodríguez–Labajos, Beatriz, Ivonne Yánez, Patrick Bond, Lucie Greyl, Serah Munguti, Godwin Uyi Ojo, and Winfridus Overbeek. 2019. "Not So Natural an Alliance? Degrowth and Environmental Justice Movements in the Global South." *Ecological Economics* 157: 175–184.

Salleh, Ariel. 2017. *Ecofeminism as Politics: Nature, Marx and the Postmodern*. 2nd ed. London, UK: Zed Books.

Scheidel, Arnim, and Anke Schaffartzik. 2019. "A Socio–Metabolic Perspective on Environmental Justice and Degrowth Movements." *Ecological Economics* 161: 330–333.

Singh, Neera. 2019. "Environmental Justice, Degrowth and Post-Capitalist Futures." *Ecologica Economics* 163: 138–142.

Stiglitz, Joseph E. 2016. "Inequality and Economic Growth." In *Rethinking Capitalism: Economics and Policy for Sustainable and Inclusive Growth*, edited by Michael Jacobs and Mariana Mazzucato. Wiley-Blackwell.

Victor, Peter A. 2019. *Managing without Growth: Slower by Design, not Disaster*. 2nd ed. Cheltenham, UK: Edward Elgar.

Wilkinson, Richard, and Kate Pickett. 2010. *The Spirit Level: Why Equality Is Better for Everyone*. London: Penguin.

Whyte, Kyle. 2019. "Way Beyond the Lifeboat: An Indigenous Allegory of Climate Justice." In *Climate Futures: Reimagining Global Climate Justice*, edited by Debashish Munshi, Kum-Kum Bhavnani, John Foran, and Priya Kurian. University of California Press.

Yellowhead Institute. 2020. *Land Back*. https://redpaper.yellowheadinstitute.org/.

Chapter 8:

Evaluating strategies for emancipatory degrowth transformations

By Panos Petridis[15]

The concept of social-ecological transformation has been central and explicit within the degrowth debate: degrowth is often said to provide a repoliticised vision for the radical transformation of society (e.g., Asara *et al.* 2015, Muraca 2013, Petridis *et al.* 2015). But *how* is this to come about? In order to facilitate a purposive transformation, we need to shift part of our attention from diagnosis to the development and evaluation of strategy. A process of social-ecological transformation as envisioned by degrowth would arguably require a synergy between the three modes of transformation introduced by Erik Olin Wright (2010, 2013), and outlined in detail in Chapter 2: ruptural, interstitial, and symbiotic.

Following this strategic canvas, the scope of the chapter is the following: First, I stress the importance of complementing strategies and argue that a synthetic viewpoint can empower individual struggles, but also help us identify points of convergence between political proposals. Then, I turn my focus, particularly to the relationship between the interstitial and symbiotic modes of transformation, and revisit the so-called "non-reformist reforms", and their potential to reinforce transformation. Finally, I discuss some tentative conditions for evaluating strategies, in light of an emancipatory horizon. My take-home message is that there is a need to understand, and support, those subversive practices and reforms that, while they can take place in the current system, at the same time modify the relations of power – and thus bring us closer to an emancipatory future.

---

15 Many thanks to Christos Zografos and the editors of this chapter for their useful comments.

Synthesis and complementarity: in search of subversive, emancipatory institutions

The core of the "degrowth" institutions that are envisioned will likely be derived from social movements and interstitial bottom-up solidarity economy initiatives that operate against the logic of capital. These are the main spaces of social and social-ecological experimentation and historically the field where progressive proposals have been advanced – in large part because a degrowth transformation is not expected to come from the elite establishment. These "nowtopias" (Carlsson and Manning 2010) are prefigurative, emancipatory initiatives that not only *envision* but also *embody* an alternative model of societal organisation in practice. They are relevant because, while providing for specific needs (for food, housing etc.), they also contain the seeds of an alternative model of social organisation and low-scale generative economy based on solidarity, collaboration and "commoning" in practice (Bauwens *et al.* 2019, Bollier and Helfrich 2015). The basic idea is that participation in such initiatives helps deconstruct the dominant consumer/capitalist mode of being and creates a new collective political project.

These initiatives can be reinforced by public awareness campaigns and activist action that may very well take the form of civil disobedience or other ruptural strategies, such as the occupation and re-imagination of defunct public assets. Perhaps even more importantly, and especially in the current socio-political context, they would greatly benefit from institutional arrangements that can support them and safeguard them from being crushed or marginalised by dominant powers, and thus avoid becoming just "exit strategies" for a few concerned (middle class) citizens.

A synthetic approach is also necessary in order to avoid co-optation, for example of solidarity economy initiatives from capitalist enterprises or of economic localisation from xenophobic administrations. Or, to take another example, the reduction of working hours with the same pay, or an unconditional basic income, can potentially free up part of our time and creativity for political participation and engagement in degrowth initiatives or provide quality time with our family and community, but – if taken alone – it can also just lead to increased private consumption, or further legitimise precarious employment. Similarly, the use of open-source technologies can make production more participatory and democratic, but it does not guarantee the production of eco-friendly products, nor does it ensure that those are not appropriated by for-profit enterprises. So tools and technologies need to be complemented with an alternative culture of production, as well as institutions that would govern their use. And vice versa, such institutional changes can also showcase more prominently during social movement mobilisations and demands. Strategic plurality is often more likely to contribute to future resilience of degrowth proposals by helping to keep the big picture in view and see the interconnections, interdependencies and obstacles that need to be overcome to achieve and maintain a common goal (see also Chapter 1).

A case in point is the building materials factory of *Vio.Me* in Thessaloniki, Greece, abandoned by its owners, leaving workers unpaid since May 2011. Through a decision by their general assembly, the workers decided to occupy the factory and operate it under direct democratic control. They resumed production in February 2013, also shifting to the use of organic materials. This unique experiment for Greece, in terms of scale, highlights the importance of complementing strategies: a ruptural occupation, coupled with interstitial self-organisation to fair and ecological production, in urgent need of symbiotic support. This in fact is a pattern commonly observed when dealing with the institutionalisation of alternative practices: such initiatives are at constant risk, as long as they are not covered by a legal framework. But, what kind of institutional changes are we talking about?

Given the necessity but also the difficulty to achieve institutional change and reform higher-level institutions, André Gorz has made a very important and relevant qualitative distinction, between conventional reforms and *non-reformist reforms* (Gorz 1967). Conventional reforms such as humanitarian aid, corporate volunteerism, responsible shopping, or "green growth" investments have at the very best an ameliorative effect, but basically legitimise existing power structures, dynamics of accumulation, and political processes, and in effect achieve no transformative change (Bond 2008). In contrast, non-reformist reforms are incompatible with the preservation of the current system. They directly empower social movements and demands and "are conceived not in terms of what is possible within the framework of a given system and administration, but in view of what *should be* made possible in terms of human needs and demands" (Gorz 1967, 7, own emphasis). They propose a way to overcome the historical problem of dualism between the tactic having to happen *now* and strategy coming *after* and intend to "simultaneously make life better within the existing economic system and expand the potential for future advances of democratic power" (Wright 2013, 20). Such "non-reformist reforms" are by nature subversive, and create the space and conditions for transformative policies to emerge.

Some relevant questions are: To which extent can reforms support the conditions for nowtopias to flourish, for example, a legal framework backing up cooperative firms? In which cases can ruptural civic action and nowtopias push for the adoption of institutional reforms, and under which conditions can positive feedback be initiated? The main challenge is that nowtopias, much like grassroots innovations, need to operate on the margins of the current system and sometimes even need to be illegal in the short term in order to induce institutional changes that will render them appropriate to a more just future (Smith *et al.* 2014). Similarly, we can only speculate about the threshold at which symbiotic transformations require the elimination of capitalism as a precondition for their own existence (Murphy 2013). In essence, we seek proposals that are at least marginally appropriate for a local situation at present, while at the same time transforming those same conditions in the future. In other words, if we understand nowtopias as expressions of the desire for a better way of living that involve the reconstruction of society *imagined otherwise* (Levitas 2005), the challenge then is how such an emancipatory "utopian" project can be grounded on existing practices but at the same time leave space for imaginary alternatives.

Tentative conditions for evaluating strategies: considerations for non-reformist reforms

Following Wright (2013, 9), I argue for placing the strategic emphasis on institutions that "envision the contours of an alternative social world that embodies emancipatory ideals and then look for social innovations that move us towards that destination", what he called "real utopias", such as participatory budgeting, solidarity finance, worker-owned cooperatives, and unconditional basic income. Wright's proposal is to further evaluate alternatives according to their *desirability*, *viability* (longer-term sustainability), and *achievability* (how do we move from here to there?), putting strategic emphasis on the viability component. If an alternative is desirable, but not viable or achievable, he argues, then it is just "utopian". Similarly, a reform can be non-reformist, or just ameliorative, depending on the set of criteria or conditions by which we choose to evaluate it. In one of his preferred examples, Gorz (1967) stated that the demand for building 500,000 new housing units every year in France to meet people's housing needs, could either be termed a *neocapitalist* or an *anti-capitalist* reform, depending on whether it would involve public subsidies to private enterprise, or if it was constructed as a socialised public service on confiscated private territory. Still, nowadays we might dismiss both options altogether on ecological grounds.

What we can learn from the above is that there is a need to constantly evaluate both our proposals and overall strategies – but based on which criteria? One suggestion, inspired by Wright's approach, is to critically examine our strategies according to their *emancipatory potential*. Note that I use the term "emancipation" in its more classical sense, referring to liberation from the alienating logics of productivism, efficiency, growth and overconsumption and not, as it has also been associated with, ever more individualised freedom, flexibility and increasingly consumerist lifestyles (Blühdorn 2011). Given that ruptural and interstitial modes of transformation are perhaps more straightforward and, at least according to the description above, are largely already "emancipatory", this task then becomes especially relevant for symbiotic strategies that often take the form of institutional arrangements and policy proposals. Here the battleground becomes more contested and lines can be blurred. To this end, it would be very useful to begin to consider the factors and conditions that would render proposed strategies "non-reformist" and emancipatory, as opposed to just "ameliorative." What could such conditions look like? Departing from Wright's principles of emancipatory social sciences, we can start developing some tentative conditions, listed below. A proposal can be hypothesised to be non-reformist or transformative if:

1. *It results from bottom-up social movement demands.* This condition addresses desirability and follows from an attempt to identify the potential of human demands, as discussed by Gorz (1967). If non-reformist reforms are to be conceived in view of what should be made possible in terms of *human needs and demands*, one would therefore need to evaluate those demands by directly listening and responding to emancipatory social and ecological movements. A relevant question would be: Does a proposal resonate *directly* with social movement demands, rather than vested interests or representatives?

2. *It contributes to a set of emancipatory moral principles.* This directly tackles the emancipatory vision of a proposal. Wright (2013) notably mentions the following three moral principles: equality, democracy and sustainability; one could

also include diversity and freedom of expression. Related questions: Does a proposal get us closer to an emancipatory vision (as shaped by these moral principles), or put us in a better position to reach it? How does a proposal contribute to one or more goals related to the above principles (e.g., decreasing inequality, increasing participation, reducing environmental impact)?

3. *It contributes to the building of democratic institutions.* The relevance of (direct) democracy for degrowth (e.g., Cattaneo *et al.* 2012) lies not only in considering the governance of future "degrowth" societies but also in its role in achieving purposive transformation. More than just contributing to an emancipatory ideal, this refers to the possibility of reinforcing values that would contribute to the building of longer-lasting, less totalitarian, more democratic, more participatory institutions. Questions: Does a proposal modify relations of power? Which proposals decentralise decision making, extending popular power against the powers of state or capital?

4. *It has a place in the current society, but also in the desired society.* This is a reality-check on the viability of a proposal. One would ask: Is a proposal applicable at present, *but also* in the envisioned society, or is it only perceived as a transitory tactic that does not have inherent value for the future?

To use an illustrative example, let us look at the issue of meaningful employment – a cornerstone of envisioned degrowth society and perhaps constituting the main link between nowtopias and non-reformist reforms. Nowtopias in a way try to redefine work, while some of the most critical non-reformist reforms are those that directly tackle the issue of employment. Take the example of worker-owned cooperatives: these result from bottom-up social movements demands, contribute to the moral principles of equality and democracy, as well as to the building of long-term counter-institutions, and have a place in the present society while also prefiguring a future mode of working conditions and relations. They have clear emancipatory potential, as they directly subvert and modify current relations of power. Similar proposals supporting solidarity economy practices (legally, institutionally and financially) essentially fall in the same category of providing work imagined differently. While the main goal of such proposals is the reduction of unemployment, they simultaneously support an alternative model of social and environmental relations.

Other examples could be *participatory budgeting* or *participatory urban planning*. They also result from long-lasting social movement demands; they reinforce a series of emancipatory moral ideals such as democracy, participation and freedom of expression; and they contribute to the building of more decentralised participatory and democratic institutions. Finally, they also embody a mode of organisation that is both applicable today and would also prefigure and be highly desirable in a future degrowth society.

The proposed conditions are meant to be used heuristically and do not intend to be complete or comprehensive, and by no means are intended as a blueprint for transformations. Still, collectively developing and elaborating such a list of considerations can be very useful in evaluating the viability of a strategy, or strategy mix. One important common point about the proposed conditions is that the main focus is on the emancipatory direction, rather than the speed of change. Changes can be sudden or gradual, but reformism is only radical as long as it modifies the relations of power, in view of an emancipatory horizon. Otherwise, it is just conventional reformism. Moreover, this focal shift also largely bypasses the longstanding debates on the role of the state versus bottom-up action by focusing instead on *subversive* strategies (both state and non-state) that would ultimately help us build more participatory institutions (see Chapter 9). This is a radically different view of the state from just being a delegator of peoples' hopes, a fact that has often led to the co-option of social demands. Still, it would require large doses of ingenuity to identify non-hegemonic ways of linking social movements with higher-level institutions.

To summarise, the development of "degrowth" as a subversive slogan over the past decade has offered us a new narrative to collectively envision an alternative form of social organisation beyond the logic of economism and towards simpler, more ecological and democratic societies. It has also provided a vocabulary that intends to give meaning to local initiatives and connect them to policy proposals. In order to further advance our understanding of the potential synthesis and complementarity of strategies for transformation, and "do things now that put us in the best position to do more later" (Wright 2013, 21) there is a need to examine those subversive practices and reforms that would be feasible today, while still, at the same time, be able to prefigure alternative social relations and enhance democratic participation, and in this way facilitate the conditions for emancipatory transformation.

References

Asara, Viviana, Iago Otero, Federico Demaria, and Esteve Corbera. 2015. "Socially Sustainable Degrowth as a Social-Ecological Transformation: Repoliticizing Sustainability." *Sustainability Science* 10, no. 3: 375–384.

Bauwens, Michel, Vasilis Kostakis, and Alex Pazaitis. 2019. *Peer to Peer: The Commons Manifesto*. University of Westminster Press.

Blühdorn, Ingolfur. 2011. "The Sustainability of Democracy: On Limits to Growth, the Post-Democratic Turn and Reactionary Democrats." *Eurozine*, July 11, 2011: 1–10.

Bollier, David, and Silke Helfrich, eds. 2015. *Patterns of Commoning*. Commons Strategy Group and Off the Common Press.

Bond, Patrick. 2008. "Reformist Reforms, Non-Reformist Reforms and Global Justice Activist, NGO and Intellectual Challenges in the World Social Forum." *Societies Without Borders* 3: 4–19.

Carlsson, Chris, and Francesca Manning. 2010. "Nowtopia: Strategic Exodus?" *An-*

tipode 42: 924–953.

Cattaneo, Claudio, Giacomo D'Alisa, Giorgos Kallis, and Christos Zografos. 2012. "Degrowth Futures and Democracy." *Futures* 44, no. 6: 515–523.

Gorz, André. 1967. *Strategy for Labor*. Boston: Beacon Press.

Levitas, Ruth. 2005. *The Imaginary Reconstitution of Society or Why Sociologists and Others Should Take Utopia More Seriously*. Inaugural Lecture, University of Bristol, 24.

Muraca, Barbara. 2013. "Décroissance: A Project for a Radical Transformation of Society." *Environmental Values* 22, no. 2: 147–169.

Murphy, Mary P. 2013. "Translating Degrowth into Contemporary Policy Challenges: A Symbiotic Social Transformation Strategy." *Irish Journal of Sociology* 21, no. 2: 76–89.

Petridis, Panos, Barbara Muraca, and Giorgos Kallis. 2015. "Degrowth: Between a Scientific Concept and a Slogan for a Social Movement." In *Handbook of Ecological Economics*, edited by Joan Martinez-Alier and Roldan Muradian, 176–200. Cheltenham, UK: Edward Elgar Publishing.

Smith, Adrian, Mariano Fressoli, and Hernán Thomas. 2014. "Grassroots Innovation Movements: Challenges and Contributions." *Journal of Cleaner Production* 63: 114–124.

Wright, Erik Olin. 2010. *Envisioning Real Utopias*. London: Verso.

Wright, Erik Olin. 2013. "Transforming Capitalism through Real Utopias." *American Sociological Review* 78, no. 1: 1–25.

Chapter 9:

Rethinking state-civil society relations

By Max Koch

Degrowth strategising has suffered from a tension between viewing the state as incapable of initiating transformational change – a view especially prominent in the Anarchist tradition – and making a political appeal to it to do precisely this. As Cosme *et al.* (2017) first observed, most of the eco-social policies that degrowth activists promote would require a great deal of intervention by states and/or international organisations. A limited number of papers have attempted to bridge this tension by addressing the state as an arena within degrowth activism.

D'Alisa and Kallis (2020; see also D'Alisa 2019) review perspectives on the state within degrowth thinking from a Gramscian perspective. My own contribution (Koch 2020a) applies materialist state theories to sketch the general direction and potential roles of the state in social-ecological transformations at various scales (local, national, European), emphasising use-value orientation, welfare and the satisfaction of human needs. I argue that, if they are able to mobilise a sufficiently large number of resources, degrowth and related movements could become strategically relevant and transformative public policies would be more likely to be implemented. These policies could help set in motion a societal transformation that would successively allow the state to step out of its current role of facilitating the socio-economic context for economic growth. Such a transformation of the roles that the state plays in society would need to be complemented by changes to the apparatuses of the state itself, for example through the addition of citizens' assemblies.

These works have proposed how degrowth might conceptualise the state in a transformation – considering both its limits and possibilities. However, neither of the papers mentioned discuss in any greater detail the strategic implications for degrowth arising from the proposed conceptualisations of the state and state-civil society relations. This chapter examines the theories of Antonio Gramsci, Nicos Poulantzas and Pierre Bourdieu in this light (see Koch 2022 for a more detailed version). It first compares and contrasts the three theories in respect to general characteristics of state-civil society relations. It then addresses related principles of domination and crises as structural openings for oppositional movements like degrowth. Emphasis is placed on the potential in periods of crisis for creating and expanding alternative spaces. The chapter concludes with a summary of the strategic implications for degrowth actors and with some suggestions for how a critical perspective of the state may be taken forward in degrowth research.

General characteristics of state-civil society relations

Civil society is often understood as a social sphere separate from politics and economy, with "solidarity" and "basic egalitarianism" (Müller 2006, 313) reigning in the former and exploitation and bureaucracy dominating the latter (this view also to some extent underlies Erik Olin Wright's framework discussed in Chapter 2). Gramsci, Poulantzas and Bourdieu take a different view, emphasising, in particular ways, interconnections between state and civil society.

Gramsci's *Prison Notebooks* (2011) contain a systematic analysis of the changes in state-civil society relationships in Western Europe after World War I. Before, the bourgeois rule was characterised by a direct economic rule coupled with military force. After the war, however, a new sort of relationship between the state and powerful classes emerged. The economic and military rule came to be complemented by hegemonic, civil and political domination. Hence, domination came to be more complex, that is, beyond the material state apparatus in a narrow sense ("political society") and including areas generally regarded as belonging to civil society. The theoretical framework describing how civil society became more closely entangled with the state is that of the "integral state" (see also D'Alisa and Kallis 2020).

By contrast, for Poulantzas, there is a clear–cut inside and outside of the state. At first sight, this makes his interpretation of state-civil society relations more compatible with mainstream interpretations. Yet, Poulantzas' definition of the state as a "condensation of social forces" (Poulantzas 1978) stresses the interdependence of the formal "state" apparatus and "civil society." State power is to be grasped as a reflection of the "changing balance of forces in political and politically–relevant struggles" (Jessop 2011, 43). Political mobilisation in a range of social spheres, Poulantzas writes, can thus strongly influence the concrete directions of state action.

Bourdieu rejects the notion of civil society altogether and instead studies relatively autonomous "fields" as social arenas in which particular activities and strategies are pursued. This is comparable to a game, the rules and stakes of which are accepted by all players. By conceptualising the state itself as a field, he draws on Weber (1991) and his definition of the modern state as an institutional association of rule (*Herrschaftsverband*), which has successfully established the monopoly of physical violence. What, according to Bourdieu, remained to be done was to understand how the state managed to also concentrate the legitimate use of "symbolic violence." The state appears here as the "culmination of a process of concentration of different species of capital" (Bourdieu 1994, 5), including physical instruments of coercion (army, police), economic capital, cultural and informational capital. This process, which Bourdieu describes in terms of a succession of socio-historical stages, culminated in the modern bureaucratic state (including welfare and environmental states), which itself was riddled with contradictions: The "left hand of the state", represented by state employees in public education, health and social welfare, came to stand in opposition to its "right hand" in the judiciary, domestic affairs and finance. With this opposition, Bourdieu's work suggests an opening for social change through struggles within the state apparatus.

Principles of domination

How do the dominant classes rule within and beyond the material state apparatus, and what makes dominated groups respect respect this rule? An advanced understanding of power positions, power relations and the role of the state within these relations can facilitate the development of strategies that challenge the status quo. Gramsci studied the ways in which the ruling class's domination of political society and its leadership of civil society came to reinforce each other and how the powers of physical coercion and the production of consent became intertwined. His famous "general notion of the state" therefore refers "back to the notion of civil society": "state = political society + civil society, in other words, hegemony armoured with coercion" (Gramsci 1971, 263). As briefly alluded to earlier, consent thereby necessarily includes the – albeit limited – consideration of the interests of subordinate groups in state strategies or, at least, the production of the appearance of such consideration.

Poulantzas takes up Gramsci's concept of hegemony and the dual notion of coercion and consent. State apparatuses "consecrate and reproduce hegemony" by "bringing the power bloc and certain dominated classes into a (variable) game of provisional compromises" (Poulantzas 1978, 140). Efforts to increase the representation of the subaltern in the institutional structure of the state may in fact pay off as it can take the form of "centres of opposition" (Poulantzas 1978, 142), from which civil society mobilisation can be reinforced.

For Bourdieu, state power exists twice: in its material or objective form and in its symbolic form or its effect on our thoughts and perceptions. The former mode structures society through, for example, "timetables, budget periods, calendars" (Bourdieu 2014, 183) or even, for example, spelling rules. One way to think of the latter (symbolic) mode of state domination is the fact that the "sentence of the judge or the grade of the professor" (Bourdieu 1994, 12) tends to be perceived as appropriate and legitimate. Hence, like Gramsci's "hegemony", symbolic capital is the power of making people see the social and natural world in a specific way, perceived as universal and natural (Koch 2018). By establishing "common forms and categories of perception and appreciation", the state creates a pre-reflexive "belief effect" on the part of the dominated, which helps to explain why the state normally does not have to use physical coercion for "generalised obedience" (Bourdieu 2014, 166).

Crises as strategic openings

Our three state theorists are in agreement that crises are the structural background for societal change and provide corresponding openings for oppositional movements. Humphrys (2018, 38) points out that Gramsci's integral state is always and "necessarily unstable." This means that in certain instances civil society can "break through the political container." This is most likely during crises, generally characterised as conjunctures (historically and/or geographically specific combinations of circumstances or events), where "no group, neither the conservatives nor the progressives, has the strength for victory" (Gramsci 1971, 211). However, crises may also serve as context and entry points for "charismatic 'men of destiny'" (Gramsci 1971, 211) and authoritarian exit strategies. This was strategically reflected in his notion of a "war of position"[16], in which a new kind of intellectual, unified with the subaltern, was to play the role of "constructor, organiser, 'permanently active persuader'" (Gramsci 1971, 10). Such "organic intellectuals" – for example, researchers, journalists and other professions that more or less directly contribute to producing and reproducing influential and especially public discourses – would find their role only in their integration with the citizenry. In this perspective, the more codified knowledge of "intellectuals" benefits more from the practical knowledge of the

---

16 By contrast, the "war of movement" may be a revolutionary alternative in societies with less developed "trenches" of civil society, such as in Russia in 1917. Gramsci (2011, 229–230) illustrates the distinction as follows: "Ghandi's passive resistance is a war of position, which at certain moments becomes a war of movement, and at others underground warfare. Boycotts are a form of war of position, strikes a war of movement, the secret preparation of weapons and combat troops belong to underground warfare."

citizenry, rather than the other way around. The former are educated just as often as they serve as educators.

Poulantzas expands Gramsci's notion of crises by discussing their threefold character: economic, political/ideological and state crises. These forms of crisis are not directly related. Economic crises do not automatically become political crises nor do the latter immediately become crises of the state. Neither do the different forms of crisis necessarily have to coincide. Given the interconnectedness of the state and civil society, he does not assign priority to struggles that are either inside or outside the state (Brand and Heigl 2011, 246), and, instead, suggests that these "two forms of struggle must be combined" (Poulantzas 1978, 260). Hence, if Gramsci argued that the dislocation of consent in civil society was to be achieved by an alternative hegemonic project and from there advanced to political society, Poulantzas (1978, 258) added that subaltern groups could occupy "centres of resistance" within the state, which were to be strategically coordinated and increased in number until they become "real centres of power", capable of staging "real breaks" with the established order – or, in the terminology of Erik Olin Wright (2012), whose work in many ways built upon Poulantzas – "ruptural transformations" (see Chapter 2). As a corollary, Poulantzas encouraged both the amplification of subaltern voices within state institutions and representative democracy as well as popular movements for establishing new forms of deliberative elements, including principles of direct democracy. While this may involve a "war of position" (Gramsci) within the state itself, this does not mean that the struggles in neighbourhoods, communities, workplaces, campuses and so on are to be neglected.

Bourdieu points out that, during periods of crisis, there is an increased chance that alternative ways of thinking and acting become influential. Acts of symbolic mobilisation are then able to "manipulate hopes and expectations", introducing a "degree of play" into the otherwise unquestioned interplay of objective chances and subjective expectations (Bourdieu 2000, 234). In this context, researchers or "intellectuals" can take the role of "professional practitioners" or "spokespersons of the dominated" (Bourdieu 2000, 188), even if such "transfer of cultural capital" is always in danger of "hijacking" due to the difference in social position and interests of intellectuals and the dominated (Koch 2020b). While Bourdieu regards intellectuals[17] as holders of cultural capital, as part of the "dominant class", that is, they are in a superior class position vis-à-vis the middle and lower classes, he nevertheless places them in a "dominated" position vis-à-vis the dominant fraction of the dominant class: the holders of economic capital. Hence, intellectuals ("dominated-dominant"), middle and lower classes, occupy different positions in the social structure and, as a consequence, personify "different experiences of domination" (Bourdieu 2000, 188). Though his insistence on this difference in social position (and, as a corollary, in the interests of intellectuals) constitutes a sociological critique of the Gramscian notion of "organic intellectuals" – as well as a qualification and further development of it, Bourdieu nevertheless formulates a similar ambition.

Expanding alternative spaces

Gramsci emphasised that the integral character of state-civil society relationships is never complete and perfect. This was already applicable to the early period of Fordism, with its "mass" parties and corporatist organisations. As the Fordist regime transitioned to a neoliberal one, this integrative function weakened even more (Crouch 2016). Such upswings and downswings of the integrative capacity at different historic stages of state-civil society relations seem to point to a dialectical reading of some of Gramsci's core

---

17 Bourdieu refuses to provide a substantial or definite definition of who and what kind of practice actually counts as "intellectual". He assumes the historical development of a relatively autonomous "intellectual field" with its own specific laws and principles of capital distribution, especially that of a symbolic kind. Though the "currency" of this capital is somewhat difficult to measure, Bourdieu (1990) emphasises that it cannot be expressed in commercial terms in the first place. More important is the recognition indicated through publications, citations, awards, appointments to academies, and so forth. An "intellectual" is then an actor who is included in and operates in the intellectual field.

concepts. Just as there are conjunctures where the economy is "embedded" and "disembedded" from society (Polanyi 1944), the "enwrapping" of civil society by the state in one political and economic conjuncture can turn into "unwrapping" in the next. Identifying the limits of the integrating effects of state-civil society relations in certain conjunctures is of great strategic significance, as each new regime of state-civil society relations corresponds with new openings for oppositional movements. This would imply dedicating more time and energy to civil society organisations such as churches, trade unions, unemployment initiatives, but also to fighting counterstrategies on the part of the dominant, for example, in the form of lobbying or climate emergency denial.

Following Gramsci, a degrowth strategy oriented around state-civil society relationships would need to be built on a combination of the theoretical knowledge of "organic intellectuals" of various kinds and the practical knowledge of subaltern groups engaged in a range of oppositional practices and struggles. To unite both sorts of knowledge, Bourdieu (2003) highlights the importance of joint practical and deliberative exercises as measures of "countertraining". These have the best chance of gaining critical amounts of support if they are tied up with traits of *habitus* that have become blocked over the course of socialisation and daily life (Koch 2020b) and can help extend social spaces in which the growth imperative and the associated values of status, competition and performance become neutralised.

One example of such collaboration between researchers, activists and other citizens is the deliberative citizen forum. In an ongoing research project, Jayeon Lindelle, Johanna Alkan-Olsson and I explore how these may be used to identify alternative and sustainable needs satisfiers as well as form the foundation for policy (Koch *et al.* 2021; Koch 2021). While such forums are by definition locally and temporally specific, their outcomes have, in different social contexts, helped to critically review policy goals, behaviours, needs satisfiers, and infrastructures, and led to adaptations in long-term policy planning (Guillén-Royo 2015). To awaken the capacities of individuals to free play and alternative thinking and to promote opportunities for mutual learning, these forums should be organised in an atmosphere as welcoming, open, and participatory as possible. This implies mixed-methods approaches beyond panel-style "exchanges of arguments" including workshops, storytelling, as well as performative methods including filming and theatre.

Taking forward a critical perspective of the state in degrowth strategies

There are four strategic implications for degrowth strategising arising from this discussion of state-civil society relationships. First, a degrowth strategy exclusively targeted at (certain areas of) civil society and not the state – or indeed vice versa – is bound to fail, because state and civil society are interconnected in myriad ways, that is, the internal structures and struggles within one are significantly co-produced by corresponding processes in the other. Bourdieu's notion of social fields with specific logics, rules, interests, forms of capital and positions is a useful specification of the rather vague notion of "civil society". Second, my plea to include the state as a central arena in degrowth activism does not mean to underestimate the risk of co-optation of civil society movements by state bureaucracies. Third, to avoid this, it is crucial that the connection of movements outside the state with their representatives within it does not weaken but indeed strengthens over time. More efforts may be dedicated to scenarios and methods where interaction and feedback between holders of public office and their electoral base could be facilitated and intensified.[18]

Finally, when it comes to broadening the social base of the degrowth movement, it would make sense to better develop eco-social policies through alternative spaces such as deliberative forums

---

18 These may include the limitation of public office to a certain amount of years and the complimenting of institutions of representative democracy with elements of direct democracy, such as deliberative citizens' forums.

between activists, researchers and citizens. It is not only single policy suggestions that are of importance here, but also their potential integration into a new "virtuous policy circle" (Hirvilammi 2020). A useful entry point is the already initiated constructive dialogue with Green New Deal proposals (Mastini et al. 2021). This could be further developed by considering a temporal dimension of social-ecological transformation, involving a short-term (in the context of the COVID-19-crisis), mid-term (including a phase-out of the most emission-intensive industries; Eckersley 2021) and long-term perspective (transformation to a provisioning economy of use-values serving as sustainable needs satisfiers). Further strategic gains could also be made by considering appropriate governance networks and divisions of labour across actors (such as private and civil society actors, commons and the state) and scales (EU, national, local). A crosscutting effort could attempt to identify a limited number of key proposals with the potential for "ruptural" transformation and around which a new virtuous circle of policies could be formulated.[19]

References

Bourdieu, Pierre. 1990. "The Intellectual Field: A World Apart." In *In Other Words. Essays towards a Reflexive Sociology*, edited by Pierre Bourdieu, 140–149. Cambridge: Polity Press.

Bourdieu, Pierre. 1994. "Rethinking the State: Genesis and Structure of the Bureaucratic Field." *Sociological Theory* 12, no. 1: 1–18.

Bourdieu, Pierre. 2000. *Pascalian Meditations*. Cambridge: Cambridge University Press.

Bourdieu, Pierre. 2003. *Counterfire: Against the Tyranny of the Market 2*. London: Verso.

Bourdieu, Pierre. 2014. *On the State. Lectures at the Collège de France 1989–1992*. Cambridge: Polity.

Brand, Ulrich, and Miriam Heigl. 2011. "'Inside' and 'Outside': The State, Move-

---

19   Hubert Buch-Hansen and I suggested caps on wealth and/or income in this context (Buch-Hansen and Koch 2019).

ments and 'Radical Transformation' in the Work of Nicos Poulantzas." In *Reading Poulantzas*, edited by Alexander Gallas, Lars Bretthauer, John Kannankulam, and Ingo Stützle, 246–216. Pontypool: Merlin.

Buch-Hansen, Hubert, and Max Koch. 2019. "Degrowth Through Income and Wealth Caps?" *Ecological Economics* 160: 264–271.

Cosme, Inês, Rui Santos, and Daniel W. O'Neill. 2017. "Assessing the Degrowth Discourse: A Review and Analysis of Academic Degrowth Policy Proposals." *Journal of Cleaner Production* 149: 321–334.

Crouch, Colin. 2016. "The March towards Post-Democracy, Ten Years On." *The Political Quarterly* 87, No. 1: 71–75.

D'Alisa, Giacomo. 2019. "The State of Degrowth." In *Towards a Political Economy of Degrowth*, edited by Ekaterina Chertkovskaya; Alexander Paulsson, and Stefania Barca. London: Rowman & Littlefield.

D'Alisa, Gicacomo, and Giorgos Kallis. 2020. "Degrowth and the State." *Ecological Economics* 169, 106486.

Eckersley, Robyn. 2021. "Greening States and Societies: From Transitions to Great Transformations." *Environmental Politics* 30, no. 1–2: 245–265.

Gramsci, Antonio. 1971. *Selections from the Prison Notebooks*, edited and translated by Q. Hoare, and G. N. Smith. New York: International Publishers.

Gramsci, Antonio. 2011. *Prison Notebooks. Vol. 2.*, translated by J. A. Buttigieg. New York: Columbia University Press.

Guillen-Royo, Monica. 2015. *Sustainability and Wellbeing: Human-Scale Development in Practice*. London: Routledge.

Hirvilammi, Tuuli. 2020. "The Virtuous Circle of Sustainable Welfare as a Transformative Policy Idea." *Sustainability* 12, no. 1: 391.

Humphrys, Elizabeth. 2018. "Anti-Politics, the Early Marx and Gramsci's 'Integral State'." *Thesis Eleven* 147, no. 1: 29–44.

Jessop, Bob. 2011. "Poulantzas's State, Power and Socialism as a Modern Classic." In *Reading Poulantzas*, edited by Alexander Gallas, Lars Bretthauer, John Kannankulam, and Ingo Stützle, 41–55. Pontypool: Merlin.

Koch, Max. 2018. "The Naturalisation of Growth: Marx, the Regulation Approach and Bourdieu." *Environmental Values* 27, no. 1: 9–27.

Koch, Max. 2020a. "The State in the Transformation to a Sustainable Postgrowth Economy." *Environmental Politics* 20, no. 1: 115–133.

Koch, Max. 2020b. "Structure, Action and Change: A Bourdieusian Perspective on the Preconditions for a Degrowth Transition." *Sustainability: Science, Practice and Policy* 16, no. 1: 4–14.

Koch, Max. 2021. "Social Policy without Growth: Moving towards Sustainable Welfare States." *Social Policy and Society*: 1–13.

Koch, Max. 2022. "State-civil society Relations in Gramsci, Poulantzas and Bourdieu: Strategic Implications for the Degrowth Movement." *Ecological Economics* 193, 107275.

Koch, Max, Jayeon Lindellee, and Johanna Alkan Olsson. 2021. "Beyond the Growth Imperative and Neoliberal Doxa: Expanding Alternative Societal Spaces through Deliberative Citizen Forums on Needs Satisfaction." *Real–World Economics Review* 96: 168–183.

Mastini, Ricardo, Kallis, Giorgos, and Jason Hickel. 2021. "A Green New Deal without Growth?" *Ecological Economics* 179, 106832.

Müller, Karel B. 2006. "The Civil Society–State Relationship in Contemporary Discourse: A Complementary Account from Giddens' Perspective." *The British Journal of Politics and International Relations* 8, no. 2: 311–330.

Polanyi, Karl. 1944. *The Great Transformation. The Political and Economic Origins of Our Time*. Boston: Beacon Press.

Poulantzas, Nicos. 1978. *State, Power and Socialism*. London: NLB.

Weber, Max. 1991. "Politics as a Vocation." In *From Max Weber: Essays in Sociology*, edited by Hans Gerth and C. Wright Mills, 77–128. London: Routledge.

Wright, Erik O. 2012. "Taking the Social in Socialism Seriously." *Socio Economic Review* 10, no. 2: 386–402.

Chapter 10:

Strategic entanglements

By Susan Paulson

This book brings together explorations of strategy and plurality to address a vital question: how can progress towards degrowth goals be strengthened and coordinated without sacrificing the diversity of positions and approaches involved? Degrowth horizons are broadened by the celebration of a rainbow of knowledges, cosmologies, and vital worlds, conceptualised as components of a pluriverse. However, in contexts where institutional power favours authoritative knowledge, and where political successes are bolstered by unified positions, plurality raises all kinds of challenges.

Contributors agree that a transformation towards worlds that prioritise good living for all will require us to find points of convergence and to activate synergies among diverse positions. There is less consensus on how to do this. To date, degrowth alliances have foregrounded principles and processes, including participatory democracy, inclusion, commoning, sufficiency, conviviality, and care. Contributors to this book explore strategies to accelerate progress towards desired outcomes by expanding scales and realms of action; interconnecting different kinds of struggle; and establishing shared frameworks, goals, or measures of progress.

Recognizing that it is unlikely (and perhaps not even desirable) for degrowth to develop into a banner of massive mobilization or an umbrella coordinating diverse movements, this chapter explores possibilities of "strategic entanglements". The metaphor alludes to quantum entanglement, a physical phenomenon that occurs when a group of particles are generated, interact, or share spatial proximity such that the quantum state of each particle cannot be described independently of the others. To make such entanglements strategic, a first move is to foster mutual learning and nourishment among interlocutors and collaborators in qualitatively different positions and places. A second move is to heighten awareness of relations of power and difference among us; this encompasses concern not only that degrowth activists and thinkers might be co-opted by powerful forces, but also that other visions and pathways might be encompassed by degrowth processes.

The first part of this chapter looks at opportunities and challenges for building alliances across differences, then addresses strategies for enhancing degrowth coordination across scales, realms, and types of transformative action. Asking what forces and factors have been frustrating such efforts, the text examines hierarchical socio-cultural systems and narratives that divide and polarise potential allies. It then makes a case for heightening awareness of relative positioning and power within these systems, and for contextualising pathways and perspectives in relevant places and social groups. The conclusion looks towards more horizontal models for mutual nourishment and mobilising for change.

Possibilities and challenges of alliances among diversely empowered positions and paths

People in different positions and contexts are exploring degrowth as a field of research, a network of social movements, a community of scholar-activists, a way of life, or a vision for desirable futures. An even broader range of people and movements may contribute to – and benefit from – degrowth, including nature-lovers, care providers, local governments, diverse workers' organisations, fighters for environmental justice, overworked professionals, vegans, hippies, families with children, biking fanatics, unemployed people, people employed in exploitative and harmful jobs, climate refugees, back-to-the-landers, senior citizens, people engaged in anti-colonial and anti-capitalist movements, members of low-income communities, feminists, and anti-racists (Kallis *et al.* 2020, 98). How can relations among some of these contribute more strategically towards desired outcomes?

There are moments for raising a big tent, jumping into indeterminate relations with all, and striving to treat everyone the same. This chapter, however, foregrounds lessons from degrowth analyses and initiatives that explicitly recognise and respect differences, and that attend conscientiously to power dynamics among them. Human biology, socio-cultural practice, and changing environments continually interact to create astonishingly diverse ways of being human. These forms of diversity – within and among societies – are essential to vitality and adaptation in human history. However, while differences among humans are good and necessary, systems that differentiate people in hierarchical and exploitative ways limit progress towards goals of care and equitable wellbeing. As chapters 1 and 7 argue, societies organised around the capitalist growth imperative have been built on, and now function to reinforce, social relations in which life opportunities and spaces of action, assets, and income are distributed in brutally uneven ways.

Strategic entanglements explicitly recognise the class, gender, colonial, and ethno-racial systems that categorise people into those unequal relationships and attend to ways in which these systems constrain and contaminate attempts at alliance-building. Experiences of mutual exchange across differently empowered knowledges and beings can nourish the adoption of healthier and more equitable socio-cultural systems (Paulson 2019). The promising news is that possibilities for innovative moves towards degrowth objectives are opened by historical crises including climate breakdown and pandemics that destabilise established orders. In chapter 9, social theory is mobilised to illuminate ways to seize such historic opportunities for social and structural change.

Beware, however, that eco-social crises also nourish reactionary alliances. As current troubles threaten the status quo, identity categories are being strategically mobilised to polarise potential allies and limit capacities to envision and enact systemic change. For example, scientists calling to limit CO_2 emissions and other forms of ecological damage are construed as elite antagonists to workers demanding jobs and security. Rather than choose sides, degrowth advocates are pursuing strategies ranging from patient listening and dialogue among opposing actors to applications of Green New Deals, job guarantees, and universal basic incomes that support viable livelihoods and sustainable ecosystems as inseparable objectives (Lawhon and McCreary 2020).

While those who deny climate change differ from those who advocate green growth via ecomodernism and geoengineering, their strategies and motives interconnect in powerful ways: they are similarly constituted by mostly white men positioned in the Global North, and their proposals are designed to avoid changing – or even questioning – the hierarchical social systems that sustain economies based on uneven distribution of benefits and burdens (Paulson and Boose 2019; Paulson 2021; see also Chapter 7). These and other actors strategically unite under banners of political-economic stability and defence of geopolitical interests in campaigns to delegitimise calls to curb growth, respond to COVID-19, and address systemic racism, sexism, and economic inequality.

On all these fronts, resistance to change is fuelled by an understandable fear of losing personal identities and relationships. Although conservative ideologies portray current roles and relations as determined by nature (and, for many of us, they come to *feel* natural), historical analyses show that they have been created by evolving societies (and adapted to support growth). The liberating empirical record shows that human identities and relations change historically and can certainly be made more equitable and reciprocal through human creativity and action. One example of strategic entanglements supporting systemic change is dialogue among radical environmentalists, eco-feminists, and masculinities on reasons and opportunities for people of all identities to adapt gender expectations and relations that are healthier for themselves, as well as for human and non-human others (Hultman and Pulé 2019; MenEngage 2022).

Interconnecting initiatives across scales and realms

To date, much attention to degrowth praxis has focused on local initiatives such as community gardens, time banks, maker spaces, and bike-repair cooperatives. In *Degrowth in Movement(s): Exploring Pathways for Transformation*, Burkhart et al. (2020) draw on participatory case studies to explore the exercise of agency in a mosaic of eco-social movements whose shared focus on emancipatory practice coexists in tension with challenging differences around moral frameworks, relations with capitalism, and organisational dynamics. In Chapter 6, lessons from this collaborative experience, including observations of unexpected synergies among local movements that lead to broader changes, are applied to challenges of moving towards degrowth – in activist communities as well as broader societies.

There is more contention around the potential of local initiatives to interconnect with social, educational, and governmental institutions operating on regional and national levels. In debates documented by Gómez-Baggethun (2020), some degrowth advocates insist that small ventures with convivial technologies are the only way to move beyond hierarchy and exploitation, while others support re-orienting large-scale industrial technologies towards healthier ends. Demmer and Hummel (2017) describe efforts to support mutual learning about degrowth across grassroots experiments and formal university training, where ways of knowing and interrelating sometimes seem incommensurable. How can we activate more synergies across these gaps and power structures?

Chapter 9 makes the case for moving beyond civil society to engage state-level actors and actions, stressing that the two realms are more intertwined than is recognised by many who reject working with state-led programmes or institutions. Other contributors to this book explore the potential for mutual benefit among Erik Olin Wright's three modes of transformation. Chertkovskaya (Chapter 2) makes a case for engaging them all by continuing interstitial action at the core of degrowth, expanding symbiotic work to adapt institutional conditions for radical possibilities, and provoking localised and temporal ruptures in dominant systems. Chapter 2 also emphasises the dangers of degrowth energy being coopted by powerful funds, forces, and bureaucracies that actually function to sustain the status quo.

To that concern, I add a warning to think critically when applying the conceptual vocabulary of evaluation that is prominent in contemporary strategising. Measures of "effectiveness," defined as the degree to which efforts are successful in producing targeted results, and "efficiency", the achievement of results with the least amount of resources (money, time, material, and energy), have become political and technical priorities in national and international development industries, foregrounded in United Nations Sustainable Development Goals, the Intergovernmental Panel on Climate Change, and similar programmes. In contrast, local, organic, or grassroots collectives often find these measures antagonistic to the above-mentioned principles of inclusion, participatory democracy, commoning, and caring. While calculations of efficiency and effectiveness may, for example, favour a group vote followed by action on the majority decision, such procedures could jeopardise opportunities to build consensus amid long hours of listening to, thinking about, and experimenting with deeply different visions and approaches. Recognition of such differently empowered logics for advancing and measuring success connects with discussions in Chapter 3 of relations between means and ends, between processes and goals, in degrowth strategy.

Logics of prefiguration guide many small-scale efforts with expectations that, as degrowth-supporting practices and relations circulate and take root in everyday practice and culture, they ripen conditions for the emergence of correlating expressions on other scales and structures. It can be hard to maintain faith that ideas and energy developed in a neighbourhood cooperative contribute to shifts in global power structures, in the way that a butterfly flapping its wings sets off a chain of events leading to a distant hurricane. Yet, there is increasing evidence that degrowth critiques and objectives are generating tension within mainstream politics and gaining prominence in parallel forums such as the Green New Deal for Europe, the EU Parliament's Post-Growth Conference, Latin America's Pacto Ecosocial del Sur, and the African Green Stimulus Programme.

In recent years, many of us have been surprised to see ideas and policies long-discussed and experimented with within so-called "alternative" forums emerge on larger scales and power structures. For example, degrowth's objective of reorienting societies around equitable wellbeing – rather than economic growth – has gained traction among participants in the Wellbeing Economy Alliance, including leaders of Finland, Iceland, New Zealand, Scotland, and Wales, who have pledged to prioritise wellbeing in future policies. Amid the COVID-19 pandemic, a range of governments have been experimenting with policies proposed in the 2020 books *The Case for Degrowth* and *Less is More*: Green New Deals, basic care incomes, job guarantees, reduced labour hours, public services, and support for community economies. In moves to "build back better," the transformative potential of these policies depends on the extent to which they are institutionalised as support for wellbeing and regeneration of human and natural resources, rather than as stimuli for economic growth. Chapter 2 points to an example of what symbiotic transformation might look like in an EU reoriented around wellbeing and sustainability, rather than growth, while Chapter 9 emphasises the potential to strengthen the impact of individual policies by integration into new policy cycles, such as a Green New Deal.

Yet, as Chapter 3 makes clear, the implemented policies are still far from those called for in the open letter *Degrowth, new roots for the economy* and the *Feminist degrowth statement on the COVID-19 pandemic*. And evidence to date suggests mixed outcomes from the implementation of promising policies within pandemic relief packages, driven by pushes to reignite economic growth. Hickel

(2020) documents huge benefits to asset owners and corporations (exemplified by Amazon), steep increases in billionaire wealth and devastating losses for the poorest 50% of humanity. In the US, moreover, governmental responses to the pandemic have included dismantling – rather than increasing – environmental protections.

Seeking ways to interact more constructively with institutions, governments, and large-scale initiatives, I now turn to underlying structures that have been operating to constrain or co-opt such collaborations.

Addressing hierarchical relations among positions and places

Differences of scale and realm, like differences of position and identity, are never innocent of power. In contemporary societies, power operates through historically specific hierarchical binaries that have been disseminated with colonial capitalism and globalisation, and internalised (or resisted) in various ways around the world. In currently predominant paradigms, superiority and domination of humans over other nature are conceptually and structurally interconnected with coloniser over colonised, white over non-white, man over woman, hetero-normative over queer, owner/executive over worker, and nation-state over community.

The abilities of government leaders, sustainability professionals, and green growth advocates to question the domination of humans over other nature have been curbed by their positions and roots in this paradigm. Of course, critical awareness could be activated via alliances with eco-feminist, anti-colonial, anti-racist and other movements that address interconnected hierarchies. Unfortunately, however, powerful institutions of knowledge production have been operating in ways that construe these perspectives as less valid than mainstream science, and that marginalise their topics – gender relations or racialisation, for example – as irrelevant to economic and ecological knowledge.

At the confluence of critiques of humans-over-nature and critiques of coloniser-over-colonised, conversations about degrowth offer ways towards deeper interrogation of these historical structures. Since its earliest articulations, *decroissance*/degrowth diverged from mainstream development and environmental stances by seeking ways for "developed" societies, positioned as colonisers, to reduce our negative impacts on other people and environments, starting with efforts to decolonise our own minds from the growth imperative and to examine our own ambitions and exploitations before intervening to fix the rest of the world (Gorz 1980; Illich 1974; Latouche 1986; and Mosangini 2012).

To honour this tradition, current concerns that degrowth may be co-opted by stronger forces must be accompanied by concerns about degrowth co-opting allied actors and movements. Dengler and Seebacher (2019, 247) make that message clear in response to common misconceptions: "degrowth is not to be misunderstood as a proposal from the Global North imposed on the Global South, but rather a Northern supplement to Southern concepts, movements and lines of thought. It is therefore imperative for degrowth to seek alliances with these Southern 'fellow travellers'".

In sum, alliances among fellow travellers working towards degrowth, decolonisation, deracialisation, and depatriarchisation synergise to resist the ongoing imposition of certain universal models. In complementary processes, mutual learning among travellers forging healthier identities and paths nourish what the Zapatistas call "a world that encompasses many worlds".

Across places and social groups

Degrowth strategies have long involved active learning from – and with – groups struggling to sustain old and to forge new paths away from growth (Gezon and Paulson 2017). This includes conversations with participants in ecological swaraj in India, ubuntu in South Africa, Gross National Happiness in Bhutan, and millennial Christian traditions of simple communal life, revitalised in contexts ranging from North American spiritual communities to Latin American responses to Pope Francis' *On Care for our Common Home* (Beling and Vanhulst 2019).

Escobar (2015) points to a convergence between degrowth in the North and post-development in Latin America. Emerging from different intellectual traditions and operating through different epistemic and political practices, they similarly combine radical questioning of economic expansionism with visions of alternative worlds that prioritise ecological integrity and social justice. Yet, even sincere commitments to dialogue across these differences meet obstacles. In interviews with environmental justice activists, Rodríguez-Labajos and colleagues found that "in parts of Africa, Latin America and many other regions of the Global South, including poor and marginalised communities in Northern countries, the term degrowth is not appealing, and does not match people's demands" (2019, 177).

These observations raise strategic challenges around vocabulary. We start by acknowledging that decades of degrowth research has produced universalising analyses of the global economy couched in Western scientific logic and expressed through specialised jargon – including the word degrowth itself. This awareness supports a conscious pivot in communication among actors with different logics and vocabularies when it comes to building strategies, defined in this book as thought constructs, with associated actions, embedded in a specific context. Chapter 7, "Why social equity is the key to degrowth," nourishes such efforts.

Another challenge raised here is to recognise differences *within* regions and groups. Amid current global dependencies, for example, many governments and households welcome access to income from international agribusinesses, sweatshops, electronic waste, and other ventures. At the same time, the 3,555 conflicts documented to date in the Environmental Justice Atlas demonstrate that many people living with very low incomes organise to resist initiatives for economic development, including mines, dams, oil-wells, ranches, factories, plantations, and highways. Participants in the global network *Feminisms and Degrowth Alliance* struggle with ways to respond to structural positions, while recognising that not all colonised people (nor all women, all whites, all Global North or South, etc.) can be understood as a single position or voice. Although racism has been explicitly recognised by environmental justice scholars and activists, serious work still needs to be done on the roles that racialisation and white privilege play in dynamics that drive growth, as well as in those that may support just and equitable degrowth (Tyberg 2020).

Valuable lessons can be learned from different logics and dynamics of change-making. For decades, for example, small farmers in various parts of the world have collaborated to forge alternatives to the green revolution by drawing on local knowledges, ritual agroecology practices, and environmental management regimes less based on the domination of humans over other nature. Slowly, through reciprocal visits, participatory gatherings, and other interactions, hundreds of nodes have been woven into horizontal networks of mutual learning and action, such as La Via Campesina (La Via Campesina n.d.) and *Movimiento Agroecológico* Campesino-a-Campesino (FAO 2015).

Soil made fertile with these alliances has nurtured reciprocal care and given rise to direct actions to resist extractivist expansion. In Latin America, conceptualizations of *Sumak Kawsay/Buen Vivir* have influenced programmes, policies, and even national constitutions that institutionalise the rights of nature. These impulses have not played out free from conflict and contradictions of political power. Chapter 2 provides tools to think about these processes as strategies that not only seek to *escape* degrading relations and systems of production, but also interact to build forms of *resistance* to the development of industry, and perhaps lead to *taming* or *dismantling* aspects of global food systems. These hope-giving processes encounter stubborn constraints in landscapes marked by inequitable power systems. No matter how vibrant and constructive, alliances of small producers around the world are a long way from halting degrading incursions into their territories and lives by extractivist governments and corporations.

Horizontal mobilising for multi-scale political change

More horizontal models for strengthening coordination and impact can help to contextualise and to question worldviews colonised by hierarchies and divided by differences. Valuable examples are found in networks and roots that Indigenous, marginalised, and other people have built as both ends and means to defend diverse lifeworlds.

Nirmal and Rocheleau (2019) offer metaphors of rootstocks that extend on or under the soil surface and develop mutually nourishing nodes from which new shoots extend vertically, exemplified by rhizomes, through which plants like bamboo and poison ivy reproduce and expand. The *Call to Participate in the 8th International Degrowth Conference in The Hague (2021), Caring Communities for Radical Change* (Undisciplined Environments 2021), creatively combined the organic metaphor of mycelium, the body of mushrooms and other fungi, with the mandala, the ancient symbol of wholeness.

> Our mycelium mandala represents the vegetative part of a fungus; it is known for being full of life – connecting a rapidly developing underground system. Mycelia play a crucial role in the decomposition of old forms of life. They decompose dead organic matter, making nutrients available again for the system and its growing life forms. It is a wonderful emblem for degrowth, a social movement that ranges from ecology to spirituality (from the soil to the soul).

Degrowth rootstocks can be nourished by enhancing synergies already operating among values, visions, and actions that are harboured and circulated through subterranean networks. One network that is self-organised in non-hierarchical ways – degrowth. info – writes in Chapter 5 about creating spaces for coordination, exchange, and learning within the degrowth movement. Such efforts prepare the ground for activating more visible sprouts of cultural, civic, and political action in response to openings that emerge from unexpected events and cracks in the system. This type of network-building is hard to eradicate. Even when visible ventures are frustrated, pieces of rhizome or mycelia – in this case, degrowth values, practices, and relationships – are left behind in the soil where they grow and emerge in new manifestations.

Such are dynamics fostered by the "Global Tapestry of Alternatives", dedicated to creating inclusive horizontal spaces of exchange and solidarity among widely ranging alternatives to dominant regimes driven by capitalist, patriarchal, racist, statist, and anthropocentric forces. By activating diverse logics, languages, and other ways of communicating, participants weave together already existing communal or collective webs, join in regional and global encounters, and develop synergistic linkages with organisations like the *World Social Forum*.

Conclusion

Degrowth visions and actions are nourished by and take root among many practices and contexts, ranging from long-established spiritual beliefs and everyday life in low-income communities to major research institutions and political leadership. Contributors to this book push for more strategic interactions among scales, realms, and types of action in order to support progress towards emancipatory social-ecological transformation. Yet, even amid passionately shared purposes, collaborations are constrained and sometimes derailed by tensions between pushes to better coordinate towards desired outcomes and the plurality of perspectives, logics, and plans involved.

To support constructive engagement across positions, places, and scales, this chapter does not encourage degrowth advocates to take centralised control of process and direction, nor does it suggest engaging with all comers in indeterminate interactions. Instead, this chapter explores ongoing practices and potentials of specific types of interactions across difference: entanglements that strategically engage in instructive dialogues across places and social groups, strategically acknowledge positioning within hierarchical systems of power, and strategically build horizontal alliances nourished through mutual flows of ideas and resources.

Conceptual and analytic tools developed in Part I of this book, together with attention to power and difference in alliances of mutual learning encouraged by this chapter, are designed to strengthen thought and action around a variety of initiatives. Tangible cases and efforts presented in the next section, Part II, offer opportunities to connect these insights with cases and efforts involving money, finance, trade, decolonisation, housing, food, agriculture, energy, technology, and more.

References

Beling, Adrián and Julien Vanhulst, eds. 2019. *Desarrollo non sancto: La religión como actor emergente en el debate global sobre el futuro del planeta*. México: Siglo XXI.

Burkhart, Corinna, Matthias Schmelzer, and Nina Treu, eds. 2020. *Degrowth in Movement(s): Exploring Pathways for Transformation*. Alresford, UK: John Hunt Publishing.

Dengler, Corinna, and Lisa M. Seebacher. 2019. "What about the Global South? Towards a Feminist Decolonial Degrowth Approach". *Ecological Economics* 157 (March): 246–252.

Demmer, Ulrich, and Agata Hummel. 2017. "Degrowth, Anthropology, and Activist Research: The Ontological Politics of Science." *Journal of Political Ecology* 24, no. 1: 610–622.

Escobar, Arturo. 2015. "Degrowth, Postdevelopment, and Transitions: A Preliminary Conversation." *Sustainability Science* 10 (April): 451–62.

FAO. 2015. *Plataforma de conocimientos sobre agricultura familiar. Escuela Campesina Multimedia*. https://www.fao.org/family-farming/detail/es/c/345402/.

Gezon, Lisa L., and Susan Paulson, eds. 2017. "Special Section: Degrowth, Culture and Power." *Journal of Political Ecology* 24, no. 1: 425–666.

Gómez-Baggethun, Erik. 2020. "More is More: Scaling Political Ecology within Limits to Growth." *Political Geography* 76 (January).

Gorz, André. 1980. *Ecology as Politics*. New York: Black Rose Books.

Hickel, Jason. 2020. "What Does Degrowth Mean? A Few Points of Clarification."

Globalizations 18, no. 7: 1105–1111.

Hultman, Martin and Paul Pulé. 2019. *Ecological Masculinities Theoretical Foundations and Practical Guidance.* London, UK: Routledge.

Illich, Ivan. 1974. *Energy and Equity.* London, UK: Calder and Boyars, Ltd.

Kallis, Giorgos, Susan Paulson, Giacomo D'Alisa, and Federico Demaria. 2020. *The Case for Degrowth.* Cambridge, UK: Polity Press.

Latouche, Serge. 1986. *Faut-il refuser le développement?: Essai sur l'anti-économique du tiers–monde.* Paris, France: Presses Universitaires de France.

La Via Campesina. n.d. *La Via Campesina. International Peasants' Movement.* https://viacampesina.org/en.

Lawhon, Mary, and Tyler McCreary. 2020. "Beyond Jobs vs Environment: On the Potential of Universal Basic Income to Reconfigure Environmental Politics." *Antipode* 52, no. 2 (March): 452–474.

MenEngage. 2022. *MenEngage. Working with Men and Boys for Gender Equality.* http://menengage.org.

Mosangini, Giorgio. 2012. *Decrecimiento y justicia norte-sur: O cómo evitar que el norte global condene a la humanidad al colapso.* Barcelona, Spain: Icaria Editorial.

Nirmal, Padini, and Dianne Rocheleau. 2019. "Decolonizing Degrowth in the Post-Development Convergence: Questions, Experiences, and Proposals from Two Indigenous Territories." *Nature and Space* 2, no. 3 (May): 465–492.

Paulson, Susan. 2019. "Pluriversal Learning: Pathways towards a World of Many Worlds." *Nordia Geographical Publications Yearbook 2018 Affirmative Political Ecology* 47 no. 5: 85–109.

Paulson, Susan. 2021. "Decolonising Technology and Political Ecology Futures." *Political Geography* 88 (June).

Paulson, Susan, and Will Boose. 2019. Masculinities and Environment. *Centre for Agriculture and Bioscience International Reviews* 14, no. 30 (October): 1–12.

Pope Francis. 2015. *Laudato si' on care for our common home.* Vatican City, Italy: Encyclical Letter, Librería Editrice Vaticana.

Rodríguez-Labajos, Beatriz, Ivonne Yánez, Patrick Bond, Lucie Greyl, Serah Munguti, Godwin Uyi Ojo, and Winfridus Overbeek. 2019. "Not So Natural an Alliance? Degrowth and Environmental Justice Movements in the Global South." *Ecological Economics* 157 (March): 175–184.

Tyberg, Jamie. 2020. "From Degrowth to Decolonization." *The Ecologist* (June). https://theecologist.org/2020/jun/12/degrowth-decolonisation.

Undisciplined Environments. 2021. "Call open for 8th International Degrowth Conference (The Hague, NL, 24–28 August)." *Undisciplined Environments* (blog), February 11, 2021. https://undisciplinedenvironments.org/2021/02/11/call-open-for-8th-international-degrowth-conference-the-hague-nl-24-28-august/.

PART II

Strategies in practice

Provisioning sectors

Chapter 11: Food

An overview of strategies for social-ecological transformation in the field of food

By Christina Plank[20]

Food is a basic need but also a driver of injustice globally. On the one hand, food provisioning is necessary for our survival on the planet. On the other hand, the current corporate food regime contributes to environmental decline and social disruptions. The climate crisis and the tremendous loss of biodiversity, land grabs, or farmers' protests are just some examples of these developments (Franco and Borras 2013; Plank *et al.* under review; van der Ploeg 2020). Food is crucial for degrowth and the degrowth movement for several reasons. First, degrowth advocates for putting the basic needs of people at the core of the economy and policies. Second, degrowth literature and activists often refer to food because there are a lot of food-related projects in degrowth practices (Nelson and Edwards 2021; Vandeventer *et al.* 2018). Third, people who are not part of the degrowth movement can easily relate to food activities connected to degrowth. This can be and is helpful in getting more people engaged with initiatives working towards social-ecological transformation.

The following contribution gives an overview of what strategies can be adopted to foster degrowth's food agenda. Food is here understood to cover all parts of the food system, i.e., the production, distribution and consumption of food. In order to analyse the existing literature on food and degrowth, I draw on the approach to degrowth strategy suggested by Chertkovskaya (Chapter 2). Chertkovskaya applies Erik Olin Wright's (2010) framework of ruptural, interstitial, and symbiotic modes of transformation to the degrowth movement. In particular, she emphasises the role of

---

20 I would like to thank the editor and the reviewer of this chapter for their helpful comments. This research was funded in part by the Austrian Science Fund (FWF) (ZK–64G).

ruptural strategies in their temporal and small-scale dimension, which would also need to be considered to facilitate interstitial and symbiotic strategies. Drawing on this literature, I differentiate strategic logics and highlight what actors, places, times, and scales are involved in them. Since most food initiatives employ several strategies, this is an ideal-typical typology. However, this reflection on the different foci of the movement can help with getting a clearer picture of where the emphasis of food-related practices is today and how they could be developed in the future.

Escaping capitalism by building alternatives and resistance

Most food initiatives mentioned in the degrowth literature (e.g., Kallis and March 2015; Nelson and Edwards 2021; Brossmann and Islar 2019) can be assigned to strategies that build alternatives on the local level such as urban gardening initiatives, food cooperatives, community-supported agriculture, or eco-villages. By building these local alternatives they try to escape capitalist structures and are therefore interstitial strategies. These initiatives are linked to degrowth principles such as autonomy, commoning, or conviviality (Nelson and Edwards 2021) and are practised within a rather small community. Usually, they are locally anchored, grassroots-driven, and can be found at the urban or peri-urban scale.

These food alternatives exist in all parts of Europe, but not all actors involved identify themselves as belonging to the degrowth movement and some are not familiar with the idea of degrowth. This is particularly the case for self-food-provisioning practices in Central Europe. Daněk and Jehlička (2021) have characterised these practices as "quiet" because they are not perceived as a form of activism, but rather they draw on a long tradition of allotments and home gardens. Whereas in degrowth initiatives actors are rather young and middle-class, the self-food-provisioning practices are socially more inclusive because they are carried out by a wider public, i.e., in the case of the Czech Republic by almost 40% of households. However, these households do not aim for changing the economic system but rather see it as a leisure activity (Daněk and Jehlička 2021). Despite criticisms such as those claiming that gardening cannot be considered a political action, initiatives like urban gardening can function as political work towards social-ecological transformation. For example, by cultivating vegetables and experiencing change in the city, degrowth can be practised and lived (Müller 2020). It can furthermore be perceived as a practical example of decommodification that establishes alternative provisioning systems outside of capitalist markets, which is a central element of degrowth.

Furthermore, it is important to note that these food initiatives are often connected to other activities that respond to the fulfilment of basic needs; in other words, different provisioning systems are or can be linked with each other. This is for example the case for co-housing projects that include food shops or shared cooking responsibilities among the different co-housing partners. These shared responsibilities can imply time-saving possibilities where the time gained could be used, for example, for relaxation or taking better care of children (Lietaert 2010). How the patriarchal organisation of society and in this way reproductive work influences alternative projects like food cooperatives, however, still needs to be better explored (Homs et al. 2021).

Such food initiatives, i.e., urban gardening initiatives, food coops, Community Supported Agriculture (CSA), eco-villages, are often considered to be niche projects. Even if these practices are shared with allied movements, such as the movement for food sovereignty which the case study below focuses on, there is, first of all the challenge to merely exist and survive within the capitalist system and, second, the danger of staying in a niche. Some alternative food networks like CSA initiatives in Austria do not aim to get out of their niche because they do not have the necessary economic, political and time resources (Plank et al. 2020). Perhaps some even prefer to remain small-scale because it makes it easier to maintain a relaxed atmosphere, trust-based cooperation or to make decisions.

Others, in turn, try to engage with municipalities to create a wider impact such as in the case of urban food councils or other public procurement initiatives (see again the case study below). Overall, there is a rather strong focus on the individual, household level, on movements, and on networks (Nelson and Edwards, 2021). There is a void in the literature on regional and national levels, in that the literature does not address the role of the state, with the exception of the case of Cuban agriculture. Biollat *et al.* (2012) argue that theoretically, the Cuban economy is better suited for degrowth agroecology than capitalist economies because the accumulation of capital is restricted. However, they also point out that Cuban agroecology would work even better with more democracy, providing more rights to small-scale farmers' cooperatives.

Resisting capitalism has not been the focus of the literature on food and degrowth but has been dealt with in critical agrarian studies. This literature explores movements against land grabbing and land concentration in Europe and in the Global South, activism for food and seed sovereignty and against genetically modified organisms, or forms of "everyday resistance" of peasants (Franco and Borras 2013; Scott, 1986; Peschard and Randeria 2020; Larsson 2016; Hall *et al.* 2015). Here, it is social movements, often from the Global South, who resist displacement and the destruction of their livelihoods. This is triggered by a form of agro-industrial development that dominates the corporate food regime (McMichael 2009). However, resistance can also take place in the Global North. An example of this, explored by the case study below, is the cooperative in Mals in South Tyrol which stood up against the use of pesticides via a referendum. More attention should thus be paid to these different possible forms of resistance to advance degrowth.

Taming and dismantling capitalism

Symbiotic strategies can only be found in the literature that uses degrowth as an analytical framework. The modes of transformation of taming and dismantling capitalism are directed towards changing institutions from within the capitalist system. In the case of degrowth and food, they have been connected to the shaping of different policies. For example, degrowth has been used as a framework to investigate the European Union's policies, including food policies, through a degrowth lens, such as examining the extent to which the European Green Deal is driven by green growth (Ossewaarde and Ossewaarde-Lowtoo 2020). Likewise, the concept of "blue degrowth" has served to critically analyse the European Union's fisheries policies oriented towards blue growth, namely, considering the sea as a potential site of economic growth (Hadjimichael 2018). Yet, degrowth has so far not been used for developing alternative food policies, and concrete suggestions for how to transform and dismantle food policies are absent in the literature.

Concrete suggestions for transforming policies, however, have been advanced by allies of the degrowth movement, for example, the movement for food sovereignty (Salzer and Fehlinger 2020; see also the case study below). As an intervention into the negotiations of the European Union's Common Agricultural Policy – crucial for defining the conditions of the food system – food sovereignty movement actors recently called for doubling the amount of money received as a direct payment for the first 20 hectares of farmland (ÖBV 2021). This would ensure access to land for small-scale farmers in the European Union and help regulate the agricultural system. With respect to policy suggestions that do not only tame but also dismantle the system, the cooperation among different actors from different fields like the scientific community, social movement, and practitioners would be crucial to advance different strategies – as exemplified by the International Panel of Experts on Sustainable Food Systems (IPES-Food) (see the case study below).

An interesting example at the national scale is the commitment of the French Ministry of Agriculture to agroecology (France. Ministry of Agriculture 2016). Here, the aim is to assist the majority of farmers to make the transition to agroecology by 2025. If radically performed, this could lead to dismantling current structures. Another example comes from the Indian state of Sikkim, which already transitioned to 100% organic agriculture through policy changes by phasing out chemical fertilisers and pesticides and banning the latter from the state (Heindorf 2019). By learning from these examples, the degrowth movement could not only expand its strategic toolkit but also explore how niche projects can be scaled up.

Future research and strategy building would benefit from an even stronger tie with the food sovereignty movement and critical agrarian studies. In this way, the degrowth movement could consider strategies that operate beyond the local scale, and more diverse transformational strategies could be employed. From an academic perspective, Gerber (2020) has pointed out that a mutual exchange between scientific communities would be desirable. By referring to "agrarian degrowth", he points to a possible common research agenda. This could entail researching how economic growth has shaped the countryside, how social metabolism shapes biophysical limits and the role of building alliances with social movements. Furthermore, from a global perspective, the role of Indigenous people would be particularly important to consider regarding non-growth oriented alternative imaginaries and food practices.

Halting and smashing capitalism

Ruptural strategies are characterised by actions that seek to halt or smash capitalism. Chertkovskaya (Chapter 2) refers to acts of disobedience as examples of halting capitalism, while she uses the example of occupying and running a factory to illustrate what smashing capitalism can look like. Both of these modes of transformation have not been focused on much in the literature on degrowth and food, nor have they been explored much in the degrowth movement. Yet, the occupation of fields, often as a temporal activity, can be thought of as a ruptural strategy for halting capitalism. For instance, in Austria, the collective, *SoliLa!* (*Solidarisch Landwirtschaften*) has reclaimed some fields in Vienna to gain access to land for growing vegetables. By occupying fields the collective further problematises land speculation and the increasing rate of sealing of soil – the covering up of soil through, for example, concretisation or urban development (Möhrs *et al.* 2013). In France near Nantes, local farmers and activists have squatted an agricultural area that was intended for the development of an airport for several decades. They also built local alternatives on the ground (Pieper 2013). As Chertkovskaya points out, these small-scale, temporary ruptural actions can enable or support further interstitial strategies, for example, land occupation can provide access to land.

Where different structures of oppression (such as capitalism, but also colonialism and extractivism) come into play, land questions have been pressing, and ruptural strategies have been employed on a long-term basis. Here, the landless workers' movement in Brazil (MST, for *Movimento dos Trabalhadores Sem Terra* in Portuguese) is certainly one of the best-known examples of fighting against capitalism through occupying land (Hammond and Rossi 2013). In view of the deepening climate crisis, social-ecological issues, and problems related to the access, ownership, and use of land will also become acute in the Global North. The urgency to fight not only *for* alternative ways of food systems but also, for example, *against* the sealing of soil or increasing CO_2 emissions through aviation as the cases of *SoliLa* or Nantes have shown, are already clear contemporary examples of initiatives that will become even more prevalent in the future. More generally, there will be a need to grapple with the dynamics and challenges associated with urban sprawl, which is followed by more traffic as well as more infrastructure like shops and supermarkets. Hence, there will be increasing emissions but less soil available for agriculture, water retention, or carbon sequestration; all of which will become even more important with the exacerbating climate crisis. Stronger alliances with the climate justice movement and social movements from the Global South would not only broaden the spectrum of strategies but would also allow these movements to better support each other in re-structuring the economic and political system towards a global degrowth society.

Conclusion

To summarise, most degrowth food initiatives can be seen as interstitial strategies that build alternatives on the local, urban and peri-urban level, which do not necessarily aim to scale up. The state represents almost a void in the literature on degrowth and food. Symbiotic strategies can only be found in the literature where degrowth serves as an analytical framework, but where this framework is not used for developing alternative policy proposals. Ruptural strategies for transformation are absent in degrowth and food literature. Within academia, the degrowth community could be more engaged with critical agrarian studies, particularly for exploring symbiotic strategies, which aim at dismantling the capitalist system. For concrete actions regarding symbiotic and ruptural strategies, the more activist-led part of the degrowth movement can learn from other social movements like the food sovereignty or the climate justice movement. The former is experienced in dealing with symbiotic strategies – which, in the context of the European Union, often means being preoccupied with the Common Agricultural Policy. By joining forces and strengthening their ties even more, both the degrowth and the food sovereignty movement might also be able to focus on dismantling these policies. From a global perspective, a stronger alliance with the food sovereignty movement could also strengthen the Global South perspective within degrowth. Finally, the use of temporal, small-scale ruptural strategies might increase in the future within the degrowth movement if it allies with the climate justice movement as a response to the increasingly severe climate crisis which can now also be more directly experienced in the Global North and which increases the pressure for urgent transformation.

References

Biollat, Sébastien, Julien-François Gerber, and Fernando R. Funes-Monzotec. 2012. "What Economic Democracy for Degrowth? Some Comments on the Contribution of Socialist Models and Cuban Agroecology." *Future* 44, no. 6: 600–607.

Brossmann, Johannes, and Mine Islar. 2019. "Living Degrowth? Investigating Degrowth Practices through Performative Methods." *Sustainability Science* 15: 917–930.

Daněk, Petr, and Petr Jehlička. 2021. "Quietly Degrowing: Food Self-Provisioning in Central Europe." In *Food for Degrowth: Perspectives and Practices*, edited by Anitra Nelson and Ferne Edwards, 33–44. London/New York: Routledge.

France. Ministry of Agriculture. 2016. *The Agroecology Project in France*. http://agriculture.gouv.fr/sites/minagri/files/1604-aec-aeenfrance-dep-gb-bd1.pdf.

Franco, Jennifer and Saturnino M. Borras Jr., eds. 2013. *Land Concentration, Land Grabbing and People's Struggles in Europe*. Transnational Institute (TNI) for European Coordination Via Campesina and Hands off the Land network. https://www.tni.org/my/node/1548.

Gerber, Julien-François. 2020. "Degrowth and Critical Agrarian Studies." *The Journal of Peasant Studies* 47, no. 2: 235–264.

Hadjimichael, Maria. 2018. "A Call for a Blue Degrowth: Unravelling the European Union's Fisheries and Maritime Policies." *Marine Policy* 94: 158–164.

Hall, Ruth, Marc Edelman, Saturnino M. Borras Jr., Ian Scoones, Ben White, and Wendy Wolford. 2015. "Resistance, Acquiescence or Incorporation? An Introduction to Land Grabbing and Political Reactions 'from below'." *The Journal of Peasant Studies* 42, no. 3–4: 467–488.

Hammond, John L., and Federico M. Rossi. 2013. "Landless Workers Movement (MST) Brazil." In *The Wiley-Blackwell Encyclopedia of Social and Political Movements*, edited by David A. Snow, Donatella della Porta, Bert Klandermans, and Doug McAdam. Hoboken, NJ: Wiley-Blackwell.

Heindorf, Ingrid. 2019. "Sikkim's State Policy on Organic Farming and Sikkim Organic Mission, India." *Panorama*, March 26, 2019. https://panorama.solutions/en/solution/sikkims-state-policy-on-organic-farming-and-sikkim-organic-mission-india.

Homs, Patricia, Gemma Flores-Pons, and Adrià Martín Mayor. 2021. "Sustaining Caring Livelihoods: Agroecological Cooperativism in Catalonia." In *Food for Degrowth: Perspectives and Practices*, edited by Anitra Nelson and Ferne Edwards, 100–111. London/New York: Routledge.

Kallis, Giorgos, and Hug March. 2015. "Imaginaries of Hope: The Utopianism of Degrowth." *Annals of the Association of American Geographers* 105, no. 2: 360–368.

Larsson, Tomas. 2016. "Who Catches the Biotech Train? Understanding Diverging Political Responses to GMOs in Southeast Asia." *The Journal of Peasant Studies* 43, no. 5: 1068–1094.

Lietaert, Matthieu. 2010. "Cohousing's Relevance to Degrowth Theories." *Journal of Cleaner Production* 18: 576–580.

McMichael, Philip. 2009. "A Food Regime Genealogy." *The Journal of Peasant Studies* 36, no. 1: 139–169.

Möhrs, Kim, Franziskus Forster, Sarah Kumnig, and Lukas Rauth, members of the SoliLa! Collective. 2013. "The Politics of Land and Food in Cities in the North: Reclaiming Urban Agriculture and the Struggle Solidarisch Landwirtschaften! (SoliLa!) in Austria." In *Land Concentration, Land Grabbing and People's Struggles in Europe*, edited by Jennifer Franco, and Saturnino M. Borras Jr. Transnational Institute (TNI) for European Coordination Via Campesina and Hands off the Land Network. https://www.tni.org/my/node/1548.

Müller, Christa. 2020. "Urban Gardening: Searching New Relationships Between Nature and Culture." In *Degrowth in Movement(s): Exploring Pathways for Transformation*, edited by Corinna Burkhart, Matthias Schmelzer, and Nina Treu, 333–346. Winchester UK, Washington US: Zero Books.

Nelson, Anitra, and Ferne Edwards, eds. 2021. *Food for Degrowth. Perspectives and Practices*. London/New York: Routledge.

ÖBV. 2021. "Doppelte Förderung der ersten 20 ha." ÖBV – Via Campesina Austria, January 21, 2021. https://www.viacampesina.at/doppelte-foerderung-der-ersten-20-ha/.

Ossewaarde, Marinus, and Roshnee Ossewaarde–Lowtoo. 2020. "The EU's Green Deal: A Third Alternative to Green Growth and Degrowth?" *Sustainability* 12, no. 23: 9825.

Peschard, Karine, and Shalini Randeria. 2020. "'Keeping Seeds in our Hands': The Rise of Seed Activism." *The Journal of Peasant Studies* 47, no. 4: 613–647.

Pieper, Anton. 2013. "Land Grabbing in France: The Case of the Notre-Dame-des-Landes Airport." In *Land Concentration, Land Grabbing and People's Struggles in Europe*, edited by Jennifer Franco, and Saturnino M. Borras Jr. Transnational Institute (TNI) for European Coordination Via Campesina and Hands off the Land Network. https://www.tni.org/my/node/1548.

Plank, Christina, Christoph Görg, Gerald Kalt, Lisa Kaufmann, Stefan Dullinger, and Fridolin Krausmann. "Biomass from Somewhere? Governing the Spatial Mismatch of Viennese Biomass Consumption and Its Impact on Biodiversity." *Land Use Policy* (under review).

Plank, Christina, Robert Hafner, and Rike Stotten. 2020. "Analyzing Values–Based Modes of Production and Consumption: Community Supported Agriculture in the Austrian Third Food Regime." *Austrian Journal of Sociology* 45: 49–68.

Salzer, Irmi, and Julianna Fehlinger. 2020. "Food Sovereignty: Fighting for Good Food for All." In *Degrowth in Movement(s): Exploring Pathways for Transformation*, edited by Corinna Burkhart, Matthias Schmelzer, and Nina Treu, 187–200. Winchester UK, Washington US: Zero Books.

Scott, Jim. 1986. "Everyday Forms of Peasant Resistance." *The Journal of Peasant Studies* 13, no. 2: 5–35.

van der Ploeg, Jan Douwe. 2020. "Farmers' Upheaval, Climate Crisis and Populism." *The Journal of Peasant Studies* 47, no. 3: 589–605.

Vandeventer, James Scott, Claudio Cattaneo, and Christos Zografos. 2018. "A Degrowth Transition: Pathways for the Degrowth Niche to Replace the Capitalist Growth Regime." *Ecological Economics* 156: 272–286.

Wright, Erik Olin. 2010. *Envisioning Real Utopias*. London, New York: Verso.

A case in the field of food: the movement for food sovereignty

By Julianna Fehlinger, Elisabeth Jost and Lisa Francesca Rail

We require a fundamental reorientation towards degrowing food systems around the globe – for the sake of soils, biodiversity, human health, animal well-being, and the fulfilment of rural livelihoods. In our contribution, we show that such a reorientation needs to be addressed on diverse levels simultaneously: on the scale of regional and city governments, of nation-states, of supranational organisations like the European Union (EU), or of international trade agreements. Furthermore, degrowing food systems must tackle issues related to production, distribution, and consumption.

Movements of resistance against intensified agrarian production have brought up a variety of alternative projects engaged in sustainable food futures. This diverse vibrancy holds great potential for alliances with the degrowth movement. As organisers of the panel on food at the *Degrowth Vienna 2020 Conference: Strategies for Social-ecological Transformation*, we aimed to represent this potential. We invited speakers from La Via Campesina, the International Panel of Experts on Sustainable Food Systems (IPES-Food), Copenhagen House of Food, and the citizens' cooperative in Mals, Italy.

In this chapter, we present these initiatives, which operate on different spatial scales and are engaged in a variety of activities, such as knowledge production and educational work, public procurement, and bottom-up movements for alternative regional development. Drawing on Ekaterina Chertkovskaya's understanding of the modes of transformation (Chapter 2) the examples can be described as interstitial and as symbiotic in their endeavours. They all strive towards food sovereignty, meaning the people's right to determine how food is produced, distributed, and consumed – in other words, the right to democratically shape one's own agricultural system without harming others or the environment (La Via Campesina 2003). We start by introducing the wider food sovereignty context before delving into the examples.

The movement for food sovereignty: an open bracket

Food sovereignty as a concept was first presented in 1996 at the World Food Summit of the Food and Agriculture Organisation of the United Nations (FAO) by La Via Campesina, a global organisation of peasants, rural workers, fishing communities, landless and Indigenous peoples. La Via Campesina is a strong transnational movement, which opposes the neoliberal tendencies that restrict the livelihoods of millions of small-scale farmers and that are worsening the situation of hungry people all over the globe. With over 200 million members, it is one of the largest social movements in the world.

La Via Campesina realised that the transformation of agricultural and food systems could only be achieved through alliances with other movements – and thus the Nyéléni Food Sovereignty Movement was born. In 2007, the first international Nyéléni Forum brought together environmental organisations, human rights organisations, consumer networks, women's movements, and urban movements. Together, they developed and defined the principles of food sovereignty as an answer to the technical term "food security" coined by the FAO, which fails to address a number of political questions concerning our food systems. Food sovereignty, instead, addresses the power structures that embed our food system; it addresses the conditions of food production, distribution, and consumption; it addresses the consequences of our production methods for future generations, and it places the people who produce and consume food products at centre stage (Patel 2009).

An essential feature of the Nyéléni process is the participation of marginalised social groups, including farmers – who typically find it difficult to access political processes – and those affected by poverty. Such broad alliances are possible within the Nyéléni Food Sovereignty Movement because they are centred around the needs and concerns of those affected. They allow politically excluded people to formulate and enact their interests as an act of practical solidarity (Nyéléni 2007).

Today the vision of food sovereignty is inspiring a growing number of social actors: civil society, local municipalities, scientists, entrepreneurs in the food system, and even national and EU-policy makers. Although the concept is often captured for green washing, the necessity for a social-ecological transformation of our food systems is omnipresent. The Nyéléni Food Sovereignty Movement seeks to enable a transformation through three different but complementary strategies: Resist – Transform – Build alternatives.

The remainder of this chapter will turn in more detail to the variegated strategies followed by movements identifying with food sovereignty at different administrative scales. The conclusion will then pick up the diverse threads laid out in the case examples, to draw together insights on transformative strategies concerning the food system.

IPES-Food: knowledge-production at the EU level

A group of renowned thinkers from the scientific community, civil society, and social movements established the *International Panel of Experts on Sustainable Food Systems* (IPES-Food) in 2015. The consortium publishes scientific reports and policy recommendations fostering a holistic perspective on sustainable reform in food and agriculture, i.e., accounting for the whole supply chain including production, processing, retail, and consumption. Their systemic analyses disclose the increasing concentration of power in the hands of large private agribusiness corporations (IPES-Food 2015; 2017a) and show how the industrialisation of our food and agriculture system has led to a large-scale, highly competitive, and uniformised agrarian structure (de Schutter 2020). IPES-Food also highlights the long-standing misalignment of European policies (regarding agriculture, but also environment, health, employment, trade, and investment), which target different segments of the food chain. This misalignment led to the known sustainability challenges associated with agriculture today: the tremendous decline of small-scale producers, the dependence on external inputs (e.g., agrochemicals, synthetic fertilisers, fossil fuels, vulnerable and thus exploitable labour force), climate change, agrobiodiversity loss, soil organic carbon loss, as well as a low-cost food economy driving increasing rates of obesity (IPES-Food 2017b).

In 2016, the IPES-Food initiated a participatory process together with over 400 farmers, food entrepreneurs, civil society activists, scientists, and policy-makers to push for a comprehensive, integrated Common Food Policy for the EU (IPES-Food 2019). They call for a reappraisal of the power of social innovations in agriculture (e.g., community supported agriculture) and aim for re-localisation of European food systems. Accordingly, EU food policy should enable coordinated change through trans-sectoral governance, the implementation of social and ecological conditions in trade agreements based on the Human Right to Food, and the active incentivisation of agroecological practices (IPES-Food 2016). Apart from shaping a democratic food environment, this would further enable the reduction of negative social and environmental impacts imposed on extra-EU territories (cf. FIAN International 2017; Fritz 2011).

The IPES-Food's strategy to influence policy-making by anchoring the expertise of, for example, smallholder farmers, Indigenous peoples, and social movements in participatory scientific knowledge production, is valuable for transformative action. The works of the IPES-Food contribute to the Degrowth debate, as they foster a paradigm shift in food systems thinking and food policy formulation (IPES-Food 2021). Using Chertovskaya's terms (Chapter 2), these proposals help to foster a symbiotic transformation by contributing to the conversation on how to dismantle capitalism. IPES-Food offers feasible solutions apart from a capitalist logic, which is framed by re-localised economic activity while manoeuvring within planetary boundaries. IPES-Food proposes a food policy that enables decent, equitable working conditions along food supply chains, diversified production, access to healthy food, and the protection of natural resources (cf. Azam 2018).

Copenhagen House of Food and Changing Food: public procurement in a city

The project Copenhagen House of Food, established in 2007 by the municipality of Copenhagen, was based on the realisation that city governments, as large-scaled food procurers for public canteens, have the power to profoundly re-shape the food product market – and thus also to transform agricultural production (Nielsen 2020). At that time, the City of Copenhagen ran about 900 public kitchens for kindergartens, retirement homes, employee canteens or social housing, serving approximately 70,000 meals per day. The vision of the Copenhagen House of Food was to raise the percentage of organic, high-quality produce distributed through Copenhagen's kitchens to at least 60% without raising the municipality's procurement budget. The project succeeded and subsequently increased the target, first to 75%, and later to 90%. By 2019, the average percentage was 86% for all publicly funded meals in Copenhagen (*Ibid.*). Through education campaigns for kitchen staff and procurement officers, employees were trained in cooking from scratch, and processed products were replaced by unprocessed ones. Meat and fish were reduced and substituted for a higher diversity in seasonal vegetables, fruits and tubers. As this improved the taste of the served meals, it also led to reductions in food waste, which again contributed to decreased spendings (*Ibid.*).

Due to a cut in municipal funding, the Copenhagen House of Food closed in 2019, but its legacy lives on in the procurement and cooking style of Copenhagen's kitchens (*Ibid.*). Additionally, the story of Copenhagen has inspired other cities like Berlin or Tallinn to follow the city's model. Members of the former Copenhagen House of Food have founded the organisation Changing Food (see Changing Food n.d.) that now advises projects that aspire to follow Copenhagen's example. This shows that movements towards food sovereignty involve not only farms as sites of production, but also nodes of buying and distribution, processing and cooking, public education, and consumption. It also reminds us of the interstitial transformative role public agencies can take in building alternatives.

Mals and Upper Vinschgau: a pesticide-free region

The village of Mals and the wider region of Upper Vinschgau in South Tyrol, Italy, is not only an impressive example of effective, bottom-up resistance against hegemonic trends of agricultural intensification but also for a site of democratically crafted alternatives. As such it provides practical visions of how to degrow rural landscapes and livelihoods. In the early 2010s, the people of Mals had witnessed the increased spread of monoculture apple plantations with a high input of synthetic pesticides. Villagers started to observe and analyse the resulting conflicts between organic and non-organic apple farmers, the detrimental effects on people's health, a steep rise in land prices, and the profound aesthetic and functional restructuring of the cultural landscape that arose. They decided to claim their right to democratic control over processes so deeply affecting their everyday lives and futures. In 2014, a plebiscite (*Volksabstimmung*) was held in which the vast majority (76%) voted for a pesticide-free region, a will that the mayor was subsequently charged with implementing in the form of a safety distance regulation. This would not de jure but de facto have made the use of pesticides almost impossible. This act of resistance did not remain unchallenged: a court case filed by farmers supporting agro-industrial production that questions the legitimacy of the municipality's ban on the use of chemicals is still ongoing (Holtkamp 2020).

In 2016, in addition to this tenacious resistance, several initiatives from the area founded the „*da*"[21] – a citizen cooperative that works on a sustainable future for the region with the goal of providing a good life for all. The cooperative's approach is holistic: its projects include small-scale farming and local crafts, integrative models for tourism, support for local markets and trade, as well as cultural and educational events. Its members stress that democratic control over the ecological, economic, cultural, and social futures of a region needs to be claimed back by the people who live there in order to

---

21 The full name is: Bürger*innengenossenschaft Obervinschgau „da"/Cooperativa di comunità Alta Val Venosta „da"

craft creative and truly resilient development models (da, n.d.; Der Malser Weg 2021; Schiebel 2019).

Conclusion

The examples show that different initiatives employ a variety of strategies when aiming for food sovereignty. Symbiotic transformations can be found in the IPES-Food initiative, which aims to inform EU policies with knowledge-based recommendations on how to shape democratic food systems and dismantle capitalist agroindustry. Interstitial transformations can be spotted in the work of the Copenhagen House of Food and the regional cooperative in Mals, which build alternatives on a municipal and regional level. The last example is particularly interesting because it combines resisting with constructing alternatives. Overall, this reflects the strategic approach of the Nyéléni Food Sovereignty movement, i.e., simultaneously resisting, transforming, and building alternatives. Growing food and degrowing food systems should thus follow this mix of strategies to approach social-ecological transformation.

References

Azam, Geneviéve. 2018. „Degrowth." In *Systemwandel: Alternativen zum globalen Kapitalismus,* edited by Pablo Solón, 72–92. Wien, Berlin: Mandelbaum.

Changing Food. n.d. *Changing Food: Copenhagen Food System Centre.* https://www.changingfood.dk/.

Da. n.d. *da – Die Bürger*Genossenschaft Obervinschgau-Genossenschaft.* https://da.bz.it/.

Der Malser Weg. 2021. *Der Malser Weg.* https://www.der-malser-weg.com/en/.

De Schutter, Olivier. 2020. "Degrowing the Food Sector: How to Build Democratic Food Policies." Presentation held at the *Degrowth Vienna 2020 Conference, Vienna* on May 31, 2020. https://www.youtube.com/watch?v=qMKQ3p0ZsF4.

FIAN International. 2017. *Land Grabbing and Human Rights. The Role of EU Actors Abroad.* Heidelberg: FIAN International for the Hands on the Land for Food Sovereignty Alliance.

Fritz, Thomas. 2011. *Globalising Hunger: Food Security and the EU's Common Agricultural Policy (CAP)*. Berlin: FDCL-Verlag.

Holtkamp, Carolin. 2020. *Der Malser Weg: Geschichte einer sozialen Bewegung für Demokratie und nachhaltige Regionalentwicklung*. Kassel: Kassel University Press.

IPES-Food. 2015. *The New Science of Sustainable Food Systems: Overcoming Barriers to Food Systems Reform*. International Panel of Experts on Sustainable Food Systems. http://www.IPES-Food.org/_img/upload/files/NewScienceofSusFood.pdf.

IPES-Food. 2016. *From Uniformity to Diversity: A Paradigm Shift from Industrial Agriculture to Diversified Agroecological Systems*. International Panel of Experts on Sustainable Food Systems. http://www.IPES-Food.org/_img/upload/files/UniformityToDiversity_FULL.pdf.

IPES-Food. 2017a. *Too Big to Feed: Exploring the Impacts of Mega-Mergers, Consolidation and Concentration of Power in the Agri-Food Sector*. International Panel of Experts on Sustainable Food Systems. https://www.IPES-Food.org/_img/upload/files/Concentration_FullReport.pdf.

IPES-Food. 2017b. *Unravelling the Food-Health Nexus: Addressing Practices, Political Economy, and Power Relations to Build Healthier Food Systems*. International Panel of Experts on Sustainable Food Systems. http://www.IPES-Food.org/_img/upload/files/Health_FullReport(1).pdf.

IPES-Food. 2019. *Towards a Common Food Policy for the EU*. International Panel of Experts on Sustainable Food Systems. https://www.IPES-Food.org/_img/upload/files/CFP_FullReport.pdf.

IPES-Food. 2021. *A Long Food Movement: Transforming Food Systems by 2045*. International Panel of Experts on Sustainable Food Systems. http://www.IPES-Food.org/_img/upload/files/LongFoodMovementEN.pdf.

La Via Campesina. 2003. "Food Sovereignty." *La Via Campesina*, January 15, 2003. https://viacampesina.org/en/food-sovereignty/.

Nielsen, Line R. 2020. "Degrowing the Food Sector: How to Build Democratic Food Policies." Presentation held at the *Degrowth Vienna 2020 Conference*, Vienna on May 31, 2020. https://www.youtube.com/watch?v=qMKQ3poZsF4.

Nyéléni. 2007. *Nyéléni 2007: Forum for Food Sovereignty*. https://nyeleni.org/DOWNLOADS/Nyelni_EN.pdf.

Patel, Raj. 2009. "Food Sovereignty." *The Journal of Peasant Studies* 36, 3: 663–706.

Schiebel, Alexander. 2019. *Das Wunder von Mals: Der Agrarlobby Widerstand leisten*. Wunderwerkstatt. http://wundervonmals.com/.

Chapter 12: Urban housing

An overview of strategies for social-ecological transformation in the field of urban housing

By Gabu Heindl

Homelessness exists not because the system is failing to work as it should, but because the system is working as it must.
Peter Marcuse (1988)

The dominant policy approach to housing worldwide has been an unquestioned pro-growth agenda within capitalist market logic: to stimulate more, faster and possibly cheaper housing construction. New housing – even if it is social housing – on greenfield sites (i.e., undeveloped land) is generally accompanied by soil sealing (where the soil is covered over with impermeable construction) for the creation of roads, parking lots, and so on.[22] An alarming number of newly built housing units are not at all constructed for addressing the housing crises, but to serve as abstract financial products (Aigner 2020). This phenomenon is a part of the broader process of the financialisation of housing, where housing is increasingly becoming a speculative commodity. Individual owner-occupiers purchase a home not only for "long-term secure housing but also as a quasi-asset (…) home-cum-commodity" (Nelson 2018). In addition to speculation on urban real estate, today's platform capitalism is contributing to the dissection of housing into many potential capital assets, techno-commodifying the home and urban space through schemes like AirBnB, private car hiring platforms such as Uber, home delivery, and dating apps (Terranova 2021).

---

22 United Nations Special Rapporteur Raquel Rolnik defines the Right to Adequate Housing as a combination of rights to spatial, environmental and infrastructural security (Rolnik 2014).

The increased attention to ecological issues within housing has opened up yet another terrain for capital. Ecological retrofitting leads to increases in rental costs, with "ecological gentrification" (Dooling 2008) causing evictions in the name of ecology. Ecological claims often reveal an imbalance between, on the one hand, those who can and want to afford ecological measures and, on the other, those for whom high environmental standards are not affordable or may even come to pose existential threats.

Most technical solutions to the environmental dimension of housing, such as the decarbonisation of the housing sector – itself an important goal – still operates within the confines of pro-growth hegemonic ideology. Critical literature links decarbonisation measures on the one side to "rebound effects" driven by the affluent (Sunikka-Blank *et al.* 2016) and on the other side to "fuel poverty", "energy poverty", and housing poverty (Boardman 2010). Together, this creates an "eco-social paradox" (Holm 2011). As long as housing remains a commodity and speculative asset regardless of social justice considerations, "greening" housing alone will not lead to housing and climate justice. In order to overcome the eco-social paradox, the degrowth movement must study and draw its conclusions from the history of housing struggles, socialist housing developments, rent strikes, class struggle and intersectionality.

"System change, not climate change" – so goes one of the more evocative slogans of the climate justice movement. Likewise, the issue of housing requires the dismantling of various existing paradigms. Yet, with every crisis, we are presented with new TINA ("There Is No Alternative") arguments for why paradigm change is impossible.

A key political approach for degrowth housing is that of radical democracy – the idea that we need to fight for even more democracy and democratic rights. This is exactly *because* neoliberalism and authoritarianism impose the idea that, mostly relying on economic logic, democracy is not possible (Mouffe 2013). In contrast to a market-based approach towards housing, the radical democratic approach aspires to housing justice. Housing justice emphasises intergenerational considerations, acknowledging that the rights of future generations are dependent on how our generation uses limited resources. Hence, the complex question is: how can social justice in housing be achieved while reducing the ecological impacts of housing?

A radical democracy framework is open to both strategies from within democratic institutions, as well as from the margins or the outside – and most of all for (often unexpected) alliances in between. In my book on radical democracy in architecture and urbanism (Heindl 2020), I laid out how the diversity of actors in housing struggles may act on three different levels: (institutional) politics, planning, and popular agency – and, whenever possible, through interactions between these different levels.[23] In other words, politics may be called "top-down" and popular agency "bottom-up", with planning operating in between.

The aim of this chapter, which is structured along these three levels, is to provide an overview of tangible strategies for the social-ecological transformation of urban housing. In the hope of turning what is sometimes diagnosed as a "strategic indeterminance" of the degrowth movement (Herbert *et al.* 2018) into a progressive and transformative bundle of strategies, we will look at specific strategies – those that were experimented with in the past, those being enacted today, and those that do not yet exist. The early 20th-century housing policy of Red Vienna and the present-day Vienna Housing Model will serve as the main guiding examples.

Politics

Housing and communication policies of historic Red Vienna

In order to address the current housing crises, we can look at and (critically) draw from historical social(ist) housing policies, such as

---

23 These different levels relate to, but are slightly different from the strategic logics outlined by Erik Olin Wright (ruptural, interstitial, and symbiotic; see Chapter 2).

Red Vienna's progressive social democratic housing politics of the interwar years (1919–1934), which was based on Austro-Marxist theory. During this period, Vienna's municipal housing programme pursued multiple objectives: supporting workers through decent and sanitary living, combined with public education infrastructure that supported political consciousness-raising in the working class, as well as the development of a sense of community.

Possibly the most essential housing policies were (and still are) tenant protections. Red Vienna inherited tenant protection as a reaction to the housing crises during World War I and it became a crucial precondition for the Red Vienna housing programme. It encompassed a set of tenant rights and a high level of rent control, such as setting caps on rent at quite a low level, security of the duration of rent and the possibility to hand over the flat within a family. These policies were complemented by a housing requisition law (the *Wohnungsanforderungsgesetz*), which allowed the municipality to claim and take over unused private housing for those in need. As a result of both, private investors did not see a profit in housing real estate and lost interest in speculative housing construction. Consequently, land prices fell. Rather than creating incentives for the private market, as would usually be done today, the social democratic administration of Red Viena bought land and constructed communal housing themselves – not privileging capital's needs, but rather workers' needs for housing.

Vienna received tax sovereignty by becoming an independent state in 1922, which helped in the financing of Red Vienna's large-scale housing programme. This made it possible for politicians to establish luxury taxes, such as the progressive housing construction tax (*Wohnbausteuer*). The tax applied to all properties within the municipal jurisdiction but assessed large and luxurious villas and private property to be in an exponentially higher bracket than small working-class housing-units.[24] The tax helped to fund

---

24 In a way the housing construction tax was indirectly fighting growth by taxing affluent housing exponentially.

the construction of 64,000 communal housing units as well as kindergartens and libraries.[25] On a more economic level, the construction of these housing blocks increased employment rates and supported local industries such as the Wienerberger brick production. Throughout its existence, Red Vienna's housing politics and policies were fought by the political opposition and finally violently ended by the right-wing authoritarian "Austro-fascist" federal government in 1933.

Taxing policies today

An example of a communication strategy around housing, as well as an example of a tax related to urban development gains, are the policies undertaken by the city of Basel. Since the 1970s, the Swiss city has implemented a land value capture tax (*Mehrwertabschöpfung*), a city-wide municipal levy that redistributes up to 70% of the profits (which would be derived from up-zoning or new-zoning from e.g., green space to housing zone) from real estate development into investment in public space and infrastructure. When communicating the benefits of this form of redistribution, city officials worked on the refinement of their communication strategy. Through this scheme, a transparent calculation of the expected profits of the property owner or developer is combined with an affect-loaded discourse on redistribution, rather than employing merely technical language. Instead of framing the policy as a public tax of 70% on private profits, the city is emphasizing in its communication the fact that the remaining 30% was, in fact, still a gift from the public to landowners. After all, the profit would be created without any work or achievement by the private landowner, but only due to the upzoning made possible by the municipality. A public act, which increases the development potential for the private piece of land. Such affective

---

25 Red Vienna's housing programme formed the basis for present-day Viennese communal housing stock of 220,000 units, making Vienna's Municipal Department 50 one of the largest public housing authorities, and hence also in a position of responsibility to reduce the housing sector's CO_2 emissions. For the relationship between Red Vienna and radical democracy, see Heindl 2020.

information strategies could be transferred to other tax policies, e.g., to introduce new taxes or to raise a CO_2 consumption tax, property tax, inheritance tax, vacancy tax or energy tax.

Another powerful communication strategy that can facilitate redistributive taxation is cost transparency. One example is to announce the actual costs of empty housing units for the public or to consider future recycling costs of building material into the calculation of construction costs. Also, municipalities could communicate the injustice of the gap between low property taxes and high-income tax.[26] This can be revealing, as it highlights an injustice that needs to be made more controversial, as speculation using housing is taxed much less than work, e.g., care work that is most relevant to society.

Use and re-distribution of existing space

To use what already exists would possibly be the most effective degrowth strategy with regard to housing, and it certainly is quite the opposite of the historically dominant growth-dependent response to housing problems. In order to redistribute what already exists, municipalities would need to end the misuse of the housing stock such as buy-to-let models (housing units which are only purchased as an investment property and managed by large companies), secondary residences, commercial AirBnB developments, or empty homes. On this front, there is a paradigm shift already happening at different scales and places. For example, Tyrol, Austria has put in place a municipal ordinance restricting secondary residences. Barcelona has temporarily expropriated flats that banks repossessed and hoarded following the 2008-2014 Spanish financial crises and has restricted short-term private room-rentals such as AirBnB. Vancouver, with its conspicuously under-used downtown core of empty houses, has implemented an Empty Homes Tax in 2017, even if it is still fairly low at three per cent of a home's assessed value.

---

26 This was lucidly documented in the exhibition "Boden für alle" at Architekturzentrum Wien (AzW), 2020/2021.

Decommodification of land within a municipal territory

An important set of policies relates to the politics of urban land use. Today's high demand for housing and insufficient rent control makes real estate investments appealing terrains for those with excess capital. Subsequently, urban land prices have skyrocketed and affordable land for subsidised housing has become rare. In Austria, this resulted in a decrease in social or communal housing run by limited-profit associations[27] while, at the same time, private market housing construction boomed. In 2018, in order to secure affordable land for subsidised housing, Vienna's city government introduced a remarkable building code amendment, creating the zoning category "subsidised housing". This effectively caps land prices, since the provisions under the amendment limit land prices for subsidised housing to 188 €/m² gross floor area. Through such zoning, the municipality aims to make two-thirds of development subsidised housing. The impact of this law became most evident when landowners called it "quasi-expropriation" of their future speculated profit. This amendment, which should be seen as only a first step, resulted from counter-hegemonic claims and actions by a differentiated group of actors. On the one hand, housing cooperatives criticised the lack of land and, on the other hand, activists criticised the lack of policies limiting free-market speculation. Additionally, workshops and public debates on urban land as a commons enabled land price caps to become a conceivable idea and thus a practical possibility.

However, this law comes quite late, as a lot of land in Vienna has already been zoned. In addition, its implementation still has to be put into effect. A law that is not executed only "tames" capitalism (see Chapter 2). Even though the law puts private property rights into question, it does not address the initial problem of turning green land into construction sites, which contradicts agricultural

---

27 In Austria subsidised housing is subjected to regulations regarding the land price, the rental price, and also limited-profit cooperations have to reinvest gains in funded housing projects.

and ecological demands (e.g., good agricultural soil for farming in Donaufeld, on Vienna's outskirts).

Generally, if new zoning for housing (or rather for "social housing" as it should be) is still to be pursued, it should at least be *limited-time* zoning and municipalities should be given the right as a priority buyer. This would make sure that land is not being hoarded and speculated on. In cases where it is not developed, the land can be – and should be – taken over by the municipality.

Planning

The main objective of degrowth and social justice strategies should be to rather abandon new construction, and instead redistribute and refurbish existing structures and possibly densify built urban areas. Density is a planning goal, which would support and impact ecological mobility strategies and resourceful use of infrastructure. Yet, it has to come along with the planning of high-quality public and green space. Concurrently, there is a boom of new housing construction in nearly every city seeing economic growth. Within this growth-driven housing sector, at least some subsidies are dedicated to decarbonisation, relating mostly to technological aspects like low-energy or passive house construction or green facades. Yet, we know that the most ecological house is the one that is not built.

Refurbishment

Refurbishment of existing housing stock may lead to some unexpected impacts. Many municipalities and governments are moving to end the subsidisation of fossil fuel-based heating in the home, which is already a positive step. However, there is a risk that this green turn in the housing industry fosters "low-carbon gentrification" (Bouzarovski *et al.* 2018). If there are no remediating policies in place, it could lead to unaffordable rent increases and, ultimately, evictions. Retrofitting must be more tightly linked to urban justice, rent safety, and rent control.

The "prebound effect", demonstrates that if energy-efficient retrofitting or affordable energy is made available to households with limited financial means, there may in fact be a less significant decrease in energy use than expected. Studies showed how households living in homes that are rated as inefficient may use much less energy than predicted (e.g., Sunikka-Blank *et al.* 2016). In terms of costs and effects, this suggests that there may be a gap between the performance of energy-saving devices and actual energy consumption, meaning that technical improvements may have a limited impact. In order to prevent the "*rebound* effect" – where efficiency improvements lead to more consumption, e.g., construction boom of detached houses "sanctioned" by passive house certification – measures must be connected to resolutions of general resourcefulness which include the calculation of grey energy and building site preparation.

In order to reduce new construction, the existing housing stock needs to be re-assessed, since the building industry continues to claim that refurbishing costs are much higher than new construction. These economic calculations can be challenged through new and all-inclusive means of calculating construction costs. Also, the protection of the existing housing stock must be customised to the appropriate context: While energy-inefficient and oil-consuming buildings (e.g., from the post-WWII-period) depend on conversion and modification, historic buildings may require proper legal protection rather than layers of insulation. If anything is to be taken down, circular economy and urban mining should be encouraged, since whatever is taken down should become upcycled for new construction. Yet, many of the current building techniques are not made for this. Hence, it would be favourable to add mandatory disassembly planning to the filing process of any new construction.

In addition, stricter laws would be needed to protect green spaces and trees as well as to prevent urban sprawl and soil sealing. And, to return to communication strategies, when it comes to negotiating it is not enough to merely call for an "end to soil sealing": degrowth means de-sealing. Some cities have already taken up some of this challenge, for example, Dresden's city council has established a "soil compensation account" (*Bodenausgleichskonto*), which involves requiring de-sealing of a certain area (soil recovery) in compensation for sealing elsewhere (European Commission 2021).

Post-growth development

From a planning perspective, the ecological crisis raises the question of how to conceptualise *doing* nothing – which is not at all the same as not doing anything. All actors that shape the city – planners, citizens, administration, politicians – face the challenge of finding ways of defining "progress" without the need for new construction. The good news is that the younger generation of planners and architects are not keen on serving as tools for growth and capitalist agendas. Recently, established architecture office Lacaton Vassal received the Pritzker Prize, the highest architectural award, for their approach of carefully doing as little (re)construction as their projects need and for their exclusive focus on refurbishing. These are signs of a change in the general discourse in architecture.

Unexpected alliances

Housing is more than housing and also relates to the quality of public space. To highlight this, I want to present the case of the rescue of Vienna's Danube Canal meadow. It is an interesting example of a bottom-up movement successfully interrupting the logic of growth in alliance with a top-down planning process – in which I played an active part as one of the planners who designed urban guidelines for the canal in 2014, commissioned by the city of Vienna.[28] While the guidelines were initially intended to regulate the aesthetics of new construction, we changed their logic to quite the opposite: a guide for the definition of areas where nothing should

---

28   Donaukanal Partitur, in collaboration with my colleague Susan Kraupp, 2014. The process consisted of around fifty meetings with planning and maintenance authorities, users and politicians.

be constructed. By means of a "non-building plan", we mapped and drew – through reversing the logic of a building or zoning plan – a clear prohibition against building within this important public waterfront of Vienna. Our non-building plan described explicitly that the few remaining non-commercialised areas along the water should not be commercially developed by private investors. This included the Donaukanalwiese, the last open-access horizontal piece of river channel bank in central Vienna. Yet, it was only after a group of activists named *Donaucanale für alle!* ("Danube Canal For All!") organised sit-ins and protests that plans for large-scale gastronomic development on this remaining area were rejected. It is interesting, especially when considered in relation to the strategic perspective of the chapter as a whole, that government-commissioned guidelines only gained momentum when the activists used them to support their demands (Heindl 2020).

Popular agency

Commoning and decapitalising

The Syndicate of Tenements (*Mietshäusersyndikat*) in Germany and its younger sister organisation in Austria, HabiTAT, work toward self-organised affordable living (and working) by creating a network of non-profit and self-managed houses, mostly by refurbishing houses. Specifically, member associations buy land and buildings from the speculative market and transform them into commons. Their collective structure guarantees the permanent commitment of its sub-associations to not profiting from the living and working space. Such decapitalizing "nowtopias" represent a goal and strategy at the same time. However, commoning needs resources and opportunities to counter exclusiveness and inaccessibility, which such projects could easily succumb to.

Some municipal governments support cooperative building initiatives (*Baugruppen*) with subsidised land, for which the initiatives are (rightly so) required to give some social benefits back to society. More often, however, such commoning projects operate without top-down support. Nevertheless, these projects are pioneers in certain social and ecological aspects, as they are experimenting with collective use of kitchens, living rooms, amenities, and so on. They are often engaged in practices such as sharing economy, solidarity economy as well as energy autonomy. In Vienna, supporting platforms such as the Initiative for Community Building and Living (*Initiative für gemeinschaftliches Bauen und Wohnen*) are important actors as they actively work on connecting bottom-up actors with the city administration in charge of official land-use policies. Additionally, they offer a platform for pressuring municipalities to continue to reserve land for collective housing.

Commoning is a precarious process that requires a lot of effort and energy – this is where all too often the participating groups consist of actors who have sufficient time resources. Hence, it is important to support the housing movement in its commoning projects and strengthen them by inserting radical democratic values and ways of organising to improve the accessibility and openness of their commoning projects. In addition, it would of course be very valuable if ways could be found for how such commoning processes could contribute their methods, knowledge, and experience to political and planning processes. In this way, lessons from small group experiments could be scaled up to the larger and more anonymous scale of social or public housing. This includes lessons for intersectional justice in housing, for example, certain small-scale experiments have developed methods for those who might not have the capacity to participate fully in collective processes to still benefit from self-governed housing models – these could be adapted to facilitate community-controlled social housing as well. Strategic alliances between degrowth actors with new housing cooperatives (for example *WoGen – Wohnprojekte Genossenschaft*, a cooperative for building initiatives in Vienna), and non-profit community land trusts – solidarity-based corporations which hold land and steer land use without profit-orientation (e.g., *Deutsche Stiftung Trias*) are vital to building bridges between individual, small-scale efforts for alternative housing and society as a whole.

Learning from past failures and successful alliances

A successful degrowth movement will, however, also rely on research and on lessons from the failures and successes of past projects. Degrowth-oriented projects are often dependent on a substantial mass of supporters and expertise and must endure for a long time to develop fully. Not all projects have the necessary perseverance. Yet, there are precedents which demonstrate how urban neighbourhoods would have developed in a very different way had there not been activist momentum by civil society: from the historic success of the protection of the Viennese Spittelberg area (including the squatted Amerlinghaus, which today remains a largely a non-profit community space), to the protest *Doncaucanale für alle!* (see above). Fridays for Future activists, mobility experts, researchers and oppositional politicians have been collectively protesting against the Lobautunnel, the construction of a highway tunnel under a natural resort in Vienna, as well as against further highway construction in Northern Vienna. This interdisciplinary and intergenerational alliance of protesters is demanding, amongst other things, a substantial upgrading of public mobility infrastructure in this area.

Protesting and squatting

Last but not least I will discuss how civil disobedience in the form of protests and squatting can help steer society toward degrowth in housing. One way of moving forward is to prevent the growth of non-social housing – for example when protest movements block neoliberal developments which would not include a single social housing unit. Beyond this, movements are also working to undo the neoliberal sell-off of social housing, which Deutsche Wohnen & Co enteignen in Berlin has demonstrated powerfully (see case, this chapter). Finally, tenant protest movements in Barcelona are an example of the power of protests, which eventually resulted in the victory of a municipalist, radical-democratic party of former activist and current mayor Ada Colau. Colau introduced redistributive policies such as the temporary expropriation of vacant flats owned by banks. We must not forget that Barcelona also has a large squatting scene, which has had a large role in the housing movement.

Squatting poses the property question in its most direct way and positions it at the centre of a radical paradigm and system change. By doing so, it smashes the system's logic as much as it acts as a useful survey of empty houses. Squatters scout for vacancies that could be used by those who urgently need housing. Squatting can also help save houses from demolition – not only because it exposes these buildings to the public's attention, but also through what has been called "convivial conservation" (Büscher *et al.* 2020), meaning: houses need people for their maintenance. How squatting becomes a useful part of the system can be seen in how certain squatted houses have developed into cultural centres in the urban fabric (in Vienna e.g., the music venue Arena). Squatted houses often have not only been witnesses to civil engagement but – when successfully turned into self-organised, non-profit housing – have also become eco-retrofitted and experimental zones for co-living and solidarity economy.

Conclusion

Degrowth strategies are not about pursuing purity, but rather embody a "use what you can" ethic. In other words – and relating directly to radical democracy – it is about a counter-hegemonic strategy. Such a counter-hegemonic strategy is especially necessary when, compared to the present context in which TINA is the norm, the reformist measures of the past look like the most daring future utopias. When travelling the path to shift the paradigm from growth to degrowth, it is important not to play the ecological question against the social question (see also Chapter 7). It also means taking the smallest steps wherever we can: we can simultaneously develop the infrastructure and conditions needed for change, form alliances with a spirit of critical pragmatism, or advocate non-reformist reforms. The latter are especially important as they can "set in motion a trajectory of change in which more radical reforms become practicable over time" (Fraser and Honneth 2003). Rosa Luxemburg offers a productive perspective on reforms: these can allow for important (next) steps and small victories – even within capitalism. But a comprehensive kind of change (for Luxemburg: the revolution) must not be left out of sight (Luxemburg 1982). Hence, a degrowth perspective on housing should connect projects, long-term visions and small steps through a comprehensive framework of radical democracy and housing beyond capitalism.

References

Aigner, Anita. 2020. "Housing as Investment: The Critique of Financialized Rental Investment in Vienna." *Eurozine*, July 1, 2020. https://www.eurozine.com/housing-as-investment/.

Boardman, Brenda. 2010. *Fixing Fuel Poverty: Challenges and Solutions*. London: Earthscan.

Bouzarovski, Frankowski, and Tirado Herrero. 2018. "Low-Carbon Gentrification: When Climate Change Encounters Residential Displacement." *International Journal of Urban and Regional Research* 42, no. 3: 845–863.

Büscher, Bram and Robert Fletcher. 2019. "Towards Convivial Conservation." *Conservation & Society* 17, no. 3: 283–296.

Dooling, Sarah. 2008. "Ecological Gentrification: Re-Negotiating Justice in the City." *Critical Planning* 15: 40–57.

European Commission. 2021. *Guidelines on Best Practice to Limit, Mitigate or Compensate Soil Sealing*. Luxembourg: Publications Office of the European Union. https://ec.europa.eu/environment/soil/pdf/guidelines/pub/soil_en.pdf.

Fraser, Nancy, and Axel Honneth. 2003. *Redistribution or Recognition? A Political–Philosophical Exchange*. New York: Verso.

Heindl, Gabu. 2020. *Stadtkonflikte: Radikale Demokratie in Architektur und Stadtplanung*. Wien: Mandelbaum.

Herbert, Joe, Nathan Barlow, Iris Frey, Christoph Ambach, and Pietro Cigna. 2018. "Beyond Visions and Projects: The Need for a Debate on Strategy in the Degrowth Movement." *Resilience*, November 5, 2018. https://www.resilience.org/

stories/2018-11-05/beyond-visions-and-projects-the-need-for-a-debate-on-strategy-in-the-degrowth-movement/.

Holm, Andrej. 2011. "An 'Eco-Social Paradox' – Urban Redevelopment and Gentrification." *Geography blog RaGeo*, March 20, 2011.

Luxemburg, Rosa. 1982 [1899]. *Sozialreform oder Revolution?* Berlin: Dietz.

Marcuse, Peter. 1988. "Neutralizing Homelessness." *Socialist Review* 88, no.1.

Mouffe, Chantal. 2013. *Agonistics: Thinking the World Politically*. London, New York: Verso.

Nelson, Anitra. 2018. "Housing for Growth Narratives." In *Housing for Degrowth: Principles, Models, Challenges and Opportunities*, edited by Anitra Nelson and François Schneider, n.a. 3-13. London, New York: Routledge.

Rolnik, Raquel. 2014. "Place, Inhabitance and Citizenship: The Right to Housing and the Right to the City in the Contemporary Urban World." *International Journal of Housing Policy* 14, no. 3: 293–300.

Sunikka-Blank, Minna and Ray Galvin. 2016. "Quantification of (P)rebound Effects in Retrofit Policies – Why Does It Matter?" *Energy* 95, no. 15: 415–424.

Terranova, Tiziana. 2021. "In the Shadow of Platform." In *Platform Urbanism and Its Discontents*, edited by Peter Mörtenböck and Helge Mooshammer, n.a. Rotterdam: nai010.

A case in the field of urban housing: Deutsche Wohnen & Co. Enteignen – Berlin's strategy for a tenants' commons

By Ian Clotworthy and Ania Spatzier

Deutsche Wohnen & Co. Enteignen (DWE, „Expropriate[29] Deutsche Wohnen & Co." in English) is a campaign in Berlin, whose strategy is discussed in this section as a social-ecological transformation of urban housing. The campaign was launched in April 2018 and at the time of writing successfully organised for its demands to be put to a citywide referendum on 26 September 2021. This is possible due to the existing direct democracy mechanisms which exist in the federal state of Berlin. Voters supported the referendum with 59.1% valid votes in favour of the campaign's proposal (Berlin, Landeswahlleiterin für Berlin 2021a).

Deutsche Wohnen is a stock market-listed housing corporation that has come to own 114,191 flats in Berlin (Trautvetter 2020). This makes it Berlin's single largest landlord. The campaign aims to take back into public ownership the entire stock of housing that belongs to this company and a number of similar corporations (referenced by "& Co. " in the campaign name) that own more than 3,000 flats each. The referendum campaign included about 250,000 flats, thereby doubling the public housing stock. DWE proposes to place the flats in the ownership of an *Anstalt des öffentlichen Rechts* (public-law institution in English, see Figure 1) which would include tenants, staff and the public in administering the housing, enabling a radical expansion of democracy (DWE 2019, 21). Such tenants' commons would mark a ruptural break from housing dominated by private speculators. With rents no longer servicing the demands of the financial markets, the result would be a permanent decrease in

---

29 In this case, expropriation is meant not as a seizure of property without compensation at all, but to indicate that the campaign demands compensation considerably below market value, as provided by the German Basic Law. Thus, Berlin would not reward speculation by providing further capital to these companies.

rents across the city (DWE 2021c). The campaign has gained support stretching well beyond the tenant activist milieu, including major trade unions Verdi, GEW and IG Metall (DWE 2021b).

Background

Through a series of privatisations, Berlin's stock of 600,000 flats in the 1990s (Sontheimer 2021) has been whittled down to 324,000, so that the majority of housing is now in private hands (74%), with about 250,000 homes held by large companies (Trautvetter 2020). Analyses of annual reports reveal that tenants pay large dividends to shareholders of companies like Deutsche Wohnen, Vonovia and Akelius. Every year, each tenant of Deutsche Wohnen pays shareholders dividends to the order of €2,100 (Meister 2021) – for Vonovia and Akelius, this comes to €2,100 and even €3,200, respectively (Kühn 2021; Akelius Residential Property AB 2021). Shareholders are largely investment management companies such as BlackRock (Trautvetter 2020).

Berlin has a large tenant population – some 85% of residents rent (Trautvetter 2020). In 2020 the average Berlin tenant paid 29.7% of their net income on rent (ImmoScout24 2020), close to the 30% at which housing costs are considered to be a major financial burden (Hans-Böckler-Stiftung 2017). Between 2008 and 2018, rents for new contracts in Berlin increased by 112% (Germany, Deutscher Bundestag 2019). This has led to widespread displacement of working-class residents, non-commercial cultural spaces, and small businesses, to make way for more affluent residents and upmarket businesses (Kotti & Co. 2017).

Since 2012, the Berlin state government has attempted to gain more control over the market by gradually buying back 40,000 flats, but it has not been enough to slow the rise in rents (Lindenberg 2019). Finally, the government introduced the *Mietendeckel* (rent cap), a law to tame the market, freezing rents for five years to their 2019 level, and even, for about 31% of flats, reducing rents (Kostrzynski *et al.* 2020). However, this period of relief came to a sudden end in April 2021, when the German federal constitutional court struck down the law on the grounds that Berlin, as a state, does not have the legal competence to pass such a law (Germany, Bundesverfassungsgericht 2021).

Movement formation and development of the proposal

The last decade has seen a rising tide of tenant activism in Berlin. The city has many long-time residents who have experienced the *Mietpreisbindung* (long-term rent control) of West Berlin, the mass provision of housing in East Berlin, and the continuous presence of the housing occupation (squatting) scene (Hoffrogge 2021). Beyond the tenants' associations which focus on providing legal aid, local initiatives arose in order to network tenants and fight collectively against the creeping phenomenon of displacement of individuals out of the neighbourhoods where they had long lived (Strobel 2020).

The epicentre of these initiatives is in the heart of the Kreuzberg district: Kottbusser Tor. Here stand many of the social apartment blocks that were sold to Deutsche Wohnen. The company has been identified as a key actor in the displacement of members of this substantially Turkish migrant community, in favour of new rental contracts with higher-paying tenants (Kotti & Co. 2012; Gürgen 2017).

From this community in 2011 arose the initiative Kotti & Co., which has become a driving force of the Berlin tenants' movement. From the beginning, it argued that the privatisation of housing at Kottbusser Tor was a mistake and demanded its democratic recommunalisation (Kotti & Co. 2019). In the following years, more initiatives such as Mieter*inneninitiative Bündnis Otto-Suhr-Siedlung (Tenant Initiative Otto-Suhr-Estate), Mieter*innenprotest Deutsche Wohnen (Tenant Protest Deutsche Wohnen) and the Akelius-Mieter*innenvernetzung (Akelius Tenant Network) were formed, joining the demand for democratic recommunalisation (Akelius-Mieter*innenvernetzung 2021). Key actors in this, besides the tenants themselves, included organisers from the Interventionist

Left (IL), who also went on to play critical roles in DWE (Strobel 2020).

In 2015, while SPD politicians were expressing their regret at selling off social housing, Kotti & Co. began to develop strategies of how exactly to achieve the demand of socialisation on a large scale in Berlin (Villinger 2016; Kotti & Co. 2019). During their research, they noticed the potential of Articles 14 and 15 of the *Grundgesetz*, Germany's constitution: the articles prescribe that private property rights are protected, but prioritised below the public interest.[30] It provides for compensation well below the market value.[31] In April 2018, following discussions with legal experts, these initiatives decided to step up the pressure on policymakers by collaborating to launch a citywide campaign for recommunalisation: Deutsche Wohnen & Co. Enteignen (Taheri 2018).

The idea of expropriation achieved such resonance with the population that the Berlin government implemented the *Mietendeckel* (rent cap) – a policy intended to absorb the momentum behind DWE (Kunkel 2021; Kusiak 2021) by immediately arresting the rise in rent prices. After the overturning of the *Mietendeckel* in April 2021, the government made a renewed attempt to placate the movement, presenting a proposal to buy back 20,000 flats from Vonovia and Deutsche Wohnen as part of the two companies' merger process (Iser 2021).

Strategy

In their brochure *Vergesellschaftung und Gemeinwirtschaft* (Socialisation and the Social Economy), DWE lay out a Vienna-inspired vision of transforming housing and related sectors to a point where profit would play no role at all. Considered at a total system

---

30 Article 14, Paragraph 2: "Property entails obligations. Its use shall serve the public good."

Article 15: "Land, resources, and means of production may for the purpose of socialisation be transferred to public ownership" *(abbreviated)*

31 Article 14, Paragraph 3, Sentence 3: "Such compensation shall be determined by establishing an equitable balance between the public interest and the interests of those affected"

level, this would represent an interstitial strategy, in which expansion of an alternative model of democratic control of housing also spurs the expansion of public housing companies and the publicly-owned renewable energy sector. This is described as already happening with the public housing companies installing solar panels on roofs, generating low-cost electricity for the apartment blocks they own (DWE 2019,18).

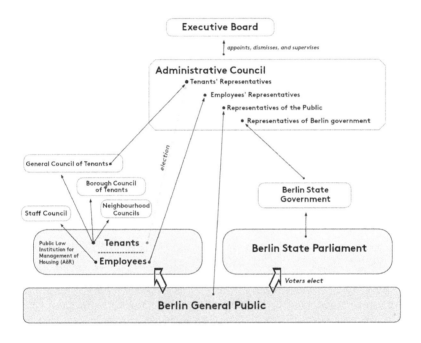

Figure 12.1.: DWE's proposal to democratically administer expropriated housing.

The campaign decided to use a legal instrument of direct democracy that specifically Berlin provides: a *Volksbegehren* (popular petition), whereby initiatives can put forth a proposal and collect enough signatures to oblige the government to hold a referendum on it. DWE decided that their *Volksbegehren* would be to call upon the legislature to write a law fulfilling certain conditions laid out in a document called the *Beschlusstext* (resolution text, Berlin,

Landeswahlleiterin für Berlin 2021a). They chose to do this rather than write a law and propose it because other initiatives had failed due to technical errors in proposed laws (Metzger *et al.* 2021). The signatures must be provided on a particular paper form along with the signer's address and date of birth so that the election office can verify them as a resident. Securing the referendum involves two windows of time, or phases, for collecting signatures. The first phase required collecting 20,000 signatures; 77,001 were collected between April and September 2019. Then the proposal spent a year in an official legal examination before being declared valid. During this time, the government attempted to have DWE agree to water down the wording of the *Beschlusstext* from a demand to pass a law to socialise housing to merely "taking measures" towards it (Joswig 2020). The campaign did not submit to this co-optation attempt – a common problem faced by symbiotic strategies (see Chapter 2).

Since the parties of the governing coalition could not agree on passing a socialisation law, the campaign initiated the second phase. This required gathering the signatures of 7% of eligible voters in Berlin, about 172,000 people, with the aim of forcing a referendum on the issue. The way this was accomplished was by organising *Kiezteams* (neighbourhood teams) in every district of the city, who could collect signatures in public places. Some of these emerged from the DW tenant initiatives discussed above. The barriers to entry were made low: every *Kiezteam* and campaign working group, as well as the whole campaign, hosted regular online meetings, and a mobile app was created in which anyone could view and join upcoming public collection drives. Besides *Kiezteams*, there are a number of thematic working groups. All working groups elect representatives to a coordination circle of twenty people that keeps the campaign together and deals with financial matters. Major decisions are made democratically at a general campaign meeting every two weeks.

The second collection phase took place between 26 February and 25 July 2021 (DWE, 2021a), by which time the campaign submitted 359,063 signatures to the election office. This was a record

– despite the long COVID-19 lockdown, DWE had collected more signatures than any other such initiative in Berlin. The referendum was quickly planned to take place for 26 September 2021 (Berlin, Landeswahlleiterin für Berlin 2021b), alongside the Berlin state and federal elections. About 2,000 activists were bound into campaign structures and collected signatures regularly.

This strong infrastructure paved the way to a decisive victory for the campaign in the referendum. On 26 September 2021, the voters of Berlin supported the motion of the referendum by 57.6%, parallel to electing a new Berlin state government (Berlin, Landeswahlleiterin für Berlin 2021c). The referendum was not legally binding but can be considered politically binding. The campaign has therefore moved into a mode of mobilising political pressure to make the socialisation of housing a reality.

Conclusion

The scale and ambition of this project to rapidly decommodify and manage housing democratically suggests a ruptural break with the status quo of increasing financialisation of the housing sector, similar to the worker takeovers of industries in Argentina (see Chapter 2). Wright suggests that this use of "ordinary democratic processes of the state" can even be a strategy to pursue ruptural outcomes (Wright 2010, 309). In this case, the means used are very much symbiotic: passing a law changing the existing institutional forms from private to public and deepening social empowerment by building democracy into the new institution that manages the housing stock (see Figure 1). Beyond Berlin, the development could have a chilling effect on real estate speculation and demonstrates new possibilities for tenant movements globally (Kusiak 2019).

DWE does not explicitly identify as a degrowth campaign, but it does identify with the degrowth goal of linking ecological limits with approaches to radical democracy (DWE 2019, 21). Its strategy to decouple housing from profit aims to tackle the problem that Berlin tenants face at its root: the fact that housing as an investment commodity causes upward pressure on rents (Taheri 2018). Stopping this dynamic even in just one economic sector goes beyond harm reduction, toward transcending structures, possibly triggering further degrowth transformations. DWE has developed an alternative vision to the dominant "build, build, build" narrative, which suggests that all of Berlin's housing problems would be solved by simply building more private housing (McGath 2021). This vision not only addresses the distribution of existing housing but would also make it possible to build new housing that most Berliners could afford. If implemented, this vision would realise housing as a right, always to be prioritised over the interests of unelected capital. As activist Ralf Hoffrogge says (Peter 2021, n.p.):

> "Our campaign's success would be a real step towards democratic deglobalisation; that capital is taken back from the financial markets and fed into the local economy, where it serves the need for housing. Making more money out of money is not a basic need, but a perversion that benefits no one. Our success would save Berlin from becoming a city of capital and would be a signal that a cosmopolitan city can also be thought of as a regional public economy."

References

Akelius Residential Property AB. 2021. "Notice of Annual General Meeting 2021." *Cision* (blog), December 3, 2021. https://news.cision.com/akelius–residential–property–ab/r/notice–of–annual–general–meeting–2021,c3304727.

Akelius-Mieter*innenvernetzung. 2021. *Stopp Akelius Berlin!*. https://www.akelius–vernetzung.de/.

Berlin, Germany. Landeswahlleiterin für Berlin. 2021a. *Endgültiges Ergebnis ermittelt: Beschlussentwurf angenommen*. https://www.berlin.de/wahlen/pressemitteilungen/2021/pressemitteilung.1135955.php.

Berlin, Germany. Landeswahlleiterin für Berlin. 2021b. *Endgültiges Ergebnis ermittelt: Volksbegehren zustande gekommen*. https://www.berlin.de/wahlen/pressemitteilungen/2021/pressemitteilung.1101919.php.

Berlin, Germany. Landeswahlleiterin für Berlin. 2021c. *Volksentscheid „Deutsche Wohnen & Co. Enteignen" 2021*. https://www.wahlen-berlin.de/abstimmungen/VE2021/AFSPRAES/index.html.

Deutsche Wohnen & Co. Enteignen (DWE). 2019. *Vergesellschaftung und Gemeinwirtschaft: Lösungen für die Berliner Wohnungskrise*. https://www.dwenteignen.de/wp-content/uploads/2020/01/Vergesellschaftung_Download_2.-Auflage.pdf

Deutsche Wohnen & Co. Enteignen (DWE). 2021a. *Etappen des Volksentscheids*. https://www.dwenteignen.de/etappen-des-volksentscheids/.

Deutsche Wohnen & Co. Enteignen (DWE). 2021b. *Unterstützer:innen*. https://www.dwenteignen.de/unterstuetzerinnen/.

Deutsche Wohnen & Co. Enteignen (DWE). 2021c. *Vergesellschaftung ist ein guter Deal*. https://www.dwenteignen.de/positionen/entschaedigung/.

Germany, Bundesverfassungsgericht. 2021. *Pressemitteilung: Gesetz zur Mietenbegrenzung im Wohnungswesen in Berlin nichtig*. https://www.bundesverfassungsgericht.de/SharedDocs/Pressemitteilungen/DE/2021/bvg21-028.html.

Germany, Deutscher Bundestag. 2019. *Drucksache 19/12786: Wohnungspolitische Bilanz der Bundesrepublik Deutschland seit 2006*. https://dserver.bundestag.de/btd/19/127/1912786.pdf.

Gürgen, Malene. 2017. „Protest gegen Verdrängung in Berlin: Kira çok yüksek – die Miete ist zu hoch." *Die Tageszeitung: taz*, May 28, 2017. https://taz.de/!5409280/.

Hans-Böckler-Stiftung. 2017. *Mieten bringen viele an die Belastungsgrenze*. https://www.boeckler.de/de/boeckler-impuls-mieten-bringen-viele-an-die-belastungsgrenze-3805.htm.

Hoffrogge, Ralf. 2021. „Dann eben enteignen." *Jacobin Magazin*, April 19, 2021. https://jacobin.de/artikel/berliner-mietendeckel-vergesellschaftung-enteignung-deutsche-wohnen-enteignen-karlsruhe-bundesverfassungsgericht-bundesdeckel-wohnungskrise/.

ImmoScout24. 2020. *Miete häufig höher als 30 Prozent des Einkommens*. https://www.immobilienscout24.de/unternehmen/news-medien/news/default-title/miete-haeufig-hoeher-als-30-prozent-des-einkommens/.

Iser, Jurik Caspar. 2021. „Mit aller Macht gegen Enteignungen." *Die Zeit*, May 25, 2021. https://www.zeit.de/wirtschaft/unternehmen/2021-05/deutsche-wohnen-vonovia-fusion-immobilienkonzerne-folgen-mieter/komplettansicht.

Joswig, Gareth. 2020. „Volksinitiative streitet mit Senat: SPD drückt sich vorm Enteignen." *Die Tageszeitung: taz,* June 26, 2020. https://taz.de/!5697334/.

Kostrzynski, Manuel, Hendrik Lehmann, Ralf Schönball, and Helena Wittlich. 2020. „Diese Vermieter treiben den Berliner Mietspiegel in die Höhe." *Tagesspiegel,* July 26, 2020. https://interaktiv.tagesspiegel.de/lab/diese-zehn-firmen-treiben-den-mietspiegel-in-berlin-besonders-in-die-hoehe/.

Kotti & Co. 2012. *Hintergrund.* https://kottiundco.net/hintergrund/.

Kotti & Co. 2017. *Pressemitteilung: Bündnis der Deutsche Wohnen Mieter*innen.* https://kottiundco.net/2017/02/14/pm-buendnis-der-deutsche-wohnen-mieterinnen/.

Kotti & Co. 2019. *Wir wollen alles.* https://kottiundco.net/2019/09/22/wir-wollen-alles/.

Kühn, Timm. 2021. „Immobilienwirtschaft in der Pandemie: 956 Millionen für die Aktionäre." *Die Tageszeitung: taz,* March 5, 2021. https://taz.de/!5750997/.

Kunkel, Kalle. 2021. „Speculators Love This Trick." *The Left Berlin,* April 22, 2021. https://www.theleftberlin.com/speculators-love-this-trick/.

Kusiak, Joanna. 2019. "Berlin's Grassroots Plan to Renationalise up to 200,000 Ex-Council Homes from Corporate Landlords." *The Conversation,* March 5, 2019. http://theconversation.com/berlins-grassroots-plan-to-renationalise-up-to-200-000-ex-council-homes-from-corporate-landlords-112884.

Kusiak, Joanna. 2021. *Housing Struggles in Berlin: Part II Grassroots Expropriation Activism Urban Political.* The Podcast on Urban Theory, Research, and Activism, May 4, 2021. https://urbanpolitical.podigee.io/42-kusiak.

Lindenberg, Hartmut. 2019. „Berlin will seine Wohnungen zurück – Die Diskussion um Rekommunalisierung und Enteignung." *Berliner Mieterverein e.V.* (blog), February 27, 2019. https://www.berliner-mieterverein.de/magazin/online/mm0319/berlin-will-seine-wohnungen-zurueck-die-diskussion-um-rekommunalisierung-und-enteignung-031912.htm.

McGath, Thomas. 2021. "How Do We Fix Berlin's Housing Crisis?" *Berliner Zeitung,* June 25, 2021. https://www.berliner-zeitung.de/en/we-cant-build-our-way-out-of-the-housing-crisis-li.166853.

Meister, Hans. 2021. „Deutsche Wohnen – Anatomie eines Immobiliengiganten." *Berliner Mieterverein e.V.* (blog), February 2, 2021. https://www.berliner-mieterverein.de/magazin/online/mm0121/alles-was-am-wohnungsmarkt-schief-laeuft-verkoerpert-die-deutsche-wohnen-anatomie-eines-immobiliengiganten-012114.htm.

Metzger, Philipp P. 2021. *Wohnkonzerne enteignen! Wie Deutsche Wohnen & Co. ein*

Grundbedürfnis zu Profit machen. Wien, Berlin: Mandelbaum.

Peter, Erik. 2021. „Kapitalismuskritik am Wohnungsmarkt: Das Problem an der Wurzel packen." *Die Tageszeitung: taz*, April 10, 2021. https://taz.de/!5760422/.

Sontheimer, Michael. 2021. „Die Berliner SPD und das Volksbegehren: Kampf gegen die Mieterschaft." *Die Tageszeitung: taz*, April 10, 2021. https://taz.de/!5760380/.

Strobel, Hannes. 2020. „Organisiert gegen einen profitorientierten Wohnungskonzern: Fünf Jahre berlinweite Vernetzung der Deutsche–Wohnen–Mieter*innen." *Sub\urban: Zeitschrift Für Kritische Stadtforschung* 8, no. 3 (December): 195–204.

Taheri, Rouzbeh. 2018. „Ein Landesenteignungsgesetz Auf Grundlage Artikel 15 Grundgesetz ist das Ziel." *Rosa-Luxemburg-Stiftung*. https://www.rosalux.de/publikation/id/38902.

Trautvetter, Christoph. „Wem gehört die Stadt?" Studie im Auftrag der Rosa–Luxemburg–Stiftung. Berlin: Rosa-Luxemburg-Stiftung, November 2020. https://www.rosalux.de/publikation/id/43284/wem–gehoert–die–stadt.

Villinger, Christoph. 2016. „Gastbeitrag Mietenbündnis: Wagt die Enteignung!" *Die Tageszeitung: taz*, February 29, 2016. https://taz.de/!5278275/.

Wright, Erik Olin. 2010. *Envisioning Real Utopias*. London, New York: Verso.

Chapter 13: Digital technologies

An overview of strategies for social-ecological transformation in the field of digital technologies and the cases of Low-Tech Magazine and Decidim

By Nicolas Guenot and Andrea Vetter

The relentless development of technology is not just a key trait of modernity, but also an essential driving force of the industrial society against which the degrowth movement stands. Consequently, one could expect to find clearly formulated analyses and visions about technology in the degrowth literature. But, surprisingly, there is little work specifically addressing technology (Kerschner *et al.* 2018) and strategic indeterminism (Herbert *et al.* 2018) on this question plagues a community that has not yet been able to properly formulate a desirable vision and related strategies – be they based on the radical critique of classic authors (Ellul 1964) or on the hopes some have put in digital commons and peer-to-peer production (Gorz 2010).

The rejection of gigantic technical infrastructures such as airports or pipelines and the use of bicycles as a symbol for a more human way of life are widespread in the degrowth movement. Yet beyond calls to limit the spread of technical devices (Latouche 2010), the dominant technological imaginary is left mostly untouched and very few manage to envision the kind of technology a world after growth would need or discuss how our current relationship with technology could be transformed. This is striking because technology, as the set of processes of producing and applying instrumental knowledge to improve the efficiency of material human action, involves and influences all of society and its institutions, so neither technology nor society can be transformed independently from the other. Therefore, a transformation strategy for technology must explain both how to reshape it and how to change its role within society.

In this chapter, we will describe the degrowth movement's

approach to the topic and then outline various strategies to transform technology. There are essentially two orientations: working with existing technology and controlling or repurposing it to progress towards a degrowth society, or struggling against the very imaginary underpinning the development of industrial technology. The former focuses on the role of technology in society, the latter on reshaping it. Thus, any strategy will have to combine both orientations to be successful.

Our analysis relies on Erik Olin Wright's typology of symbiotic, interstitial and ruptural transformations (Wright 2010) presented in Chapter 2, but also on a set of criteria used to evaluate how strategies address various aspects of the politics of technology. Noticeably, the strategies considered mostly involve actors from outside the degrowth movement who pursue different agendas – which reflects the weakness of the degrowth narrative in the field of technology. In order to convey a sense of the challenges ahead, we will end with a more detailed survey of two projects demonstrating the strengths and weaknesses of a particularly interesting strategy in the field of digital technology and suggest some leads for a sorely needed debate on desirable technological futures and the means to achieve them.

The degrowth movement between primitivism and techno-utopianism

Degrowth can be seen as a call to critically reassess the idea of progress as it was forged in the ideological framework of industrial societies. Too often, this is mocked as an attempt to "take us back to the dark ages", in a striking expression of the pervasive fear of losing a way of life defined by devices such as cars or televisions. This fear is rooted in the narrative that presents the continuous development of productive forces through science and technology as the essential condition of human wellbeing (Sahlins 1972). Support for this "myth of progress" is not limited to the heralds of capitalist production – it is also part of a certain Marxist teleology of human development, despite the relation between technology and alienation pointed out by Marx himself (Wendling 2009). Technology thus plays a central role in the conflict between those seeking to downscale industrial production and those advocating the expansion of productive forces beyond capitalism (Bastani 2019). But which criteria should be considered in this debate? Here, we will foreground two: the relation of technology to resources and energy use, and its impact on society.

The general attitude of the degrowth movement towards technology hinges on the environmental question: what level of consumption of energy and natural resources is possible within planetary boundaries? The technologies underlying the expansion of capitalism have always been based on fossil fuels (Malm 2016) and scarce resources. Can these be replaced, and if so, how? No future can be imagined without first answering these questions. There is a widespread tendency to believe that the energy efficiency of technical devices can steadily increase, even though it is undermined by rebound effects (Herring and Roy 2007). But few answers are available and divergent views on the future of technology often boil down to a question of faith, as illustrated by the dominant cornucopian imaginary of always expandable natural boundaries (Jochum 2020). In our analysis, we will operate under the assumption that there will not be significantly more energy available in the future than today, due to fossil fuels being phased out and physical limits on renewable energy.

In the face of ecological uncertainties, another criterion is often used to assess the role of technology: its impact on human relations and the shaping of societies. Again, divergent views coexist in the degrowth movement. Whereas the figure of Skynet, an artificial superintelligence wiping out humankind in the movie *The Terminator*, echoes the ambivalent relation of humans with their own creations (Anders 1956), information technology is the cornerstone of many post-capitalist visions of society (Mason 2015) with which many in the degrowth movement sympathise. On a strategic level, it seems difficult to make a new imaginary appealing if it is widely deemed too technophobic, and the global blending of cultures already achieved by modern means of communication (Appadurai 1996) should not be overlooked and cannot be rolled back. Moreover, the socio-political implications of introducing new technology cannot be fully determined in advance (Winner 1986). This all makes transforming and directing technology towards degrowth rather difficult.

The sheer amount of distinct technological fields forces us to focus our attention, and here we will mostly choose examples from one specific form of technology – digital technology, which encompasses all processes collecting and manipulating information using electronic devices. There would be much to say about bio- and nanotechnology, or space exploration, but nothing within current discourses appears as likely to reshape society and help to overcome the climate crisis as digital technology. And indeed, it is increasingly transforming democracy, work, and our use of resources. So what potential lies in this process? Digital technology is the foremost strategic field of our times, because it is at the heart of the green growth narrative, promising the dawn of a dematerialised and cognitive capitalism (McAfee 2019). It has been mobilised to support the ideological function of technological discourse, reframing industrial economic policies as paths towards sustainability, using for example the vocabulary of *smart cities* (European Commission 2020). Questioning the transformative potential of digital technology should thus be a priority for the degrowth movement.

However, from the radical democratic aspirations of the internet culture of the 1990s to the data monopolies of giant digital platforms (Srnicek 2016), and from staggering energy consumption to the promise of a dematerialised economy (Hickel and Kallis 2019), the gap between discourse and reality makes it difficult to define strategic goals. More than any other artefact, computers can shape very different technological imaginaries. But a path between fear and frenzy must be found: a radically primitivist narrative ignores too many realities, while techno-utopias mostly ignore natural boundaries and run counter to degrowth principles by demanding ever more technology to balance the unpredictable effects of technology itself. As we will see in our analysis of strategies for transforming technology, navigating the contradictions of possible (digital) futures is an ongoing challenge.

The difficulty of shaping technology from a degrowth perspective

While degrowth as a slogan has played an important part in questioning various economic orthodoxies and suggesting new paths in the face of social and environmental disasters, in the field of technology it often appears limited to a critique of planned obsolescence and totalitarian tendencies to surveil or control our lives. The primary cause for the prevalent strategic indeterminism – the lack of a clear goal or of the means to achieve it – ironically seems to be deterministic views on modern technology, tending to describe it as either entirely dispensable or absolutely necessary (Eversberg and Schmelzer 2018). Both options are obviously unfit to support a reasonable strategy, the challenge being to envision the kind of technology that can be deemed necessary in a degrowth society.

How can the development of technology be reappropriated by the many? Inventing convivial tools means being able to assess their impact on the natural and human world (Vetter 2018). Our analysis distinguishes between four interlocking dimensions. *Ecological sustainability* is a measure relating the quantity of natural resources used in producing and deploying technology to their regeneration rate. *Social justice* addresses the ties of technical systems to privileges and power relations. *Self-determination* describes the individual and collective degree of control over the course of our own lives. Finally, *interdependency* defines the structure of necessary interactions among humans through and with the artefacts they create. It is not easy to balance these dimensions, and transformation strategies usually prioritise some over others, depending on their goals and ideological contexts. The four following strategies take these different aspects of technology into account in very different ways.

Green New Deals: industrial sustainability through efficiency

A first strategy is the symbiotic one, often labelled as the Green New Deal. Something akin to it is currently advocated for by many states and environmental organisations attempting to reach a transformative threshold through small steps, beyond which an industrial society would become sustainable (European Commission 2019). It focuses mostly on ecological sustainability and often focuses on demanding legislation against planned obsolescence – as the *Right to Repair* campaign does in the European Union – or improving recycling or upcycling rates and making cities *smart*. Crucially, energy and resource efficiency must steadily increase. Pressure on the industry is ensured through economic means, increasing prices for natural resources through taxes. The threshold is crossed when all energy is renewably produced, goods are durable and all materials cyclically reused without losing their integrity or quality. This strategy applies to technology in general, but the focus on ecological efficiency is usually associated with the transition to a digital post-industrial economy striving for qualitative development.

However, even digital technology is not immaterial but requires massive infrastructure and the industrial production of countless devices (Bratton 2016). Further developing our technical infrastructure or even just maintaining current technological standards in the Global North under this strategy illustrates the lock-in of technological thinking: all of it relies on efficiency gains and renewable energy production which themselves require sustaining a complex industry, while full recycling amounts to a technical miracle we cannot reliably hope for (Bihouix 2014).

This efficiency-oriented strategy is in practice hegemonic when it comes to sustainable technology. Interestingly, it is at the heart of the green growth narrative but also seems to appeal to those who see degrowth as a welcome attempt to decrease the ecological footprint of capitalism. In a sense, it makes degrowth attractive to those not ready to confront their own technological imaginary by channelling demands for transformation towards an optimistic agenda tailored for capitalist modernity and its impressive track record in increasing efficiency. But despite the importance of recycling and parsimonious use of resources, there is probably no path towards degrowth following this strategy without a dramatic change in production and consumption patterns to avoid rebound effects, because all existing technologies consume non-renewable resources. Indeed, technological change without a deeper transformation, which at least accounts for social justice, can only crash into the social and physical limits to growth.

Accelerationism: repurposing technology for the common good

So as we have seen a new level of efficiency reached by a full-fledged digital infrastructure is still very likely bound to fail due to the irrational productive compulsion of capitalism. So a new question arises: Could technological progress solve our problems under another mode of production? Addressing social justice dramatically shifts previous assumptions about the kind of production that needs to be made sustainable. Could the transformation of technology just hinge on economic democracy? This is argued by left-wing accelerationists (Srnicek and Williams 2015). Their idea of repurposing technology to serve the common good rather than profit interests leads to a very ambitious symbiotic strategy aimed primarily at social justice and economic democracy. Beyond full automation to reduce working hours and a universal basic income, a characteristic demand would be for workers to take control of giant digital corporations currently organising the logistics of capital and of platforms running global communications. Such a strategy has an immense potential to become hegemonic if it can be harnessed by a political party drawing power from the ever-growing class of precarious workers (Standing 2011).

Obviously, this strategy focuses on redefining the function of technology within society rather than reshaping technology itself. One could hope that, if form follows function, this would lead to a transformation of technology – and indeed, accelerationists argue for a combinatory approach to repurposing existing pieces of technology. However, the high-tech character of the envisioned future is likely to induce a hierarchical division of labour and is thus difficult to reconcile with a brand of grassroots democracy widely supported in the degrowth movement and rejected by accelerationists as naive *folk politics*. The central role of expertise and efficiency in a technological society thus warrants a critical approach to the accelerationist strategy within the degrowth movement.

The question of the ecological feasibility of this project is even more controversial and has just started being debated – with the promises of digital technology at the centre of the discussion. Accelerationism does not only provide a vision of high-tech and mostly digital commons liberating everyone from the drudgery of work but also promises sustainability through limitless renewable energy production. Even reformulated to avoid disregarding care work and physical realities, both aspects should be critically discussed. But reducing working hours and clean energy production are indeed important topics. So is there a middle ground between degrowth and the reappropriation of high-tech infrastructures? The essential contradiction might lie deeper, in an unabashed promotion of technological progress that should be carefully assessed. First, the development of modern technology should be replaced in the history of colonialism (Arnold 2005) and its often-disastrous impact on the Global South should be acknowledged (Fritz and Hilbig 2019). Second, the concept of progress played a central role in the victory of historical capitalism over its socialist alternatives (Wallerstein 1983) and still acts as an ideological safeguard against any attempt to overcome the industrial mode of production. The question of whether digital technology could be the cornerstone of a new socialism (Morozov 2019) beyond growth leads to a productive controversy, and yet it is clear that accelerating towards degrowth would require rethinking our relationship with technical artefacts.

The two strategies above – Green New Deals and accelerationism – suggest transformations on the basis of existing technologies and therefore do not address the dimensions of self-determination and interdependency. The two following strategies focus on overcoming high-tech imaginaries and thus introduce a vision of alternative technologies taking these aspects into account.

Luddism: controlling and downgrading technology

The pervasiveness of the idea of progress in the development of historical capitalism foregrounds high-tech imaginaries and leads to symbiotic strategic approaches, where the industrial state is key. This can be the case even when striving to overcome capitalism, as the Soviet Union did. The paradigmatic ruptural strategy concerning technology, the opposite of "Soviet power plus electrification", emerged in an organised form at the very beginning of the industrial revolution in Great Britain. The struggle of the Luddites (Sale 1996) against the introduction of machines in manufactures and their own degradation illustrates the strained relation of workers to technology and the still-ongoing production of the working class through industrial discipline. The smashing of machines is a direct action strategy to reclaim self-determination and social justice by workers and simple citizens lacking democratic control over new technologies, and, in time, sabotage spread from the workplace to modern infrastructures such as digital communication networks (Çapulcu Redaktionskollektiv 2018).

There is a distinctive degrowth touch to the Luddite strategy of smashing the technological order, and workers burning down their factories to claim their "right to be lazy" (Paul Lafargue) would be a most apt romanticisation of a degrowth revolution. But the underlying theory of change is fuzzy, with answers pending for a few questions. What is lost when a given technology is destroyed or rejected? How far should technological development be reverted? Although turning back the clock to before the industrial revolution would indeed be a safe path to avoid a climate catastrophe, the social and human price might be too high, and even the most controversial technological developments seem difficult to revert.

So what could be viable strategies for a Luddite approach to technology? Winning over relevant sections of society to such a radical agenda implies focusing on widely rejected technologies: any device or software making work feel like slavery or serving mass surveillance could and should be targeted. And if the historical Luddites failed on a practical level, they left their mark in the form of a powerful counter-imaginary undermining the myth of technological progress and fuelling neo-Luddite attitudes (Mueller 2021). The key to successful strategies in line with a Luddite vision of technologies is to insist on radical democratic control and to show that it is more often industrial modernity than its rejection that leads to reactionary politics (Herf 1984). In an age of permanent climate crisis and digital precarity, ever more people can be convinced that new technologies are not always beneficial to humankind.

Given the centrality of technology in industrial societies, a number of variations on the Luddite theme could be considered as ruptural strategies as well. The individual refusal of technological innovations can hardly account for a systemic strategy, but a collective critical approach as a form of "methodological Luddism" could – that means, not literally destroying things, but sceptically evaluating promises of technology and rationally limiting the power of technologies (Winner 1977). Simple demands such as a moratorium on new technologies (Latouche 2010) can have massive political implications and represent real steps towards making technologies compatible with degrowth. Indeed, continued growth often relies on coercing ever more regions of the world into the world economy through technology. Can there be an effective defence of non-industrial livelihoods? Luddite strategies offer a narrative that can be useful for some extractivist struggles and post-development approaches in the Global South and helps with escaping historical determinism (Fisher 2009).

Open-source low-tech: growing appropriate technology from below

One of the most remarkable legacies of the Luddite threat to industrial societies is the space it opened for interstitial strategies within the field of technology. Disillusionment with and sometimes unfaltering opposition to existing technologies led to calls for an alternative approach (Illich 1973) breaking with oppressive technical structures (Mumford 1967). The idea of building technology outside of the industrial mode of production has spread widely – sometimes as a subculture under the slogan "do it yourself" but also out of necessity for the economically disenfranchised. To a certain extent, even large futuristic projects such as the Cybersin system in Chile had to resort to outdated technology when unable to access state-of-the-art equipment (Medina 2011).

Digital technology is at the forefront of this appropriation movement working with tinkering, hacking and bricolage to gain control over technological systems, but also illustrates its ambiguities. The relative freedom of research at institutions where early software was collaboratively developed, the introduction of personal computers and above all the internet gave rise to a particularly active community in which software was built for users, by users (Himanen 2001) – a group restricted at first to computer scientists, then wealthy enthusiasts and, by the end of the century, the global middle classes. The *Free Software* movement and its best-known achievement, the GNU/Linux operating system, takes a political stance on digital technology and directly addresses issues of social justice and self-determination (Stallman 2002). However, the transformations within capitalism driven by emerging platform corporations (Srnicek 2016) have deeply impacted hacker culture, and call for a critical evaluation of such a digital appropriation strategy. Also, technologies like blockchain and cryptocurrencies, at least to some degree addressing issues of self-determination, fail regarding their ecological impact, being very data- and therefore resource-intensive.

While the digital economy has indeed started restructuring labour relations, it is now clear that the collaborative and commons-oriented approach of the hacker community is not immune to capitalist co-optation (Terranova 2004). As opposed to the concept of free software, which prevents for-profit uses, the more pragmatic vision of open-source software offers technology companies the opportunity to reincorporate the creations of Internet culture. Another benefit of collaborative software development concerns sustainability and planned obsolescence: freed from profit constraints, hardware can be used much longer because updates can still be produced. But few are free to choose the technology they use, and the imperatives of progress undermine this practice of sustainability.

Beyond digital technology, the high-tech paradigm of implementing the latest scientific developments in complex production processes is omnipresent in industrial societies. This manifestation of the never-ending growth principle tends to disregard older or other forms of knowledge and divergent perspectives on the place of technology in our daily lives. The low-tech approach (De Decker 2019) delivers a strong critique of the high-tech imaginary and the problems it induces when applied indiscriminately to any situation, but also a positive vision of ingenious applications of simple but adequate technology to very concrete problems. With a pragmatic attitude, the low-tech movement offers a thorough reflection on the myths of growth and progress and their consequences for the human and natural world.

These observations lead us to consider an open-source low-tech interstitial strategy, which would consist of contextualising technical needs within social and environmental constraints (Bihouix 2014), democratically creating appropriate technologies, and spreading them from below. It would focus on the community of its users and developers, in much the same way as the free software movement did, but seek to lower the requirements to use and co-develop technologies rather than competing with high-tech developments. The flexibility of the low-tech concept is of strategic importance:

devices that were once high-tech can sometimes be repurposed, so that an adaptive response to the crisis of industrial societies can be developed by reusing existing components. For many digital devices already produced, such as certain standardised chips, software updates allow for an extended lifetime, while recycling is impossible. From this perspective, much can also be learned from non-industrial or low-budget technologies that can be found in many places, in particular in the Global South (Pansera *et al* 2020).

This approach is inherently oriented towards ecological sustainability and social justice because it strives to fairly distribute access to technology within natural boundaries. Its very *modus operandi* is self-determination, with an emphasis on individual and collective autonomy in the establishment of technopolitical institutions (Castoriadis 1987). But, above all, it acknowledges the complex system of interdependence induced by technical infrastructures and avoids pursuing the illusion of an individual made absolutely free and all-powerful by high-tech enhancements of its natural abilities. Rather, a low-tech tool is meant to enable fair collaboration between all those using it or affected by it. However, there is a problem with this strategy: if it questions the progress narrative, how can it become hegemonic?

The emancipation of our imaginaries from high-tech patterns requires expanding the spaces where low-tech can spread, which can be achieved by combining various strategies. Reforms establishing a right to repair within a Green New Deal strategy would strengthen the "do it yourself" culture and help share technical skills. A radically democratic reappropriation and repurposing of technology would help create new sustainable technopolitical institutions, under the influence of the critical stance and "propaganda of the deed" of the Luddite strategy. Moreover, the open-source low-tech strategy can only gain wider support in the face of digital corporations expanding their power over society and of a looming "degrowth by disaster" – for example, if high-tech infrastructures crumble under extreme weather conditions and resource exhaustion.

Synergies towards a low-tech digital democracy?

In order to illustrate some of the strategies described above, we now consider two examples showing how the hardware and software of digital technology can be transformed through following degrowth principles. In combination, they hint at a reorientation of the dominant digital imaginary towards a sustainable Internet culture built on the emancipatory ideals of the beginnings of the digital era.

Building a low-tech digital infrastructure

Low-Tech Magazine (Low-Tech Magazine n.d.) is a website presenting research into the problems and limitations of the high-tech paradigm and promoting low-tech solutions, often drawing on pre-industrial technological knowledge. It was launched in 2007 by Kris de Decker, a journalist specialised in technology, as a means to question the progress narrative – in the best critical tradition of the Enlightenment. What was at first a practically-minded discussion took a turn towards prefigurative politics in 2018 with the development of a low-tech solar-powered version of the website that would practice what it teaches, in collaboration with designer Marie Otsuka and artist Roel Roscam Abbing.

The holistic approach of Low-Tech Magazine makes this proof-of-concept particularly interesting. Beyond the carefully selected hardware components, hosted at home on a balcony near Barcelona, the solar website project is an experiment with minimalistic software design. Indeed, its energy consumption is drastically reduced through design choices, made transparent to the visitor, and the display of a battery metre as the background is in itself a political statement. The architecture of the website is perfectly adapted to its contents, and the abundant documentation provides insights and inspiration to those wishing to learn more about the thought-provoking idea of a website actually going offline during longer periods of bad weather. The idea that we can adapt our behaviour to available natural resources is made clear by presenting the printed version of the website as a legitimate offline version – a solution as much social as it is technological.

The project obtained some funding from a design institution in its starting phase and is still ongoing. The achievements and open problems of the project are evaluated and communicated regularly, making it a long-term experiment. It could be seen as a practical campaign promoting low-tech ideas, and has been very successful in this regard, garnering international attention from the media and being discussed at conferences. The website itself has hundreds of thousands of visitors a year and inspired the development of several other websites using solar-powered servers or minimalistic designs. The project has limited resources and clearly states that it has no ambition to scale things up, but also provides ideas for others to expand the experiment.

The solar Low-Tech Magazine project embodies the interstitial open-source low-tech strategy, building a small-scale alternative at the margins of an Internet dominated by the high-tech narrative. Some sites it inspired restrict themselves to reducing their ecological footprint, but the true emancipatory potential of this experiment lies in its exemplary value. It shows in great detail how a digital infrastructure based on a completely different technological assumption could be built, and scaling up the experiment could only lead to an attempted ruptural transformation. Indeed, the backbone of the world economy has been thoroughly digitalised and the infrastructure needed to maintain it could not be rebuilt on low-tech principles. Interestingly, the Internet is an incredibly heterogeneous network in which low-tech servers can easily be integrated. Obstacles to the spread of such servers are thus social and ideological rather than technical – but as energy and other resources become scarce with the end of fossil fuels, such a spread might be triggered by necessity.

Even though the principles of this website naturally hint at a degrowth narrative about technology, the project does not explicitly self-identify with degrowth. However, it definitely contributes to a shift in our technological imaginaries. So much so that it paradigmatically displays the weakness of any degrowth discourse: as long as disasters stay unseen, the degrowth discourse can be dispelled by capitalism and remains unattractive to most people. Only when one notices that there cannot be a high-tech solution to all problems – if any – can the low-tech idea gain traction. This strategy is thus highly context-sensitive: it has more potential in regions with unstable energy grids or undeveloped communication infrastructures and offers a response to the degrading conditions induced by environmental crises.

Strengthening local democracy through digital platforms

Our second example is the software platform Decidim, developed from 2017 onwards in Barcelona to foster participatory democracy in the city. It allows an institution to manage large group processes such as planning, budgeting, assemblies, elections or consultations so that a given instance can be seen as a dedicated social network for a democratic entity. The components of these processes structure interactions between users of the platform in a transparent and traceable manner. The platform was initially created by the city of Barcelona and supported by regional public institutions but evolved into a sustainable software ecosystem driven not only by institutions using it but also by an active community – based on the observation that open-source projects dependent on few public institutions are often discontinued, for example, due to lack of funding. It is now also used by other cities, governments or cooperatives throughout Europe.

This project reflects the entanglement of technical and political processes inherent to the use of digital technology for mass communication and organisation. Attempting to develop tools for participatory democracy, it made its own technopolitical dimension transparent and democratic by establishing a self-governance system for its own technical development, called Metadecidim – itself using Decidim as a decision-making platform, allowing for autonomous decision-making and conflict resolution. The purely technical process of maintaining the source code is hosted on an external collaborative development platform. Using or contributing to the project requires endorsing a social contract describing its guiding principles. Today Decidim is a rather large project that involves many people and institutions and managed to secure funding for itself from public institutions and has been able to take a long-term approach.

The strategy underlying Decidim lies at the crossroads of interstitial and symbiotic approaches to transformation. Indeed, it focuses on concretely building alternative forms of politics through software development and serves as a model for implementing the principles of the future society it strives for, and yet its driving force is governmental institutions attempting to reform their political process. The changes in institutional forms and the ongoing social empowerment Decidim induces have opened spaces for alternative politics and support transformational processes in local politics. Thus, we could expect that if Barcelona were to become the centre of a ruptural transformation once more, as it was in 1936, the interstitial transformations achieved through Decidim would support its move towards a more democratic organisation of society. From this perspective, it should not come as a surprise that Decidim originated in a city that once was the centre of one of the most successful anarchist experiments in history (Bookchin 1976): culture and historical experiences are also key for strategic orientation.

Interestingly, this project can be interpreted as repurposing the platform technology used by social media networks towards a participatory form of local democracy that embodies much of the ideals of the degrowth movement – is this an accelerationist means to a *folk-political* end? This is a consequence of the versatility of web technology and yields a number of questions regarding the relevance of digital technology for the construction of a degrowth society. Crucially, Decidim is not oriented towards the development of productive forces or efficiency but aims at facilitating participation in political processes: even though the ecological costs of running such software on a large scale and in countless institutions should be critically investigated, its design cannot trigger in itself the need for consuming more resources. Therefore, its contribution to the transformation of politics towards a form of collective organisation involving a high level of individual autonomy – a central principle for the degrowth movement – is not tainted by the economic bias of usual platforms and social networks.

It is also important to note that the democratic governance of Decidim has its limitations in the gap between collective design decisions and the actual implementation undertaken by a technical team. Avoiding leaving decisions of programming and implementation to a small group of developers, with their inevitable biases, requires reducing the gap between developers and stakeholders. Therefore, this necessitates technical competence to be shared and disseminated across a larger group of people. This would be a challenge for any attempt to support democratic processes through digital technology, as significant learning and skill-sharing are pre-requisites.

Inventing technology for a new Great Transformation

The examples of Low-Tech Magazine and Decidim illustrate two very different aspects of digital technology and its role in the struggle for a degrowth transformation. But even though the approaches they embody are far from being dominant in discourse and reality, both contain seeds of a radical transformation of technology. Indeed, one can envision a technological future where digital democratic platforms running on a low-tech infrastructure of servers and networks would play a prominent role in organising society in an integrated way. However, as the lack of societal control over technological development is a consequence of the separation of labour from democracy inherent to capitalism, achieving such a goal crucially depends on a larger transformation.

Just as the Great Transformation (Polanyi 1944) gave rise to market societies by introducing new economic mechanisms, this new transformation will need to redefine how societies coordinate needs and resources. A digital infrastructure, from servers and networks to platforms such as Decidim, could support this transformation by combining transparency and democratic control with efficient coordination of production and consumption – advantageously replacing the invisible hand of the market (Daum and Nuss 2021). But the degrowth movement should not lose sight of the relative technical simplicity of Decidim and the role this plays in achieving its goals: making such a platform into a full-fledged techno-utopia by extending it with algorithmic control and comprehensive data collection would most likely be counter-productive with respect to essential democratic and ecological principles.

The most pressing problem to address in the field of technology is the high-tech imaginary and its elitist, centralised conception of knowledge, preventing the democratic process of establishing new techno-political institutions. This is why symbiotic and interstitial strategies must be combined to create space for alternative views of technology. The main challenge lies in making alternatives attractive, but the economic and ecological devastation of the planet – through which capitalism brings its own demise – are also powerful incentives for a deep cultural and political change in attitudes towards technology. Although rethinking and reappropriating technology is only a piece of the puzzle, reinventing socially and ecologically resilient technology is central to any serious attempt at transformation and is one of the most urgent tasks we face.

References

Anders, Günther. 1956. *Die Antiquiertheit des Menschen* (The Outdatedness of Human Beings). München: C.H. Beck.

Appadurai, Arjun. 1996. *Modernity at Large.* Minneapolis: University of Minnesota Press.

Arnold, David. 2005. "Europe, Technology and Colonialism in the 20th Century." *History and Technology* 21, no. 1: 85–106.

Bastani, Aaron. 2019. *Fully Automated Luxury Communism: A Manifesto.* London: Verso.

Bihouix, Phillipe. 2014. *L'âge des low tech. Vers une civilisation techniquement soutenable*. Paris: Éditions du Seuil.

Bookchin, Murray. 1976. *The Spanish Anarchists: The Heroic Years 1868–1936*. Edinburgh: AK Press.

Bratton, Benjamin. 2016. *The Stack: On Software and Sovereignty*. Cambridge, MA: MIT Press.

Çapulcu Redaktionskollektiv. 2018. *DELETE! Digitalisierte Fremdbestimmung*. Münster: Unrast.

Castoriadis, Cornelius. 1987. *The Imaginary Institution of Society*. Cambridge: Polity.

Daum, Timo, and Sabine Nuss, eds. 2021. *Die unsichtbare Hand des Plans. Koordination und Kalkül im digitalen Kapitalismus*. Berlin: Dietz.

De Decker, Kris. 2019. *Low-Tech Magazine 2007–2012*. North Carolina: Lulu.

Ellul, Jacques. 1964. *The Technological Society*. New York: Vintage Books.

European Commission. 2019. *The European Green Deal*.

European Commission. 2020. *100 Climate-Neutral Cities by 2030 – by and for the Citizens*.

Eversberg, Dennis, and Matthias Schmelzer. 2018. "The Degrowth Spectrum. Convergence and Divergence Within a Diverse and Conflictual Alliance." *Environmental Values* 27, no. 3: 245–267.

Fisher, Mark. 2009. *Capitalist Realism: Is there no Alternative?* Ropley: Zero Books.

Fritz, Thomas, and Sven Hilbig. 2019. *Global Justice 4.0. The Impacts of Digitalisation on the Global South*. Berlin: Brot für die Welt, Evangelisches Werk für Diakonie und Entwicklung e.V.

Gorz, André. 2010. *Critique of Economic Reason*. London: Verso.

Herf, Jeffrey. 1984. *Reactionary Modernism: Technology, Culture and Politics in Weimar and the Third Reich*. Cambridge: Cambridge University Press.

Herring, Horace, and Robin Roy. 2007. "Technological Innovation, Energy Efficient Design and the Rebound Effect." *Technovation* 27, no. 4: 194–203.

Hickel, Jason, and Giorgos Kallis. 2019. "Is Green Growth Possible?" *New Political Economy* 25, no. 7576: 1–18.

Himanen, Pekka. 2001. *The Hacker Ethic and the Spirit of the Information Age*. Random House.

Illich, Ivan. 1973. *Tools for Conviviality*. London: Marion Boyars

Jochum, Georg. 2020. "(Techno-)Utopias and the Question of Natural Boundaries." *Behemoth* 13, no. 1: 7–22.

Kerschner, Christian, Petra Wächter, Linda Nierling, and Melf-Hinrich Ehlers. 2018. "Degrowth and Technology: Towards Feasible, Viable, Appropriate and Convivial Imaginaries." *Journal of Cleaner Production*, 197: 1619–1636.

Latouche, Serge. 2010. *Farewell to Growth*. Cambridge: Polity.

Low-Tech Magazine. n.d. *Low-Tech Magazine. Doubts on Progress and Technology*. https://www.lowtechmagazine.com/.

Malm, Andreas. 2016. *Fossil Capital: The Rise of Steam Power and the Roots of Global Warming*. London: Verso.

Mason, Paul. 2015. *Postcapitalism: A Guide to our Future*. London: Lane.

McAfee, Andrew. 2019. *More from Less: The Surprising Story of how we learned to proper using fewer resources – and what happens next*. New York: Scribner.

Medina, Eden. 2011. *Cybernetic Revolutionaries. Technology and Politics in Allende's Chile*. Cambridge, MA: MIT Press.

Morozov, Evgeny. 2019. "Digital Socialism?" *New Left Review* 116/177. https://newleftreview.org/issues/ii116/articles/evgeny-morozov-digital-socialism

Mueller, Gavin. 2021. *Breaking Things at Work: The Luddites Are Right about Why You Hate Your Job*. London: Verso.

Mumford, Lewis. 1967. *The Myth of the Machine. Technics and human development*. London: Secker&Warburg.

Pansera, Mario, Keren Naa Abeka Arthur, Andrea Jimenez, Poonam Pandey, Stevienna de Saille, Fabien Medvecky, Michiel van Oudheusden et al. 2020. "The Plurality of Technology and Innovation in the Global South." In *Responsibility Beyond Growth: A Case for Responsible Stagnation*, 91–110. Bristol University Press.

Polanyi, Karl. 1944. *The Great Transformation: The Political and Economic Origins of Our Time*. Boston: Beacon Press.

Sahlins, Marshall. 1972. *Stone Age Economics*. Chicago and New York: Aldine Atherton.

Sale, Kirkpatrick. 1996. *Rebels Against The Future: The Luddites and Their War on the Industrial Revolution: Lessons for the Computer Age*. Basic Books.

Srnicek, Nick, and Alex Williams. 2015. *Inventing the Future: Postcapitalism and a World without Work*. London: Verso.

Srnicek, Nick. 2016. *Platform Capitalism*. Cambridge: Polity.

Stallman, Richard. 2002. *Free Software, Free Society.* Free Software Foundation.

Standing, Guy. 2011. *The Precariat: The New Dangerous Class.* Bloomsbury Academic.

Terranova, Tiziana. 2004. *Network Culture. Politics for the Information Age.* New York: Pluto Press.

Vetter, Andrea. 2018. "The Matrix of Convivial Technology-Assessing Technologies for Degrowth." *Journal of Cleaner Production* 197, no. 2: 1778–1786.

Wallerstein, Immanuel. 1983. *Historical Capitalism.* London: Verso.

Wendling, Amy E. 2009. *Karl Marx on Technology and Alienation.* Basingstoke: Palgrave Macmillan.

Winner, Langdon. 1977. *Autonomous Technology. Technics-out-of-Control as a Theme in Political Thought.* Cambridge, MA: MIT Press.

Winner, Langdon. 1986. *The Whale and the Reactor. A Search for Limits in an Age of High Technology.* Chicago: University of Chicago Press.

Wright, Erik O. 2010. *Envisioning Real Utopias.* London: Verso.

Chapter 14: Energy

An overview of strategies for social-ecological transformation in the field of energy

By Mario Díaz Muñoz

Introduction

During the last 150 years, the availability of cheap and high energy density fossil fuels has enabled a dramatic increase in global primary energy use. This fuelled the uneven global development of modern industrial economies. While providing enormous amounts of goods and material wealth, this development is posing existential threats to humankind, such as climate change and the ecological crisis (Clark and York 2005). The shift away from fossil fuels to renewable energy sources is a crucial step in the right direction, but one to tread carefully. Renewable energy production has a lower energy return per energy invested (EROI) as compared with fossil fuels, reducing the overall net energy available to sustain high levels of energy use. In addition, the production of renewable energy rests on the extraction of vast amounts of non-renewable raw materials such as lithium, cobalt, neodymium or nickel which are used for batteries, solar panel cells and wind turbines, respectively. These raw materials are mostly extracted in Global South countries, resulting not only in environmental degradation during their extraction and allocation of waste, but also leading to social conflicts that involve notions of (in)justice, sovereignty and distributional conflicts. A low-carbon economy must be, therefore, a socially just and low-energy use economy.

Under capitalism, economic growth is necessary to keep the system stable, as well as being deemed as a precondition to satisfy human needs and well-being. However, the economy is embedded in the biophysical reality, which means that all economic processes require energy and materials and produce waste. This makes absolute decoupling of growth from its environmental impacts – in other words, green growth, supported by techno-optimists – impossible. Furthermore, under capitalism, the way energy is produced, transformed, distributed, and eventually consumed, prioritises logics of power and profit maximisation over the satisfaction of human needs and well-being.

Degrowth is put forward as an alternative to tackle not only decreasing energy and material throughput, but also the enormous lock-in around production, finance, and the governance of energy to accommodate a plurality of low-energy visions of society in which social institutions are not reliant upon growth. While there is an increasing amount of literature that explores the theoretical and material feasibility of low energy use scenarios (Millward-Hopkins *et al.* 2020), degrowth scenario analysis (D'Alessandro *et al.* 2020) and complex modelling analyses (Nieto *et al.* 2020), there is a challenge regarding the socio-political feasibility of those scenarios. This poses a serious question, and the object of this chapter: what strategies could the Degrowth movement pursue to achieve its energy-related goals while securing living conditions and basic needs?

This chapter discusses a variety of strategies aimed at transforming energy systems away from fossil fuels and capitalist relations into low-carbon and low-energy use social arrangements. I conclude by highlighting the mutually interdependent and interconnected nature of these strategies as the key feature of their potential for being effective.

Resisting and disrupting energy capital

Scientific evidence suggests that, to avoid exceeding a 2°C global warming, more than a third of oil reserves and 50% of gas reserves need to remain in the ground (McGlade and Ekins 2015). Yet, the fossil fuel industry keeps heavily investing in new infrastructure to expand fuel supply (Piggot *et al.* 2017). Simultaneously, investment in renewable energy is at its record high (BNEF 2019). Resistance movements emerge against the backdrop of environmental degradation, irreversible environmental-social impacts, territorial dispossessions and issues of control and access rights to resources, often triggered by fossil fuel projects (Temper 2019) and, more recently, low-carbon energy projects (Del Bene et al. 2018). Resistance movements threaten to disrupt the circuits of energy capital – understood as energy-related infrastructure and financial assets – while raising the question of who produces energy and for what purposes.

Resistance movements and actions are formed by Indigenous people, frontline communities and a wide variety of collectives such as environmental activists, journalists or social movements – 350.org, Fridays for Future, Extinction Rebellion, or the campaign Chiloé Libré de Saqueo Energético, which the second half of this chapter focuses on. The Environmental Justice Atlas project, launched in 2015, currently documents over 2046 cases of resistance around the globe over energy-related projects. It is widely recognised that these actions and movements influence the politics and practices of resource use towards less destructive social and ecological outcomes (Villamayor-Tomas and García-López 2018).

The organisation of workshops and discussion groups, civil disobedience, direct confrontational tactics such as mass arrests, marches, lockdowns and blockades are part of the extensive repertoire of strategies. However, there is an uneven distribution of the consequences of activism. Whereas in some parts of the world, activists may mainly deal with mass arrests, in other areas, defenders face physical violence or even murder. In 2018 alone, 61 environmental defenders against energy-related projects (disproportionately located in the Global South) were murdered (Global Witness 2019) and the trend has increased over the last fifteen years (Butt et al. 2019).

Additional resistance strategies involve the creation of politically effective – and unexpected – coalitions driven by common interests, such as the Cowboys and Indians Alliance to stop the Keystone XL project (Lukacs 2014). Resistance movements tend to reframe their demands in terms of collective rather than individual preferences. Frequently those preferences cannot be reduced to monetary terms, widening the scope of the political debate for the inclusion of different languages of valuation (Martinez-Alier 2008). In addition, the effectiveness of resistance actions is often influenced and increased by the level of connectedness between bottom-up decentralised actions and transnational networks and coalitions. This last strategy adds an important element to resistance strategies that signals a shift from "not in my backyard" to "not on my planet" (Vedder 2019) or NOPE (Not On Planet Earth).

Legal strategies are double-edged means to stop or slow down the construction of energy projects. Investor-State Dispute Settlement mechanisms protect energy capital when energy infrastructure projects are blocked or interrupted and tend to compensate – frequently with public money – the financial investors for their "lost" potential returns. On the other hand, there are successful cases of litigation such as the outlawing of the expansion of London Heathrow airport for not meeting the government's climate commitments, the permanent ban on fracking in the state of Paraná in Brazil, or the Kenyan tribunal cancelling a developer's licence to build a new coal plant at Lamu.

Economic strategies are exemplified by the fossil fuel divestment movement, a broad-based civil society movement aimed at redirecting finance away from fossil fuels (Healy and Barry 2017). The movement is currently an international network of campaigns and campaigners involving 1,327 institutions with divestment pledges reaching US$14.58 trillion by mid-2021 (Global Divestment Commitments Database 2021). Typical strategies within the divestment movement involve the creation of alliances within members of the targeted institution (e.g., senate members of a university and their finance staff), awareness-raising events, marches, training workshops on the consequences of divestment – e.g., stranded assets which in turn increase the uncertainty around the long-term financial viability of fossil fuel projects, press releases to local media and/or open letters from academia that pressure the institution to divest. In addition, the divestment movement can simultaneously be understood as a strategy to reframe climate change as a moral issue by raising questions of legitimation and reputation and stigmatising the fossil fuel industry while socialising the idea that fossil fuels are at their endgame (Helm 2017).

There is, however, an important potential drawback of the divestment movement (as briefly explained in Chapter 18). The strategy could backfire if small companies or state-owned companies, which are subject to less public scrutiny, buy these assets and start maximising the returns exploiting the reserves. This could lead to unintended consequences for the divestment movement (Raval 2021).

It is crucial to point out that all strategies described above depend on transnational networks of alliances to avoid cost-shifting and spatial fixes driven by Northern elites (and increasingly Southern elites too) as a response to disruptions of energy capital. One case in point is the Fossil Fuel Non-proliferation Treaty, a global initiative that aims at (1) Preventing the global proliferation of coal, oil and gas by ending all new exploration and production; (2) Regulating the phasing-out and dismantling of fossil fuel production infrastructure while defending the rights of Indigenous peoples and impacted communities; and (3) Fast-tracking collective action for developing low-carbon pathways that are fair for workers, communities and countries. These overarching strategies open the possibility of broadening the social-ecological transformation beyond *solely* transitioning away from fossil fuels, while facilitating the emergence of collective autonomy and processes of collective self-limitation, which could be key for low energy use visions.

Building alternatives

Under capitalism, energy systems are predominantly organised through symbiotic relationships between profit-oriented transnational corporations and States aiming to control and secure the flows and stocks of energy to maximise profit and power to maintain their competitive advantage (Riffo 2017). This is predicated on the private ownership and control of productive technologies. Therefore, tackling the issue of ownership and control is key to any degrowth strategy aiming at decreasing energy and material throughput.

Community energy projects have proliferated over the last years. These involve control and ownership over energy utilities, while also allowing communities to collectively benefit from the outcomes – such as autonomous control and organisation over energy production and consumption (Seyfang *et al.* 2013). Collective ownership is not a panacea. It could be the case that a collectively owned enterprise is organised around growth. However, collective ownership is likely to be the precondition for gaining political agency and collectively deciding upon goals that would not just limit energy use, but would also include social measures of redistribution, reciprocity, equity and justice, opening up possibilities for social-ecological transformations (Kunze and Becker 2015).

Strategies towards community energy involve governance tactics at various scales. At the national scale, centralised governments can support and enable community energy projects through research, policy efforts and financial incentives, grants or direct support. However, as a response to policy uncertainty – the lack of policy, planning and intermittent financial support from national governments – there has been a mushrooming of transnational networks of governance amongst relevant cities around the world such as Cities Climate Leadership Group (C40), Cities for Climate Protection, Fearless Cities network or the Global Covenant of Mayors for Climate and Energy. The main goal is to align policy plans with climate targets.

Public participation in policy development is essential to put an end to the social exclusion of marginalised groups in the development of energy systems (Pandey and Sharma 2021). Public participation raises the issue that hierarchical government-led or expert centred approaches are not always adequate to address policy issues and energy developments. One of the main strategies put forward is the creation of climate assemblies/citizens' assemblies.

The creation of climate/citizens assemblies is a strategy aiming to set climate-related mandates for national and local governments while improving their legitimacy. The set of demands posed by citizens' assemblies can range from the creation of debates and informative sessions, the development of adaptation, mitigation and resilience plans against climate change, the allocation of funds towards climate action or pressuring the higher-level government to take action. However, even if some demands are accepted and agreed upon with local government officials, serious challenges can appear that impede their implementation. Neoliberal pressures of privatisation and outsourcing limit the capacity of institutional actors to change locked-in inertia. While it is strategically important to pursue these pathways for change, community-based responses are emerging to find other ways to influence policy or directly build parallel alternatives.

At the community level, the strategies are manifold. On one hand, there is the creation of civil-society-led initiatives such as Transition Towns and carbon rationing groups (Bulkeley and Newell 2015). Transition Towns have grown from only 400 communities in May 2010 to more than 2,000 spread over more than 50 countries today. They constitute a "quiet, networked revolution" of communities of practice around the globe and play a key role in mobilising finance, setting standards of community governance and enabling political engagement (Rapid Transition Alliance 2019). In terms of energy-oriented plans, some initiatives aim at developing community energy plans for energy descent scenarios – low-energy use communities powered by renewable energy sources – and for taking back democratic control over decentralised renewable energy production. These types of community-based initiatives form the context in which social innovations flourish, leading to strategies of scaling-up demands through all governance levels.

One key community-based social innovation is the development of Public-Common Partnerships (PCPs). These are alternative institutional designs that go beyond state/market dichotomies to include Commoner Associations – ordinary people associated with the energy project – and third parties (trade unions or expert groups). The objective is not just collective ownership, but a decentralised democratic governance model that embodies new common senses about energy, democracy, and collective control (Milburn and Russell 2019). This is a crucial strategy to build energy democracy and energy sovereignty at the heart of new energy systems.

Culturing low-energy use practices

Beyond challenging the very structures of control and growth-oriented relations that govern energy systems, Degrowth strategies need to be complemented with demand-side strategies aimed at drastically reducing energy use and consumption to stay within planetary boundaries (Grubbler *et al.* 2018).

Strategies pertaining to individual behaviour and lifestyles, such as consumption patterns – e.g., start a vegan diet or lower household electricity use as well as mobility choices, i.e., more cycling and less car use, are seen as potential "low-hanging fruits" that could be applied without significant trade-offs. Dubois *et al.* (2019) found that these voluntary decisions could lead to significant results by potentially reducing up to 50% of lifestyle-related emissions. However, excessive focus on individual behaviour has provoked criticism due to the individualisation of responsibility and issues of virtue signalling.

In this respect, degrowth strategies need to follow a dual approach that recognises both: (1) the transformative role of individual actions through empowerment and increased political agency and awareness; and (2) the acknowledgement that individual behaviours are conditioned by *practices,* which in turn are embedded in social, cultural and economic contexts that reproduce certain patterns of demand.

From practice theory (Shove *et al.* 2012), we know that norms, values and belief systems play a crucial role in shaping, reproducing or questioning everyday practices of producing and consuming resources. *Practices* need to be first imagined as *concepts* against the backdrop of the dominant "common senses" that rule our imagination. That is why concepts such as *decentralisation, decommodification, relocalisation* of renewable energy sources and *visions of low energy use* societies are prerequisites for building alternatives. Then, the materialisation of those alternatives – cooperatives, networks of care, etc. – act as positive feedback loops that can establish and reinforce different kinds of cultures that displace the hegemonic one.

Due to the centrality of energy in the way modern economies and societies function, cultural shifts around it may necessitate re-culturing different ideas about technology, social practices around mobility, comfort, etc. In this sense, for example, reflecting on the role of technology in transformative post-growth energy systems is essential to go beyond simplistic techno-optimistic approaches, towards more a nuanced understanding of the *potentials* and *engrained logics* of technology as embedded in social contexts.

Demand-side structural changes towards climate compatibility, such as measures to accelerate the decline of particular industries or new taxes imposed on fuels, can however have regressive consequences, often affecting poorer members of society. These measures can trigger popular backlashes in the form of protests, which may be amplified by the absence of a cultural shift, and by vested interests and incumbent actors who make alliances with disinformation-based extreme right media to stigmatise specific measures or foster voting mobilisation against them. Here, the material and cultural aspects of energy are both sides of the same coin. One important political strategy to overcome these issues – disinformation campaigns, top-down regressive measures, etc.

– is the proliferation of Just Transition Alliances (JTA) that bring together environmental advocacy groups, urban dwellers, trade unions and peoples affected by energy projects. This strategy focuses on people and power and pays special attention to the history and concrete context in which the strategy is taking place. JTA are based primarily on community regeneration, which becomes a precondition and an antidote to social fragmentation driven by the interests of the few, opening the possibility of collectively designing low-energy use communities.

Conclusion

It is essential to highlight the interconnected, mutually dependent, context-specific nature of strategies and tactics (Newell 2021). Political praxis is full of contradictions due to competing mental models between actors about how change emerges, which scales of action to prioritise, or which concrete next steps are to be followed. In this chapter I propose how these contradictions can be strategically minimised by: (1) building politically effective coalitions between broad-based movements that reflect ideological diversity; (2) recognising that the main driver for political mobilisation could be issues of sovereignty, justice or self-determination rather than climate concerns (see case example below); (3) promoting bottom-up decentralisation, connected through transnational webs of actions; and (4) following a dual cultural strategy where individual actions are both important and embedded in complex culturally – and materially – based practices.

The development of social boundaries through collective self-limitation should be at the centre of the energy transition. Since "there is nothing automatically emancipatory about renewable energies" (Abramsky 2010), any transformative strategy needs to keep in check the social relations that set the governance of production and consumption (e.g., avoid a productivist approach to energy, albeit in public hands) and avoid the spatial fixes driven by financial elites as a response to disruptions of energy capital.

To conclude, how energy is produced and consumed is embedded in the structures of energy systems. A shift in the use of energy production and consumption means a shift in the balance of power of who gets to organise society, what values they espouse, and what social outcomes they want to fulfil. Any strategy aimed at transforming energy systems needs to be located in the here and now while occupying all possible political spaces.

References

Abramsky, Koyla. 2010. *Sparking a Worldwide Energy Revolution: Social Struggles in the Transition to a Post-Petrol World.* Chico, CA: AK Press.

BNEF (Bloomberg New Energy Finance). 2019. *Electric Vehicle Outlook 2019.* New York, NY: Bloomberg Finance L.P.

Bulkeley, Harriet, and Peter Newell. 2015. *Governing Climate Change.* 2nd ed. London: Routledge.

Butt, Nathalie, Frances Lambrick, Mary Menton, and Anna Renwick. 2019. "The Supply Chain of Violence." *Nature Sustainability* 2, no. 8: 742–747.

Clark, Brett, and Richard York. 2005. "Carbon Metabolism: Global Capitalism, Climate Change, and the Biospheric Rift." *Theory and Society* 34, no. 4: 391–428.

D'Alessandro, Simone, André Cieplinski, Tiziano Distefano, and Kristofer Dittmer. 2020. "Feasible Alternatives to Green Growth." *Nature Sustainability* 3, no. 4: 329–335.

Del Bene, Daniela, Arnim Scheidel, and Leah Temper. 2018. "More Dams, More Violence? A Global Analysis on Resistances and Repression around Conflictive Dams through Co-Produced Knowledge." *Sustainability Science* 13, no. 3: 617–633.

Dubois, Ghislain, Benjamin Sovacool, Carlo Aall, Maria Nilsson, Carine Barbier, Alina Herrmann, Sébastien Bruyère *et al.* 2019. "It Starts at Home? Climate Policies Targeting Household Consumption and Behavioral Decisions Are Key to Low–Carbon Futures." *Energy Research & Social Science* 52: 144–158.

Global Divestment Commitments Database. 2021. *The Database of Fossil Fuel Divestment Commitments Made by Institutions Worldwide.* https://gofossilfree.org/divestment/commitments/.

Global Witness. 2019. *Enemies of the State?* London, Washington, DC: Global Witness. https://www.globalwitness.org/en/campaigns/environmental–activists/enemies–state/.

Grubler, Arnulf, Charlie Wilson, Nuno Bento, Benigna Boza–Kiss, Volker Krey, David L. McCollum, Narasimha D. Rao et al. 2018. "A Low Energy Demand Scenario for Meeting the 1.5°C Target and Sustainable Development Goals without Negative Emission Technologies." *Nature Energy* 3, no. 6: 515–527.

Healy, Noel, and John Barry. 2017. "Politicizing Energy Justice and Energy System Transitions: Fossil Fuel Divestment and a 'Just Transition'." *Energy Policy* 108: 451–459.

Helm, Dieter. 2017. *Burn Out: The Endgame for Fossil Fuels*. Yale University Press.

Kunze, Conrad, and Sören Becker. 2015. "Collective Ownership in Renewable Energy and Opportunities for Sustainable Degrowth." *Sustainability Science* 10, no. 3: 425–437.

Lukacs, Martin. 2014. "Keystone XL Pipeline Opposition Forges 'Cowboys and Indians' Alliance." The Guardian, November 17, 2014. https://www.theguardian.com/environment/2014/nov/17/keystone-xl-pipeline-opposition-cowboys-indians-alliance-oil.

Martinez-Alier, J. 2008. "Languages of Valuation." *Economic and Political Weekly* 43, no. 48: 28–32. https://www.epw.in/journal/2008/48/global-economic-and-financial-crisis-uncategorised/languages-valuation.html.

McGlade, Christophe, and Paul Ekins. 2015. "The Geographical Distribution of Fossil Fuels Unused When Limiting Global Warming to 2 °C." *Nature* 517: 187–190.

Milburn, Keir, and Bertie Russell. 2019. *Public-Common Partnerships: Building New Circuits of Collective Ownership*. Common Wealth. https://www.common-wealth.co.uk/reports/public-common-partnerships-building-new-circuits-of-collective-ownership.

Millward-Hopkins, Joel, Julia K. Steinberger, Narasimha D. Rao, and Yannick Oswald. 2020. "Providing Decent Living with Minimum Energy: A Global Scenario." *Global Environmental Change* 65: 1–10.

Newell, Peter. 2021. *Power Shift: The Global Political Economy of Energy Transitions*. Cambridge University Press.

Nieto, Jaime, Óscar Carpintero, Luis J. Miguel, and Ignacio de Blas. 2020. "Macroeconomic Modelling under Energy Constraints: Global Low Carbon Transition Scenarios." *Energy Policy* 137: 1–16.

Pandey, Poonam, and Aviram Sharma. 2021. "Knowledge Politics, Vulnerability and Recognition-Based Justice: Public Participation in Renewable Energy Transitions in India." *Energy Research & Social Science* 71: 1–11.

Piggot, Georgia, Peter Erickson, Michael Lazarus, and Harro van Asselt. 2017. "Addressing Fossil Fuel Production under the UNFCCC: Paris and beyond." SEI Working Paper. Stockholm Environment Institute, Stockholm. https://researchspace.auckland.ac.nz/bitstream/handle/2292/56341/SEI-2017-WP-addressing-fossil-fuel-production.pdf?sequence=1.

Rapid Transition Alliance. (2019). "Transition Towns – the Quiet, Networked Revolution." *Rapid Transition Alliance*, October 9, 2019. https://www.rapidtransition.org/stories/transition-towns-the-quiet-networked-revolution/.

Raval, Anjli. 2021. "A $140bn Asset Sale: The Investors Cashing in on Big Oil's Push to Net Zero." *Financial Times*, July 6, 2021. https://www.ft.com/content/4dee7080-3a1b-479f-a50c-c3641c82c142.

Riffo, Lorena. 2017. "Fracking and Resistance in the Land of Fire." *NACLA Report on the Americas* 49, no. 4: 470–475.

Seyfang, Gill, Jung Jin Park, and Adrian Smith. 2013. "A Thousand Flowers Blooming? An Examination of Community Energy in the UK." *Energy Policy* 61: 977–989.

Shove, Elizabeth, Mika Pantzar, and Matt Watson. 2012. *The Dynamics of Social Practice: Everyday Life and How It Changes*. SAGE Publications Ltd.

Temper, Leah. 2019. "Blocking Pipelines, Unsettling Environmental Justice: From Rights of Nature to Responsibility to Territory." *Local Environment* 24, no. 2: 94–112.

Vedder, Meike. 2019. "From 'Not in My Backyard' to 'Not on My Planet': The Potential of Blockadia for the Climate Justice Movement: A Case Study of Fossil Fuel Resistance in Groningen, the Netherlands." *Lund University Student Papers*. http://lup.lub.lu.se/student-papers/record/8982818.

Villamayor-Tomas, Sergio, and Gustavo García-López. 2018. "Social Movements as Key Actors in Governing the Commons: Evidence from Community–Based Resource Management Cases across the World." *Global Environmental Change* 53: 114–126.

A case in the field of energy: the struggle against energy extractivism in Southern Chile

By Gabriela Cabaña

Chiloé, an archipelago of over 40 islands in the south of Chile, has been the setting of several waves of plunder and ecological destruction, and is now facing the possibility of becoming a sacrifice zone in the name of the decarbonisation of the national energy grid. This section analyses the ongoing campaign *Chiloé Libre del Saqueo Energético* – Chiloé Free of Energy Sacking – (Chiloé Libre del Saqueo Energético 2021) to stop the construction of a new electricity transmission line. This transmission line would be a mega-infrastructure facilitating the further expansion of huge renewable energy generation plants on the archipelago. The *Chiloé Libre* campaign was initiated in January 2021 as a response to the presentation of the new transmission line by the company Transelec to the Environmental Impact Assessment System (*Sistema de Evaluación de Impacto Ambiental*-SEIA) four months earlier. SEIA depends on the state's Environmental Evaluation Service (SEA) and is in charge of giving environmental clearance to projects. Transelec, a transnational consortium composed of Canadian and Chinese investors, is the main power transmission company in the country. If constructed, this new line would connect the northern part of Chiloé's largest island (Ancud) to the continent (SEA Chile 2020). The need to start a coordinated work against the Transelec project started after a conversation with Longko (Mapuche–Huilliche–Chono ancestral authority) Clementina Lepío Melipichún, who knew that some people in the affected area were worried and sought to stop the project. Conversations between members of the CESCH (*Centro de Estudios Sociales de Chiloé*, a local, research-oriented NGO) and ancestral authorities of the archipelago followed. In a couple of months, we gathered a team of roughly 15 people, some that would be directly affected and others from different regions of the archipelago, including people and ancestral authorities from communities in and outside Ancud.

The key objective of the campaign is the cancellation of the Transelec project and, more widely, a moratorium on new energy generation projects until a proper land use plan in the archipelago (truly democratic and ecologically pertinent) is implemented and working effectively (Resumen 2021). This is important because even though the project we are trying to stop is about energy transmission and not energy generation, it will make the installation of new infrastructure like large wind farms feasible, as the current electricity line that connects to the continent is at the top capacity. This is concerning for the known negative impact that such large projects can have on the ecosystems and communities (Avila 2018). When we started organising, the first and urgent step we identified was the need to take part in the "citizen's participation", a space opened by the SEIA as part of the wider environmental impact assessment process, in order to receive anyone's comments and concerns on the Transelec project, as reported to the SEIA. We contacted NGOs with different expertise and grassroots organisations with experience with similar processes[32]. We worked to present citizens' observations (as guaranteed by the process of environmental assessment) while we simultaneously created social media content[33] to alert people about this project and the many untold consequences it would have. Our observations mainly focused on (1) the lack of proper baseline observations and incorrect determination of the "influence area" of the project (underestimated by Transelec) (2) the lack of coherence with existing planning documents, and the lack of comprehensive land planning documents more generally, (3) the impact on landscape, biodiversity and water bodies, unacknowledged or downplayed in Transelec's report, (4) the violation of Indigenous people's rights, including insufficient compensation for the damages they would suffer and (5) the grave limitations to citizens' participation due to the COVID-19 pandemic. Getting as many observations and as precise as possible was considered a key step

---

32   FIMA (Fiscalía del Medio Ambiente), Micófilos Chile, Insurgentes Chilwe among others.
33   All pieces can be found on our Facebook page (Chiloé Libre del Saqueo Energético 2021).

to both stop the project (our priority) and maintain high chances of using legal resources in the future. A key resource was some members' prior experience in territory defence, such as the collective *Salvemos Mar Brava* that has been opposing the construction of a wind park (*Parque Eólico Chiloé*) in Ancud since 2013.

Due to the several stages of approval needed for a project like this, we foresee the campaign will last at least a few years. We are still waiting for the report from the SEA and the eventual approval or rejection by the Minister's Commission (the final decision body). Even if the transmission line is approved and built, the objective of stopping the proliferation of wind farms will remain. Official policy revolves around the push for the rapid installation of renewable energy infrastructure to stimulate an exit from fossil fuels, the "greening" of mining, future economic growth, and the creation of a green hydrogen industry in which Chile would be a "world leader" (Ministerio de Energía 2020). A key element for the financial attractiveness and feasibility of green hydrogen is catering to foreign buyers, especially in Europe. Therefore, we expect the interest of large transnational investors in installing wind farms in the Chiloé province to only increase in the future.

From local impacts to the wider picture of energy planning

As noted, because the Transelec project has not yet been accepted or rejected, it is still too soon to say whether the campaign has been effective in its initial goal of stopping the transmission line. But at least we have broadened a debate that has little visibility in Chile, as most activist campaigning focuses (with good reason) on stopping existing coal power plants and fossil infrastructure. An unforeseen difficulty has been the pandemic and its multiple consequences. Besides affecting communities in their everyday lives, it has made any organising extremely difficult. Most of our meetings have been online, in a mostly rural setting where access to good quality internet is rare. This makes overcoming the lack of information about the new line – or plain disinformation in the report presented by

Transelec to the SEIA – very difficult. Many of the documents of the report are extremely opaque and technical, and finding information to criticise them is very demanding and slow.

Chiloé is a territory facing multiple ecological crises – from ecologically predatory salmon farming to illegal dumping sites, and infrastructure projects such as new highways and a bridge to the mainland (Mondaca 2017). This is why a key focus of our campaign has been to call for respecting local autonomy and self-determination, and beyond this particular project, to connect with wider and older struggles. This is also why we have focused and insisted on the respect of the rights of Indigenous people in the archipelago, the Mapuche–Huilliche–Chono. But the protection of rights of these *pueblos-nación* (First Nations) by officials is extremely poor and negligent. We know of other energy-related projects where the procedures to safeguard their rights (like the 169 ILO Convention) were violated (Radio JGM 2020).

Another key lesson is that we need to locate this project in the larger picture, at the insular, national, and even international levels. Recurrent comments in reaction to our social media campaign argue that ours is a case of "Not In My Backyard"; but nothing could be further from the truth. Both transmission lines and wind farms are heavy infrastructural interventions in delicate and already very stressed ecosystems. In existing wind farms in Chiloé, the evaluation of impacts and the monitoring of changes in elements like soil and peatlands has been omitted (Durán Sanzana *et al.* 2018). In the larger picture and public debate, and as Chile is planning its way out of fossil fuels, the social and environmental impact of renewable energies' infrastructure remains downplayed.

This neglect also hides the fact that, in most cases (including Chiloé), the energy generated is not destined for local needs. It is fundamental to make explicit that most energy demand (and expected increase in this demand) goes to industry and mining (Comisión Nacional de Energía 2020); sectors that leave little benefit to the territories where they function, but rather perpetuate ecological disasters and the relegation of some places and communities to being "sacrifice zones".[34] But the actual need for such activities is never questioned. This corporate-led energy "transition" uses "green" as a way of covering the continuation of their extractive and destructive relation with territories that have been earmarked for serving as "energy generation nodes" to sustain future growth.

Resistance as a way of "making space" for a different future

According to Wright's (2010) typology, this campaign's vision of change follows a symbiotic approach because while it uses existing institutions to express dissent, it also aims to harness experience to push for deeper political transformation of those same institutions. Our current capacity to act is limited by institutional and political constraints. There are no regular spaces to prevent or anticipate predatory projects like this, much less institutional safeguards to give political power to communities opposing them. Our defence of the territory can be understood as a way of reducing immediate and direct harm, but also as a way of creating space for different futures that break from the history and present of plunder and ecological destruction. There is no possibility for transcending structures of capitalist growth if we permit the invasion of megaprojects like wind farms and transmission lines that would crowd out the creation of more localised, democratic and ecologically pertinent forms of livelihood. The installation of several wind parks across the main island of the Chiloé archipelago could result, as in other places, in the "emptying" of the countryside and displacement of traditional ways of life. This alteration of rural life, in addition to the impacts on biodiversity, is a serious threat to any possibility of a democratically managed or popular energy transition (Bertinat *et al.* 2020).

---

34   Most places labelled as "sacrifice zones" in Chile today are affected by fossil fuels (Fuentes, Larraín & Poo, 2020).

Connecting struggles for social-ecological transformation

While our campaign does not identify with degrowth, it aligns with it as it shows the contradictions and shortcomings of implementing energy transitions without questioning the imperative of economic growth and its growing energy needs. In Chile's policy circles and elsewhere, there is an assumption that energy consumption will continue to increase in the future, regardless of the uneven ecological impacts this might have. There is no exploration of what a future of lower energy demand might look like, one that, following the principles of degrowth, manages to give decent lives to all without sustaining and entrenching existing structures of dispossession and inequality.

In that sense, the campaign *Chiloé Libre* has located itself in explicit dialogue and continuation with other local struggles around social-environmental conflicts. This is why we chose the term "sacking" and have warned against the emergence of new sacrifice zones, a phrase that has gained currency in Chile's public debate. The campaign's strength draws significantly from the wider network of social and political movements based in the archipelago. At the moment, and as a way of moving towards a wider alliance, we are articulating a network of recently elected members of local councils to push together for stronger actions against this and similar projects.

While it is location-specific by nature, our campaign also offers a window to other situations of dispossession that could emerge in Chile in the context of the national green hydrogen strategy, which relies on a dramatic increase in electricity generation to be viable. Therefore, a lesson from this campaign is that interaction and solidarity with similar issues across the country can help anticipate and prevent common mistakes or omissions in our actions.

The main limit we have faced is the overwhelming disadvantage that the institutional architecture gives to organised communities against mega projects like this. The lesson from this is that existing legal tools can be a focus of action, but that real pressure can only be exercised through public exposure of the injustice of the situation, and by setting the conflict on the agendas of people who are not directly affected.

References

Avila, Sofia. 2018. "Environmental Justice and the Expanding Geography of Wind Power Conflicts." *Sustainability Science* 13, no. 3: 599–616.

Bertinat, Pablo, Jorge Chemes, and Lyda Fernanda Forero. 2020. *Transicion Energetica Aportes Para Una Reflexión Colectiva*. Transnational Institute y Taller Ecologista (con el apoyo de Fundación Boell Cono Sur). https://tallerecologista.org.ar/wp-content/uploads/2020/11/TransicionEnergetica-Reporte-comp.pdf.

Chiloé Libre del Saqueo Energético. 2021. «Chiloé Libre de saqueo energético. Community organisation. Facebook page." https://www.facebook.com/Chilo%C3%A9-Libre-de-saqueo-energ%C3%A9tico-103545675138623/.

Comisión Nacional de Energía. 2020. *Variación del consumo energético*. http://energiaabierta.cl/visualizaciones/consumo-por-sector-de-energia/.

Durán Sanzana, Vanessa, Eduardo Mondaca Mansilla, and Federico Natho Anwandter. 2018. «Megaparques Eólicos, Destrucción de Turberas y Conflictividad Sociopolítica: La Urgencia de Un Ordenamiento Territorial Democrático.» In *Archipiélago de Chiloé: Nuevas Lecturas de Un Territorio En Movimiento*, edited by Eduardo Mondaca, Esteban Uribe, Sebastián Henríquez, and Vladia Torres, 1st ed., 129–160. Chiloé: Editorial CESCH.

Fuentes, Claudia, Sara Larraín and Pamela Poo. 2020. *Transición justa desafíos para el proceso de descarbonización, la justicia energética y climática en Chile*. Santiago: Programa Chile Sustentable. https://www.chilesustentable.net/wp-content/uploads/2020/12/Transicion-Justa-baja.pdf.

Ministerio de Energía. 2020. *Gobierno presenta la Estrategia Nacional para que Chile sea líder mundial en hidrógeno verde*. https://energia.gob.cl/noticias/nacional/gobierno-presenta-la-estrategia-nacional-para-que-chile-sea-lider-mundial-en-hidrogeno-verde.

Mondaca, Eduardo. 2017. "The Archipelago of Chiloé and the Uncertain Contours of Its Future: Coloniality, New Extractivism and Political–Social Re-Vindication of Existence." In *Environmental Crime in Latin America: The Theft of Nature and the Poisoning of the Land*, edited by David Rodríguez Goyes, Hanneke Mol, Avi Brisman, and Nigel South, 31–55. Palgrave Studies in Green Criminology. London: Palgrave Macmillan UK.

Radio JGM. 2020. «Corte suprema deberá dictarminar sobre conflicto de transnacional en Chiloé.» March 10, 2020. https://radiojgm.uchile.cl/corte-suprema-debera-dictaminar-sobre-conflicto-de-transnacional-por-proyecto-electrico-en-chiloe/.

Resumen. 2021. «Pese a resistencia de comunidades: Empresa Transelec busca instalar línea de transmisión que uniría isla grande de Chiloé con el continente.» *Resumen*, April 16, 2021. https://resumen.cl/articulos/pese–a–resistencia–de–comunidades–empresa–transelec–busca–instalar–linea–de–transmision–que–uni-279ria–isla–grande–de–chiloe–con–el–continente/.

SEA Chile. 2020. *Ficha del Proyecto: Sistema de Transmisión S/E Tineo – S/E Nueva Ancud.* https://seia.sea.gob.cl/expediente/expedientesEvaluacion.php?modo=-ficha&id_expediente=2147998098#-1.

Wright, Erik Olin. 2010. *Envisioning Real Utopias*. London, New York: Verso.

Chapter 15: Mobility and transport

An overview of strategies for social-ecological transformation in the field of transportation

By John Szabo, Thomas SJ Smith and Leon Leuser

Introduction

A destructive and wasteful transportation model has developed across the Global North and further afield over the last 150 years, emerging hand-in-hand with a society reliant on fossil fuels. The proliferation of privately owned, combustion engine-propelled passenger vehicles, for instance, drives a highly individualised, resource-, time-, and space-intensive system, as well as one that perpetuates an unjust and growth-oriented capitalist society. Distances travelled, whether by land, sea or by air, have been on the rise, and the means to facilitate this have rapidly expanded (see e.g., USA. FHA 2018). Today, nearly a quarter of global CO_2 emissions originates from the transportation sector (Solaymani 2019). In the face of climate change, it has therefore never been more urgent to take action to reconfigure the mobility system. The COVID-19 pandemic offers yet another fork in the road. It can provide a structural opening for change, since it has forced many to travel less at a point in time when the technology capable of substituting travel is available to many. It also further exacerbates inequalities.

In this chapter, we provide a humble point of departure for further action that drives social-ecological change by harnessing degrowth strategies. Current transportation systems need to be radically transformed, prioritising social justice and ecological soundness, and thus decoupled from various forms of exploitation. We explore strategies that can be adopted to support such a transformation. Like other authors in this book, we draw on Erik Olin Wright's four strategic logics (2019), which offer valuable insights on how societies can move towards "Real Utopias" (2010). We highlight that strategies are variegated, as are the movements and organisations that employ them.

Travelling in the wrong direction?

Transportation, in its current form, is destructive on multiple fronts, which we will briefly introduce in this section to contextualise strategies we explore below. Amongst the most destructive components of the sector are individually owned fossil fuel combustion-propelled vehicles – cars, in other words. In the European Union, 72% of CO_2 emissions in transportation are linked to road transport, of which passenger vehicles are responsible for 61% (EP 2019). The situation is similar in the USA (USA. EPA 2021). The material throughput of vehicles is large and growing, with the rising popularity of larger sport-utility vehicles (SUVs) (Cozzi and Petropoulos 2021). Individual ownership exacerbates the material demands of the industry – making the "green growth" vision of a shift to electric vehicles (EVs) only a piecemeal solution. Furthermore, the widespread use of cars is highly dangerous to humans and wildlife: 3,700 people die in traffic accidents every day (WHO 2020). Air pollution has been on the rise and the negative implications of this are becoming clearer, with particulate pollution linked to 18% of deaths globally in 2018 (Vohra *et al.* 2021). While data on wildlife deaths is scarce, it was estimated that across just 13 countries around 400 million animals are killed on roads annually (Schwartz *et al.* 2020), with further destruction reverberating through ecosystems as the expansion of road systems and associated pollution drives habitat loss.

Looking more broadly, time-space compression (Harvey 1991) via increasingly rapid and large-scale transportation systems has enabled a shift of production to far-flung places to reduce production costs and underpin an immense freight industry. Bulk and just-in-time shipping have allowed for goods to be transported to consumers, who have been able to access products at lower prices as environmental and labour standards are circumvented by producers. Meanwhile, the management of firms that developed these global value chains monitors production and expands relations with overseas producers through continuous air travel. Combined with rising demand from consumers for inexpensive goods, this has supported the expansion of a transportation system that is extremely environmentally and socially destructive. If we seek to decarbonise shipping and aviation while remaining within the confines of current consumer-capitalist logics, there appear to be few quick fixes or technologically palatable alternatives available. A systemic rethinking, backed up by a spectrum of strategic and radical intervention, is instead required across the transport sector.

André Gorz noted that the key to dealing with the contemporary problems of transportation is to consider it alongside other pressing issues. He argues "never (to) make transportation an issue by itself. Always connect it to the problem of the city, of the social division of labour, and to the way this compartmentalises the many dimensions of life" (Gorz 1980, 77). The strategies we have gathered aim to support this very vision.

Taming transportation

Taming the transportation sector entails the introduction of sweeping interventions (often top-down, though against the background of wider public pressure) that confine it and the damage that it yields. A point of departure is the phasing out of subsidies for highly emitting modes of transportation – such as diesel vehicles or air travel (Transport & Environment 2019) and levying taxes on polluting means of transport or outright capping them (Gössling and Humpe 2020; Stay Grounded 2021). Taming road transport has begun with the introduction and tightening of emissions standards – although recent emissions scandals show how far producers will go to circumvent regulation. Less polluting vehicles can yield incremental benefits, such as newly popular electric passenger vehicles offering some environmental gains vis-à-vis their internal combustion counterparts. However, their diffusion will not allow for climate targets to be met due to the so-called "long tailpipe" effect[35] (Milovanoff *et al.* 2020). The bare minimum of vehicles necessary could be electric, but the transition in propulsion systems has to be paired with the reduction of vehicle ownership and a shift to alternative modes of travel (Henderson 2020).[36]

Communities can tame road transport by regulating space and access to space. Some urban areas already do so by limiting access by particular vehicles. Cities can adopt measures to make car use unattractive through parking space management, congestion charges, the closing of roads, and the establishment of speed limits. Historically, heavy-duty vehicles have been banished from urban areas, but local residents and city councils are gradually pushing to ban (emitting) passenger vehicles from urban spaces as well. Oslo and Ljubljana, for instance, have been leaders in going car-free within the city centre. Car-free zones are essential in limiting pollution and allowing dwellers to reverse current car-centred infrastructure's colonisation of urban space. Restrictions should not be tied solely to emissions standards or vehicle-based charges, since this tends to privilege the wealthy. Rather, sweeping restrictions on all but essential vehicles ought to be introduced, paired with social policies which compensate those less well-off who need to adjust to a new setting. In tandem, complementary enabling infrastructure, such as bicycle paths, (regional, affordable or free[37], and accessible) rural-urban public transportation, as well as "park and ride" infrastructure need to be introduced to facilitate a transformation.

Strategic potential for taming the transportation system cannot be assessed in isolation from the relative political-economic power of the automotive and aviation sectors. Six of the world's fifty largest

---

35 The long tailpipe refers to the need to consider emissions and pollution during the entire life-cycle of vehicles and the sources of electricity on which electric vehicles run on to obtain an idea of whether they indeed contribute to lower emissions.

36 Vehicle sharing can also play a crucial role, as discussed in the case study below.

37 A number of cities and regions (such as Luxembourg and Tallinn, Estonia) have experimented with free public transport in recent years, deeming public transport infrastructure to be a default public resource akin to street lighting or footpaths. In other cases, the objective has been to ensure very low prices.

companies, by revenue, are in the automotive sector (Fortune 2021). This inherently drives a growth-oriented model of vehicle ownership, as politicians have an interest in stabilising employment and economic growth, while firms seek to increase shareholder value. The issue needs to be tackled from a number of fronts. A greater voice for labour and the support of unionisation should be linked to long-term strategic thinking that pressures company executives to re-consider social-ecological aspects of their current operations. NGOs, new mobility actors (e.g., car-sharing, bicycle manufacturers, or public transport companies), and social movements can highlight bad practices and offer palatable alternatives, although we must be wary of the likes of Uber co-opting a language of transport sharing in support of their models based on the wide-scale exploitation of people. Citizens can also introduce product purchasing boycotts regarding vehicles in general, but specifically directed towards problematic firms and models. While not wanting to overly emphasise individual action to achieve political goals, boycotts and their associated political mobilisation have been proven effective in the past (Tomlin 2019).

Dismantling the transportation system

Taming transportation has to be paired with its dismantling, that is to say, establishing alternative modes of organising the sector. Overall, kilometres travelled by people and freight need to be reduced. A part of this can be linked to the use of technology, but it also entails that communities are empowered to explore the joys the "local" has to offer. The COVID-19 pandemic has shown that virtual meetings can offer a substitute to in-person meetings with a substantially lower environmental footprint (Faber 2021). These should not substitute all human interaction, and such technologies have their own ecological impacts, but they may be used to minimise travel, especially in the case of business dealings. Simultaneously, in the right social conditions, individuals can free up time to participate and re-discover the pleasure of community-building and activities taking place in local neighbourhoods (Soper 2020).

The reconfiguration of national and regional transportation could be supported by the rapid deployment of a railway system developed as part of a degrowth-oriented Green New Deal (Mastini *et al.* 2021). This may not be a suitable solution in all contexts and must take shape through transparent and democratic citizen engagement. Politicians and activists have called for private jets and short-haul flights to be phased out, to be replaced with comprehensive funding for rail network expansion (Asquith 2019) – France seems to be making shy headway on this front by banning some short-haul flights where substitutable by rail. This would re-establish rail as the prime form of long-distance travel, including greater frequency and streamlined services, a renaissance in night trains, high-speed lines, and rail-based freight. Democratic ownership would provide the backbone for a just development of this system, allowing for the engagement of impacted communities and the introduction of cross-subsidisation to ensure equitable access for all. Public ownership is essential more broadly for the erosion of the current transportation system, as it allows the public to exert greater pressure on the incumbent system and shape it according to social needs, rather than to profit.

Another key form of parallel transportation institution is support for bicycles and e-bikes, often through dismantling car-centric infrastructures. As Ivan Illich (1974) points out, the bike is an especially convivial mode of transportation and it is also amongst the most efficient modes of urban transportation. The COVID-19 pandemic has begun a renaissance of the bicycle, momentum which policy-makers should maintain by providing support for further infrastructure (e.g., the repurposing of roads) and subsidies for bicycles. A number of successful initiatives throughout the world have shown that there is ample demand for cargo bicycles, which could alleviate the space, material, and energy-intensity of intra-urban transportation of goods as well.

Resisting the transportation system

Resisting the current transportation model has become paramount. Social movements of various kinds have taken to disrupting emission-intensive modes of transport, targeting them for symbolic and practical reasons. Street protests and occupations in the 1960s and 1970s played a key role in resisting the ubiquity of the car in cities like Amsterdam and Copenhagen, with visible effects to the present day. Movements need not only be in resistance to specific causes, but also in support of certain ones. Since the early 1990s, Critical Mass events have been important points of departure in reclaiming the streets and raising awareness for the support of bicycles and requisite infrastructure through direct action. Such inclusive mass mobilisation has been crucial in empowering pro-bicycle movements globally, essential to moving the transportation system away from its entrenched practices.

Airports have also been at the heart of social resistance, and the willingness of locals to participate in demonstrations is heavily shaped by the negative ramifications of airports (Liebe *et al.* 2020). Given the close links between climate action and social justice, strategies need to involve, empower, and amplify the voices of those most affected by negative repercussions. Here, again, localised forms of pollution, such as noise or heightened traffic, can be key instigators of protests to the expansion of airport infrastructure. In recent years, we have seen a number of campaigns emerge around such causes (e.g., protests against London Heathrow or Vienna Airport). Contesting these projects through demonstrations have not always been successful but can clearly bear fruit, especially in a post-pandemic world where the normality of air travel is questioned. A notable instance of strategic resistance was the ZAD (*zone à défendre*) in opposition to a proposed airport near Nantes in France. Building on decades of local resistance, zadists squatted land and led the opposition, which ultimately resulted in the cancelling of the airport by the French government (ZAD 2021).

The disruptiveness of social movements will certainly have to be scaled up. Chenoweth and Stephan (2011) argue that peaceful resistance works, given the low barriers to entry and the rising engagement from all across the social spectrum, but movements are effective when they have leverage – that is, when they can disrupt and compromise the system in place. Extinction Rebellion's actions to shut down circulation and travel reflect the power social movements can assert. The determination to protest is increasingly evident, as we have seen with the Fridays for Future movement, but these movements need to be supported by a broader social base and include more targeted direct action as well, as suggested by Chenoweth and Stephan and others. Broader support for actions to change our transport system can be achieved by highlighting the importance of addressing the social justice aspects of changes in transport systems whilst limiting its environmental impacts. The poorer strata of society who bear the brunt of climate events and air pollution, as well as being under-served by mobility systems, should be the first to benefit from more thorough intervention.

In parallel to underpinning the legitimacy of movements, more militant action can be taken by social movements as well. "Sabotage can be done softly" (Stern 2021, n.a.) as has been argued and shown by Andreas Malm and other activists. Interventions such as releasing the air from the tires of expensive SUVs target both strata of society (the wealthy) and emitting sources (SUVs) that are amongst the most harmful artefacts in the transportation system. These "nudges" can spark debate and deter ownership of highly emitting vehicles, which can be paired with public media campaigns that underscore just how dangerous these vehicles are for others on the road. Introducing soft nudges and resistance through interventions such as painting guerilla bicycle lanes, closing roads and so on can be essential to averting deeper social conflicts in the future.

Escaping transportation

Escaping transportation relates to attempts to escape the dominant structures of transport and introduce solutions outside the system.

Often emerging in the form of various "nowtopian" initiatives, formed in protective niches, these are attempts to build parallel institutions and practices outside the mainstream transport sector. In its most extreme forms, escape entails eliminating motorised travel from one's life. Henry David Thoreau's *Walden* (1971 (1854)) is one influential guide to such "simple living". In it, Thoreau (1971 (1854), 92) asks, "if we want to stay at home and mind our business, who will want rail roads?" Similar to Illich's (1974) analysis of the counter productivity of cars, Thoreau argued that at the time he was writing, travel by foot would actually be the fastest means, when the wages required to pay for more industrial means of transport were taken into account – a point that continues to be prescient (see e.g., Heller 2019). Thoreau also criticises the mechanisation and labour required for constructing railways, arguing that "(w)e do not ride on the rail road; it rides upon us … if some have the pleasure of riding on a rail, others have the misfortune to be ridden upon" (92).

In a similar vein of escape, François Schneider, a pioneering degrowth activist and thinker, set out for a year-long tour of France on foot in 2004, accompanied by a donkey, to research and propagate the virtues of slowness and degrowth (Demaria *et al.* 2013). This may seem quirky or irrelevant to broader change. However, a related ethos of encouraging walking and slow mobility can be seen in the recent drive to create "superblocks" by the municipal government of Barcelona – territorial units of nine blocks which restrict traffic and aim to increase walkability, social cohesion, and green spaces. Initially facing opposition from local businesses, creating a culture of walkability has produced a broadly win-win situation, enhancing local vibrancy, local business, and human health. If coupled with the relocalisation of food production and other needs – rather than gentrification and new forms of exclusion – this can be a powerful tool.

Similarly, for the last fifty years, Freetown Christiania, an autonomous 20-acre community in the centre of Copenhagen, has banned the internal combustion engine from within its self-governed vicinity (Smith 2020). Engagement with such experiments can also bear the seeds for wider change: still needing to move goods and people around the large site, one Christiania resident invented a robust type of cargo bike – the Christiania Bike – which is now popular around the world. Christiania's experiment thrived alongside Copenhagen's bike culture, which is one of the most successful in the world. In a similar way, volunteer-run community bike kitchens and repair cooperatives around the world have created parallel infrastructures for bike maintenance and repair infrastructure.

Conclusion

In this chapter, we have made a brief attempt to lay out some possible battlegrounds and strategic opportunities in the search for degrowth of transportation. There is much more, of course, that could (and should) be said. Reflecting on the open-endedness of social transformation, the social ecologist and critic of growth Murray Bookchin outlined that it is advantageous to establish a flexible programme in this search. While posing certain "minimum" and "transitional" demands (taxing airline fuel for instance, or incentivising night trains), he said we should always be guided by "maximum demands", in this case for a thoroughly democratic and degrowth-oriented mobility sector. We also ascribe to this ethos and call for these and further strategies to be considered by communities across the globe, so as to impede the destruction perpetuated by the growth-oriented fossil fuel-based transportation system currently in place.

We admit that distinctions between the various strategic logics laid out above are not necessarily clean cut. Any one space, movement or initiative can incorporate aspects of taming, dismantling, resistance, and escape, all at the same time. Given the widespread nature of capitalist mobility, action for degrowth in the transportation sector will need to be contextual and broad-based – aimed at a variety of political and institutional levels, from the grassroots to the more institutional, and from reformism to revolution. We also believe that it is crucial to acknowledge that these strategies may be contradictory on occasion. For instance, there is an evident conflict between most forms of escapism and the build-out of a larger railway network. But we posit that when developed in accordance with the core objectives of democratisation and degrowth, they are reconcilable in the long term.

References

Asquith, James. 2019. "Should Private Jets be Banned?" *Forbes*, November 7, 2019. https://www.forbes.com/sites/jamesasquith/2019/11/07/should-private-jets-be-banned/.

Chenoweth, Erica and Maria J. Stephan. 2011. *Why Civil Resistance Works: The Strategic Logic of Nonviolent Conflict*. New York, NY, USA: Columbia University Press.

Cozzi, Laura and Apostolos Petropoulos. 2021. *Carbon Emissions Fell across all Sectors in 2020 except for one – SUVs*. Paris: International Energy Agency. https://www.iea.org/commentaries/carbon-emissions-fell-across-all-sectors-in-2020-except-for-one-suvs.

Demaria, Federico, François Schneider, Filka Sekulova, and Joan Martinez–Alier. 2013. "What Is Degrowth? From an Activist Slogan to a Social Movement." *Environmental Values* 22, no. 2 (April): 191–215.

EP (European Parliament). 2019. *CO_2 Emissions from Cars: Facts and Figures (Infographics)*. Strasbourg, France: European Parliament Headlines. https://www.europarl.europa.eu/news/en/headlines/society/20190313STO31218/co2-emissions-from-cars-facts-and-figures-infographics.

Faber, Grant. 2021. "A Framework to Estimate Emissions from Virtual Conferences." *International Journal of Environmental Studies* 78, no. 4: 608–623.

Fortune. 2021. *Fortune Global 500*. https://fortune.com/global500/.

Gorz, André. 1980. *Ecology as Politics*. Boston, USA: South End Press.

Gössling, Stefan and Andreas Humpe. 2020. "The Global Scale, Distribution and Growth of Aviation: Implications for Climate Change." *Global Environmental Change* 65 (November): 102–194.

Harvey, David. 1991. *The Condition of Postmodernity: An Enquiry into the Origins of Cultural Change*. Cambridge, MA, USA: Wiley-Blackwell.

Heller, Nathan. 2019. "Was the Automotive Era a Terrible Mistake?" *New Yorker*,

July 22, 2019. https://www.newyorker.com/magazine/2019/07/29/was-the-automotive-era-a-terrible-mistake.

Henderson, Jason. 2020. "EVs Are Not the Answer: A Mobility Justice Critique of Electric Vehicle Transitions." *Annals of the American Association of Geographers* 110, no. 6: 1993–2010.

Illich, Ivan. 1974. *Energy and Equity*. London, UK and New York, NY, USA: Marion Boyars.

Liebe, Ulf, Peter Preisendörfer, and Heidi Bruderer Enzler. 2020. "The Social Acceptance of Airport Expansion Scenarios: A Factorial Survey Experiment." *Transportation Research Part D: Transport and Environment* 84.

Mastini, Riccardo, Giorgos Kallis, and Jason Hickel. 2021. "A Green New Deal without Growth?" *Ecological Economics* 179 (January), 106832.

Milovanoff, Alexandre, I. Daniel Posen, and Heather L. MacLean. 2020. "Electrification of Light–Duty Vehicle Fleet Alone Will not Meet Mitigation Targets." *Nature Climate Change* 10, no. 12 (December): 1102–1107.

Schwartz, Amy L. W., Fraser M. Shilling, and Sarah E. Perkins. 2020. "The Value of Monitoring Wildlife Roadkill." *European Journal of Wildlife Research* 66, no. 18.

Smith, Thomas S. J. 2020. "Freetown Christiania: An Economic 'Nowtopia' at the Heart of a European Capital City." *OpenDemocracy*, January 7, 2020. https://www.opendemocracy.net/en/oureconomy/freetown-christiania-economic-nowtopia-heart-european-capital-city/.

Solaymani, Saeed. 2019. "CO_2 Emissions Patterns in 7 Top Carbon Emitter Economies: The Case of the Transport Sector." *Energy* 168: p989–1001.

Soper, Kate. 2020. *Post-Growth Living: For an Alternative Hedonism*. London, UK: Verso.

Stay Grounded. 2021. *Stay Grounded*. https://stay-grounded.org/.

Stern, Scott W. 2021. "Sabotage Can Be Done Softly: On Andreas Malm's 'How to Blow Up a Pipeline'." *LA Review of Books*, January 5, 2020. https://lareviewofbooks.org/article/sabotage-can-be-done-softly-on-andreas-malms-how-to-blow-up-a-pipeline/.

Thoreau, Henry David. 1971 (1854). *Walden*. Princeton, NJ, USA: Princeton University Press.

Tomlin, Kasaundra M. 2019. "Assessing the Efficacy of Consumer Boycotts of U.S. Target Firms: A Shareholder Wealth Analysis." *Southern Economic Journal* 86, no. 2: 503–529.

Transport & Environment. 2019. "How to Tax Aviation to Curb Emissions." *Transport & Environment*, July 11, 2019. https://www.transportenvironment.org/discover/how-tax-aviation-curb-emissions/.

USA. EPA (Environmental Protection Agency). 2021. *Green Vehicle Guide: Fast Facts on Transportation Greenhouse Gas Emissions*. https://www.epa.gov/greenvehicles/fast-facts-transportation-greenhouse-gas-emissions.

USA. FHA (Federal Highway Administration). 2018. *Annual Vehicle–Miles of Travel, 1980 – 2018*. https://www.fhwa.dot.gov/policyinformation/statistics/2018/pdf/vm202.pdf.

Vohra, Karn, Alina Vodonos, Joel Schwartz, Eloise A. Marais, Melissa P. Sulprizio, and Loretta J. Mickley. 2021. "Global Mortality from Outdoor Fine Particle Pollution Generated by Fossil Fuel Combustion: Results from GEOS–Chem." *Environmental Research* 195 (April).

WHO (World Health Organisation). 2020. *Road Traffic Injuries*. Geneva, Switzerland: World Health Organisation Fact Sheets. https://www.who.int/news-room/fact-sheets/detail/road-traffic-injuries.

Wright, Erik Olin. 2010. *Envisioning Real Utopias*. London, UK: Verso.

Wright, Erik Olin. 2019. *How to Be an Anticapitalist in the Twenty–First Century*. London, UK: Verso.

ZAD (Zone A Défendre). 2021. *Who Are We?*. https://zad.nadir.org/?lang=en.

A case in the field of mobility and transport: the Autolib' car-sharing platform

By Marion Drut

Vehicle sharing exists at the intersection between private cars and public transport. Such initiatives have multiplied over the last decade with growing citizen participation (Firnkorn and Shaheen 2016; Drut 2018; 6t-bureau de recherche 2019). Degrowth calls for more collective property and sharing (Jarvis 2019). Vehicle sharing offers the potential of wider processes of social-ecological transformation, propelled by two drivers of change. First, sharing vehicles means fewer vehicles will be needed in the economy to meet the same level of needs. The second lever is the demotorisation that it causes. Estimates of several case studies throughout Europe and Canada highlight a decrease in the distance travelled by drivers enrolled in a car-sharing system from 11 to 50% (Sioui *et al.* 2013, Meijkamp 2000). This chapter analyses to what extent the experience of the Autolib' platform, a one-way station-based car-sharing system[38] in Paris, can be a potential strategy towards degrowth. As such, the case study is necessarily limited to a Western context.

The Autolib' platform

The Autolib' project was first conceived in early 2008 by Bertrand Delanoë, leftist mayor of Paris, as a follow-up to the bicycle-sharing Velib' system set up in Paris in 2007. The main objective was to reduce car ownership in the Paris region. As more Autolib' cars are available for public use, at a fair price and with dedicated parking spaces, car drivers are encouraged to abandon their privately owned cars. The issue of parking spaces is of particular concern in densely populated areas such as the Paris urban area. According to official communication, each Autolib' car would replace 10 cars. The secondary objective was to substitute fossil fuel cars for electric cars

---

38 Vehicles can be driven back to any station.

in order to cut down CO_2 emissions. Setting up a large-scale car-sharing system was thought of as one possible project to achieve a low-carbon mobility strategy in the Paris urban area.

The Autolib' platform was a public car-sharing service implemented in December 2011 and closed in July 2018. The platform offered a fleet of almost 4,000 electric cars spread over 1,100 stations located in 103 municipalities (Paris and its surroundings). Autolib' cars were available for public use on a spontaneous basis (subscription effective immediately) and at a quite low price.[39] The Autolib' platform was operated by the Autolib' company, a subsidiary of the multinational transportation company Bolloré, through a public service delegation contract (public-private partnership) covering the period from December 2011 to the end of 2023. It employed 500 workers.

Autolib's successes and failures

The Autolib' platform showed mixed results. In the short run, the achievement of the initial objective (decrease in car ownership rates) was questioned by a study from the City of Paris published two years after the implementation of the platform (Razemon 2013). Although Autolib' targeted existing car drivers, 60% of Autolib' drivers did not own any car and mainly used public transport, and, even worse, 18% of Autolib' drivers seemed to get used to automobility and considered buying a car in the future. Among the 40% of Autolib' drivers who did own a car, only a third had considered selling it. An explanation for this failure is that the Autolib' platform operated mainly in the city centre: 700 out of the 1,000 Autolib' stations were located in Paris. Autolib' was a transport mode mainly used by Parisians moving within Paris, and used only to a lesser extent in the suburbs. In the city centre, alternative modes are available like public transport, cycling and walking. Consequently, Autolib' competed not

---

39 The cost includes an annual subscription (120 € in 2017) and a variable cost increasing with the time spent using the car (6 € for each 30 minutes), or a fixed reservation cost of 1 € and a variable rate of 9 € for each 30 minutes for occasional drivers.

only with private cars, but also with more sustainable transportation modes. Second, the potential of attracting non-car users to using cars is particularly strong when car ownership rates are low because there is a greater proportion of potential new drivers: only 37.4% of Parisians owned a car in 2013 (INSEE 2013). As suggested by the experience of other car-sharing systems, car-sharing would have created more desirable outcomes if operated in peri-urban locations where car ownership rates are higher and where low-carbon transport alternatives are scarcely used.[40]

On the other hand, a study published in 2014 by an independent consulting firm providing expert services on transport policies showed different results. They clearly observed a 23% decrease in the number of private vehicles owned by Autolib' users after their subscription to the car-sharing system (6t-bureau de recherche 2014). According to the study, an Autolib' vehicle replaces three private cars and frees two parking spaces. In addition, after subscribing to the platform, an Autolib' driver travels 43 km less per month compared to before, which corresponds to an 11% reduction in the vehicle-kilometre travelled (both from their private car and the Autolib' car) (*Ibid.*). This reduction in mileage does not occur because Autolib' drivers travel less, but rather because they tend to shift to other mobility modes, like public transport and walking (Louvet 2018). 13% of Autolib' drivers used their private car daily before subscribing to the platform, against 5% after their subscription, indicating a 63% decrease in daily private car use (*Ibid.*). Other transportation modes used daily by Autolib' users saw a much smaller decrease. Car sharing builds on long-term changes in mobility patterns towards low car-usage lifestyles, and lower car ownership rates (Firnkorn and Shaheen 2016; Martin and Shaheen 2010; Meijkamp 2000). The Autolib' platform competed primarily with private motorised modes – that was one of its successes. Another

---

40   Mobizen, now Communauto, a car-sharing system mainly used by Parisians to go outside the city centre, showed a higher shift from private cars (6t-bureau de recherche 2014): the share of drivers using their private car daily decreased by 93% after subscribing, while the share of most alternative modes increased from 30% for bicycle-sharing to 2–4% for walking and public transport. Only the daily use of private bicycles slightly decreased (–6%).

success of the project was the effective sharing of cars: each Autolib' car was used on average between 3 and 5 times a day (Louvet 2018). All other things equal, meeting the same level of mobility needs with both fewer vehicles and lower car usage reflects a wider process of social-ecological transformation.

Last but not least, the Autolib' company claimed a 50 million annual loss in 2018 and forecasted future yearly losses that went beyond what the Autolib' firm had agreed to support. This situation was in conflict with the engagement of the municipalities to provide a no-cost public service for their citizens and resulted in the termination of the contract and the end of the Autolib' service. One reason – probably not the only one – for these losses was the decreasing number of Autolib' users (150,000 subscribers but only 11,000 trips a day in 2018), due to the rise of private hire services and of free-floating bicycles and motor-scooters (Farge 2018). The quick end of this project due to financial reasons shows another kind of failure as well. Private industrial stakeholders seek short term monetary profits and may not settle for long term non-economic benefits. Profitability is usually not a criterion – much less a purpose – for public services, for instance, public transport. Rather, social utility is central. Considering social and environmental costs and values as well may have led to a more desirable scenario. A social-ecological transformation would benefit from cooperation rather than competition. As they become capitalised and institutionalised, vehicle sharing systems must comply with capitalist and institutional requirements. This may contribute to, even hasten, their fall – as described in the Autolib' case study.

In conclusion, the Autolib' project experienced mixed results, with failures such as encouraging people to become drivers and operating an inadequate business model that led to the end of the initiative, and also limited successes – but still successes – in demotorising Autolib' drivers who owned private vehicles, and by proving that large-scale use of shared cars was a possible mobility option at the level of an urban area (Louvet 2018).

Autolib': A symbiotic strategy based on a ruptural element

Cars are overwhelmingly the dominant mode of transport in western societies, including in cities where many alternative travel options are provided, from public transport to cycling and walking. The car is used for 83% of passenger-kilometres in the European Union in 2018 (Eurostat 2021) and for 63% of trips in France (France. Ministère de la transition écologique 2020). Western societies are still embedded in private individual automobility, where individual cars often remain a genuine societal cult object which conveys symbolic representations. The observed reduction in car use reflects a change in the relation the driver has to the vehicle. The shift is from owning to accessing, from individual to collective, from monetary exchange value to social use-value.[41] Nikolaeva *et al.* (2019) define the concept of "commoning mobility", based on the idea that mobility is not only a question of individual freedom but can be considered as a collective good, ie. as a common. Shared mobility allows – forces – us to have a systematic approach to mobility and encourages a logic of commoning. Vehicle sharing thus entails a ruptural element at the individual level as it disrupts and opens up a space that is inherently individualistic.

The Autolib' project involved powerful actors: the Bolloré company and the City of Paris. The former, as a private firm, was seeking short term profit while the latter, as a public body, was aiming to reduce car ownership. Such a compromise between private actors whose concerns drastically diverge from degrowth and others who support degrowth objectives, although not explicitly, falls within what Erik Olin Wright (2010) calls a symbiotic transformation. The Autolib' example highlights that symbiotic transformations have features that can either lead to success (powerful actors have the potential to be heard and followed) or failure (private actors are profit-seekers and their core beliefs and objectives contradict degrowth). Pushing such transformations towards success is a hard task.

---

41 Using a shared vehicle rather than a private one creates benefits not only for the driver but also for others in society (ie. through reduced congestion).

Towards social-ecological transformation: a road paved with challenges

Presenting a car-sharing project as a degrowth strategy for mobility is challenging. Indeed, car-sharing as it is currently experienced and implemented has the impression of being far from desirable social-ecological transformation. To my mind, however, shared mobilities convey a ruptural element at the individual level and therefore have the potential to lead to broader and more desirable social-ecological transformation. Fostering commonly shared mobilities – including automobility – can represent a transition towards degrowth. However, when strategising for degrowth and following a symbiotic strategy, one must take care not to jeopardise degrowth's aims (sufficiency, social justice, ecological justice, commoning, well-being etc.). Autolib' was not a satisfactory degrowth strategy. Indeed, although the Autolib' project induced long-term changes in mobility patterns towards low car-usage lifestyles, outcomes were limited and subject to criticism.

Deep knowledge of the local context appears decisive, although not sufficient, to engage citizens. Autolib' was operated in the Paris region only, in partnership with local authorities, but failed to engage local stakeholders on a long-term basis.

Another core limit to vehicle-sharing as a degrowth strategy is the positioning of stakeholders. Operators of car-sharing platforms (private or public bodies) generally do not identify with degrowth, although the initial objective, car reduction, overlaps with degrowth objectives. Nonetheless, several studies highlight the ecological convictions of shared vehicle users (Kawgan-Kagan 2015; Schaefers 2013). This limit can turn into an opportunity: successful degrowth-oriented projects would multiply if stakeholders identified with degrowth and conducted strategies explicitly in line with degrowth principles.

References

6t-bureau de recherche. 2014. *One-Way Carsharing: Which Alternative to Private Cars? Executive Summary*. Angers, France: ADEME.

6t-bureau de recherche. 2019. *Enquête nationale sur l'autopartage – Edition 2019, final report*. Angers, France: ADEME.

Drut, Marion. 2018. "Spatial Issues Revisited: The Role of Shared Transportation Modes." *Transport Policy* 66, 85–95.

Eurostat. 2021. *Modal Split of Passenger Transport*. Eurostat Data Browser. https://ec.europa.eu/eurostat/databrowser/view/t2020_rk310/default/table.

Farge, Loïc. 2018. «Paris : le modèle Autolib' est-il mort ?» *RTL*, June 5, 2018. https://www.rtl.fr/actu/economie-consommation/paris-le-modele-autolib-est-il-mort-7793640458

Firnkorn, Jörg. And Susan Shaheen. 2016. "Generic Time- and Method- Interdependencies of Empirical Impact-Measurements: A Generalizable Model of Adaptation-Processes of Carsharing-Users' Mobility-Behavior over Time." *Journal of Cleaner Production* 113, 897–909.

INSEE. 2013. *Taux de motorisation des ménages*. Institut national de la statistique et des études économiques. https://www.data.gouv.fr/fr/datasets/taux-de-motorisation-des-menages/.

Jarvis, Helen. 2019. "Sharing, Togetherness and Intentional Degrowth." *Progress in Human Geography* 43, no. 2: 256–275.

Kawgan-Kagan, Ines. 2015. "Early Adopters of Carsharing with and without BEVs with Respect to Gender Preferences." *European Transport Research Review* 7, no. 33: 1–11.

Louvet, Nicolas. 2018. *Autolib' : puisqu'un service public n'a pas vocation à être rentable, quelle est son utilité sociale ?* 6t bureau de recherche. https://6-t.co/rentabilite-ou-utilite-sociale-autolib-fevrier-2018/.

Meijkamp, Rens. 2000. "Changing Consumer Behaviour through Eco-Efficient Services: An Empirical Study on Car Sharing in the Netherlands." PhD thesis, Delft University of Technology.

Nikolaeva, Anna, Peter Adey, Tim Cresswell, Jane Yeonjae Lee, Andre Nóvoa, Cristina Temenos. 2019. "Commoning Mobility: Towards a New Politics of Mobility Transitions." *Transactions of the Institute of British Geographers* 44, no. 2: 346–360.

Razemon, Olivier. 2013. «On a raté l'objectif. Autolib' ne supprime pas de voitures.» *Le Monde*, March 26, 2013. https://www.lemonde.fr/blog/transports/2013/03/26/

on-a-rate-lobjectif-autolib-ne-supprime-pas-de-voitures/.

Schaefers, Tobias. 2013. "Exploring Carsharing Usage Motives: A Hierarchical Means-End Chain Analysis." *Transportation Research Part A: Policy and Practice* 47, 69-77.

France. Ministère de la transition écologique. 2020. *Enquête mobilité des personnes 2018-2019.* https://www.statistiques.developpement-durable.gouv.fr/comment-les-francais-se-deplacent-ils-en-2019-resultats-de-lenquete-mobilite-des-personnes.

Sioui, Louiselle, Catherine Morency, Martin Trepanier. 2013. "How Carsharing Affects the Travel Behavior of Households: A Case Study of Montreal." *International Journal of Sustainable Transportation* 7, 52–69.

Wright, Erik Olin. 2010. *Envisioning Real Utopias*. London, New York: Verso.

Economic and political reorganisation

Chapter 16: Care

An overview of strategies for social-ecological transformation in the field of care

By Corinna Dengler, Miriam Lang and Lisa M. Seebacher

Introduction

We are living through multiple and overlapping crises, which are further exacerbated by the COVID-19 pandemic. In seeking transformative solutions, we need to move away from the growth-dependent economic system that is structurally based on extractive capitalism, white supremacy, coloniality, and patriarchy. This chapter focuses on degrowth strategies for the highly gendered sphere of care/care work and puts an emphasis on strategies that prioritise people and the planet over profit. After briefly introducing the concepts of care/care work and outlining how we combine Erik Olin Wright's and Nancy Fraser's views on strategies of transformation, we discuss and evaluate degrowth strategies contributing to Christa Wichterich's (2015, 86) triple-R goal of redefining, redistributing, and revalorising, thereby contributing to care and health for all.

Care and care work: a brief introduction

The concept of care/care work is sometimes used synonymously with social reproduction/reproductive work and indeed there are many overlaps: Raising children, caring for the elderly, cooking for flatmates or in a community kitchen – if unpaid, these activities are both unpaid care work and social reproduction. However, there are differences in the socio-historical evolution of these concepts. Social reproduction/reproductive work emerges from a feminist Marxist tradition that conceptualises work performed without remuneration as a counterpart to production/wage work. The concept of care/

care work is broader and arguably less political. In emphasising the content of work, it refers not only to unpaid but also to paid care work provided, for example, by the state, the market, or the non-profit sector.

Although it is hard to find a general definition of care work, a common denominator is the relationality and (inter-)dependency inherent to care. In a narrow sense, care is often defined as caring activity provided by a caregiver to a care receiver, involving emotions and intimacy as well as asymmetrical power relations, limited autonomy, and vulnerability (Tronto 1993, Jochimsen 2003). Dependency on care – framed as exceptional in a society that regards independent, autonomous, and self-sufficient hetero-masculinities as ideal – is something *all* lives begin with, and most lives end with. Broader conceptions of care go beyond human subject-subject relations: Care as a keystone of social-ecological transformation is not only directed towards persons, but also to non-human life-forms and the complex web that makes life on the planet possible (Pacto Ecosocial del Sur 2021, The Care Collective 2020).

In the current economic system, unpaid care work is invisibilised and highly gendered. Being the necessary precondition for *every* production process in the monetised economy, unpaid care work is regarded as a free subsidy, performed mostly by women in heteronormative households, without monetary compensation and/or social recognition (Himmelweit 1995, Jochimsen and Knobloch 1997, Dengler and Strunk 2018). Time use studies, employing a binary understanding of gender, indicate that women perform ¾ of the unpaid care work globally (ILO 2018, 53f). In the paid care sector roughly ⅔ of the care workers are women (*ibid.*, 167f). The liberal feminist "emancipation through wage work" – narrative from the 1970s – has left many women with the unsatisfactory choice to either perform unpaid care work in *their* "second shift" (Hochschild 2003) or to outsource this work to paid care workers, e.g., poorly paid (often migrant) women in elderly care or early childcare institutions.

The COVID-19 pandemic highlights the feminist argument that

the wealth and well-being of the world are fundamentally built upon the invisibilised and feminised sphere of social reproduction (FaDA 2020). Closed childcare facilities and schools have exacerbated the gendered division of labour in the "private sphere" of households (Bahn *et al.* 2020), sometimes coupled with problematic tendencies such as rising levels of gendered violence in families during the pandemic (Roesch *et al.* 2020). However, even when unpaid care work is shifted to the paid care sector it is often "valorised but not valued" (Dowling 2016). This particularly holds for marketed care, which is systematically underpaid and often pressured for profitability and efficiency. Regarding public provisioning, it is noteworthy that welfare states are historically patriarchal and colonial, reproduce binary heteronormativity, and claim unjust amounts of global resources (Koch and Mont 2016, Bhambra and Holmwood 2018, Dengler and Lang 2022). Neither marketised care nor welfare states are a blueprint for a Just Transition around care, let alone global social welfare. A degrowth society ideally values care work without valorising it and collectively shares the joys and burdens that care work entails beyond the "private sphere" of heteronormative families on the one hand and "public" market, state, and non-profit organisation provisioning on the other, focusing on collective forms of caring.

Conceptual notes on strategies for transformation

We propose to read the categorisation of strategies for anti-capitalist transformation formulated by Wright (2013) as a descriptive, explanatory framework, whose categories are not mutually exclusive and should not be hierarchised. Wright's definition of *ruptural transformation* seems the most radical strategy at first. In the long history of 20th-century revolutions, however, it has merely led to reconfigurations of power and new elites, neither overcoming the growth imperative nor building sustainable modes of social reproduction. *Interstitial transformations* which operate from the margins can cover a broad range of strategies. They can aim at "escaping" capitalism in rather self-centred ways or at multiplying horizontally (scaling-out) until they create the opportunity for *systemic change*. In prefigurative spaces where logics of conviviality, solidarity, and reciprocity are practised, they potentially produce transformative subjectivities (Global Working Group Beyond Development 2018). We agree with Ekaterina Chertkovskaya (Chapter 2) that *symbiotic strategies,* operating within the realm of existing institutions, run the risk of co-optation. Nevertheless, they are needed to generate conditions that allow *interstitial strategie*s to scale out and thrive. In this chapter, we combine Wright's ideas with Fraser's (1997) framework, which is more common in feminist reasoning: *Affirmative strategies* work within a given structure, while *transformative strategies* aim at changing the structure itself. However, affirmative strategies potentially "give rise to transformative effects because they alter relations of power and thereby open a path for further struggles that become increasingly radical over time" (Fraser and Jaeggi 2018, 174). We, therefore, sympathise with concepts like "non-reformist reforms" (Gorz 1967), "concrete utopias" (Bloch 1959), or "revolutionary realpolitik" (Luxemburg 1903).

Strategies towards care for all and their relevance for degrowth

The following section introduces and evaluates three strategies that seek to redefine, redistribute, and revalue unpaid care work by establishing different (1) wage systems, (2) time regimes, and (3) modes of organising care in a degrowth society. Though not being the main focus of this chapter, we deem it necessary that waged work in the health and care sector needs to be thoroughly revalued in terms of fair wages, dignified working conditions, and more time for preventive and holistic care.

Changing wage relations and redefining work

Wage labour is a dominant structure of capitalist growth-based societies that forces people who depend on wages to prioritise wage work over all other forms of work and activities (Weeks

2020). Hence, changing wage relations is a central precondition of redefining, redistributing, and revaluing all kinds of socially necessary work. In this section, we discuss the Wages for Housework (WfH) campaign, the Care Income (CI), and a Universal Basic Income (UBI) as means towards this end.

The international "Wages for Housework" (WfH) campaign drew on the intellectual ideas of Mariarosa Dalla Costa (1972), Selma James (1972) and Silvia Federici (1975), who co-founded the International Feminist Collective (IFC). The IFC launched the WfH-campaign in 1972 and soon had WfH-working groups across Europe, North America and even in, for example, Mexico and Argentina, and thematic groups such as the *Wages Due Lesbians* and *Black Women for Wages for Housework* (Toupin 2018). Before the term "care work" was coined, the campaign had the dual aim of making reproductive work – until then considered a "labour of love" – visible as the foundation of the economy *and* subverting the capitalist system. In the context of the feminist movement in the 1970s, WfH can be read as a critique of the liberal feminist notion of integrating women into the unquestioned category of (male-connoted) wage labour. WfH was criticised for aiming at institutionalising the gendered division of labour and for asking to include reproductive work into capitalist valorisation (e.g., Davis 1983). However, WfH was not intended as *realpolitik* or a symbiotic strategy in Wright's terms, but as a radical provocation both to the capitalist system (by exposing that it was nurturing on invisible constant subsidies) and to patriarchy (by questioning the gendered division of labour). In this sense, WfH aimed at ruptural, transformative change in a historical period when interstitial transformation was thriving.

Building on WfH and the the Bejing platform 1995 consensus to "make unpaid care work count" in national accounting, the Care Income (CI) is a symbiotic proposal aiming at compensation for unpaid care work supported by the Global Women's Strike (2020), several degrowth scholars (e.g., Barca 2020), and the Green New Deal for Europe (2019). The CI is a form of "participation income"

(Atkinson 1996), issued to carers by state institutions. By demanding capital for socially necessary yet appropriated and invisibilised care work, the CI aims to redistribute wealth to those caring for "people, the urban and rural environment, and the natural world" (Global Women's Strike 2020), thereby strengthening the social position of carers and the recognition of care work. By putting an emphasis on people who perform care work, the proposal directly addresses the gendered distribution of care work and raises transformative and ruptural questions of power. However, the CI also exhibits affirmative elements as it aims at monetising care rather than widening the decommodified dimensions of life. Wichterich (2015, 88) points out that conditional cash transfers always bear the risk of "neoliberal co-optation that seeks individual and monetary solutions to problems of social inequalities." Moreover, the practical necessities to prove one's eligibility for a care income in practice bear problematic dimensions of surveillance, humiliation, and bureaucracy (Baker 2008). Hence, the transformative potential of a CI largely depends on its concrete design. Up to date, a CI has not been implemented but is advocated for by several groups around the globe (e.g., IWRAW Asia Pacific 2020, Barca *et al.* 2020).

The proposal of a Universal Basic Income (UBI) avoids the pitfalls of eligibility as it envisions a regular, fixed, age-dependent amount of cash granted to everyone (Torry 2019). Due to the harsh economic crisis and the massive increases in inequality in the COVID-19-context, debates around UBI were boosted in different world regions and gained support from international institutions (e.g., ECLAC 2020). Whilst the UBI is not specifically focused on care, several feminist scholars discuss it as a strategic possibility to reorganise, revalue, and redistribute care work (Zelleke 2021; Winker 2015). Like the CI, the UBI is a symbiotic proposal distributed by state institutions, however, without investing those with the power to decide on eligibility, as it is universal. From a feminist perspective, the ruptural transformative potential of a UBI lies in the possibility to decouple social security from wage labour (e.g., Schulz 2017,

Winker 2015). It allows for socially re-valuing unpaid forms of work without monetising them and, more generally, for interstitial strategies to thrive. However, a UBI is no automatism for a gender-just redistribution of care work among all members of society and crucially depends on a cultural shift and complementary measures (Katada 2012). More recent proposals underline the centrality of care within UBI arrangements by reformulating it as "Universal Care Income" (Kallis *et al.* 2020, 71). Some applications of UBI in peripheral regions of the Global South (e.g., in Kenya, see Lowrey 2017) subsidise growth by mitigating poverty and improving productivity, e.g., by including subsistence peasants into exploitative and environmentally damaging wage work (Lang 2017). This is incompatible with degrowth visions, which seek to dignify and recognise unpaid work and livelihoods based on non-commodified economies, proving the need to change wage relations context-sensitively.

Changing time regimes and redistributing care work

Another central strategy to redefine, redistribute, and revalue care aspires to dethrone wage work by freeing up time spent in wage work that can then be devoted to all other forms of work. Throughout the 20th century, demands for a general reduction of working hours often came up in the context of productivity gains or as short-term economic policy in times of economic crises (Zwickl *et al.* 2016). The degrowth proposal of work-sharing (WS) as "redistribution of work between the employed and the unemployed" (Kallis *et al.* 2015, 13) differs from this perspective as it aims to push back the dominant role of wage labour as such. Implementing WS through legislation is a symbiotic proposal that, by reducing *everyone's* time spent in wage work, allows all kinds of interstitial strategies to flourish. Seemingly gender-neutral proposals like WS, however, can have highly gendered effects. As Dengler and Strunk (2018) argue, a *daily* reduction of hours spent in wage work has more transformative potential regarding the redistribution of unpaid care work than, for example, the proposal to have "Fridays off" (Kallis *et al.* 2013). Moreover, in order not to reproduce socio-economic inequalities, WS requires full wage compensation for low-income earners or other ways, by which wage work is decoupled from livelihood security (Winker 2015).

Instead of only reducing time spent in wage work, Frigga Haug (2008) aspires to a radical and holistic (re-)distribution of socially valuable work and to a transformation of the ways societies organise themselves and interact with nature. Her "4-in-1 perspective" envisages that everyone engages four hours each in paid work necessary to produce means for life, care work for humans and more-than-humans, communal and political activities, and time for leisure and self-development (Haug 2011). The realisation of 4-in-1 is necessarily tied to a basic income, which, according to Haug (*Ibid.*), would be universal, but not unconditional, as it relies on the social obligation for each person to perform their share of every kind of work, including care work. By claiming four hours/day for political work, she emphasises the importance of political engagement "from below" (Haug 2008) where everyone gets involved with shaping the transformation of time regimes. Hence, the proposal for changing economies of time is formulated as a revolutionary *realpolitik* that starts from the status quo but has the potential to subvert diverse power relations.

Re-organising societies around care

The strategies of changing wage relations and time regimes feed into the major degrowth strategy to reorganise societies around care, which requires democratic and collective care arrangements beyond the dichotomy of money-mediated care work in the market/state/non-profit sector on the one hand and unpaid care work in heteronormative nuclear families on the other. Founded in 2012, Care Revolution (CR) is a political strategy that aims at transforming care as the basis for a society grounded in solidarity and, at the same time, a social movement closely linked to a variety of care strikes in

Germany, Austria, and Switzerland, as well as a political network with more than 80 cooperation partners. Gabriele Winker's (2015) book *Care Revolution: Schritte in eine solidarische Gesellschaft* is foundational for the Marxist feminist analysis behind CR. The vision of a CR is sketched as a "radical democratic society oriented towards human needs, ... in which the division between paid and unpaid care work no longer applies" (Winker *et al.* 2018, 421). Whilst CR applies a broad concept of care that respects planetary boundaries (Winker 2021), it decidedly takes human life and needs as a starting point. By acknowledging that some non-reformist reforms such as a UBI or WS could pave the way towards a solidarity-based care economy, CR offers a broader context for thriving interstitial spaces of transformation. Local care councils, such as the *Care-Rat* in Freiburg (Winker *et al.* 2018), are an example of how CR seeks to democratise existing care infrastructures and strive towards a collective reorganisation of care – a strategy that is closely linked to discussions of commoning care.

Research on the commons has flourished over the last decades. In contrast to debates that regard commons as a type of good/resource, we consider commons as social relations and processes of democratic self-government which enable the sharing of (re-)production of life (Caffentzis and Federici 2014, Bollier and Helfrich 2019, Perkins 2019). Day-to-day caring activities and parts of the health care sector can be organised beyond the market, state, households, and non-profit organisations as Caring Commons (CCs) (Akbulut 2016, Gutiérrez Aguilar 2017, Dengler and Lang 2022). Examples of the strategy to re-organise care work as commons are the community-based health care system in the cooperative Cecosesola in Barquisimeto, Venezuela (see the second half of this chapter) and the Poliklinik in Hamburg Veddel, Germany, as well as the *Ollas Comunes* (popular kitchens in Chile in the 1970s), commonised childcare, or co-housing projects for elderly people in Spain today. These examples are not primarily focused on the common administration of goods, but on transforming and (re-)

building relations of care and conviviality in day-to-day life. CCs are, as Silvia Federici (2019, 4) reminds us, "an already present reality ... and a perspective anticipating in an embryonic way a world beyond capitalism." In decidedly acknowledging the interdependence of human and non-human forms of life, CCs can be read as an interstitial strategy that, when scaled out, have transformative and ruptural potential. Symbiotic strategies that aim at changing wage relations and time regimes enhance the conditions of possibility for such commoning practices and, more generally, a re-organisation of care to thrive.

Conclusion: care for all

Strategies around care for a degrowth society adopt a non-anthropocentric and non-binary perspective to build caring relations with humans and more-than-humans, acknowledging multiple interdependencies. Experiences and debates from the last decades show that a redefinition and reorganisation of work and a restructuration of day-to-day activities have the potential to place the ethics of care at the centre of social-ecological transformation, thereby overcoming the asymmetries and injustices along the lines of gender, class, race, and coloniality that currently characterise care work. To move towards a feminist degrowth society, the different strategic levels described by Wright and Fraser complement each other. Symbiotic demands that push back wage work generate the structural conditions of possibility for a broader transformation of day-to-day relations, habits, and routines, where urban and rural communities multiply caring commons according to their specific, situated needs in a democratic, self-governed manner. In this degrowth future, people of all genders dedicate part of their lifetime to care work, thereby contributing to the necessary cultural change to redefine, redistribute, and revalue care.

References

Akbulut, Bengi. 2016. "Carework as Commons: Towards a Feminist Degrowth Agenda." Paper presented at the 5*th* Degrowth Conference, Budapest.

Atkinson, Anthony B. 1996. "The Case for a Participation Income." *The Political Quarterly Publishing* 27, no. 1: 67–70.

Bahn, Kate, Jennifer Cohen, and Dana Rodgers. 2020. "A Feminist Perspective on COVID-19 and the Value of Care Work Globally." *Gender, Work & Organisation* 27, no 5: 695–699.

Baker, John. 2008. "All Things Considered, Should Feminists Embrace Basic Income?" *Basic Income Studies* 3, no.3.

Barca, Stefania. 2020. *Forces of Reproduction: Notes for a Counter-hegemonic Anthropocene.* Cambridge: Cambridge University Press.

Barca, Stefania, Giacomo D'Alisa, Selma James, and Nina López. 2020. *Rente de los Cuidados ¡ya!* Barcelona: Icaria Editorial/El Viejo Topo/Montaber.

Bhambra, Gurminder, and John Holmwood. 2018. "Colonialism, Postcolonialism and the Liberal Welfare State." *New Political Economy* 23, no. 5: 574–587.

Bloch, Ernst. 1959. *Das Prinzip Hoffnung.* Frankfurt: Suhrkamp.

Bollier, David, and Silke Helfrich. 2020. *Free, Fair, and Alive: The Insurgent Power of the Commons.* Gabriola Island: New Society Publishers.

Caffentzis, George, and Silvia Federici. 2014. "Commons Against and Beyond Capitalism." *Community Development Journal* 49, no. 1: 92–105.

Dalla Costa, Mariarosa. 1972. "Women and the Subversion of Community." In *The Power of Women and the Subversion of the Community*, edited by Mariarosa Dalla Costa, and Selma James, 19–45. Bristol: Falling Wall Press.

Davis, Angela. 1983. *Women, Race & Class.* New York: Vintage Books.

Dengler, Corinna, and Miriam Lang. 2022. "Commoning Care: Feminist Degrowth Visions for a Socio-Ecological Transformation." *Feminist Economics* 28, no. 1: 1–28.

Dengler, Corinna, and Birte Strunk. 2018. "The Monetized Economy Versus Care and the Environment: Degrowth Perspectives on Reconciling an Antagonism." *Feminist Economics* 24, no. 3: 160–183.

Dowling, Emma. 2016. "Valorised but not Valued? Affective Remuneration, Social Reproduction and Feminist Politics Beyond the Recovery." *British Politics* 11, no. 4: 452–468.

ECLAC (Economic Commission for Latin America and the Caribbean). 2020. *The Social Challenge in Times of COVID-19*. United Nations. https://www.cepal.org/en/publications/45544-social-challenge-times-covid-19.

FaDA (Feminisms and Degrowth Alliance). 2020. "Feminist Degrowth Reflection on COVID-19 and the Politics of Social Reproduction." *Degrowth.info* (blog), April 20, 2020. https://www.degrowth.info/en/2020/04/feminist-degrowth-collaborative-fada-reflections-on-the-covid-19-pandemic-and-the-politics-of-social-reproduction

Federici, Silvia. 1975. *Wages Against Housework*. Bristol: Falling Wall Press.

Federici, Silvia. 2019. *Re-Enchanting the World. Feminism and the Politics of the Commons*. Oakland: PM Press.

Fraser, Nancy. 1997. *Justice Interruptus. Critical Reflections on the "Postsocialist" Condition*. New York, London: Routledge.

Fraser, Nancy, and Rahel Jaeggi. 2018. *Capitalism. A Conversation in Critical Theory.* Cambridge: Polity Press.

Global Women's Strike. 2020. "Open Letter to Governments – a Care Income Now!" *Global Women's Strike*, March 27, 2020. https://globalwomenstrike.net/open-letter-to-governments-a-care-income-now/.

Global Working Group Beyond Development. 2018. "Beyond Development. Stopping the Machines of Socio-Ecological Destruction and Building Alternative Worlds." In *Alternatives in a World of Crisis* edited by Miriam Lang, and Claus-Dieter König *et al*, 258–306. Brussels and Quito: Rosa Luxemburg Foundation and Universidad Andina Simón Bolívar.

Gorz, André. 1967. *Strategy for Labor: A Radical Proposal*. Boston: Beacon Press.

Green New Deal for Europe. 2019. *A Blueprint for Europe's Just Transition*. https://report.gndforeurope.com/cms/wp-content/uploads/2020/01/Blueprint-for-Europes-Just-Transition-2nd-Ed.pdf

Gutiérrez Aguilar, Raquel. 2017. *Horizontes comunitario-populares. Producción de lo común más allá de las políticas estado-céntricas*. Madrid: Traficantes de Sueños.

Haug, Frigga. 2008. *Die Vier-in-einem-Perspektive. Politik von Frauen für eine neue Linke*. Hamburg: Argument Verlag.

Haug, Frigga. 2011. „Die Vier-in-Einem Perspektive und das Bedingungslose Grundeinkommen, Notizen aus einem Diskussionsprozess." In *Den Maschinen die Arbeit ... uns das Vergnügen! Beiträge zum Existenzgeld,* edited by Anne Allex, and Harald Rein, 49–62. Neu-Ulm: AG SPAK Arbeitsgemeinschaft sozialpolitischer Arbeitskreise.

Himmelweit, Susan. 1995. "The Discovery of 'Unpaid Work': The Social Consequences of the Expansion of 'Work'." *Feminist Economics* 1, no. 2: 1–19.

Hochschild, Arlie. 2003. *The Second Shift*. New York: Penguin Books.

IWRAW Asia Pacific. 2020. *"Wages for Caring Work": An Exploration of the Care Income Campaign*. https://www.iwraw-ap.org/wages-for-caring-work/.

ILO. 2018. *Care Work and Care Jobs for the Future of Decent Work*. Geneva: ILO.

James, Selma. 1972. "A Woman's Place." In *The Power of Women and the Subversion of the Community*, edited by Mariarosa Dalla Costa, and Selma James, 55–77. Bristol: Falling Wall Press.

Jochimsen, Maren. 2003. *Careful Economics. Integrating Caring Activities and Economic Science*. Dordrecht: Springer.

Jochimsen, Maren A., and Ulrike Knobloch. 1997. "Making the Hidden Visible: The Importance of Caring Activities and Their Principles for Any Economy." *Ecological Economics* 20, no. 2: 107–112.

Kallis, Giorgos, Federico Demaria, and Giacomo D'Alisa. 2015. "Introduction: Degrowth." In *Degrowth: Vocabulary for a New Era*, edited by Giacomo D'Alisa, Federico Demaria, and Giorgos Kallis, 1–17. New York/London: Routledge.

Kallis, Giorgos, Michael Kalush, Hugh O'Flynn, Jack Rossiter, and Nicholas Ashford. 2013. "'Friday Off': Reducing Working Hours in Europe." *Sustainability* 5, no. 4: 1545–1567.

Kallis, Giorgos, Susan Paulson, Giacomo D'Alisa, and Federico Demaria. 2020. *The Case for Degrowth*. Cambridge: Polity Press.

Katada, Kaori. 2012. "Basic Income and Feminism: In Terms of 'The Gender Division of Labor'." *Basicincome.org*. https://basicincome.org/bien/pdf/munich2012/katada.pdf.

Koch, Max, and Oksana Mont. 2016. *Sustainability and the Political Economy of Welfare*. London/ New York: Routledge.

Lang, Miriam. 2017. *Erradicar la pobreza o empobrecer las alternativas?* Quito: Abya Yala.

Lowrey, Anna. 2017. "The Future of Not Working." *New York Times,* February 23, 2010. https://www.nytimes.com/2017/02/23/magazine/universal-income-global-inequality.html?_r=0.

Luxemburg, Rosa. 1903. „Karl Marx." *Vorwärts* 64.

Pacto Ecosocial del Sur. 2021. *Pacto Ecosocial del Sur: América Latina y Caribe*. https://pactoecosocialdelsur.com/#1591241016278-e6c4e5dd-de46.

Perkins, Patricia Ellie. 2019. "Climate Justice, Commons, and Degrowth." *Ecological Economics* 160: 183–190.

Roesch, Elisabeth, Avni Amin, Jhumka Gupta, and Claudia García-Moreno. 2020. "Violence against Women during COVID-19 Pandemic Restrictions." *British Medical Journal* 369: 1712.

Schulz, Patricia. 2017. "Universal Basic Income in a Feminist Perspective and Gender Analysis." *Global Social Policy* 17, no. 1: 89–92.

The Care Collective. 2020. *The Care Manifesto. The Politics of Interdependence.* London, New York: Verso.

Torry, Malcolm. 2019. "The Definition and Characteristics of Basic Income." In *The Palgrave International Handbook of Basic Income. Exploring the Basic Income Guarantee*, edited by Malcolm Torry, 15–30. Cham: Palgrave Macmillan.

Toupin, Louise. 2018. *Wages for Housework. A History of an International Feminist Movement 1972–1977.* London: Pluto Press.

Tronto, Joan C. 1993. *A Political Argument for an Ethic of Care.* New York, London: Routledge.

Weeks, Kathi. 2020. "Anti/Postwork Feminist Politics and a Case for Basic Income." *triplec* 18, no. 2: 575–594.

Wichterich, Christa. 2015. "Contesting Green Growth, Connecting Care, Commons and Enough." In *Practicing Feminist Political Ecologies: Moving Beyond the "Green Economy"*, edited by Wendy Harcourt, and Ingrid Nelson, 67–100. London: Zed Books.

Winker, Gabriele. 2015. *Care Revolution: Schritte in eine solidarische Gesellschaft.* Bielefeld: transcript.

Winker, Gabriele. 2021. *Solidarische Care-Ökonomie: Revolutionäre Realpolitik für Care und Klima.* Bielefeld: transcript.

Winker, Gabriele, Brigitte Aulenbacher, and Birgit Riegraf. 2018. „Care Revolution." *Equality, Diversity and Inclusion* 37, no. 4: 420–428.

Wright, Erik Olin. 2013. "Transforming Capitalism through Real Utopias." *American Sociological Review* 78: 1–25.

Zelleke, Almaz. 2021. "Basic Income, Care, and Wages for Housework." *LPE Project*, October 2, 2021. https://lpeproject.org/blog/basic-income-care-and-wages-for-housework/.

Zwickl, Klara, Franziska Disslbacher, and Sigrid Stagl. 2016. "Work-Sharing for a Sustainable Economy." *Ecological Economics* 121, no. 1: 246–253.

A case in the field of care: the Health Centre Cecosesola

By Georg Rath

Cecosesola is not a model, it is an inspiration. And what inspires most is not just the fact that it has been working for so long, but the care with which they do things differently, they create something that is completely mediated by the base.
– *John Holloway, epilogue to Cecosesola (2012)*

As probably the first of its kind, our communitarian-cooperative integral health centre *Centro Integral de Salud* (CICS) was opened in the Venezuelan city of Barquisimeto, in the North-Western state of Lara, on 2 June 2009. This holistic health centre combines conventional medicine and alternative therapies and offers treatments and care to the city's 1.5 million inhabitants. In addition to general medicine, the cooperative health centre offers paediatrics, gynaecology, natural birth, X-ray diagnostics, laboratory work, Tai-Chi, music therapy, urology, orthopaedics, psychology, and physiatry. As the heart of a healthcare network that also includes six smaller facilities, this health centre is a self-organising and self-financed communitarian initiative whose services have been fully maintained even in times of the pandemic. The fact that the CICS is a cooperative makes it rather different from existing public or private health centres. We are neither guided by the principle of profit maximisation, which drives private clinics, nor by the logics of public welfare that underlie state health policies. The services are not only open to members of the cooperative, but to everyone who hopes to receive support for their healing processes. For us, the primary aim is to create a space for communal encounters in health, which includes the possibility of transforming traditional relationships shaped by hierarchies into democratic processes of collective provisioning. This focus on democratic and collective provisioning is, no doubt, a perspective that we share with the degrowth movement.

The CICS is part of the *Central Cooperativa de Servicios Sociales del Estado Lara* (Cecosesola), born in 1967. A total of 40 cooperatives with about 20,000 members in and around Barquisimeto make up the Cecosesola cooperative network. Many activities work in synergy, such as the supply of food (especially fruit and vegetables at our community markets), funeral services, and healthcare. Our health network started in 1995 as a collective health fund for members. Over the years, six decentralised locations for medical consultation emerged in some of the cooperatives, until the CICS was built in 2009 as the heartpiece of the network.

This network logic is what allows us to self-finance every new activity, such as the sales of our eight market halls with an average of 100,000 customers per week. These are the backbone of the network, which ensure the livelihoods of members who sustain the network with their labour and engagement in rotative shifts. They also provide start-up funding for new projects like the construction of the CICS, which cost approximately 7 million USD. New activities are supported through fundraising actions like food sales or t-shirt campaigns and can receive temporary loans from other cooperatives in the network. But the goal is to be financially self-sufficient, and the CICS has achieved that for five years now. This, and our capacity to constantly adapt to changing circumstances through flexible self-government, have allowed us to be resilient even throughout the huge economic crisis Venezuela has experienced in the last years (Lander 2018).

It is characteristic of Cecosesola's strategy that its initiatives almost always arise from a communitarian, collectively felt necessity of life. Originally, Cecosesola started out as a communal funeral parlour in December 1967. Since then, public transportation, food, and health initiatives have emerged, all of which – except the public transportation – are ongoing. Only three years after the founding of Cecosesola, the question arose whether cooperatives should generally offer services exclusively for their members (the classic position represented and practised by most cooperatives and commoning initiatives), or if we should make these services available to the general public. After long discussions, we decided on the latter and, since then, we have opened our services to everyone in need, a decision that became ever more important for the organisation. This also applied to our commitment to health, which was initially limited to providing health care only for our members. As this proved incompatible with our communitarian logic, we then continually expanded our health services to the general public.

The cooperative-communitarian process of the CICS health centre allows for treatment prices to be about half the price of other, non-governmental health facilities. As the respective activities are seen primarily as community engagement with the "side effect" of an income opportunity (prices should cover material costs, there are only small excess margins, and there are no specialised "top earners"), some dominant market mechanisms are undermined. Prior to the COVID-19 pandemic in 2020, an annual average of 200,000 people visited our health centre – a number that shows the scope of our transformational aspirations.

Due to its cooperative-communitarian character, the CICS management is a collective, too. A "medical director" only formally appears when required by government authorities. Internally, however, all management decisions are made based on consensus. The self-organisation of the CICS primarily consists of plenary discussions of all those members involved in a particular issue. They take place several times a week and can last several hours until all pending questions have been (temporarily) clarified. These plenary sessions neither have an agenda, nor a facilitator. Everyone can contribute their opinion at any time. The quality of self-organisation improves with collective experience. As in the upward movement of a spiral, we get back to the same relational topics from time to time but do so on a higher level of reflection. This form of organisation sometimes lacks the ability to respond quickly, but it also enables an approach to health that meets everyone's needs and expectations.

The integral approach of health in Cecosesola and its dimensions

For us, an integral approach goes beyond a combination of individual services. It describes the synergy of different strategies that do not result from a quantitative striving for growth, but from a striving for a certain quality of relationships. Integrality for us includes:

1. Patients are at the centre of our approach and relationships with everyone are carefully nourished. Appreciation, support, and respect are key terms forming the relationship between therapists and patients. Thereby, those terms themselves (therapist/patient) and the type of relationships they stand for tend to be replaced while creating a subject-subject relationship. This is part of the cultural transformation in Cecosesola – a transformation that, based on everyday experience, constantly reflects and deconstructs utilitarian relations which degrade the other into an object of one's own expectations, goals, ambitions, and emotions.

2. A second axis is that consciousness, knowledge, and feelings converge; people who want to work at CICS need to understand that the team not only needs the necessary expertise, but also a heart that is sensitive enough to serve sick people with an attitude of mindfulness. Mindfulness is not understood as an attitude of compassion towards the "poor little you", but as solidarity with one another in situations of imbalance. We need people who are willing to become aware of the civilisational patterns that impair humanity so deeply: the pursuit of one's own benefit, the lack of altruism and the unnecessary accumulation of goods, power, and knowledge as

a supposed safety belt of our existence. We cannot design an integral health centre with the primary aim of earning money. The real goal is to rebuild life out of a sick and sickening situation.

3. Integrality also refers to the aspect of community, which goes beyond solidarity pricing. It is about turning the centre into a space of encounter and community with neighbours, friends, and residents of Barquisimeto's districts, in which access to health services is generally difficult. The community and its rich and diverse experiences are part of our activities, and we are part of the community if we only allow ourselves to see health as an opportunity to learn and share knowledge, wisdom, and experiences from within the community. In Spanish, the term *comunidad* emphasises two essential components of community: what we have in common and what we want to do together. Based on our experience as a cooperative, we contribute tools that improve organisational processes in the community. For example, having solid principles while at the same time being flexible in terms of living these principles without dogmatism; or building organisational processes that respect transparency, honesty, and sharing based on solidarity.

4. Another axis of the integral approach is directly related to health: the axis of body, mind, and spirit, which is the axis of healing. Healing has a broader and deeper meaning for us rather than just making one healthy. It is about not regarding the sick person (which we all are, to a certain degree) as an "object to be healed", as a number in a medical record, as a "next one, please." Healing processes understand illness as a possibility and opportunity for the transformation of the person, and our task in health is to help the person to decipher the message that is contained in the complaints.

Neither public nor private, but cooperative and communitarian

The cooperative originates from a free and egalitarian agreement between people who decide to form an organisation under cooperative law, whose activities must be carried out for purposes of social interest and collective benefit, without privileging one or more of its members. In practical terms, this implies that all people who educate themselves – regardless of whether they work as doctors, nurses, dentists, cleaners, or technicians – work as equals. They do so in a team with collective discipline in a self-governed manner, which supports creativity, the creation of holistic wellbeing, solidarity, and a feeling of identity and belonging. A rather practical consequence of this structure is that in Cecosesola – except for a few doctors and technicians – all receive the same remuneration for our communitarian-cooperative commitment. The exceptions mentioned are the subject of collective discussions to gradually create a balance of remuneration in the future.

However, none of this is a linear process. There were many ups and downs, or unexpected obstacles, caused by new state regulations that needed to be overcome through negotiations or actions of civil disobedience. For example, new tax regulations for cooperatives were introduced in 2018 without any specific relation to Cecosesola, but which translated into a huge threat to its financial sustainability. There are also problems in everyday life, for example, due to deeply rooted patriarchal structures that we carry along with us. Based on our patriarchal, racist, hierarchical culture, it is no easy task to create a process leading towards a culture of participation that transcends relationships of domination. For instance, an area of tension that continues to challenge us lies in the elitist self-conception of doctors, who perceive themselves as superior based on their expertise, thereby enacting power.

Venezuela has, from 2013, been going through the most severe economic and political crisis in its history (Lander 2018). Shortages of all kinds of goods, including medical supplies, hyperinflation (over one million % in 2018), and strict state control of all economic activities mark the context in which Cecosesola and the CICS currently operate. The pandemic has further challenged our ability to mature and reinvent ourselves, with a drastic quarantine that includes a curfew in our city. Within the few hours the CICS is currently allowed to open, we are hardly able to cope with the approximately 700 persons that visit us per day and sometimes must resort to civil disobedience. As it has already happened quite frequently in the history of Cecosesola, such challenges invite us to deepen our communitarian engagement and to meet them with collective creativity. For example, when patient numbers dropped in the first weeks of the pandemic, we invited doctors to work at the grocery markets so they could maintain their income.

Our strategy neither aims at symbiotic laws or government policies nor at a ruptural break. Abandoning the power relations that shape our society is a shared, time-consuming process of interstitial everyday learning that follows the principles of transparency, responsibility, respect, and mutual help. In doing so, we are not guided by a ready-made imperative of how everything should turn out, but by a sincere desire to change ourselves in relation to others. Transforming our relations in Cecosesola according to these principles leads us to move away from the growth imperative, both in what concerns production, distribution, and consumption as well as the social imaginaries of endless personal needs. Importantly, we do not consider ourselves as a closed collective, but, through the means of all our cooperative activities, we interact with the people in our city and regard every crossroads of our path as an invitation for everyone to get involved.

References

Cecosesola. 2012. *Auf dem Weg – Gelebte Utopie einer Kooperative in Venezuela*. Berlin: Die Buchmacherei.

Lander, Edgardo. 2018. "The Longterm Crisis. The Venezuelan Oil Rentier Model and the Present Crisis the Country Faces." *Transnational Institute Longreads*, January 4, 2018. https://longreads.tni.org/longterm-crisis-venezuelan-oil-rentier-model-present-crisis-country-faces.

Chapter 17: Paid work

An overview of strategies for social-ecological transformation in the field of paid work and the case of Just Transition in the aviation sector

By Halliki Kreinin and Tahir Latif

Introduction

Work forms a central component of social organisation and welfare in growth-dependent societies, with adverse environmental and social outcomes. The way work is structured today and the division of labour lie at the crossroads of environmental crises (climate breakdown, resource exploitation, biodiversity loss, food distribution) and social crises (gender and income inequality, labour exploitation, mental health) while work also conversely provides people with meaning, income and identity. Although there is agreement about the need to *transform* work amongst a variety of actors on the political spectrum, *what* kinds of work should be transformed, *why*, *how*, and *who* should do the transforming (as well as *what* counts as work) remain a terrain of debate and struggle. This is particularly true when one seeks to envision a degrowth society where work will be substantially different from the way work is currently organised.

In the following, we first briefly outline the interrelation of work to the different crises, then we will elaborate on the directions in which work could or should be transformed, as well as strategies to get there. We argue that interstitial and symbiotic strategies can work together and strengthen the potential for the transformation of work, for example, through amplifying workers' voices and providing alternatives that undermine the logic of capitalist economic production. While symbiotic transformation can be critiqued as reformist, currently there is no realistic way out of the conundrum of transforming capitalism in line with environmental and social considerations without implementing reforms that empower and broaden democracy. These reforms, however, may end up ameliorating and potentially reproducing existing capitalist relations of production (McCabe 2013). In what follows, we consider the combination of interstitial and symbiotic strategies for the transformation of work – primarily through the activities of labour unions. As the case study of the aviation sector workers will show, interstitial and symbiotic strategies often work together – momentum built up by interstitial transformation may eventually result in symbiotic transformation.

How paid work is currently organised

It is not news that the way work is currently organised has detrimental effects on the environment, as well as on society. Work and production play a crucial role in perpetuating the growth-based economic system – both as an input in production and as a consumption-causing activity (Hoffmann and Paulsen 2020). The need to secure full-time paid employment in line with productivity growth is one of the central mechanisms of the growth economy in the Global North, with disastrous environmental consequences (Jackson and Victor 2011).

In the growth-dependent capitalist economy "coercion, rules, ideology and material interests" interact in the terrain of work, thus reproducing exploitation by tying society's interests to the interests of capital (and against nature); this renders exploitation in waged labour economically and socially more desirable than unemployment (Wright 2010, 277; 279). In the Global South, the capitalist drive for growth and production is powering the destruction of subsistence communities and forced proletarianisation in the name of development. Lower-income countries are locked into a system of exploitation to supply cheap labour, materials, energy, and land, reinforcing inequality and the advantaged position of the Global North (Hoffmann and Paulsen 2020).

On the other hand, work that is socially accepted as prestigious and thus well paid often undermines or fails to contribute to social provisioning and may even lack internal meaning on its own terms, while also being environmentally or socially exploitative. According to Graeber (2018) more than half of the performed paid work in the Global North are "bullshit jobs" – outwardly well-regarded and paid, but often considered meaningless or not of social value, even by those who hold those jobs themselves. "Batshit work" has been used to refer to work that destroys the environment and human health for short-term economic profit (Hansen 2019). Bullshit and batshit jobs stand in contrast to the many unpaid (or low paid) activities that form the foundation of provisioning, but which are devalued by society – work historically performed largely by women (see Chapter 16).

Although multiple social and environmental crises highlight the urgent need for societies to transform work, the focus on productivity as a goal, and the primacy of paid labour in material provisioning, means that it is unlikely that paid work will disappear as a form of social organisation in the near future (Barca 2019). Within the individualist framework of capitalist society, a person's work is considered to provide the material basis for a good life and – rightly or wrongly – defines meaning, community, and identity (Fellner 2017). As a result, the transformation of current work relations is made more difficult by the immediate material interests of workers being tied to the continuation of the system. The direct material pressures that enforce the work ethic, as well as the growth imperative (see Chapter 1) render policies such as working time reduction, or limiting production for environmental reasons, contested – subjugating ecological interests to economic interests. Long working hours, unhealthy working conditions, and physically damaging labour are not only environmentally harmful, but have serious mental and physical health implications, both for the employed and unemployed (such as social exclusion, loss of meaning and identity) (Frayne 2015, Weeks 2011).

Working time reduction, work-sharing, the provision of universal basic services (or income), offer potential solutions to liberating society from the worst aspects of waged work (Kallis 2011, Schor 2005). As Barca (2019) explains, much degrowth scholarship and imaginary on work and its transformation have focused on this "liberation *from* work" perspective; the next task for the degrowth movement, she argues, is to also focus on the "liberation *of* work" from the capitalist growth imperative and work discipline, as a basis for alliances with other social struggles and an eco-socialist transition. Rendering waged work environmentally and socially sustainable (instead of exploitative and alienating) is a key element in challenging the socio-economic orthodoxy of productivity and GDP growth as supreme societal goals (Barca 2019).

It is workers who have intimate knowledge of the sites of production, how production could be transformed, or where to exert pressure to bring *batshit* production to a halt, thus workers are key agents for the social-ecological transformation (Hansen 2019, Pichler *et al.* 2021). Work as an institution also helps to passively reproduce exploitative social structures, making work the key terrain of strategic action for change and human liberation (Wright 2010, 276).

In the following section, we will elaborate on the "liberation *of* work" perspective, starting from the ground up as the basis for strategic alliances that challenge the existing exploitative institutions of work.

Towards the liberation of work: What do we mean by transforming waged work?

When considering the potential for a transformation of work, we can identify three main kinds of transformations:

1. *Changing the actual work that is done* – this is the fundamental underpinning for a transformation of work, from one activity (environmentally destructive) to another (socially useful), e.g., from fossil fuel production to renewable energy, from

plane and car to train and bus construction and maintenance, underpinned by a guarantee of continued employment and of any retraining required.

2. *Changing the character of work* – moving away from an ethos of excessive measurement and continuous acceleration of pace and expectation, and thereby eliminating bullshit/batshit jobs, automating routine tasks where technologically or ecologically feasible to release people for more fulfilling work, proper and equal treatment in the workplace including guaranteeing decent basic wages instead of performance-based "incentivisation".

3. *Transitioning to a more democratic workplace* – replacing hierarchical structures with workplace democracy, using workers' knowledge as the basis of decision-making within a sector, and actively promoting and progressing towards alternative models of ownership (nationalised, local or regional, community-based, worker-owned co-ops) and democratic accountability.

The first is the easiest to deal with – in theory, if not in practice – as it describes the physical switching of production from one activity to another. This could possibly be done without implementing the other two kinds of transformation of work. However, such a change in isolation would not be sufficient to deliver the post-carbon society that is needed for social-ecological transformation. Changes in lifestyle, social organisation and workplace democracy are implicit in any serious attempt to decarbonise work.

The other issue with *changing the actual work that is done* is the resistance that would be (and is) encountered from vested interests that profit from current activities. There is no shortage of evidence for the lengths to which some corporations go to protect their interests, such as Shell's or Chevron's knowledge of climate change in the early 1970s, or the aviation industry's greenwashing regarding biofuels and technological developments (Franta 2021). Governments are often deeply entwined in complex relationships with these corporations, and consequently will either resist change or do the minimum required. It is highly possible that they would seek to implement climate policy through market principles. Such an approach will likely deliver limited success – both in terms of social and environmental outcomes. For these reasons, a transformation that targets the form and purpose of work is essential, which would replace simple profiteering with broader social and environmental goals from which all benefit.

Strategies to liberate work

To transform work, the first key task is to understand the contradictions, limits and gaps in the system that reproduce the hegemony of current economic and work relations, in order to find and open up spaces for truly transformative strategies (should be (Wright 2010, 290). According to Wright's typology, we now consider different types of transformation in the field of work – interstitial, ruptural, and symbiotic.

Practices of interstitial transformation are important as lived utopias, which increase social empowerment, extend the degrowth imaginary and realms of possible action. Interstitial strategies offer parallel solutions to transforming the institution of waged work. Cooperative ways of organising production, consumption, and distribution have long provided viable alternatives to capitalist or centrally planned economies (Vieta 2010). Eco-villages and forms of labour exchange through practices such as time-banking, provide visions of a possible social organisation of tasks outside waged labour that transcend current structures. However, there is a risk for interstitial strategies to remain marginal or function simply as an escape from the yoke of capitalist relations (Wright 2010). While an important element showcasing how work can be transformed, on their own these are unlikely to bring about changes on a societal level.

Similarly, it is difficult to consider ruptural transformations of work on a societal scale. An emancipatory metamorphosis will require some elements of rupture, as contesting the growth paradigm and current institutions of waged labour will be a conflictual process. Ruptural strategies that make a complete or sharp break with existing social and economic relations at this point in history not only "seem implausible in the world in which we currently live, at least in the developed capitalist economies" (Wright 2010, 320), but are also likely to have unintended consequences (Wright 2010, 309). With this in mind, possibilities for rupture (breaks with the capitalist growth imperative) that are temporally or spatially limited are both more desirable, and likely – even if still relatively rare. These localised and temporally limited ruptures can help bring about interstitial transformations on a local scale (see Chapter 2). Promising and successful local ruptures leading to interstitial strategies of transformation in the recent past have included workers taking over companies to transform production. These instances are most often related to financial failure or the pressures of globalisation, for example, the Argentinian tile factory FaSinPat, the Greek soap factory Vio.me (see Chapter 8), as well as the French worker-recuperated tea company SCOP TI (Hansen 2019, Neumann 2020, Vieta 2010). These small-scale local ruptures have been most effective in bringing about transformation when they have joined up with other local ruptural projects and existing causes – including civil society. Local civil society action and trade union support were crucial in supporting SCOP TI during the 3.5 years of struggle against Unilever, in the example of the French tea company.

Finally, symbiotic transformations through trade unions and workers movements have been some of the largest and most successful emancipatory forces in history, but which have also regulated capitalism and helped it to evolve and survive (Wright 2010). The tension between large-scale change and co-optation in symbiotic transformations is referred to throughout this book (e.g., Chapter 2 and Chapter 9).

Trade unions and the transformation of work

Workers constitute the fundamental element around which the system hinges, while worker movements, including trade unions, are crucial as vehicles for the transformation of work. Withholding labour is the one action that brings everything to a halt. It is no surprise that great efforts have been made in many countries to strictly circumscribe the scope for industrial action, and to prevent unionisation.

There are examples of labour environmentalism and labour-environmental coalitions – struggles for protecting workers' and communities' livelihoods and the environment together, which have used "old" methods of union action – such as negotiating with employers for workplace improvements (recycling facilities, renewable energy provision), or strike action (where serious health and safety consequences are at stake) – to fight for environmentally just outcomes (e.g., Räthzel, Cock, and Uzzell 2018). Different unions in the same sector have acted both as "defenders of the status quo" as well as "agents of green transition": in aviation, for example, described below, some unions support the expansion of flying to increase jobs in the sector while others see this as an employment dead end given that climate change will force a constraint on flying at some point. These differences depend on both the specific sectoral interests, the union's internal identity, organisational structure and coalition partners, as well as external factors such as the political climate, governance and socio-economic contexts (Kalt forthcoming).

Historically, workers' movements have been at the forefront of struggles for emancipation and the social forces capable of changing work relations, including working time reduction, campaigning for improved working conditions, mobilising member awareness of working circumstances, and organising direct action and strikes (McAlevey 2020). However, industrial action is a long way from where most trade unions are today. The co-option of labour as the fundamental driver of the treadmill of capitalism, particularly in the last forty years, has meant that the tradition of radical labour organising has been "beaten, jailed, and (depending on the country) murdered out of the movement" – with the complicity of some trade union leaders, who hoped that business unionism would mean security for life (*Ibid.*).

Short-term economic necessity (exacerbated in an era of austerity and precarious labour markets), as well as leadership self-interest, have all combined to propel many unions towards relatively conservative positions, such as support for the expansion of aviation or the UK Conservative government's nuclear programme (GMB 2021). In this context, trade unions at best make a case for workers getting a greater share of the fruits of their labour. At worst, they replicate the language and priorities of employers to maintain the status quo.

Despite some successful ruptural strategies of taking over sites of production, or of organising interstitial strategies (such as starting a cooperative without taking over the site of production), in many cases workers have been excluded from decision-making when plant closures are negotiated. Where decisions were made to relocate or close down production, there has often been little that workers or their unions could do. Appeals to employers' humanity have had little effect; occasionally an economic case can be constructed to persuade the employer to change strategy, but this is rare. For example, unions at the Rolls-Royce manufacturing plant in Barnoldswick (UK) were able to prevent the closure of the factory and job losses by persuading management of the value in utilising the highly skilled workforce for "emerging and green technologies" – following the decision to transfer its historic jet engine work to Singapore (Unite, 2021). Despite successes in, for example, the SCOP TI French tea company, more often, such victories tend to be temporary and limited, in spite of the potential perceived by workers, as with the limited additional life granted to the Oshawa General Motors plant that, for a short period, redirected part of the workforce towards the manufacturing of masks. In these cases, the temporary reprieve tends to be part of an uphill struggle for survival (Leedham 2020).

Given the limited degree of success from such efforts, proposals to transform and recontextualise work, therefore, have to not only challenge the existing hierarchies of power, but also often sceptical workers and their representatives. This is clearly demonstrated by the antipathy, if not outright hostility, exhibited by many workers towards the concept of Just Transition (Cohen 2019, Kalt 2021). The transformation of work, including transition out of environmentally harmful work, is not a smooth process but "shaped and obstructed through conflicts," where in some regions environmentalists and unions are pitted against each other in a discursive battle of claims to "justice", to the benefit of the fossil fuel industry (Kalt 2021, 16).

Workers and their union leaders commonly perceive a Just Transition as a threat to livelihood that needs to be opposed, or a threat to the commonly accepted social "good life" as a lifestyle with high individual consumption (GMB 2020, Keil and Kreinin 2022). This is the case even in instances where those same workers are facing threats to their jobs, pay and conditions from the very employer they are aiming to align with, and against whom they are taking industrial action. For example, despite the action taken by workers against the "fire and re-hire" tactics undertaken in the face of the COVID-19 pandemic by British Gas and British Airways, the unions concerned remain committed to the expansion of those industries in spite of their own advocacy of green policies (Robson 2021).

Transforming work in practice

A combination of interstitial strategies (showing the possibility of organising work differently) and symbiotic strategies (bringing about wide-reaching change in the organisation of work through collaboration with existing institutions at the local level), will be of crucial importance in the social-ecological transformation of work. Governments cannot be relied on to enact appropriate policy unless prompted to do so from below (see Chapter 9). In fact, it was just such pressure from workers' movements in the 1930s that compelled Roosevelt to enact the New Deal. Today, the situation is more complex, with networks of global interconnectedness, which suggests that such forces have to emerge in a wide range of local circumstances. This is why cooperation between workers and environmental movements is a key strategy when aiming to transform work.

Plans to improve local or regional economies can be collaboratively developed by local authorities, trade unions and community groups, with a view to solving specific localised problems and redirecting the workforce towards those solutions. One such plan is the Green New Deal for Gatwick, as described in the following section on aviation, which has generated significant support among workers, communities, and local authorities representing the region. This is because the direct benefits of taking the steps proposed can be seen, including workers themselves who can recognise in their everyday reality where the current shortfalls in social and public services are. Against the work ethic, environmental justice claims must be formulated in a way that considers workers' interests, contextualising the environmental crisis within local settings, to help overcome the logic of short-term economic rationality, and strengthen long-term social-ecological rationality.

In terms of climate justice, this recognition of local circumstances can manifest through an identification of the work required to, say, generate energy locally to satisfy people's needs, transform local transport systems, and retrofit homes. In broader terms, it means addressing the shortfalls in public service that have been allowed to develop over the last four decades of neoliberal capitalism as a result of privatisation and commercialisation – restoring decent health facilities, care for the elderly and children, education, and so on. Importantly, developing plans in this way lends itself to communal ownership, by citizens and/or the workforce, and a place for workers in making the decisions that impact their working lives (Wolff 2012).

In bypassing central government through local action, such

localised plans build pressure for a response at the national level. This is important in order to provide the joined-up thinking required to guarantee the provision of high-quality public services and carbon-free industries, to legislate and regulate in the interest of workers and alternative ownership models, and to run those aspects of the economy that naturally require national coordination.

Just Transition in the aviation sector

The need for aviation to evolve from its current model of indefinite expansion given the challenge of climate change provides an example of the way in which degrowth implies the potential transformation of work.

Aviation is among the fastest-growing contributors to global carbon emissions. Pre-COVID-19 industry growth aspirations would have seen a 300% increase in emissions from air traffic by 2050 (ICAO 2019). At the same time, aviation is also one of the most efficient mechanisms for the reproduction of global inequalities. Research commissioned by the climate charity *Possible* has demonstrated, first in the UK (Devlin and Bernick 2015), then subsequently for several other industrialised countries (Hopkinson and Cairns 2021), that around 10-15% of the population of those countries take 70–75% of the flights, while about 50% do not fly at all in any given year. It has also been shown that just 1% of the world's people cause half of the global aviation emissions, while 80% have never set foot on an aeroplane (Stay Grounded and PCS 2021). Taken together, the level of emissions and the identification of those responsible clearly shows a sector that exemplifies global inequality and the privilege of the few.

National plans are currently not enough to achieve the Paris Agreement target of staying within the 1.5°C limit. Technological solutions and alternative fuel sources are being developed but are decades away from implementation and would be insufficient to achieve the reduction in emissions required in any meaningful time and scale – leaving only the reduction of overall levels of flying as the solution (Stay Grounded 2017).

Presently, the more growth there is in aviation, the more workers are required; more pilots, cabin crew, baggage handlers, air traffic controllers, security and associated roles. Aviation is a highly liberalised and deregulated industry where the service providers (airlines and airports) are rigorous in the pursuit of profits. This means that if traffic levels remained stable, the imperative to achieve efficiencies would result in a decline in the number of workers due to automation and improved processes. Workers and their unions are aware of this and, to protect job security, are largely supportive of the expansion of the industry, paradoxically aligning with employers who are attacking their jobs and terms and conditions. As a result, aviation workers are suspicious about proposals for a Just Transition into other forms of employment, for the reasons discussed above. The advent of the COVID-19 pandemic has brought these workers and unions some recognition of the need for a Just Transition accompanied by the demand for a government-backed jobs guarantee (Chapman and Wheatley 2020) but they are unlikely to fully support such proposals until that guarantee becomes official government policy.

Leaving aside the practical barriers, the conversion of the industry would require a very different workforce, on three counts:

1. The transfer of workers into other, sustainable modes of transport (predominantly rail) as these come to replace flying.

2. The transfer of workers into other, socially useful and less environmentally harmful sectors (e.g., flight attendants to the care sector).

3. The development of new skills and adaptation of existing skills for the green transition of the remaining aviation sector (e.g., for different infrastructure and possibly new fuels).

These changes constitute the first of the three categories noted previously – *changing the work that is actually done*. In terms of *changing the character of work*, an ethos of public service rather than private profit would provide a different motivation for workers, with an emphasis on safety, security and good practice rather than speed and quantity of traffic. If unlimited expansion is legally rendered impossible, the growth-based dominant metrics would no longer apply. As with replacing GDP with some broader measure of social satisfaction, the success or failure of aviation could be recontextualised within its role as part of an integrated transport system and the service it provides to people in satisfying human needs within the planetary boundaries.

As for *changing to a democratic workplace*, this might be more contentious but also crucial. In theory, aviation could achieve the first two aims while retaining its internal hierarchies and mode of organisation. However, limiting the amount of flying is contradictory to the success criteria of capitalist enterprises. A different ownership model would be necessary if aviation formed part of an integrated transport system rather than being in competition with other modes of transport. As a field that utilises a range of highly skilled labour, in order to fundamentally transform the industry, it may be appropriate that workers be able to participate in decisions regarding the future of the industry, or even be part of the ownership structure. In fact, such proposals were advanced by the Lucas Aerospace workers in the UK as part of their plan for worker-directed socially useful production in the 1970s (Wainwright and Elliott 1982), and were actively considered by the Corbyn-led Labour party in the 2010s. As such, the basis upon which work is predicated could be removed from its current limitations and motivations.

No such actions are being considered by national governments despite a stated commitment to climate targets. In their absence, local and regional development plans for job creation, driven by a pandemic-induced decline in aviation and based around the real needs of local communities, are emerging. The Public and Commercial Services union (PCS) in the UK seeks to reconcile opposition to aviation expansion with the need to defend jobs, and has worked with the think tank Greenhouse and the campaign group Green New Deal UK to develop an alternative employment plan, following the massive job cuts at Gatwick airport post-pandemic (Latif et al. 2020). Their report sought to identify the jobs that would be required in the region around the airport to both provide much-needed social and public services impacted by years of privatisation (primarily in care, but also in health and education services) and to provide an effective local response to climate change (in energy provision, upgrade of buildings and public transport). It estimated that over 16,000 jobs could be created to fulfil these needs at a cost of less than half of the annual tax break the government provides to Gatwick airport, identified skill sets among the former airport employees that might be conducive to a transition to these jobs (e.g., cabin crew to care services) and the training requirements to qualify workers for activities such as retrofitting homes.

The Gatwick Green New Deal plan is gaining significant traction among not only local communities but their representatives in local councils and Members of Parliament for the area in a way that the more abstract general demands have not been able to. In this sense, we are seeing interstitial strategies at play that have the potential to combine to bring about symbiotic transformation of the aviation industry. These actors are making the links between the report's findings and their everyday lived experiences in the communities around the airport. As a consequence, campaigners against expansion at Heathrow and Leeds Bradford airports are actively developing similar alternative employment proposals, with input and support from the collaborators on the Gatwick report. Other single-industry dependent communities such as the Suffolk towns around the Sizewell nuclear plant, the proposed re-opening of a coal mine in West Cumbria, and opposition to the building of an incinerator in Edmonton, North London, are building links with these anti-airport expansion groups, recognising a commonality of interest and the need to propose active alternatives. As such localised plans become more numerous, the likelihood is that they will merge into a large-scale movement demanding the transformation of work – and, potentially, ownership – needed to meet the societal challenges and, in the process, they demonstrate the bottom-up source of radical change.

Conclusion

In this chapter, we have reflected on the strategies and possibilities for the social-ecological transformation of work. Yet, realistic discussions about transforming work present a challenge. Examining the potential for such transformation through the lens of interstitial, ruptural and symbiotic modes of transformation suggests that it is most likely to emerge from a combination, and interaction, of these rather than being confined to a single approach, with a combination of interstitial and symbiotic approaches appearing the most promising. While the successes of labour organising via trade unions have largely been confined to addressing workers' immediate needs (food, shelter etc.), the centrality of work to meeting the fundamental needs of society means that workers' movements, such as unions, provide the most likely basis for successful society-wide struggle. The example of the aviation sector shows the uphill battle of generating radical change, but also points towards joint environmental-union action and co-mobilisation providing the potential for displacing the segmented organisation of work with a more coordinated and social-ecologically viable approach, society-wide. This can be considered to be part of an interstitial transformation activating symbiotic transformation on a different scale. Such an approach could open up a number of possibilities, including replacing the profit motive, GDP and growth, with well-being as the primary measure of success, to enhancing workplace democracy, and enhancing worker participation in implementing a socially just Green New Deal, which could alter the basis upon which work is carried out.

References

Barca, Stefania. 2019. "An Alternative Worth Fighting For: Degrowth and the Liberation of Work." In *towards a Political Economy of Degrowth*, edited by Ekaterina Chertkovskaya, Alexander Paulsson, and Stefania Barca, 175–192. Rowman & Littlefield International.

Chapman, Alex, and Hanna Wheatley. 2020. "Crisis Support to Aviation and the Right to Retrain." *New Economics Foundation*, June 10, 2020. https://neweconomics.org/2020/06/crisis-support-to-aviation-and-the-right-to-retrain.

Cohen, Rachel M. 2019. "8 Unions Have a Plan for Climate Action–But It Doesn't Mention Fighting the Fossil Fuel Industry." *In These Times*, August 26, 2019. https://inthesetimes.com/article/blue-green-alliance-labor-climate-seiu-green-new-deal.

Devlin, Stephen, and Sandra Bernick. 2015. *Managing Aviation Passenger Demand with a Frequent Flyer Levy*. New Economics Foundation.

Fellner, Wolfgang J. 2017. "Work and Leisure: Money, Identity and Playfulness." In *Routledge Handbook of Ecological Economics*, edited by Clive L. Spash, 214–224. London: Routledge.

Franta, Benjamin. 2021. "Early Oil Industry Disinformation on Global Warming." *Environmental Politics* 30, no. 4 (January): 663–666.

Frayne, David. 2015. *The Refusal of Work: The Theory and Practice of Resistance to Work*. London: Zed.

GMB. 2020. "GMB Warns Just Transition Commission to Face Up to 'Hard Truths' on Renewables Jobs & Subsidies Failure." *GMB*, February 27, 2020. www.gmbscotland.org.uk/newsroom/just-transition-commission-renewables-jobs-and-subsidies-failure.

GMB. 2021. "Chinese Nuclear Block a 'Staggering U-Turn'." *GMB*, July 26, 2021. https://www.gmb.org.uk/news/chinese-nuclear-block-staggering-u-turn-conservatives.

Graeber, David. 2018. *Bullshit Jobs*. New York: Simon & Schuster.

Hansen, Bue R. 2019. "'Batshit Jobs' – No-One Should Have to Destroy the Planet to Make a Living." *OpenDemocracy*, June 11, 2019. www.opendemocracy.net/en/opendemocracyuk/batshit-jobs-no-one-should-have-to-destroy-the-planet-to-make-a-living/.

Hoffmann, Maja, and Roland Paulsen. 2020. "Resolving the 'Jobs-Environment-Dilemma'? The Case for Critiques of Work in Sustainability Research." *Environmental Sociology* 6, no. 4 (August): 343–354.

Hopkinson, Lisa, and Sally Cairns. 2021. *Elite Status – Global Inequalities in Flying*. Report for Possible. https://policycommons.net/artifacts/1439908/elitestatusglobalinequalitiesinflying/2067509/.

Jackson, Tim, and Peter Victor. 2011. "Productivity and Work in the "Green Economy": Some Theoretical Reflections and Empirical Tests." *Environmental Innovation and Societal Transitions* 1, no. 1: 101–108.

Kallis, Giorgos. 2011. "In Defence of Degrowth." *Ecological Economics* 70, no. 5: 873–880.

Kalt, Tobias. 2021. "Jobs vs. Climate Justice? Contentious Narratives of Labor and Climate Movements in the Coal Transition in Germany." *Environmental Politics* 30, no. 7: 1135–1154.

Kalt, Tobias. 2022. "Agents of Transition or Defenders of the Status Quo? Trade Union Strategies in Coal Transitions." Working paper.

Keil, Katharina, and Halliki Kreinin. 2022. "Slowing the Treadmill for a Good Life for All? German Trade Union Narratives and Social-Ecological Transformation." Journal of Industrial Relations, April. https://doi.org/10.1177/00221856221087413.

Latif, Tahir, Jonathan Essex, Robert Magowan, Sam Mason, and Jack Baart. 2020. *A Green New Deal for Gatwick: An Urgent Call for Jobs Investment in Response to COVID-19*. The Public and Commercial Services Union, Green House Think Tank, and Green New Deal UK. https://www.greennewdealuk.org/wp-content/uploads/2020/11/A-Green-New-Deal-for-Gatwick.pdf.

Leedham, Emily. 2020. "'A Great First Step': Workers Respond to GM Oshawa Plant Conversion for PPE." *Rank and File*, April 25, 2020. https://www.rankandfile.ca/a-great-first-step-workers-respond-to-gm-converting-oshawa-plant-to-produce-ppe/.

McAlevey, Jane. 2020. "It's Not Enough to Fight – Labor and the Left Have to Be Serious About How to Win." *Jacobin*, October 19, 2020. https://jacobinmag.com/2020/10/jane-mcalevey-strike-school-organizing-mobilizing.

McCabe, Conor. 2013. "Transforming Capitalism through Real Utopias: A Critical Engagement." *Irish Journal of Sociology* 21, no. 2 (November): 51–61.

Neumann, Michaela. 2020. "Putting Postcapitalist Values and Practices to Work: The Case of the French Worker-Recuperated Company SCOP TI." MSc Thesis, Vienna University of Economics and Business.

Pichler, Melanie, Nora Krenmayr, Etienne Schneider, and Ulrich Brand. 2021. "EU Industrial Policy: Between Modernization and Transformation of the Automotive Industry." *Environmental Innovation and Societal Transitions* 38 (March): 140–152.

Räthzel, Nora, Jacklyn Cock, and David Uzzell. 2018. "Beyond the Nature-Labour Divide: Trade Union Responses to Climate Change in South Africa." *Globalizations* 15, no. 4 (April): 504–519.

Robson, Tony. 2021. "GMB Union Complicit in Imposing British Gas Fire and Rehire Contracts." *World Socialist Web Site*, April 6, 2021. https://www.wsws.org/en/articles/2021/04/07/bgas-j01.html.

Schor, Juliet B. 2005. "Sustainable Consumption and Worktime Reduction." *Journal of Industrial Ecology* 9, no. 1–2 (January): 37–50.

Stay Grounded. 2017. *The Illusion of Green Flying*. Vienna: Finance & Trade Watch. https://stay-grounded.org/wp-content/uploads/2019/02/The-Illusion-of-Green-Flying.pdf.

Stay Grounded and PCS. 2021. *A Rapid and Just Transition of Aviation – Shifting towards Climate-Just Mobility*. https://stay-grounded.org/just-transition/.

Unite. 2021. "Ground-Breaking Deal by Unite Saves Barnoldswick's Rolls-Royce Factory and 350 Jobs." *Unite*, January 14, 2021. https://www.unitetheunion.org/news-events/news/2021/january/ground-breaking-deal-by-unite-saves-barnoldswick-s-rolls-royce-factory-and-350-jobs/.

Vieta, Marcelo. 2010. "*The New Cooperativism.*" *Affinities: A Journal of Radical Theory, Culture and Action* 4, no. 1: 1–11.

Wainwright, Hilary, and Dave Elliott. 1982. *The Lucas Plan: A New Trade Unionism in the Making?* London: Allison & Busby.

Weeks, Kathi. 2011. *The Problem with Work: Feminism, Marxism, Antiwork Politics, and Postwork Imaginaries*. Durham: Duke University Press.

Wolff, Richard D. 2012. *Democracy at Work: A Cure for Capitalism*. Chicago: Haymarket.

Wright, Erik O. 2010. *Envisioning Real Utopias*. London: Verso.

Chapter 18: Money and finance

An overview of strategies for social-ecological transformation in the field of money and finance and the case of the Austrian Cooperative for the Common Good

By Ernest Aigner, Christina Buczko, Louison Cahen-Fourot and Colleen Schneider[42]

Introduction

In most contemporary economies, production and consumption occur through the means of money. These economies are therefore also market economies: what is produced is to be sold to acquire the money that makes it possible to buy goods and services produced by others. The use of money expresses the agents' participation in the market economy, including its division of labour, but also allows market and non-market productions (e.g., public services) to cohabitate (Théret 1999, Aglietta 2003). Money thereby ties together producers and consumers through interconnected balance sheets.

These monetary relations are debt relations. Indeed, any payment is a debt settlement (Aglietta *et al.* 2018), not only reimbursements of formal debts. For instance, when one buys bread, the buyer is indebted until they give the money to the baker. Paying for the bread settles the debt. Therefore, strategies for achieving degrowth have to acknowledge that money and monetary practices are, first and foremost, a social institution to evaluate and settle debts between parties whose value rests on trust. Trust in money is enforced by public authorities. Money is therefore fundamentally a public good and needs to be understood as such. Money is also pervasive in growth-based societies – it appears almost impossible to imagine a

---

42 All authors contributed equally.

world without this social relation (Project Society after Money 2019).

In capitalism, the ever-expanding market sphere triggers commodification processes and thus extends the realm of what can be purchased with money. The financial system plays an instrumental role in the *commodification of everything*. This is a key issue for degrowth. Strategies are therefore needed to forestall these developments. Our chapter will review strategies to democratise, definancialise, demonetise, decommodify, defossilise, and repurpose money with the aim of restructuring economic processes. Acknowledging that money is a social relation enables one to reflect upon possible strategies to achieve degrowth through monetary regulations or repurposing money's use.

With that aim in mind, we outline three broad strategies. We explain various measures necessary to implement the strategies (with ten measures in total) and discuss their symbiotic, interstitial or ruptural nature. We then introduce the Austrian Cooperative for the Common Good (Genossenschaft für Gemeinwohl) as an example of a symbiotic strategy. We conclude by discussing to what extent different interstitial and symbiotic strategies, considered in combination, can produce ruptural effects.

Democratising money

Despite the fact that money is a public good, control over monetary flows is largely privatised. To enable a transformation towards a degrowth society, money as a public good needs to be manifested in institutions and norms that shape its use. In that vein, democratising control of monetary institutions is a critical strategy. A broader understanding of democracy, to include the realm of the economy as well as politics, must include monetary democracy; meaning (direct) democratic control over institutions that shape the creation, flows and use of money.

Democratising money is organised in this text along two levels:

democratising how money is created through public banking[43] and democratising how public money is spent through direct citizens' control over municipal budgets.

Public banking

Reforming banking is, critically, about strengthening monetary democracy and empowering the local in relation to the national, and the public in relation to the private. A social contract exists between governments and banks, whereby central banks guarantee at-par convertibility of bank deposits into settlement reserves (Chick 2013, Gabor and Vestergaard 2016). Indeed, "one of the most important and oft-forgotten truths about any banking system is that it simply cannot exist without the government" (Baradaran 2018, 11). Despite this fact, banking regulation occurs independently of democratic accountability and oversight. Importantly, when the banking system falters, the public collectively bears responsibility.

Claiming public control over money creation through public banks can serve to democratise and re-embed the monetary system in local economies. It can ensure that public responsibility for the banking system is matched by public benefit (Mellor 2010). This would enable the creation and use of money for public purposes. Historically, public banks have supported small businesses, the upgrading of public infrastructure and affordable housing, and changes to food and transportation systems. For example, the Bank of North Dakota is a state-owned public bank established in the U.S. in 1919. All of the state's revenues are deposited into the bank by law, and municipal government deposits go to local community banks. Whereas other states rent money from private banks at great cost, North Dakota is able to borrow at zero interest, and thus fund projects without raising taxes or taking on debt. The profits of the bank belong to citizens. Practices focusing on small and medium-sized enterprises and "main street banking" have resulted in North

---

43   While not addressed in this chapter, democratising central banks is also an important strategy, see Cahen-Fourot (2022) for further discussion.

Dakota having the lowest foreclosure rate, lowest credit card default rate, and lowest unemployment rate in the U.S. (Harkinson 2009, Marois and Güngen 2019). Recently there has been renewed interest in public banking in the United States. In 2019, backed by grassroots advocacy groups, a bill was passed in California to legalise and support public banks (California 2019).

A (supra)national framework could ensure environmental and social banking guidelines while empowering and prioritising local decision-making. For example, the United Kingdom's Labour Party proposed a tiered system of local, regional and national public banks, under public ownership and with a democratic control structure, to embed institutions in the community they serve (Berry and Macfarlane 2019). Rather than a mandate focused upon profit, public banks can be mandated to serve social and environmental goals, with a focus on meeting the needs of disenfranchised communities and peoples. The Cooperative for the Common Good follows this principle in its cooperation with banks. For instance, banks commit to granting loans in the amount of all deposits in common good accounts exclusively to sustainable, regional projects. Public good oriented banking can be aided by a "public taxonomy" with preferential lending conditions for investments such as affordable and sustainable housing, care-sites, sustainable local food production, worker-owned companies and public transit infrastructure. These preferential conditions may include lower interest rate payments, no collateralisation and longer maturities of loans while prohibiting speculation and "dirty investments." Strengthening public banking is an important element for transformation. That said, a clear mandate and appropriate regulatory guidelines are necessary to mitigate the governance failures that have, for example, affected the German public banking system (Behr and Schmidt 2016, Scherrer 2017).

Another step towards banking serving the public good is the creation and support of privately-owned banks that serve the public interest. Such "ethical banks" are usually established as institutions that allow for broad participation from shareholders or members, and also employees, and have been initiated mostly by citizen-led movements. The Italian Banking Act of 2016[44] marks an important milestone in regulating ethical and sustainable banking and financial services and establishing a legal differentiation between *for-profit* and *public interest* banks. The law defines criteria for ethical and sustainable financial institutions, such as ethical credit assessment, transparent investment policy, no-distribution of profits to owners, and a participation-friendly organisational and governance model. It would be beneficial for such criteria to be established at the European Union level.

People's budgets and citizens' councils

People's budgets and citizens' councils are means to expand democracy into the determination of flows of money, and to operationalise money as a public good. People's budgets – also called participatory budgets and public budgets – are ongoing initiatives to democratise public money. In this case, democratic deliberation and decision-making processes are used to decide upon municipal budgets. Government budgets are understood as public money, and municipal budget allocation is seen as a reflection and declaration of local values (Congressional Progressive Caucus 2019). Such decision processes can be inclusive of low-income, minority, non-citizen and youth residents. They have the ability to fund community-led solutions and care-based solutions, focusing on, *inter alia*, child and elder care, common spaces for non-market-based leisure and recreation activities, and "greening" infrastructure, while moving away from supporting the police-prison nexus.

Participatory budgeting was first realised in the city of Porto Alegre, Brazil in 1989, involving over 17,000 citizens through neighbourhood assemblies, thematic assemblies, and city-wide delegates. Marginalised communities were at the heart of decision-making processes that they had previously been excluded from, with

---

44   Legislatura 17ª – Disegno di legge n. 2611

redistributive effects (Abers *et al.* 2018). More recently, residents of a number of cities throughout the United States have worked through the Black Lives Matter movement to enact people's budgets to shift municipal spending away from policing and towards community-based care measures. In 2020, advocacy groups won over $840m in direct cuts from US police departments and at least $160m investments in community services and alternatives to incarceration through budget votes (Interrupting Criminalization 2021). It is important to note that this approach is limited by the extent to which policy can be influenced at the local level.

While people's budgets address public control of funds, this can be complemented by citizens' councils, which facilitate public control over banking and financial regulation, as well as broader decisions around socio-economic goals (see Chapter 9).

The transformative nature of democratising money

The strategies outlined here for democratising money creation and the spending of money are largely symbiotic strategies. The measures of people's budgets and citizens' councils both rely on the existing government apparatus and political figures to implement the will of the councils, and thus, aim at reducing harms by "taming" capitalism. Depending on how a people's budget is enacted, it is potentially an interstitial strategy as well – for example, through directing public funds to create common and non-marketed spaces and processes to meet local needs. Public banking has the potential to be both a symbiotic and an interstitial strategy. As banks are established and enacted through government regulation, they rely on juridical and regulatory conditions. However, a broad system of public banking has the potential to form a counter-power to global finance and to the private accumulation of capital, and in this way can be a part of a more radical strategy for degrowth.

Definancialisation of the economy

Financialisation of the economy refers to a dual process: the rise of the financial industry and associated sectors (e.g., the FIRE sectors: Finance, Insurance and Real Estate), and the rise of financial motives in the management of non-financial corporations (Krippner 2005, Lazonick and O'Sullivan 2000). This process thoroughly transformed capitalism from the 1970s onwards. In high-income countries a major change has been the decrease of workers' share in aggregate income and the increase of capital's income share (Kohler *et al.* 2019).

Financialisation contradicts degrowth in at least two ways. First, the search for short-term financial returns and the primacy of liquidity is contradictory to long-term planning, financial stability, and the alignment of the economy with environmental sustainability and social well-being. Shareholders' expectations of returns on investment are disconnected from the economic reality (e.g., a 15% return on investment when the economy grows at less than 2% per year). Also, the desire to retrieve liquidities in the short run will push firms to prioritise financial profitability over long-term investment and innovation. This can impede reorganising production to meet social needs and the principles of sustainability. Second, financialisation furthers the commodification of everything. For instance, the environment becomes subject to financial capital accumulation: the atmosphere, ecosystem services and natural events (e.g., storms), are cut into quantifiable pieces and abstracted into financial assets (for instance, derivatives to insure against weather events). These assets negate the complexity of natural processes and create an incentive to maximise the income generated by them (Kemp-Benedict and Kartha, 2019), thereby paving the way for further exploitation.

This section reviews strategies for definancialising the economy and for halting ongoing processes that subject everyday life to financial logics. It explores how these processes can instead come to serve societal goals of environmental, social and economic relevance.

Definancialising the economy requires several steps that can be taken together or separately in three main areas: financial markets and the finance industry; state financing; practices in the non-financial economy.

In the financial sphere, definancialisation requires returning to an era in which finance is controlled, with extremely tight regulation and renewed control over financial institutions (see section 2 above). All privately owned banks and institutional investors would be *small enough to fail* – meaning they would be small enough so that they would not need to be bailed out with public money. Further, regulations could aim to reduce the complexity of financial markets and ban financial products whose immediate purpose for real economies cannot be identified. In contrast, ethical, regional, and public good-oriented banks could be promoted and allowed to operate under less stringent conditions than private, for-profit financial institutions (Benedikter 2011, Weber 2014). Systematic assessments based on social, ecological and ethical criteria would be mandatory for every loan granted. Analogously, financial products of any kind would undergo a legally regulated approval procedure according to these criteria (Epstein and Crotty 2009).

State financing would also be taken away from global financial markets. Public bond issuance is critical for the financial industry, as it provides the risk-free asset the financial industry needs to run financial valuation models and diversify their portfolios. Transparency on who holds public bonds and policies to redirect public bonds to domestic individual households would reduce the supply of risk-free assets to financial markets and emancipate governments from the political influence of global financial corporations. Alternatively, financing fiscal spending without issuing government bonds could limit the capacity for public debt to be used as a speculative financial asset (Lerner 1943, Mitchell 2020).

Last but not least, definancialising the economy also requires changing practices in the non-financial economy. The legal definition of a private firm would be revised to include social wellbeing and sustainability concerns, in order to foster firms' production and management according to economic, social and environmental criteria. However, this alone would be insufficient as it would create contradictions between the legal object of a firm and the expectations of shareholders. Therefore, the ownership structure of firms needs to be adjusted to ensure that social provisioning is aligned with social wellbeing and sustainability. Alternative ownership structures, such as cooperatives and co-management practices between shareholders and workers, should be encouraged to reform firms' management, increase economic democracy, and foster long-term goals. This kind of ownership and management already exists in many countries in cooperative firms of various sizes and keeps them away from financial markets and purely financial logics.

Definancialisation of everyday life through decommodification

The financialisation of everyday life (van der Zwan 2014) is about how financial aspects of individual life, such as insuring against an uncertain future, increasingly become organised via financial markets. This financialisation is fostered by the retreat of the state from key sectors providing basic social needs.

For instance, pensions are being increasingly financialised through the rise of funded pension systems (financial market-based pension systems). These subject future pensions to the dynamics of financial markets. These pension systems are based on a promise of future production that leaves no space for political compromise. Indeed, any degrowth of production would leave stranded a significant part of the real assets underlying the financial assets (Cahen-Fourot et al. 2021). Stranded real assets would lose their value. This would significantly reduce the claim attached to financial assets and thus decrease the value of the pensions.

In contrast, pay-as-you-go pension systems are based on a political compromise about the share of current production devoted to financing current pensions: the share of GDP devoted to funding pensions is decided politically in discussions about how to fund and allocate public budgets (Barr and Diamond 2006, Husson 2020). This compromise can be revised and adapted in line with the reorganisation of the production and distribution of essential goods and services. In a pay-as-you-go system, the share of the aggregate income devoted to funding current pensions could be debated and set to fit with a degrowth economy while ensuring decent pensions.[45] In other words, in a pay-as-you-go pension system current production and negotiated social contributions determine current pensions; in a capitalisation-based pension system future pensions determine future production. This essential difference makes pay-as-you-go systems compatible with a degrowth economy and capitalisation-based systems most likely incompatible.

For degrowth to be a liveable option, it is therefore crucial to definancialise everyday life. This will require the socialisation of sectors fulfilling basic social needs such as health, education, housing, food, transport, energy and insurance against life risks such as unemployment and old age. In other words, definancialising everyday life requires separating the ability to take part in social life from the ability to take part in labour and financial markets.

Obtaining control over international finance

International trade and currency exchange rates are subject to, and regulated in, the interest of finance-led capital accumulation. Two implications of this are discussed here. First, the current international monetary system limits the sovereignty of nation-states over budget decisions. International institutions such as the IMF and the World Bank condition access to loans for emerging

---

45 This would certainly be a contentious political issue, but two things must be considered. First, many needs would be decommodified and would not, therefore, require money to be satisfied. Certain monetary losses in pensions could then be compensated by increased in-kind social provisioning. Second, increased rates of social contributions could compensate for the lower aggregate income upon which pensions are levied to maintain their level. This latter case corresponds to a new social compromise about an increased share of GDP devoted to pensions.

market economies (EMEs) using austerity-based policies (Chang 2002). Allowing EMEs greater levels of monetary sovereignty, for example by issuing loans in sovereign currency and allowing the implementation of capital controls, would empower self-directed development. This is addressed further in this chapter's sub-sections on complementary currencies. Second, the current system reinforces post-colonial hierarchies in international trade. International flows of capital, along with flows of natural resources, move from the Global South to the Global North, advantaging the historically colonial nations at the expense of those that have been (or still are) colonies (Dorninger *et al.* 2021, Svartzman and Althouse 2020).

Hence, international reforms of monetary flows must restrict the possibility of currency exchange as a tool for speculation. An international clearing union (ICU), as was proposed by Keynes (1941), could accomplish this by equalising the burden between debtor and creditor nations. Special Drawing Rights (SDRs) for the IMF could be more broadly used to promote anti-cyclical international liquidity, rather than heavily relying upon the US dollar for this purpose. SDRs could also be used for the payment of reparations to the Global South. More to the point, a debt jubilee in which multilateral institutions, including the IMF and World Bank, permanently cancel principal and interest on all payments owed by debtor nations would be a step towards equity. This would remove the debt-extractivism nexus in low- and middle-income countries. Of course, this can also strengthen economic growth in the respective countries, as additional funds would be available to invest and grow the economy. However, this need not be problematic *per se* if it reflects the development of the necessary provision of goods and services such as health, education, social security and so on.

<u>The transformative nature of the definancialisation strategy</u>

Measures aimed at definancialisation are rather symbiotic: all of them could be implemented in the current socio-economic system. All of these measures would also stabilise existing capitalism and make it more liveable for the many. In that sense, their transformative potential may appear weak.

However, these measures also contradict some of the key capitalist logics, such as commodification, the infinite spread of the market sphere, and the quest for short-run financial returns. Further, measures such as socialising key sectors and fostering workers' direct ownership of firms and decision power in firm management would constitute radical changes if implemented at the whole economy scale.

Redirecting and repurposing

In monetary economies, the purpose of money, i.e., what it is used for and what is financed by its use, is barely subject to political debate, despite its impact on the economy. Money's use and investment decisions are left to private actors that decide, for instance, on how much should be invested and for which purpose. Degrowth can target the way in which money is used by pushing for divestment, fossil-free monetary policy and financial regulation, or by fostering special-purpose moneys.

Divesting from fossil fuel-related activities

Fossil-free finance means removing companies directly or indirectly involved in the use or extraction of fossil fuels from financial flows. It is far from a trivial move: fossil fuels became the principal energy source in industrialised societies in the early 19th century and still account for 84% of primary energy consumption and 63% of electricity generation worldwide (2019 figures from BP Energy Review 2020).

This can be achieved in several ways. First, actions of civil disobedience and climate activism are already driving divestment campaigns globally (Healy and Barry 2017). This is an important movement as it signals growing social demand for exiting the fossil economy and highlights the issue of continued reliance on fossil fuels. However, as divesting means selling any financial asset linked to fossil fuel companies, this requires a counterpart to buy those assets. Therefore, the real effect on fossil fuel-related financial assets' liquidity – and ultimately on the ability of these companies to finance their activities – is unclear.

Defossilising monetary policy and financial regulation

The second way to remove financing options for fossil fuel companies is to act at the level of monetary policy and financial regulation. Monetary policy is the set of instruments central banks use to ensure the correct functioning of the payment system. Financial regulation concerns all the rules the financial system must abide by – in particular concerning financial risks.

One key idea is to reform the eligibility rules for asset purchasing programmes by central banks (such as quantitative easing) to exclude fossil fuels and carbon-intensive activities. Other possibilities include differentiating between interest rates depending on the nature of the activity to be financed, implementing credit controls to direct financial flows in sectors deemed sustainable, and including green-supporting and dirty-penalising factors in risk assessment in order to foster financing of sustainable activities. A major unresolved challenge is to come up with a clear and operational definition of what are "green" and "dirty" activities. Many proposals exist to remedy the carbon impact of monetary policy (see e.g., Cahen-Fourot 2022; Campiglio 2016; Dafermos *et al.* 2020), and several central banks in the world have already implemented such measures (Barmes and Livingstone 2021, Dikau and Volz 2019, D'Orazio and Popoyan 2019).

Repurposing money: from general to special-purpose money

Current monetary economies are based on general-purpose money – money that can be used for any legal purpose and that unites all functions of money into one form of money (Saiag 2014). As a consequence, general-purpose forms of money make all goods and services commensurable (O'Neill 2017) and reduce political control over economies. This could be overcome by implementing or strengthening special-purpose moneys. These have a definitive standard of value, and can only be used for particular goods and services or in a particular sphere of society (Saiag 2014). Further, they can be under community or public control (Blanc 2018) and complement or replace general-purpose money.

Special purpose currencies under community control are often referred to as Local Exchange Trading Schemes (LETS).

Depending on the number of stores and active users, the durability and significance of the currencies vary widely. One reason is that there may be no need to adopt the currency since the general-purpose currency remains a more attractive alternative. As a consequence, the circulation of the respective currency then slows down, limiting its relevance and impact on economic development.

Special purpose currencies can also be issued by state authorities in many forms. One form is vouchers that can be used only for specific goods and services by a given person (Bohnenberger 2020). A well-known (and often criticised) example are food stamps, a form of voucher issued by certain authorities that can be used to buy food. Depending on the way eligibility is designed and how they are used, they may be discriminatory and worsen the situation of already-discriminated groups. However, vouchers can also be distributed on a universal basis and strengthen certain economic spheres. For instance, in Vienna, during the COVID-19 pandemic, the local authorities issued a restaurant voucher (*Gastro Gutschein*) to all citizens, which could be used to purchase food in local restaurants. Alternately, public authorities could issue special purpose money to local associations that can only be used in stores of the respective village, as in the case of *Langenegger Talenten*[46] in the Austrian province of Vorarlberg. Such quasi-currency vouchers ensure the sustainability of basic local economic infrastructure since the associations use public subsidies in local stores. Since *Langenegger*

---

46 Unlike vouchers, the latter can be traded and any owner can use the *Langenegger Talenten*, i.e., eligibility is not limited to a particular person.

Talenten is issued by a public authority, its circulation is not dependent on voluntary adoption.

The most comprehensive proposal for state-issued complementary currencies has been made by Hornborg (2017). He suggests implementing a regional currency, through a universal basic income, as a complement to general-purpose money. The purpose of the currency is to strengthen local economies, relocalise economic production chains and ultimately gain democratic control over economic processes. This SPM is valid only for goods and services produced within a certain distance from the place of purchase and distributed to everyone that is living within a particular territory. Authorities that are managing this complementary currency could regulate its use through its exchange rate with the national currency. Further, depending on the particular design, the currency can be used only for goods, services, land, wages, or all of them. Overall, the currency would facilitate local economic development, align production with locally available goods, and, if needed, foster the development of local production. Localising production potentially increases democratic control over the production process, since cost- and problem-shifting is limited. Such a strategy could help achieve degrowth as it would start a slow process of relocalising economic activities, likely one of the preconditions for well-being for all in a degrowth world.

The transformative nature of repurposing money

Measures aiming at adapting the monetary policy of general-purpose money (i.e., most currencies) and financial regulation to environmental issues are, in themselves, symbiotic. However, they may have deeper, highly transformative implications. In western high-income countries, cheapness and abundance of fossil fuels were key factors in the high productivity gains that formed the backbone of the social compromise of the post-war era at the root of the welfare state (Cahen-Fourot and Durand 2016). Cutting access to fossil fuel-related activities from money and finance means effectively removing them from the division of labour and from socially accepted economic activities. Based on the historical importance of fossil fuels, this would therefore most likely trigger very deep changes in our societies.

Depending on the design and issuer, complementing or replacing general-purpose money with special-purpose moneys can be a symbiotic, interstitial or ruptural strategy. Special purpose currencies focusing on particular goods have symbiotic character, as they limit the impact of economic crises on particular sectors but have no impact on the economic processes at large. LETS schemes and currencies issued by local authorities would be located in the realm of interstitial transformations, driven by the motive that large numbers of "small transformations cumulatively generate qualitative shifts" (Wright 2010, 322). Such schemes, however, currently have limited geographical reach and are located in niches with little impact on global capitalism. LETS schemes further lack incentives to be adopted and thus often have little durability, in contrast to more durable currencies issued by local authorities.

Under given circumstances the implementation of a complementary currency as suggested by Hornborg (2017) is not ruptural: it would rely on the current administration to manage the currency. Nevertheless, such a currency could provide the ground for a second circuit of value that provides the precondition for a degrowth society. Particularly in the long run, it could lead to degrowth, as it allows for the formation of local production and consumption structures despite current capitalism. Hence, such a strategy could contribute to the formation of degrowth societies as it would start a slow process of relocalising economic activities.

Transforming the financial system from below: the Austrian Cooperative for the Common Good

Since its founding in 2014, the Cooperative for the Common Good (GfG) has pursued as its primary goal a change in the current monetary and financial system shaped by the principles of sustainability, democratisation and orientation for the common good. The idea of founding a democratic bank in Austria emerged in 2008, as a reaction to the financial and banking crisis and, more specifically, to Deutsche Bank CEO Josef Ackermann's call for the establishment of a "bad debt bank" for Germany. In 2011, the "Association for the Promotion and Foundation of a Democratic Bank" was created, and a bank strategy and business plan were developed. In 2014, the cooperative "Bank for the Common Good" was founded. By the end of 2018, the cooperative had about 6,000 individual and corporate members.

Using money as a means to shape the financial system for the common good

In 2016, a crowdfunding platform and a common good audit were developed and established. The creation of a payment institute, following the Austrian Payment Services Act of 2018, was considered in order to open a common good account. This was planned as a preliminary step towards a full banking licence for a bank oriented towards the common good, owned and supported by a civil society movement – the cooperative members – and strongly committed to democratic and ethical principles. Cooperations with partner banks were initiated, for example with GLS, Germany's largest social-ecological bank, which participated as one important investor in the development of the payment institution. By the end of 2018, the Austrian Financial Market Authority (FMA) rejected the application of the cooperative for a payment institute licence for formal reasons. The extensive additions and preliminary work required would have meant high investments, and it would still have remained uncertain whether the licence would have been granted. This is why the cooperative's general assembly ultimately decided against continuing the application process. In general, the FMA is rather reluctant to grant new banking licences – among other things using the argument that Austria is already over-banked.

Following the rejection, the name of the initiative was altered to

"Cooperative for the Common Good", and the strategy changed towards establishing cooperation with existing banking institutions. Today the cooperative operates in three different areas: First, by providing and facilitating common-good oriented financial goods and services in cooperation with existing banking and financial institutions. The first Common Good Account, Common Good Student Account and Common Good Savings Account in Austria were launched in cooperation with the Environmental Center of the Upper Austrian Raiffeisenbank Gunskirchen in May 2019. Negotiations with other banks in Austria and Germany are underway, as well as the elaboration of guidelines for a lending policy for common good-oriented companies and projects.

The second scope of activity is advocacy for a democratic reshaping of the financial system through political work. This is being realised through the analysis and critical appraisal of political and economic activities in the financial sector, participating in networks (such as the NGO Finance Watch), and developing positions and communicating proposals for the implementation of a common good-oriented monetary and financial system, such as the "Moneyfest" (Genossenschaft für Gemeinwohl 2020).

The third area of work consists in offering policy education about critical financial literacy and transformative learning in the Academy for the Common Good. This includes public lectures, workshops, online courses, cooperation with the international summer school "Alternative Economic and Monetary Systems (AEMS), and the certificate "Money and the Common Good" in cooperation with Steinbeis University (Germany).

<u>A shift in strategy: from creating a bank to advocating for the monetary system as a democratically regulated public infrastructure for the common good</u>

According to its self-image, the Cooperative for the Common Good sees itself as part of an economic system based on solidarity as an alternative to prevailing neoliberal and growth-based capitalism.

The overall aim of changing the monetary and financial system by founding a democratic banking institution "from below" could be characterised as an interstitial transformation. The basic idea was to trigger change by building up a democratic bank – as already existed in several other countries – as a concrete alternative for customers.

In line with the core principles of interstitial transformation, namely the building of new forms of social empowerment on the margins of capitalist society (see Chapter 2), participation and transparency have been seen as fundamental values of the Cooperative for the Common Good since its beginnings. It aims at contributing to a revitalisation of the cooperative system and movement within the financial sector as the highest participatory form of organisation and enterprise. Therefore, the cooperative contributes to further development of the already more than 170-year-old organisational form of the cooperative in order to innovatively design and specifically expand democratic participation and opportunities for co-determination on the part of its members by introducing new methods of decision-making and by shaping the organisation according to the principles of sociocracy.

After this strategy failed, a change in strategy was developed and extensively discussed within the cooperative's member community. Instead of pursuing the establishment of its own bank, the Cooperative for the Common Good now seeks to cooperate with existing banking institutions. The main principle behind it is that deposits on all common good bank accounts are allocated by the partner banks as loans exclusively given to ecologically and socially sustainable projects. The strategy of the cooperative is now to change the banking system "from within"; a symbiotic strategy nudging existing banking institutions through cooperation to include, step-by-step, an orientation towards the common good, sustainability and ethical values in their business models. The central element of this strategy is creating and expanding such niches within the existing system and winning over more banks that offer common good-oriented accounts and conditioned lending in order to guarantee sustainable use of funds. In the long-term, this should lead first to redirect an increasing amount of money flows into targeted sustainable projects and activities, and second to change existing institutions and deepen social empowerment within the current system so as to ultimately transform it.

This example shows that the implementation of transformative strategies of the monetary and financial system depends significantly on external conditions, such as, in this case, legislation and financial market policies. It also shows the need for a certain kind of flexibility for transformative actors. The shift from interstitial towards symbiotic strategies was not a consciously analytical decision of the Cooperative of the Common Good, but a strategic adjustment to manoeuvre in their given context. However, this meant compromising on one of their areas of activities – the provision of financial goods and services. Their organisational development, as well as advocacy and educational work themselves can be seen as partial symbiotic strategies. Both interstitial and symbiotic strategies are aimed, in a general sense, at raising awareness of the importance of the financial and monetary system for our economy and hence society as a whole. What remains central, however, is what money is used for and where it flows.

Conclusion: transformation as an emergent property

In recent history, deep modifications in the rules governing money were often associated with a deeper change in the economic system (Guttmann 2002). We think that the measures and underlying strategies outlined in this chapter are likely to change the monetary and financial system to work towards economic degrowth. However, any of these measures and related strategies need to be assessed both contextually and relationally, in combination with other strategies. Assessing the transformative nature of these measures is therefore speculative.

Wright's categories are ideal types but, in reality, strategies can have interstitial, symbiotic and ruptural aspects within them. For instance, a shift of the monetary regime towards sustainability-based rules may constitute initial steps towards a more sustainable (or, at least, fossil-free) capitalism. Although not aimed at overcoming capitalism itself, it would create a rupture within capitalism between different growth regimes. In turn, breaking with the fossil economy would challenge many of the existing power relations built into it and could be an opportunity for more radical agendas. Indeed, the history of sociopolitical changes indicates that the ruptural, interstitial or symbiotic nature of strategies is more an emergent property observed *ex-post* than an *ex-ante* decision by agents of change, whatever their initial intentions might be.

References

Abers, Rebecca, Robin King, Daniely Votto, and Igor Brandão. 2018. *Porto Alegre: Participatory Budgeting and the Challenge of Sustaining Transformative Change*. World Resources Institute. https://www.wri.org/wri-citiesforall/publication/porto-alegre-participatory-budgeting-and-challenge-sustaining.

Aglietta, Michel, Pepita Ould Ahmed, and Jean-François Ponsot. 2018. *Money: 5,000 Years of Debt and Power*. London/New York: Verso.

Baradaran, Mehrsa. 2018. *How the Other Half Banks: Exclusion, Exploitation, and the Threat to Democracy*. Cambridge, MA: Harvard University Press

Barmes, David, and Zack Livingstone. 2021. *The Green Central Banking Scorecard. How Green Are G20 Central Banks and Financial Supervisors*. Positive Money UK.

Barr, Nicholas, and Peter Diamond. 2006. "The Economics of Pensions." *Oxford Review of Economic Policy* 22, no. 1: 15–39.

Behr, Patrick, and Reinhard H. Schmidt. 2016. "The German Banking System." In *The Palgrave Handbook of European Banking*, edited by Thorsten Beck and Barbara Casu, 541–66. London: Palgrave Macmillan UK.

Benedikter, Roland. 2011. *Social Banking and Social Finance: Answers to the Economic Crisis*. Springer Briefs in Business. New York: Springer-Verlag.

Berry, Christine, and Laurie Macfarlane. 2019. *A New Public Banking Ecosystem*. Report to the UK Labour Party. https://labour.org.uk/wp-content/uploads/2019/03/Building-a-new-public-banking-ecosystem.pdf

Blanc, Jérôme. 2018. "Making Sense of the Plurality of Money: A Polanyian Attempt." In *Monetary plurality in local, regional and global economies,* edited by Georgina M. Gómez, 48–66. Routledge. https://halshs.archives-ouvertes.fr/halshs-01555623.

Bohnenberger, Katharina. 2020. "Money, Vouchers, Public Infrastructures? A Framework for Sustainable Welfare Benefits." *Sustainability* 12, no. 2: 596.

Cahen-Fourot, Louison. 2022. "Central Banking for a Social-Ecological Transformation." In *The Future of Central Banking,* edited by Sylvio Antonio Kappes, Louis-Philippe Rochon, and Guillaume Vallet. Cheltenham: Edward Elgar.

Cahen-Fourot, Louison, Emanuele Campiglio, Antoine Godin, Eric Kemp-Benedict, and Stefan Trsek. 2021. "Capital Stranding Cascades: The Impact of Decarbonisation on Productive Asset Utilisation." *WU Wien Ecological Economic Paper* 37.

Cahen-Fourot, Louison, and Cédric Durand. 2016. «La transformation de la relation sociale à l'énergie du fordisme au capitalisme néolibéral : une exploration empirique et macro-économique comparée dans les pays riches (1950–2010).» *Revue de la Régulation* 20.

Campiglio, Emanuele. 2016. "Beyond Carbon Pricing: The Role of Banking and Monetary Policy in Financing the Transition to a Low-Carbon Economy." *Ecological Economics* 121: 220–230.

California. 2019. *AB-857 Public banks.* http://leginfo.legislature.ca.gov/faces/billNavClient.xhtml?bill_id=201920200AB857

Chick, Victoria. 2013. "The Current Banking Crisis in the UK: An Evolutionary View." In *Financial Crises and the Nature of Capitalist Money,* edited by Jocelyn Pixley and G. C. Harcourt, 148–161. London: Palgrave Macmillan UK.

Congressional Progressive Caucus. 2019. *A Progressive Path Forward: The People's Budget.* https://progressives.house.gov/the-people-s-budget-a-progressive-path-forward-fy-2019#:~:text=The%20Fiscal%20Year%202019%20Congressional,the%20sidelines%20of%20our%20economy.

Dafermos, Yannis, Daniela Gabor, Maria Nikolaidi, Adam Pawloff, and Frank van Lerven. 2020. *Decarbonising Is Easy: Beyond Market Neutrality in the ECB's Corporate QE.* London: New Economics Foundation.

Dikau, Simon, and Ulrich Volz. 2019. "Central Bank Mandates, Sustainability Objectives and the Promotion of Green Finance." *SOAS Department of Economics Working Paper Series* 222.

D'Orazio, Paola, and Lilit Popoyan. 2019. "Dataset on Green Macroprudential Regulations and Instruments: Objectives, Implementation and Geographical Diffusion." *Data in Brief* 24.

Dorninger, Christian, Alf Hornborg, David J. Abson, Henrik von Wehrden, Anke Schaffartzik, Stefan Giljum, John-Oliver Engler, Robert L. Feller, Klaus Hubacek, and Hanspeter Wieland. 2021. "Global Patterns of Ecologically Unequal Exchange: Implications for Sustainability in the 21st Century." *Ecological Economics* 179, 106824.

Epstein, Gerald, and James Crotty. 2009. "Controlling Dangerous Financial Products through A Financial Pre-Cautionary Principle." *EKONOMIAZ* 3, no. 72.

Gabor, Daniela, and Jakob Vestergaard. 2016. "Towards a Theory of Shadow Money." *Institute for New Economic Thinking Working Paper* 24: 41–76.

Genossenschaft für Gemeinwohl. 2020. *Moneyfest der Genossenschaft für Gemeinwohl*. https://www.gemeinwohl.coop/sites/www/files/downloads/moneyfest_der_genossenschaft_fur_gemeinwohl_0.pdf

Guttmann, Robert. 2002. "Money and Credit in Régulation Theory." In *Regulation Theory: The State of the Art*, edited by Robert Boyer and Yves Saillard, 57–63. London, NewYork: Routledge.

Harkinson, Josh. 2009. "How the Nation's Only State-Owned Bank Became the Envy of Wall Street." *Mother Jones*, March 28.

Healy, Noel, and John Barry. 2017. "Politicizing Energy Justice and Energy System Transitions: Fossil Fuel Divestment and a 'Just Transition'." *Energy Policy* 108: 451–459.

Hornborg, Alf. 2017. "How to Turn an Ocean Liner: A Proposal for Voluntary Degrowth by Redesigning Money for Sustainability, Justice, and Resilience." *Journal of Political Ecology* 24, no. 1: 623–632.

Husson, Michel. 2020. «La capitalisation ou la pensée magique.» *Alternatives économiques*, January.

Interrupting Criminalization. 2021. *The Demand Is Still #DefundThePolice: Lessons from 2020*. https://communityresourcehub.org/resources/the-demand-is-still-defundthepolice-lessons-from-2020/.

Kohler, Karsten, Alexander Guschanski, and Engelbert Stockhammer. 2019. "The Impact of Financialisation on the Wage Share: A Theoretical Clarification and Empirical Test." *Cambridge Journal of Economics* 43, no. 4: 937–974.

Krippner, Greta R. 2005. "The Financialization of the American Economy." *Socio-Economic Review* 3, no. 2: 173–208.

Lazonick, William, and Mary O'Sullivan. 2000. "Maximizing Shareholder Value: A

New Ideology for Corporate Governance." *Economy and Society* 29, no. 1: 13–35.

Marois, Thomas, and Ali Riza Güngen. 2019. "A US Green Investment Bank for All: Democratized Finance for a Just Transition." *The Next System Project*, September 20, 2019. https://thenextsystem.org/green-investment-bank.

Mellor, Mary. 2010. *The Future of Money: From Financial Crisis to Public Resource*. London ; New York : New York: Pluto Press.

O'Neill, John. 2017. "Pluralism and Incommensurability." In *Routledge Handbook of Ecological Economics: Nature and Society*, edited by Clive L. Spash. London, New York: Routledge.

Project Society after Money, eds. 2019. *Society after Money: A Dialogue*. Thinking Media. New York: Bloomsbury Academic.

Saiag, Hadrien. 2014. "Towards a Neo-Polanyian Approach to Money: Integrating the Concept of Debt." *Economy and Society* 43, no. 4: 559–581.

Scherrer, Christoph, ed. 2017. *Public Banks in the Age of Financialization: A Comparative Perspective*. Advances in Critical Policy Studies. Cheltenham, UK, Northampton, MA: Edward Elgar Publishing.

Svartzman, Romain, and Jeffrey Althouse. 2020. "Greening the International Monetary System? Not without Addressing the Political Ecology of Global Imbalances." *Review of International Political Economy*, 1–26.

Weber, Olaf. 2014. "Social Banking: Concept, Definitions and Practice." *Global Social Policy* 14, no. 2: 265–267.

Wright, Erik O. 2010. *Envisioning Real Utopias*. London, New York: Verso.

Zwan, Natascha van der. 2014. "Making Sense of Financialization." *Socio-Economic Review* 12, no. 1: 99–129.

Chapter 19: Trade and Decolonialisation

An overview of strategies for social-ecological transformation in the field of trade and decolonialisation

By Gabriel Trettel Silva

Decoloniality and anti-colonialism have recently gained more attention from degrowth scholars. The time is ripe to advance an anti-colonial position for the degrowth movement. Accomplishing this task is strategic for two reasons. First, it allows us to draw a clearer line separating degrowth from imperialist visions of environmentalism. Such visions go from "one-world" discourses that erase the colonial nature of the global economy under the banner of (sustainable) development to ecofascist narratives that pursue stability in the Global North, where the political economy of growth is facing its contradictions, while at the same time arguing that the Global South represents an ecological threat. The second strategic reason is that it lets us move forward with building solidarity and stronger alliances with peripheral movements. If red and green social movements in the Global South still have difficulties seeing degrowth as an anti-imperialist ally in the North, as pointed out by Rodrígues-Labajos *et al.* (2019), it may be a sign that the above-mentioned line between degrowth and imperialist environmentalism has, in the worst case, not been drawn well enough, or, in the best case, has been miscommunicated.

But where to begin? I take as a starting point one key aspect of colonialism that is already familiar to degrowth: ecologically unequal exchange and the imperialist logic of global trade. Some ecological economists have, for decades already, scrutinised the social metabolism of the world economy and denounced the transfers of resources from peripheries to capitalist centres of accumulation as the ultimate result of international trade (Hornborg 1998). A small group of high-income countries that concentrate one-sixth of the world's population are net appropriators of resources and labour embodied in trade from all the rest of the world. Such patterns of unequal exchange can be traced and quantified: high-income countries consume approximately 52% more raw materials than they produce domestically, 28% more labour[47], 19% more land and 10% more energy (Dorninger *et al.* 2021). All this surplus is acquired in the global market, which means that the rest of the world needs to work more hours and extract more resources from their territories than their populations consume to transfer it to the richest countries, without equivalent material compensation.[48]

This perverse international division of labour is neither natural nor inevitable – quite the opposite. It is an order that is violently imposed and ideologically justified by core states in the Global North and transnational corporations. They accomplish this using a selection of instruments from their imperial toolbox: racist ideology, military enforcement, colonial occupation, control over financial systems, intellectual property and patents, trade agreements and hybrid war, depending on the geographic context, point of history and balance of power. One ideological tool from that box that has been addressed in the degrowth critique is *development*. Development is capitalism's utopian horizon that justifies international trade and gives meaning to peripheral countries' engagement with global markets as exporters of commodities (Prado 2020). Development ideology promises that, within capitalism, all countries may eventually reach the standards of welfare and

---

47   Here I refer to the concept of labour embodied in traded products, as traced by Dorninger *et al.* (2021). However, the same imperial structures push migrant workers from the peripheries to core countries, where they provide both cheap and qualified labour more directly.

48   Even though it is possible to argue that the world economy is more complex than binaries such as "Global South–North", "Core–Periphery" or "Richer–Poorer countries" might suggest, the global patterns of ecological unequal exchange establish a material basis to distinguish a group of countries that are net appropriators of resources and work (core, Global North) from a second group of countries that are net suppliers (periphery, Global South). Further, the existence of these patterns at the global level do not deny the existence of similarly unequal dynamics at sub-national or intra-group levels.

consumption experienced by the middle classes of the core countries, regardless of their position in the world economy.

We know this promise is false. First, it is ecologically impossible to universalise those standards since the material footprint required would go way beyond planetary boundaries. This argument has been extensively repeated by environmentalists in the Global North since the conservative conclusions of the report on Limits to Growth in the 1970s.[49] Another reason is that the ways of living in the North depend on ecologically unequal exchange and on the international division of labour that deprives other peoples of self-determination and keep them trapped in selling their labour and resources for cheaply in the global market. So, a mode of living that requires exploitation cannot be universalised, otherwise, there would be no one left to be exploited. Therefore, if the economics of growth and development hide colonial core-periphery relations, it is a task for the degrowth movement to unveil these relations and tackle their roots. However, this task should not be taken for granted as if the politics of degrowth were inherently anti-colonial.[50] They are not.

Scholars and activists sometimes repeat in publications and conferences the idea that degrowth is a project "in the Global North, for the Global North" replying to the common accusation that degrowth imposes a new agenda on the Global South.[51] However, this reply is a trap that leads degrowth back to Eurocentric strategies for a social-ecological transformation. For instance, work time reduction policies in the Global North have been largely discussed without considering the colonial reliance on cheap labour from the South – both directly in the form of migrant labour in the North

---

49 Pointing out the ecological impossibility of universalisation of Western consumption standards is not an anti-colonial statement. As pointed by Furtado (1983), this same finding may be used to support the conservative position that the "development of the Global South" represents an ecological threat.

50 In a recently published opinion piece, Jason Hickel suggests that degrowth politics is essentially anti-colonial, describing it as "the sharp edge of anti-colonial struggle within the metropole" (Hickel 2021, 2).

51 This accusation is raised by environmental justice organisations in the Global South, see Rodrígues-Labajos et al. (2019).

and indirectly in the form of labour embodied in products traded with the South (Dorninger *et al.* 2021, Pérez-Sánchez *et al.* 2021). Some post-growth scholars do not acknowledge how global patterns of unequal exchange relieve the burden of work in the Global North and argue that work time reduction policies only concern high-income countries.[52] This reflects a Eurocentric framing and a too narrow sense of solidarity towards the Global South, which is quite far from the anti-colonial politics of degrowth described by Hickel (2021).

Degrowth cannot focus on the Global North because degrowth is about the world economy. It is impossible to address the global and colonial nature of capitalism and the social-ecological crisis only accounting for processes in the Global North, expecting for the South to harvest the benefits of freed ecological and conceptual space. Embracing an internationalist perspective means creating a framework for a social-ecological project that accounts fully for each country's engagement with globalisation, fighting imperialism from within the core countries where most of the degrowth movement is based.

So, how can degrowth fight ecologically unequal exchange and imperialism? We can refer to Wright's (2019) framework to distinguish different modes of transformation. While ruptural and interstitial modes of transformation seek to break away from capitalist institutions and create alternatives in their margins, they do not spare us from changing the existing institutional forms, which requires operating under a symbiotic mode of transformation. The latter relates both to taming strategies that aim to reduce capitalism's harms, and dismantling strategies that aim at transcending capitalism's structures. I argue that, when it comes to unmaking ecologically unequal exchange and imperialism, the potential of

---

52 Such a view was held by Juliet Schor in the thematic panel on Work at the Degrowth Vienna 2020 Conference. Similar assumptions are found in Knight et al. (2013) and Van Den Bergh (2011). It is fair to point exceptions in the degrowth literature such as Kallis (2011) that suggests a 21-hour work week as possible common ground for a North-South common struggle.

degrowth relies on the strength of strategies operating under the logic of dismantling, while relying solely on strategies that focus on taming may contribute to greenwashing colonial relations in the name of degrowth.

This point can be illustrated with the energy transition within the framework of a Green New Deal (GND) without growth. The GND for Europe proposal – which was engaged with by degrowth scholars (Mastini *et al.* 2021) – acknowledges that raw materials for a renewable energy transition in Europe would come from outside its borders, calling for a principle of "supply chain justice" to "ensure that materials required are handled with a commitment to social and environmental justice in the rest of the world" (Adler *et al.* 2019, 66). Even though this principle sets the ground for strategies focused on reducing harm, it does not denaturalise the very function of global supply chains – unequal exchange and appropriation of resources from global peripheries. What kind of "just" supply chain can ensure that the resources for a green energy transition in the Global South are also secured? Minerals that flow from the South for a "pioneering" green transition in the North will not be available when the time comes for the South itself to move away from fossil fuels, threatening energy security and sovereignty in the peripheries.

This is clear in the case of copper, one of the key materials for an energy transition based on renewable energy technologies as we know them. Current copper stocks in use are already unevenly distributed worldwide, following colonial patterns of ecologically unequal exchange: lower-income countries count on 30–40 kg/person, while higher-income countries range from 140 to 300 kg/person (Exner *et al.* 2014). From a degrowth perspective, which aims for ecological sustainability and social equity, equalising metal stocks among countries should be achieved without further copper extraction[53]. This goal, however, could only be accomplished under the condition of returning copper from core countries back to the

---

53 Convergence of stocks does not mean that all countries should apply equal amounts of metals per capita in their economies, but it is a requisite for social equity that a fair share is at least available for everyone.

peripheries (*Ibid.*). A "supply chain justice" strategy is not enough to ensure that. To transcend structures, a green energy transition must revert the unequal distribution of resources and stop perverse flows from the poorest to the richest regions. Without doing so, a green transition may be just another name for a new wave of colonial appropriation of resources in a post-fossil fuel global economy, maintaining core-periphery relations.

Degrowthers might find inspiration in anti-imperialist movements in the Global South that explicitly refuse such international division of labour from the other end, calling for strategies that are closer to the logic of dismantling. In Brazil, for instance, The Movement for Popular Sovereignty in Mining (MAM, *Movimento pela Soberania Popular na Mineração*) promotes a critical debate within the Brazilian society about the primary exports of minerals, fostering a project of popular power. They argue that "only with popular organisation can we gradually build the proposal for a new model for the use of mineral goods, in the form of social property and for the benefit of the entire Brazilian people, which represents popular and national sovereignty over all mineral goods" (MAM n.d., translation by the author). Another Brazilian movement, The Landless Workers' Movement (MST, *Movimento dos Trabalhadores Rurais Sem-Terra*) advocates for food sovereignty and agroecology as a national social-ecological project, directly fighting export-led agribusiness, demanding a popular agrarian reform that may distribute and democratise land. According to their vision, "the export policy for agricultural products should only be complementary, seeking the greatest possible added value and avoiding the export of raw materials" (MST n.d., translation by the author). Both MAM and MST have anti-imperialism at the core of their programmes and challenge the colonial character of international trade using a different vocabulary, but with many points that connect to the degrowth framework.

Finally, strategies that employ the logic of dismantling would require that degrowth proposals expose deeper tensions in North-

South relations. Looking at the evidence on ecologically unequal exchange, an anti-colonial perspective could suggest that pushing for reducing consumption and decreasing reliance on imported labour in the Global North are requirements to enable the rest of the world to get rid of the burden of colonial appropriation of resources and labour. Only after that would it be ethical from a global point of view to advocate for further reduction in consumption and working time in the North for the sake of ecological sustainability and improving domestic wellbeing. The inversion of these priorities denotes indifference or complicity with colonial structures, relegating the "good life" to core countries and making degrowth a project "in the North, for the North." The politics of degrowth do not carry anti-colonial values by default. Shaping degrowth as an anti-imperialist and anti-colonial movement depends heavily on a commitment to dismantling ecologically unequal exchange rather than reducing its harms.

References

Adler, David, Pawel Wargan, and Sona Prakash. 2019. "Blueprint for Europe's Just Transition." *The Green New Deal for Europe*.

Dorninger, Christian, Alf Hornborg, David J. Abson, Henrik Von Wehrden, Anke Schaffartzik, Stefan Giljum, Robert Feller, Klaus Hubacek, Jan-Oliver Engler, and Hanspeter Wieland. 2021. "Global Patterns of Ecologically Unequal Exchange: Implications for Sustainability in the 21st Century." *Ecological Economics* 179, 106824.

Exner, Andreas, Christian Lauk, and Werner Zittel. 2014. "Sold Futures? The Global Availability of Metals and Economic Growth at the Peripheries: Distribution and Regulation in a Degrowth Perspective." *Antipode* 47, no. 2: 342–359.

Furtado, Celso. 1983. *O mito do desenvolvimento econômico*. Rio de Janeiro: Paz e Terra.

Hickel, Jason. 2021. "The Anti-Colonial Politics of Degrowth." *Political Geography* 88, no. 3.

Hornborg, Alf. 1998. "Towards an Ecological Theory of Unequal Exchange: Articulating World System Theory and Ecological Economics." *Ecological Economics* 25, no. 1: 127–136.

Kallis, Giorgos. 2011. "In Defence of Degrowth." *Ecological Economics* 70, no. 5: 873–880.

Knight, Kyle W., Eugene A. Rosa, and Juliet B. Schor. 2013. "Could Working Less Reduce Pressures on the Environment? A Cross-National Panel Analysis of OECD Countries, 1970–2007." *Global Environmental Change* 23, no. 4: 691–700.

MAM (Movimento pela Soberania Popular na Mineração). n.d. *Quem somos.* https://www.mamnacional.org.br/mam/quem-somos/.

Mastini, Riccardo, Giorgos Kallis, and Jason Hickel. 2021. "A Green New Deal without Growth?" *Ecological Economics* 179, 106832.

MST (Movimento dos Trabalhadores Rurais Sem Terra). n.d. *Quem somos.* https://www.mamnacional.org.br/mam/quem-somos/

Pérez-Sánchez, Laura, Raúl Velasco-Fernández, and Mario Giampietro. 2021. "The International Division of Labour and Embodied Working Time in Trade for the US, the EU and China." *Ecological Economics* 180, 106909.

Prado, Fernando C. 2020. *A ideologia do desenvolvimento.* São Paulo: Lutas Anticapital.

Rodríguez-Labajos, Beatriz, Ivonne Yánez, Patrick Bond, Lucie Greyl, Serah Munguti, Godwin U. Ojo, and Winfridus Overbeek. 2019. "Not so Natural an Alliance? Degrowth and Environmental Justice Movements in the Global South." *Ecological Economics* 157: 175–184.

Van den Bergh, Jeroen. 2011. "Environment versus Growth – A Criticism of 'Degrowth' and a Plea for 'A-Growth'." *Ecological Economics* 70, no. 5: 881–890.

Wright, Erik O. 2019. *How to Be an Anti-Capitalist in the 21st Century.* London: Verso.

A case in the field of trade and decolonialisation: litigation as a tool for resistance and mobilisation in Nigeria

By Godwin Uyi Ojo

Introduction

In the Global South, there is a growing resistance to Transnational Corporations' (TNCs) extractivist development model embedded in the colonial legacy of resource expropriation and unequal exchange of goods and services. Oil exploitation activities result in environmental degradation and pillaging of natural resources by TNCs and structures of imperialism often supported by European and North American national governments, which has resulted in the pauperisation of Africa.

Nigeria's politics and economy revolve around oil dependency. Notwithstanding the benefits from oil and the projections of impressive economic growth rates, such benefits are short-lived and unsustainable due to growing poverty and environmental degradation. Despite trade imbalance, revenue from oil is significant for the Nigerian economy and accounts for 90% of GDP, 65% of government expenditures and 88% of foreign exchange earnings (Ajayi 2019). Yet, it is the communities that bear the brunt of environmental degradation and human rights abuses from persistent gas flaring and frequent oil spills. The untold effect of "violent environments" is severe on the local people and has led to the destruction of their sources of livelihoods, including farmlands, rivers, and streams, which they depend on for fishing and farming occupations. From persistent despoliation and the onslaught against the local people, TNCs continue to laugh on their way to the banks as they count their profits while local communities, especially in Ogoniland, cry in mortuaries on a daily basis.

This chapter draws on multiple cases in Nigeria and focuses on environmental justice, social movement-building and strategies of litigation to address environmental degradation, social inequalities, and the protection of livelihoods – many of which are in line with degrowth proposals. A mix of approaches is applied by these movements that aim towards decolonisation and reversing the plunder of natural resources. I discuss the various strategies of resistance, in this case by the NGO Environmental Rights Action/Friends of the Earth Nigeria, while adopting Wright's strategies and logic of anti-capitalist transformation (2010). In particular, I show how, in the case of Nigeria's environmental justice movements, the ruptural mode of transformation, which seeks a sharp confrontation or a break with existing institutions, seems to combine well with aspects of symbiotic transformations, which seek to reform institutions within the current system (see also Chapter 2). My experience in combining activism and research, as well as through observing trends across three decades of being actively involved in environmentalism, contribute to my framing of these strategies. In most contexts discussed here, there is a plurality of strategies, each with varying degrees of success.

Advocacy as resistance and as a degrowth strategy

Decolonisation of trade through environmental justice struggles against capitalist exploitation of people and the environment is a major concern. Such efforts are wide-ranging, from actions seeking to hold TNCs accountable to claims of injustice, to those seeking to roll back their operations, or even dismantle them. TNCs' practices of environmental racism lead to double standards in their responses to environmental degradation. Environmental racism is the practice of lowering environmental standards and locating harmful projects in mostly black populated communities, or environmental injustice that occurs within a racialised context both in practice and in policy (Beech 2020). Environmental standards deployed in the Global South are different from those deployed and specified by the OECD guidelines as operating principles in Europe. While TNCs rely on their national governments to conduct trade in Africa, the situation is compounded by a neocolonial legacy of empire-building, where resources are carted away from poor communities, with increasingly violent resource conflicts at the sites of extraction. Indeed, corporatisation, or corporate capture of the state and natural resources, only empower the state and corporations to suppress and silence dissenting voices.

One important strategy for degrowth is indirectly linked to the concept of ecological debt, demanding environmental justice and payment of ecological debts incurred by industrialised countries due to the exploitation of natural resources in the Global South. Nigerian writers such as Festus Iyayi (2001) applied the concept to challenge capitalism and the "incalculable and indemnifiable damage" done to Africa supported by state structures of imperialism and called for a development paradigm shift. In the last two decades, from a political ecology perspective, I have been evolving demands for a switch from a fossil-based economy to a post-extractivist economy based on energy democracy in Nigeria, with several transition manifestos that call for an end of oil exploitation (Ojo 2018, 2016, 2015, 2010).

I describe a strategy of litigation that employs advocacy as resistance. On the surface, legal demands for clean-up in the case of spills, environmental remediation, and compensation including administrative costs and fines serve as a deterrent in the future. Advocacy involves internationalising campaigns from the local to the global. Those seeking to promote an economic system that is in line with degrowth principles in Nigeria and Africa are internationalising their advocacy and campaign strategies to build local resistance against TNCs and the state. It is important to note that such social actors, activists, grassroots movements, and civil society groups have no ready notion of the concept of degrowth, nor do they designate themselves as such. Nonetheless, they are engaged with disruptive tendencies and increasingly deploy strategies of resistance to halt or slow down the process of the vociferous capitalist system. They aim to disrupt, even if temporarily, the "rhythm of extractive capitalism" (see Chapter 2).

In the process of litigation, access to justice is critical. At the national level, Fagbohun and Ojo (2012, 270) list some scenarios of people losing access to justice due to "sleeping on their rights" or responses that are later than the specified time window to litigate in oil-related court arbitration processes in Nigeria. We argue that access to justice is restricted when violations appear apparent, but victims are unable to seek legal action, or when cases are brought to court and compensation is paid, but without due regard to the extent of environmental damage. In some cases where court action is used, cases are deliberately delayed on technical grounds as a means of buying time and frustrating the litigant. These cases are more serious in jurisdictions where governance structures are inadequate, as is often the case in the Global South, but less so in the North. This may have prompted growing efforts by claimants to seek redress in countries in the North.

A fundamental part of the strategy is social mobilising across spatial scales. Multi-scalar social mobilising and persistence of international and local civil society groups in the form of large demonstrations is one clear strategy of degrowth actors. In Nigeria, our pioneering effort during the formative stages of the NGO Environmental Rights Action/Friends of the Earth Nigeria in 1993 was coupled with the legacy of Ken Saro Wiwa. Environmentalism from the mid-1980s internationalised the environmental justice campaigns that directly attacked the market premium of Shell products, eroding its corporate image, social premium, and the social licence to operate. The ultimate goal was to make the extraction unviable and decolonise trade. Although these activists paid the supreme price through state repression and the hangman's noose through a kangaroo court verdict under a military regime, their legacy of local resistance to Shell is emblematic of a most formidable resistance, on a global scale, to a TNC, and this effectively locked in thousands of barrels of productive capacity per day. Although litigation efforts are currently ongoing to redress the wrongful, extrajudicial killing of Ken Saro Wiwa and eight compatriots, oil and gas extraction continue unabated in parts of the Niger Delta where oil reserves are located. That said, in the Ogoniland community, community actions and civil society groups' concerted efforts forced the government to embark on a clean-up, which started in 2019. Vegetation is gradually recovering decades after the end of oil exploitation in the area.

TNCs often externalise production costs to third parties and environmental activists confront capitalism through court action to account for such externalities. In the difficult political terrain associated with bad governance in Nigeria, litigation was initially deployed as a non-violent advocacy tool to draw public awareness to support a cause of action, put environmental issues on the political front burner, and not necessarily to win cases. This was because in the early 1990s during the military dictatorships, it was foolhardy to contemplate winning environmental justice cases against TNCs, which enjoy tremendous support from their parent companies and countries of domicile.

Litigation can be seen as a central degrowth strategy. It seeks ways to make "justice and sustainability comparable" (Demaria et. al. 2013, 200). This is related to environmental justice struggles and the climate change movement seeking redistributive income for the impacted communities dispossessed of their natural resources. The Bodo vs. Shell case provides an example. A major oil spill in 2008 destroyed the environment and rural livelihoods, such as polluting the Bodo communities' fish ponds and farms. Eventually, Shell was forced to make a payment of GBP 55 million. Shell sought to redistribute income in an out of court settlement in London in 2015. After this court case, a flood gate of court cases against TNCs was opened to redress harm and recoup losses (Vidal 2015). However, there is an inherent contradiction since there was no actual redistributed income. The monetary sum paid by Shell only compensated for the damages of livelihoods of farming and fishing from 2008 and 2009 oil spills.

In another court case involving four fishermen against Shell over a major 2008 oil spill across coastal communities in the Niger Delta, community representatives from Ikot Ada Odo, Goi and Oruma sought redress in Dutch courts. The landmark judgement in favour of the fishermen and their entitlements to fair compensation in 2021 was a radical revolutionary shift because it established precedence of international jurisdiction against Shell (and TNCs) over the environmental atrocities committed overseas (Agency Report 2021).

Activists involved in the litigation process describe the court case as a victory for the environment. Shell spills destroyed ecosystems, wetlands, farmlands and crops and fishing ponds of the litigants, who represent hundreds of impacted community members. By seeking to account for externalised production costs and deploying litigation to attract environmental remediation and restitution to victims of environmental degradation, the aim is to disrupt and make the sector increasingly unviable. Such actions encourage others to do the same so that TNCs can possibly be overwhelmed with, for example, a floodgate of court cases, bad publicity, public odium, rising production costs, considerable legal fees, and payment for damages and restitution.

It is important to also note that litigation helped to secure local productive assets, the preservation of ecosystem goods, services, and nature as well as the survival of local people. When compensation is paid as a form of redistributive income, impoverished locals taste from the pot of honey that they were denied during the production phase.

Apart from these mainstream strategies, some others seek a far more radical resistance to capitalism through agitations, insurgences, and arms against the state and the TNCs, as well as shutting down oil facilities or dismantling corporate power (Tamuno 2011). This approach has been expanded to include a challenge against the appropriation of a communities' natural resources, otherwise called "resource control" or local resources for local control. Such "relocalisation and repoliticisation" of resources (Chertkovskaya

2020) has in many ways led to, ownership and control over natural resources based on the commons. If communities control their local resources, ultimately, they will have the right to exploit them for themselves or the right to say no to harmful development by locking away potential harmful carbon. This "closed-door" strategy shuts out TNCs and aims to curb capitalist orientation that thrives on more trade, production, and even more consumption.

These struggles face some limits due to limited resources and the ubiquitous forces of capitalism. TNCs are neither state nor non-state actors but wield enormous political and economic power over states in the Global South – and also in the North. As a response, there is a global push within the framework of the United Nations for a global legally binding treaty to hold corporations accountable for their environmental degradation and human rights violations in their sites of operation. This has been taken up in Nigeria as part of the strategies of resistance and efforts to dismantle corporate power (Ojo 2016). Although the treaty has been discussed for decades, it is yet to see the light of the day due to the undue corporate influence. A similar due diligence law in the European Union is in the making, which would bind TNCs with uniform regulations at home and overseas. The aim is to subject TNCs to a supra-national governance approach, rather than individual nations having to confront these giants by themselves. Global legally binding mechanisms will bring TNCs under global supervision, enhance the chances of more successful litigation through expanding access to justice, and in turn, incur additional costs in remediation and legal fees that push production costs upward.

Conclusion

The mix of approaches and strategies introduced relate to the wider processes of social-ecological transformation. The disparate efforts are not necessarily termed degrowth per se by writers, activists, or environmental defenders. However, collectively, from the local to the global, they address the disillusionment, poverty and widening inequality gap perpetrated by capitalism that they contend with.

Litigation strategies have been largely successful but, invariably, these go only as far as formal state and corporate structures will accommodate. In the case of the four fishermen against Shell that was won in 2021, it was the Dutch government that picked up the legal bills through a specialist legal agency, which could be translated as a form of corporate capture, minimising damages to Shell's advantage. In this way, the symbiotic transformation that involves litigation could be limited in scope and practice because it seeks transformation within existing institutions and structures that invariably reinforce capitalism. It is tokenistic and changes depend on TNCs and state institutions for incremental victories which could come at great costs to the degrowth movement.

Legal battles against TNCs are often drawn out over long periods, up to and sometimes over ten years, and tend to reduce profits through legal costs. However, sometimes litigation against TNCs seems to favour them due to their financial war chest to confront litigants, which allows them to frustrate litigants and buy time. Further, TNCs' payment for damages often translates only to monetary compensation to victims of environmental injustices while environmental remediation and preservation, which is more costly, is largely ignored or if at all, done perfunctorily. This places the heavy burden of climate change vulnerability, loss, and damage on the poor.

A global legally binding mechanism is both ruptural and symbiotic. The symbiotic approach can be highly susceptible to co-optation, which could reinforce corporate capture and dispossess local people of natural resources, to the advantage of the state and at the behest of neocolonial powers. Decolonisation of trade could help hone degrowth strategies and present bottom-up alternatives to the prevailing economic model through decentralised energy democracy. The emerging forms of energy democracy that involve community energy cooperatives in both production and supply at local scales represent a major shift, yet they are still within a symbiotic transformative agenda.

At another level, a dismantling of the prevailing capitalist model – reinforced by the demands for local resources and for local control – would enable a bottom-up approach to development, as an interstitial approach to transformation. A post-petroleum economy for Nigeria has been proposed, with government officials recognising the potential of the campaign but without any policy commitment. Ultimately, ecosystem preservation, reduction of corporate profit and redistribution of wealth all add up as degrowth strategies to dismantle corporate power and capitalism.

To conclude, a post-extractivist agenda, encapsulated by the concept of "leave the oil in the soil", should gain more traction and may serve as a rallying call for degrowthers' social mobilisation for resistance at the local, national, and international levels.

References

Agency Report. 2021. "Oil Spill: Environmental Rights Group Hails Judgement against Shell." *Premium Times Nigeria,* January 29, 2021. https://www.premiumtimesng.com/news/top-news/439477-oil-spill-environmental-rights-group-hails-judgement-against-shell.html.

Ajayi, Wale. 2019. "Nigerian Oil and Gas Update".*KPMG,* April 23, 2019. https://home.kpmg/ng/en/home/insights/2019/04/Nigerian-Oil-and-Gas-Update.html.

Beech, Peter. 2020. "What is Environmental Racism and How Can We Fight it?" *World Economic Forum,* July 31, 2020. https://www.weforum.org/agenda/2020/07/what-is-environmental-racism-pollution-covid-systemic/.

Chertkovskaya, Ekaterina. 2020. "From Taming to Dismantling: Degrowth and Anti-capitalist Strategy." *Degrowth.info* (blog), September 21, 2020. https://degrowth.info/blog/from-taming-to-dismantling-degrowth-and-anti-capitalist-strategy.

Demaria, Federico, Francios Schneider, Filka Sekulova and Joan Martinez–Allier. 2013. "What Is Degrowth? From an Activist Slogan to a Social Movement." *Environmental Values* 22, no. 2: 191–215.

Fagbohun, Olanrewaju and Godwin U. Ojo. 2012. "Resource Governance and Access to Justice: Innovating Best Practices in Aid of Nigeria's Oil Pollution Victims." *Nigeria Institute of Advanced Legal Studies journal of Environmental law* 2: 257–302.

Iyayi, Festus. 2001. "Ecological Debts and Transnational Corporations in Africa." *Niger Delta Peoples World Congress.* http://www.nigerdeltapeoplesworldcongress.org/articles/ECOLOGICAL%20DEBTS%20AND%20TRANSNATIONAL%20CORPORATIONS%20IN%20AFRICA.htm.

Ojo, Godwin U., ed. 2010. *Envisioning a Post Petroleum Nigeria: Leave the Oil in the Soil.* Ibadan: Kraftbooks.

Ojo, Godwin U., ed. 2015. *Climate Change and Energy Democracy: A Pathway to Development.* Bénin, Lagos, Port Harcourt, Yenagoa: Environmental Rights Action and Friends of the Earth Nigeria.

Ojo, Godwin U. 2016. "Access to Environmental Justice in Nigeria: The Case for a Global Legal Environmental Court of Justice." *Environmental Rights Action and Friends of the Earth Nigeria* (October). https://www.foei.org/wp-content/uploads/2016/10/Environmental-Justice-Nigeria-Shell-English.pdf.

Ojo, Godwin U. 2018. *Just Energy Transition for Nigeria: A Manifesto.* Benin, Lagos, Port Harcourt, Yenagoa: Environmental Rights Action and Friends of the Earth Nigeria. https://erafoen.org/wp-content/uploads/2018/07/JUST-ENERGY-.pdf.

Tamuno, Tekena N. 2011. *Oil Wars in the Niger Delta.* Ibadan, Nigeria: Stirling-Horden publishers Ltd.

Vidal, John. 2015. "Shell Announces 55m Pounds Payout for Nigeria Oil Spills." *The Guardian*, January 7, 2015. https://www.theguardian.com/environment/2015/jan/07/shell-announces-55m-payout-for-nigeria-oil-spills.

Wright, Erik O. 2010. *Envisioning Real Utopias.* Verso.

About the Authors

Ernest Aigner is a research associate at the Research Institute for Law and Governance (Vienna University of Economics and Business – WU) and the Institute for Economic Geography and Geoinformatics (WU). He holds a PhD in Socioeconomics. His dissertation examined the state of global economics using bibliometric methods. He also teaches Ecological Economics and Sustainable Work, and is a lecturer at the Alternative Monetary and Economic Systems Summer School.

Viviana Asara is Assistant Professor in Sociology at the University of Ferrara and a research affiliate of the Institute for Multi-Level Governance and Development at the Vienna University of Economics and Business. Her work has focused on political ecology and environmental governance. In particular, she has undertaken research on degrowth, democracy, social movements, commons, social innovations, and political parties. Together with Luigi Pellizzoni and Emanuele Leonardi, she has recently edited the *Handbook of Critical Environmental Politics* (Edward Elgar), forthcoming in autumn 2022.

Carol Bardi is a Brazilian feminist economist and researcher currently finishing her master's at the Copernicus Institute in Utrecht University through a Utrecht Excellence Scholarship. Carol enjoys discussing ways to build a decolonial society based on happiness for all beings. She believes in autonomous movements, commonality, and sport as a tool for community building.

Nathan Barlow (he/him) is a PhD candidate in Socioeconomics at the Vienna University of Economics and Business, researching the role of strategies for social-ecological transformations. He is interested in the relationship between radical long-term systemic change and short-term necessary steps. Nathan is on the editorial team of *degrowth.info*, was a coordinator of the *Degrowth Vienna*

2020 Conference: Strategies for Social-ecological Transformation, and has been coordinating this collected volume together with Livia Regen.

Ulrich Brand (he/him) is a Professor of International Politics at the University of Vienna. His main research interests are the crisis of liberal globalisation, (global) social-ecological topics such as resource politics and the green economy, critical state and governance studies, and Latin America. Together with Markus Wissen, he introduced the concept of the "imperial mode of living", on which a book was published in 2021 with Verso, London. He is a member of the "Global Working Group Beyond Development" and of the "Latin American Working Group Alternatives to Development", both coordinated by the Rosa Luxemburg Foundation.

Christina Buczko is coordinator of the Academy for the Common Good, the educational institution of the Cooperative for the Common Good, which provides political education on the finance sector and economics. She is a sociologist and political scientist. In the past, she worked in sustainability research, advocacy and human rights observation in Central America.

Corinna Burkhart has been active in the degrowth movement since 2012. She is currently completing her PhD in Human Geography at the University of Lund in Sweden. She has worked at the Konzeptwerk Neue Ökonomie and edited *Degrowth in Movement(s)*, together with Nina Treu and Matthias Schmelzer.

Gabriela Cabaña (she/her) is an anthropologist and PhD researcher at the London School of Economics and Political Science, currently studying energy policy and planning in Chile from an ethnographic perspective. She is a member of the Centro de Análisis Socioambiental (CASA), an organisation researching and building critical perspectives for social-ecological transformation in Chile, and of the campaign *Chiloé Libre del Saqueo Energético*.

Louison Cahen-Fourot (he/him) is an assistant professor in Economics at Roskilde University (Denmark) and a guest researcher at WU Vienna's Institute for Ecological Economics (Austria). He works on ecological macroeconomics and the political economy of capitalism and the environment. He acknowledges funding by the Österreichische National Bank's Anniversary Fund (OeNB Jubiläumsfonds project number 18651).

Ekaterina Chertkovskaya (she/her) is a researcher based at Lund University, working on degrowth and critical organisation studies. Her research addresses contemporary crises and explores paths for social-ecological transformation. She has been writing on corporate violence, problems with work and employability, and the plastic crisis, on the one hand, and focusing on degrowth as a vision for transformation, its political economy, and alternative models of work and organising, on the other. Ekaterina is also a member of the editorial collective of *ephemera: theory & politics in organisation.*

Ian Clotworthy is an activist and photographer in the campaign Deutsche Wohnen & Co. Enteignen. He originally comes from Ireland and is a longtime resident of Berlin. He holds a B.Sc. In Physics from the Humboldt University of Berlin. He is currently completing a M.Sc. In Cognitive Systems and Natural Language Processing at the University of Potsdam. He has experience volunteering in the climate justice movement, and is not yet formally affiliated with degrowth.

Corinna Dengler (she/her) is a feminist ecological economist and degrowth scholar-activist, who just moved (back) to Vienna, Austria. She works as a postdoctoral researcher at WU Vienna, is interested in topics at the intersection of feminisms, the environment, and decoloniality, and co-coordinates the network Feminisms and Degrowth Alliance (FaDA).

Marion Drut is an associate professor of economics at Institut Agro Dijon, France. Her research interests include sustainable mobility and vehicle sharing, and her research is conducted within the CESAER research lab, convened by three institutions: Institut Agro Dijon, INRAE and University Bourgogne Franche-Comté.

Julianna Fehlinger is a social ecologist and works as a managing director of Via Campesina Austria (ÖBV – Austrian Association of Mountain and Small-Scale Farmers). She is part of the organising team that develops a participatory supermarket in Vienna. She previously worked on a collective ecological farm in Upper Austria and on alpine summer pastures in Switzerland.

Nicolas Guenot works for the Konzeptwerk Neue Ökonomie in Leipzig, Germany, on digitalisation and social-ecological critiques of digital capitalism. He is also a computer scientist and co-organised the *Bits & Trees conference* in 2018 in Berlin.

Gabu Heindl (she/her) is an architect and urban planner in Vienna with a PhD in philosophy. She teaches at the Architectural Association in London and is a professor of Urbanism at the Nuremberg Institute of Technology. As an activist, she is involved in housing and urban struggles. As an architect, she is involved in realising non-market housing projects. She is the author of *Stadtkonflikte: Radikale Demokratie in Architektur und Stadtplanung* (City conflicts: Radical Democracy in Architecture and Urban Design, 2020).

Constanza Hepp studied Journalism in Santiago, Chile, and completed an MSc in Human Ecology in Lund, Sweden. She is currently living in Northern Italy, establishing a community-supported agriculture project and facilitating environmental education workshops in local public schools. She is also a member of the editorial team at *degrowth.info*, working to bridge academic activism and social practices that have the potential for systemic change.

Joe Herbert holds a PhD in Human Geography from Newcastle University, UK. His research interests centre around degrowth, climate justice and radical imaginations. He is on the editorial team at *degrowth.info* and a co-founder of the *degrowthUK* online platforms.

Elisabeth Jost (she/her) is a PhD candidate at the Institute for Sustainable Economic Development at the University of Natural Resources and Life Sciences, Vienna. She is a board member of FIAN Austria and is engaged in the Nyéléni movement for food sovereignty.

Max Koch is a sociologist and professor of social policy and sustainability at Lund University. His research addresses patterns of capitalist restructuring and how these are reflected in social structures and the environment. His books include *Capitalism and Climate Change: Theoretical Discussion, Historical Development and Policy Responses* and *Postgrowth and Wellbeing: Challenges to Sustainable Welfare* (with Milena Büchs). His articles on degrowth appeared in journals such as *Ecological Economics, Global Environmental Change, Futures, Environmental Values, Environmental Politics, Social Policy and Society* and *British Journal of Sociology*.

Halliki Kreinin (she/her) is a founding member of the Vienna Degrowth Association and a Postdoctoral Researcher at the University of Münster, where she works on the "1.5° Lifestyles" project, aiming to analyse barriers and enablers of degrowth lifestyles and their public acceptance. She received her PhD ("Trade unions and the social-ecological transformation of work") from the Ecological Economics Institute at the Vienna University of Economics and Business.

Miriam Lang (she/her) is a professor of Environmental and Sustainability Studies at the Universidad Andina Simón Bolívar in Quito, Ecuador. Her current research focuses on the critique of development and growth, systemic alternatives, and the territorial implementation of Buen Vivir.

Tahir Latif is Secretary of the Greener Jobs Alliance in the UK and a co-author of the report *Climate Jobs: Building a Workforce to Meet the Climate Emergency*, produced by the Campaign Against Climate Change Trade Union Group. He was previously on the National Executive Committee of the Public and Commercial Services Union (PCS) and President of PCS's Aviation Group, representing workers across the aviation sector.

Leon Leuser is a freelance sustainability researcher and consultant based in Strasbourg.

Samantha Mailhot (she/her) is pursuing a PhD in Environmental Studies at York University, Toronto. From a political ecology perspective, she studies degrowth policy structures and public opinions on degrowth in the Canadian context. Samantha is also on the editorial team of *degrowth.info*.

Mario Díaz Muñoz is a PhD candidate and researcher at the Department of Sustainability,
Governance and Methods at Modul University in Vienna. He is also an Early Stage Researcher within Marie Skłodowska Curie ITN in the i-CONN Network.

Tonny Nowshin is an economist by training, development sector specialist by profession and degrowth and climate justice activist by passion. She has been working to centre anti-racist and decolonial perspectives in the degrowth and climate movement since 2018.

Godwin Uyi Ojo is a political ecologist and co-founder of Environmental Rights Action/Friends of the Earth Nigeria and is currently its Executive Director. He is an environmental human rights advocate fighting for social justice, involved in social movement building, championing a system change with a community-driven Just Transition that resonates with degrowth strategies. He was a discussant during the virtual *Degrowth Vienna 2020 Conference* and panellist during the *European Conference on Due Diligence Regulations* held in 2020.

Susan Paulson (she/her/they/them) is a Professor at the University of Florida's Center for Latin American Studies. She researched and taught about human-environment relations during 15 years in Latin America, and she then taught sustainability studies during 5 years in Europe. Recent books include *Masculinities and Femininities in Latin America's Uneven Development* (2016) and *The Case for Degrowth* (2020).

Patricia E. (Ellie) Perkins (she/her) is a Professor in the Faculty of Environmental and Urban Change, York University, Toronto, where she teaches Ecological Economics, community economic development, climate change science and policy, and critical interdisciplinary research design. Her areas of research include feminist ecological economics, climate justice, degrowth, commons, and participatory governance.

Panos Petridis is a post-doctoral interdisciplinary researcher, working at the interface between science, society and the environment. As part of the Institute of Social Ecology of the University of Natural Resources and Life Sciences (BOKU) in Vienna, his work has focused on island studies, socio-ecological transitions, participatory research and degrowth transformations.

Christina Plank (she/her) works as a postdoctoral researcher at the Institute for Development Research at the University of Natural Resources and Life Sciences, Vienna. Her research and teaching focus on state theory, political ecology, social-ecological transformation and critical agrarian studies.

Lisa Francesca Rail is a doctoral student at the Institute for Social & Cultural Anthropology at the University of Vienna, researching alpine pasture commons in Austria. Additionally, she works for the Österreichische Berg- und KleinbäuerInnenvereinigung, the Austrian chapter of La Via Campesina.

Georg Rath has been a cooperativist in Cecosesola since 1999 and was trained there as an acupuncture therapist. He has cooperated in the Health Centre since its founding in 2009, and has been engaging with degrowth since 2013.

Andro Rilović (he/him) is a lecturer in Degrowth and European Economics at the University of Amsterdam. He is interested in degrowth and anarchism, and how they can be applied to creating new community development models.

Matthias Schmelzer is an economic historian, social theorist and climate activist. He works at Friedrich-Schiller University Jena and is active with Konzeptwerk Neue Ökonomie and Network for Economic Transformation. He has authored *The Hegemony of Growth*, co-authored *The Future is Degrowth*, and co-edited *Degrowth in Movement(s)*.

Colleen Schneider is a PhD student at the Institute for Ecological Economics (WU). Her research and teaching focus on the political economy of monetary and fiscal policy in a social-ecological transformation.

Joëlle Saey-Volckrick (she/her) is a lecturer in Ecological Economics at the Berlin School of Economics and Law and an independent researcher associated with the Institute for International Political Economy Berlin (IPE) and the Research Center for Social Innovation and Transformation (CRITS). She works in a local food cooperative in Grenoble and is an editor at *degrowth.info*.

Lisa M. Seebacher (they/them) works as a social scientist at the Centre for Social Innovation (ZSI) in Vienna, Austria and are currently studying early-childhood education. They were involved with organising the *Degrowth Vienna 2020 Conference*.

Thomas SJ Smith is a Marie Skłodowska-Curie postdoctoral researcher in the Department of Geography at Ludwig Maximilian University (LMU), Munich, Germany. He is a member of the Community Economies Research Network (CERN) and his research interests relate to social-ecological transformation, the social and solidarity economy and post-growth economies. His involvement in this book was influenced by work undertaken on the EUKI-funded project "Just Transition in the European Car Industry" alongside colleagues from Croatia, Hungary, Slovakia, Czech Republic and Germany.

Ania Spatzier is an activist for Deutsche Wohnen & Co. Enteignen. By academic training, she is a political sociologist with her research interest lying mainly in the field of social movements as actors for a social-ecological transformation.

John Szabo is a PhD Candidate at the Central European University and a Junior Fellow at the Centre for Economic and Regional Studies.

Gabriel Trettel Silva is a researcher and lecturer at the School of Sustainability, Governance and Methods at the Modul University, Vienna. He is a PhD candidate in Socioeconomic Sciences, investigating imperialism and anti-imperialism in global social-environmental struggles. His master's thesis explored how the degrowth framework approaches the Global South. In São Paulo, he worked as a consultant in solidarity economy projects and with UNESCO on the integration of the SDGs into public education. Gabriel was also part of the editorial team of the *degrowth.info* web portal.

Nina Treu (she/her) is part of the degrowth and climate justice movement and is active as a coordinator, facilitator and networker. She is a co-founder of the Konzeptwerk Neue Ökonomie in Leipzig, Germany, and has been working there since 2011. In her belief, the only way to achieve the much needed social-ecological transformation is by bringing different social movements together.

Andrea Vetter writes, researches, narrates, organises and bakes cheesecakes for social-ecological change. She designs interfaces for transition theory and practices, mainly for the cultural hub Haus des Wandels in East Brandenburg, the think tank Konzeptwerk Neue Ökonomie in Leipzig and the magazine Oya.

About the Editors

Nathan Barlow (he/him) is a PhD candidate in Socioeconomics at the Vienna University of Economics and Business, researching the role of strategies for social-ecological transformations. He is interested in the relationship between radical long-term systemic change and short-term necessary steps. Nathan is on the editorial team of *degrowth.info*, was a coordinator of the *Degrowth Vienna 2020 Conference: Strategies for Social-ecological Transformation,* and has been coordinating this collected volume together with Livia Regen.

Noémie Cadiou (she/her) is currently finishing her undergraduate degree in Human Geography at UCL (University College London). Her dissertation looks at the potential of citizens' assemblies for climate and environmental policy-making. She is a convinced cyclist and has joined Degrowth Vienna and the editorial team of this collected volume in late 2020.

Ekaterina Chertkovskaya (she/her) is a researcher based at Lund University, working on degrowth and critical organisation studies. Her research addresses contemporary crises and explores paths for social-ecological transformation. She has been writing on corporate violence, problems with work and employability, and the plastic crisis, on the one hand, and focusing on degrowth as a vision for transformation, its political economy, and alternative models of work and organising, on the other. Ekaterina is also a member of the editorial collective of *ephemera: theory & politics in organisation.*

Max Hollweg (none/he/him) works on various projects for social-ecological transformation with Degrowth Vienna, Attac Austria and other groups. Max was also a coordinator of the *Degrowth Vienna 2020 Conference* and holds a master's degree in Socioeconomics from the Vienna University of Economics and Business.

Christina Plank (she/her) works as a postdoctoral researcher at the Institute for Development Research at the University of Natural Resources and Life Sciences (BOKU), Vienna. Her research and teaching focus on state theory, political ecology, social-ecological transformation and critical agrarian studies.

Livia Regen (she/her) studied Socio-Ecological Economics and Policy (SEEP) at the Vienna University of Economics and Business. She was part of the *Degrowth Vienna 2020 Conference* organising team and has been coordinating this collected volume together with Nathan Barlow. She is an editor at *degrowth.info* and engages in paid labour researching the technology-society-ecology nexus in the context of urban transformations.

Merle Schulken (she/her) is an MA Economics candidate at the New School for Social Research in New York. She is interested in the question of how different modes of social provisioning interact in the context of a social-ecological transformation. She also holds a master's degree in Socio-Ecological Economics and Policy (SEEP) from the Vienna University of Economics and Business and has been an active member of Degrowth Vienna for the past two years.

Verena Wolf (she/her) is currently pursuing a PhD on the interrelation of global commons, property and climate change as a researcher in the SFB294 "Structural Change of Property" at Friedrich-Schiller University of Jena, Germany. She was a coordinator of the *Degrowth Vienna 2020 Conference* and completed her master's degree in Socio-Ecological Economics and Policy (SEEP) at the Vienna University of Economics and Business.

Acknowledgements

We would like to sincerely thank the following people, institutions and funding bodies, without whom this endeavour would have been incomplete to impossible. Thank you for journeying with us and making the idea for this book transform into reality.

Firstly, we would like to thank **all contributing authors** – for your knowledge, for your time, for your openness to embarking on this journey and for your patience during our sometimes non-linear review processes. In particular, we would like to thank authors contributing to Part II of this publication who were thrown into an experimental collaboration process that required building bridges between academia and activism and the integration of their vocabularies.

Secondly, we would like to express our gratitude to all **supportive reviewers**; your expertise has been invaluable to making this book cohesive and substantive. Thank you, **Stefania Barca, Hauke Baumann, Anton Brokow-Loga, Sara Dahlman, Santiago Gorostiza, Daniel Gusenbauer, Joe Herbert, Katharina Mader, Manuel Scholz-Wäckerle, Lisa M. Seebacher, Susanne Siebel, Tone Smith, Jacob Smessaert and Ersilia Verlinghieri**.

Thirdly, we thank **our main funding body, MA7, the Culture Department of the City of Vienna**. Your generous support rendered this project possible in the first place.

Fourthly, we thank **Rosa Luxemburg Stiftung** for enabling a smooth project start in the autumn of 2020 thanks to their financial contribution.

Similarly, we thank the **ÖH Universität Wien** who supported us financially in the cover design process. For the beautiful cover design resulting from several rounds of revisions that required patience and an eye for detail we are indebted to **Dana Rausch**.

Fifthly, we are immensely grateful to **our language editor Aaron Vansintjan** for his excellent editing work, but also for his critical reading and his always poignant suggestions.

Sixthly, we are full of gratitude for **our colleagues from Degrowth Vienna** who have gently, supportively and constructively accompanied the book compilation process. Without Degrowth Vienna as a backbone, this writing process would have been infinitely more complicated.

We would like to sincerely thank **MayFly** and in particular **Toni Ruuska** and **Mihkali Pennanen** for their generosity and patience in the process of working with us.

Last but not least, we would like to thank the members of the *Degrowth Vienna 2020 Conference*'s **Advisory Board** who in different ways contributed to the realisation of this project. In particular, we would like to thank **Uli Brand** for his trust in the process and helpful guidance.

Supporting organisations

CPSIA information can be obtained
at www.ICGtesting.com
Printed in the USA
BVHW080939131022
649271BV00004B/452